# Conducting Child Custody Evaluations

*To Damon—May the Force Always Be With You.*

*With Love, Your Saba*

# Conducting Child Custody Evaluations

## From Basic to Complex Issues

## Philip M. Stahl, PhD

*Forensic Programs, Steve Frankel Group, LLC*

Los Angeles | London | New Delhi
Singapore | Washington DC

*For information:*

SAGE Publications, Inc.
2455 Teller Road
Thousand Oaks, California 91320
E-mail: order@sagepub.com

SAGE Publications Ltd.
1 Oliver's Yard
55 City Road
London EC1Y 1SP
United Kingdom

SAGE Publications India Pvt. Ltd.
B 1/I 1 Mohan Cooperative Industrial Area
Mathura Road, New Delhi 110 044
India

SAGE Publications Asia-Pacific Pte. Ltd.
33 Pekin Street #02-01
Far East Square
Singapore 048763

Printed in the United States of America.

*Library of Congress Cataloging-in-Publication Data*

Stahl, Philip Michael.
Conducting child custody evaluations: From basic to complex issues / Philip M. Stahl.
    p. cm.
Includes bibliographical references and index.
ISBN 978-1-4129-7433-2 (cloth : acid-free paper)
ISBN 978-1-4129-7434-9 (pbk. : acid-free paper)
    1. Child welfare—United States. 2. Custody of children—United States—Evaluation.
3. Parent and child (Law)—United States. I. Title.

HV741.S727 2011
362.82′94—dc22                    2010015056

This book is printed on acid-free paper.

10  11  12  13  14  10  9  8  7  6  5  4  3  2  1

| | |
|---|---|
| *Acquisitions Editor:* | Kassie Graves |
| *Editorial Assistant:* | Veronica Novak |
| *Production Editor:* | Karen Wiley |
| *Copy Editor:* | Kristin Bergstad |
| *Typesetter:* | C&M Digitals (P) Ltd. |
| *Proofreader:* | Gail Fay |
| *Indexer:* | Rick Hurd |
| *Cover Designer:* | Michelle Kenny |
| *Marketing Manager:* | Stephanie Adams |

# Contents_____

Preface                                                          xiii
    A Note on Language Used in This Book                          xvi
    Acknowledgments                                              xvii

**PART I. Critical Professional and Ethical Issues**

  1. **Introduction to the Role, Ethics,
     and Professional Responsibility**                             3
     How the Court Benefits From an Evaluation                     4
     How the Family Benefits From an Evaluation                    4
     When Is an Evaluation Harmful?                                6
     Who Is the Client/Consumer?                                   7
     Practice Standards and Ethical Issues                         7
     Evaluator Biases                                             13
         Gender Bias                                              13
         Cultural Bias                                            14
         Primacy or Recency Bias                                  14
         Confirmatory Bias                                        14
         Bias From Psychological Test Data                        15
         "Truth Lies Somewhere in the Middle" Bias                15
         "Attila the Hun Doesn't Marry Mother Theresa" Bias       16
         "For the Move" or "Against the Move" Bias                16
     Reducing the Risk of Bias                                    17
     The Bottom Line                                              18

  2. **The Mental Health Expert's Many Possible Roles**           19
     Therapists                                                   19
     Therapeutic Reunification                                    22
     Collaborative Law Coach                                      22
     Psychologist Evaluator/Psychiatrist/Vocational Evaluator     23
     Mediator                                                     24
     Consultant to Attorney/Expert Witness                        25
     Parent Coordinator (PC)                                      26
     The Custody Evaluator                                        27
     Dual Relationships                                           28

The Bottom Line 31
Notes 31

3. Fundamental Questions in Most Custody Evaluations 33

The Best Interests of the Child 33
The Family's Relationships 37
Parenting Strengths and Weaknesses 39
The Co-Parental Relationship 40
Time-Sharing Recommendations 41
The Bottom Line 42

4. General Divorce-Related Research and Basic Statutory and Case Law 43

A Quick Primer on Research 43
Risks of Divorce to Children 44
Risk Versus Resilience 45
Mitigating Factors 45
Research on Parents' Relationships After Divorce 46
Basic Statutory and Case Law 46
Uniform Child Custody Jurisdiction and Enforcement Act (1997) 47
Parental Kidnapping Prevention Act 47
*Troxel v. Granville* (2000) 48
Hague Convention on the Civil Aspects
of International Child Abduction 48
California Statutes 49
California Case Law 51
The Bottom Line 54

5. Children's Developmental Needs 55

A Developmental Framework 55
Infants and Toddlers (0–3 Years) 56
Never Paint by the Numbers 59
Preschoolers (3–5 Years) 61
School-Age Children (6–12 Years) 63
Adolescents (13–17 Years) 65
Children's Reactions to Parental Conflict 68
Giving Children a Voice Versus Protecting Their Privacy 69
Weighing the Needs of a Single Child Versus
the Needs of a Sibling Group 71
Balancing the Individual Child's Real Needs With the Ideal 73
The Bottom Line 75

PART II. Conducting the Child Custody Evaluation

6. Conducting the Evaluation: Part I. Observations
and Techniques With Adults 79

The Court Order and Initial Contact With Attorneys 79
The Initial Phone Call and Contacts With Parents 80

The Initial Contract 82
The First Conjoint Appointment 82
The Initial Individual Appointment 84
The Second Interview and Beyond 86
What to Believe? 87
Collateral Information 89
The Use of Psychological Tests 90
The Bottom Line 91

7. **Conducting the Evaluation: Part II. Observations and Techniques With Children** 93

Significant Issues in the Assessment of Children/Gaining
   Rapport at the Beginning of the First Interview 94
Children and the Potential for Suggestibility 97
Children and Their Language 99
Gathering Information About the Child's Experiences 100
Directly Assessing the Parent–Child Bond 103
Siblings Together, or Not? 105
Use of Play and Other Techniques in Understanding Children 105
Home Visits 106
The Preference of the Child 107
Cautions in Interviewing Children 110
The Bottom Line 110

8. **The Use of Psychological Testing in Custody Evaluations** 111

Review of the Literature 112
Traditional Psychological Tests 114
   Objective Personality Tests 114
   Projective Personality Tests 117
Tests Designed Specifically for Custody Evaluations 117
Parenting Inventories 118
Tests for Children 120
Benefits of Using Tests 121
Risks in Using Tests 122
Computerized Test Results 123
The Bottom Line 124

9. **Gathering Collateral Data** 125

What Are Collateral Data? 126
Benefits of Using Collateral Data 127
Record Review 128
Gathering Lists of Collateral Sources 128
Who to Talk To: A Concentric-Circle Approach 129
Interviewing Collateral Sources 131
The Bottom Line 131

10. **Sharing the Results of the Evaluation: The Evaluation Report**    133

    AFCC *Model Standards*    134

    Basic Characteristics of a Quality Report    134

    Information That Must Be in Every Report    135

        Identifying Information and Statements
            of Informed Consent    135

        Procedures    135

        Background Information    136

        The Parents    136

        The Children    139

        Collateral Information    141

        Analysis and Summary    141

        Recommendations    143

    The Bottom Line    146

**PART III. Complex Issues to Be Evaluated**

11. **Nonviolent High-Conflict Families**    149

    Contribution of Personality Features    151

    Contribution From Other Sources    154

    Recommendations for High-Conflict Families    155

        Therapy    155

        Structured Recommendations    156

        Neutral Decision-Maker (Parent Coordinator)    158

        Parallel Parenting    161

        Using a Parent Communication Notebook    162

    A Case for Sole Legal Custody or Decision-Making
        to One Parent    162

    The Bottom Line    164

12. **Domestic Violence**    165

    The Concept of Differentiation    166

        Situational Couples Violence (SCV)    168

        Coercive–Controlling Violence (CCV)    169

        Separation Instigated Violence (SIV)    170

    Approaching the Family's Domestic Violence Issues    171

    Parenting Problems of CCV Domestic Violence Parents    171

        Perpetrators    171

        Victims    172

    Gathering the Data    173

        History of the Family's Domestic Violence    173

        Specific Questions to Ask Parents    174

        The Children in These Families    175

    The Alphabet Soup of Data Used to Formulate Conclusions    176

        Pattern    176

        Potency    177

Primary Perpetrator     177
Parenting Problems     177
Perspective of the Child     177
Reflective Functioning     178
Responsibility     178
Repair     178
Using the PPPPP Analysis With the RRR Concepts
    to Reach a Decision About the Parenting Plan     178
Therapeutic and Structural Interventions     179
The Bottom Line     181

**13. The Alienated Child**     **183**

Contribution to the Child's Alienated Response     184
Parent Contributions to the Development of
    Alienation     186
Child Contributions to the Development of Alienation     187
Typical Alienated Behaviors in Children     188
Emotional Impact of Alienation on Children     189
Dynamics of the Larger System     190
Evaluation of Alienation     191
    The Aligned Parent     192
    The Rejected Parent     194
    The Children     195
Other Reasons for Alignment With One Parent:
    What to Look for in the Children     197
Concluding the Evaluation     198
    When Alienation Is Present     198
    Recommended Interventions and
       Custodial Options     199
Parentectomies: Do They Help?     201
Some Promising Alternatives     203
The Bottom Line     203
Note     204

**14. Relocation Evaluations**     **205**

Legal Considerations in Relocation Evaluations:
    Relevant Case Law     206
Legal Considerations in Relocation Evaluations:
    Relevant Statutory Law     212
The Psychological Literature Related to Relocation     214
Societal Issues That Often Lead to Requests to Move     223
Factors for the Evaluator to Consider     224
    The Actual Time-Sharing Arrangement by the Parents
       and the History of That Arrangement     224
    The Age, Maturity, Interests, Activities,
       and Special Needs (When Relevant) of the Child     225

Social Capital in Each Location                                    226
Gender, Temperament, and Fit Between
   Each Parent and Child                            226
Potential Loss to the Child: What Is the Child Likely
   to Experience if the Proposed Move
   Does or Does Not Take Place?                      227
The Child's Adjustment to Home, School,
   and Community and the Length of Time That
   the Child Has Been in a Stable Environment        228
The Preference of a Mature Child                                   228
The Reasons for the Proposed Move, and Whether
   or Not the Proposed Move Is in Good Faith
   or Designed to Thwart the Legitimate Relationship
   Between the Child and the Other Parent            228
The Reasons for Opposing the Move and Whether
   or Not the Opposition Is in Good Faith or
   Designed to Thwart the Legitimate Need
   of the Custodial Parent to Move                   229
The Advantages of Moving for Both
   the Parent and the Child                          229
The Distance of the Move, Including the Travel Time
   and Cost of Travel Between Homes                  229
Is the Move Representative of Stability or a Pattern of
   Instability on the Part of the Moving Parent?     230
The Feasibility of a Move by the Noncustodial Parent               230
Whether or Not the Moving Parent Is Likely to
   Comply With an Access Order                       230
The Permanence (or Lack Thereof) of
   the Proposed Situation                            231
The Mental and Physical Health of All Persons Involved             231
Whether or Not There Are Any False Allegations of Abuse            231
Gatekeeping                                                        231
Special Issues in International Cases                              232
Avoiding Bias                                                     233
The Bottom Line                                                   235
Notes                                                             236

**PART IV. Other Critical Issues**

15. Tackling the Terror of Testifying                              239

The Deposition                                                    240
The Process at Trial                                              241
Preparing for the Testimony                                       243
Testifying Procedures                                             245
Stick to the Data                                                 247
Avoid Ipse Dixit Assertions                                       249

Dealing With Hypothetical Questions                          250
Remain Professional                                          251
Trick Questions                                             252
Do's and Don'ts for Testifying in Court                     253
The Bottom Line                                             254
Note                                                        254

16. Critiquing Evaluations                                  255
Boy Scout Oath                                             260

17. Conclusions                                             263
Special Needs Issues of Children                            263
Substance Abuse Issues                                      264
Sexual Abuse Allegations                                    264
Longitudinal Evaluations                                    265
Conclusion                                                 265


Appendix A: Sample Court Order Appointing
Mental Health Professional                                   269

Appendix B: Sample Custody Evaluation Informed
Consent and Retainer Agreement                              275

Appendix C: Sample Custody Evaluation Face Sheet            281

Appendix D: Sample List of Questions to Ask Children        291

Appendix E: Sample List of Questions to Ask Parents         295

Appendix F: Sample Alienation Analysis and Recommendations  299

Appendix G: Sample Relocation Analysis and Recommendations  305

Appendix H: Recommended Reading                             311

References                                                  313

Name Index                                                 325

Subject Index                                              329

About the Author                                           347

# Preface

This is my third book on child custody evaluations. In the more than 25 years that I have done child custody evaluations, and in the 15 years since publication of my first book, *Conducting Child Custody Evaluations: A Comprehensive Guide* (Stahl, 1994), there has been considerable research on divorce, children's adjustment to divorce, parenting plans, domestic violence, alienated children, and relocation. Along with *Complex Issues in Child Custody Evaluations* (Stahl, 1999), there has been a growth in the literature associated with child custody and child custody evaluations. Much of this literature has been in books by Ackerman (2001), Gould (1998, 2006), and Gould and Martindale (2007). Additionally, there has been considerable writing in *Family Court Review,* the journal of the Association of Family and Conciliation Courts (AFCC), and a new journal which was first published in 2004, the *Journal of Child Custody.* AFCC has issued new *Model Standards for Child Custody Evaluations* (2006), and the American Psychological Association has issued new *Guidelines for Child Custody Evaluations* (2009) to help guide the practice for child custody evaluators. Additionally, the state of California (Rule of Court 5.220) has promulgated rules designed to improve the quality of child custody evaluation work.

During this time, I have been fortunate to present at and attend many multidisciplinary conferences, legal conferences, and judicial education programs across the country. I have presented numerous workshops on a variety of topics associated with child custody and child custody evaluations. I have benefited from exposure to thinking in the field from across the country and around the world. I continue to do evaluations and learn from the families, judges, attorneys, and other evaluators with whom I work. In recent years, I have had an opportunity to critique many evaluations conducted by child custody evaluators across the country. I have seen many excellent evaluations and, unfortunately, some very poor ones. All of this has continued to inform my thinking about child custody and child custody evaluations.

In some ways, however, the more things change, the more they stay the same. Families continue to be complex, as are their child custody issues. Judges increasingly look for multiple ways to help families solve their problems, and practitioners in the field continue to look for ways to ease the burden of litigation for families. Whereas mediation was in use in a limited number of jurisdictions in 1994, nearly all states now have authorized the use of mediation to help families solve their differences around child custody. There has been growth in collaborative law, in which attorneys and parents use a collaborative approach with mental health and other experts to help coach families through the difficult times. Even with these beneficial changes, however, many families continue to struggle and litigate their way through child custody cases. Family violence continues to be problematic and occasionally misunderstood, some parents have substance abuse problems, some children become alienated or estranged from one parent, and some parents remain in high conflict, often the result of significant personality traits exhibited by one or both parents. In spite of continued support for shared custody, parents continue to argue over and have difficulty resolving disputes about custody and parenting of their children.

With the many changes, new research, and a continued focus on helping families resolve their differences, it is time to update my books. Whereas my first book focused on basic "how to" issues in conducting evaluations and my second book focused primarily on more "complex" issues in child custody evaluations, this comprehensive book addresses all of these significant issues for child custody evaluators. This book is presented in four parts. Part I is focused on critical professional and ethical issues. This includes:

- The purpose of the evaluations, practice standards, confidentiality, and bias (Chapter 1)
- The mental health expert's many possible roles (Chapter 2)
- Fundamental questions that surface in nearly all evaluations (Chapter 3)
- General divorce-related research (Chapter 4)
- Children's developmental needs (Chapter 5)

Part II focuses on the basic tasks of conducting the child custody evaluation. This includes:

- Observations and techniques with adults (Chapter 6)
- Observations and techniques with children (Chapter 7)
- Psychological testing (Chapter 8)
- Gathering collateral data (Chapter 9)
- Sharing the results of the evaluation—The evaluation report (Chapter 10)

Part III focuses on complex issues, including:

- Nonviolent high-conflict families (Chapter 11)
- Domestic violence (Chapter 12)
- The alienated child (Chapter 13)
- Relocation evaluations (Chapter 14)

Part IV focuses on two other critical tasks facing the evaluator, including:

- Tackling the terror of testifying (Chapter 15)
- Critiquing child custody evaluations—the good, the bad, and the ugly (Chapter 16)

Along with this, as in my first book, I will include appendixes. These appendixes include sample forms and informed consent documents, sample questions to ask parents and children, sample report analysis and recommendations in alienation and relocation cases, and recommended reading that is not included in the references.

As before, this book will focus on the complexities involved in conducting child custody evaluations. I still believe that many areas need to be explored in every evaluation, including the psychological functioning of each parent; the history of the parents' relationship; the parenting skills and relative parenting strengths and weaknesses of each parent; the attachment and quality of the relationship between the child and each parent; the child's relationships with siblings, peers, and others; the existence of family violence and the intensity of the parents' conflict and the degree to which the child is exposed to it; the child's temperament and developmental needs; logistical issues, including parents' work schedules and the distance between parents' homes; and the ability (or inability) of the parents to work together to meet their child's needs.

As I stated in my previous books, all of these issues must be addressed and integrated into a discussion related to the "best interests of the child." Each evaluation must be guided by the statutes of the state in which the court orders the evaluation. The evaluator must also know relevant case law pertinent to specific evaluations. For example, in Arizona, the "best interests of the child" statute is found in AZ 25-403, which defines the factors associated with that particular state's definition of best interests. This is different, for example, from either Michigan's best-interests statute or California's best-interests statute. Similarly, if doing a relocation evaluation in Arizona, the evaluator must know the factors outlined in AZ 25-408, but if doing a similar evaluation in California, there is considerable case law that must be understood (e.g., *LaMusga* [*In re Marriage of LaMusga*, 2004]).

Since my last book, I continue to recognize that some people do not understand how complex and difficult child custody evaluations and child custody litigation can be. I have seen evaluators write very brief reports, oversimplifying the family's issues and failing to provide a rationale for the evaluator's recommendations. I also continue to see legislators try to oversimplify the issues in ways that might interfere with the evaluators doing the complex task in front of them. I continue to worry when courts try to oversimplify family issues by encouraging evaluators to be short and brief in their reports or by making rulings that tend to polarize family problems. I continue to worry when judges, attorneys, and evaluators do not understand the limitations of an evaluator's knowledge, pushing experts to reach conclusions and make recommendations beyond what the data will allow.

I am concerned when evaluators have little or no training in child custody evaluations yet believe they are qualified to perform such evaluations simply because they have read a book or two, know how to perform family interviews, and perform psychological testing. Novices need experience gained by work in the field, an understanding of the research, participation in continuing education workshops, and the assistance of consultation and supervision by more experienced evaluators. I also worry that licensing boards continue to be overwhelmed with complaints by angry litigants and yet do not understand the complexity of child custody evaluation work and do not have the ability to differentiate between ethical and competent evaluations and evaluations that may be below the standard of care.

Finally, I continue to worry about the children of divorce, for whom many decisions are being made that are based on research that still has limitations. I worry about the lack of appropriate integration of children's voices in the courts. At the time this book is being written, the United States still has not ratified the UN Convention on the Rights of the Child (1989). Article 12 of that Convention requires that children's voices be heard when courts will be making decisions that affect children's lives. It is critical, in my opinion, to have a forum in which children's voices are heard when court proceedings will be affecting the children. Other countries are doing a much better job of including children's voices in court proceedings (R. M. Stahl, 2007). I also worry that children do not get adequate information about their parents' divorce, decisions of the court, or other relevant information that affects their lives. Regardless of where parents live and the nature of family problems, we still must understand the family divorce through the eyes of the children. As I stated in my first book,

> We must understand how the children feel, what they fear and wish, and what makes conflict resolution difficult to achieve. We need to stay focused on the needs of the children, who are vulnerable to the actions of their parents, and who have the most to gain with a healthy resolution of the divorce conflict. (P. Stahl, 1994, p. x)

With this book, I hope to bring greater understanding of these multiple issues so that child custody evaluators, attorneys, and family law judges can better understand the complexities associated with child custody and continue to improve the lives of children caught in the middle of their parents' divorce.

## A Note on Language Used in This Book

Throughout this book I will be addressing the issues associated with children whose parents live apart. Some parents were never married, some barely knew each other, and some were married for many years. Some children are the result of a heterosexual relationship by their parents and some children are born in same sex unions and marriages. While there may be issues unique to each of these circumstances, I will use the term *divorce* to address all of these families.

Similarly, I will interchange genders throughout the book, recognizing that both mothers and fathers can contribute to their child's alienation from the other parent and both mothers and fathers can be violent or engender conflict. Additionally, though there are differences found in the way mothers and fathers generally raise children, I recognize that both mothers and fathers are important to children and that both will have relevant strengths and potential weaknesses in their parenting capacity and functioning.

Finally, even though I do not like the language of custody, I will be referring to it in this book. Most states continue to use the language of custody, while some are shifting to a more appropriate focus on parenting rights and responsibilities (see, e.g., Florida Statute 61.13, enacted in 2008). I will not use the word *visitation;* instead I will use the words *access* or *parenting time* to refer to each parent's time with their children, except when referring to a parent's contact as supervised visitation, since that is the general term used in such circumstances.

# Acknowledgments

I wish to thank Kassie Graves and the staff at SAGE Publications for their continued support of my work. Kassie has been instrumental in encouraging and guiding me in this task, gently but firmly reminding me of important deadlines. I would like to thank copyeditor Kristin Bergstad who helped correct many literary errors and made suggestions for clarifying the description of my ideas. I would also like to thank the following reviewers for their comments and suggestions: Martha Laughlin, Valdosta State University; Ann Rambo, Nova Southeastern University; Mary Ballou, Northeastern University; M. K. Hamza, Lamar University; Lina Hartocollis, University of Pennsylvania; Lynelle C. Yingling, J&L Human Systems Development; Angela R. Ausbrooks, Texas State University; and Gerald Michaels, California School of Professional Psychology, Alliant International University.

I also wish to thank my wife, Ruth, for her continued editing assistance, and the families of divorce for all they have taught me over the years. In addition, I wish to thank my own children, Jason and Rebecca, who continue to push me to learn new things and consider new ways of thinking about these, and many other issues in my work and in my life. Rebecca, in particular, since she has attended law school and become a lawyer, has furthered my understanding of the importance of having a venue for the children's voice in court, and I have enjoyed the opportunity and the pleasure of presenting with her on children's issues at conferences and judicial education programs.

# PART I

## Critical Professional and Ethical Issues

# 1

# Introduction to the Role, Ethics, and Professional Responsibility

Child custody evaluations are time intensive, potentially intrusive to the family, expensive, and risk putting the children right into the middle of their parents' conflicts. When ordered by the court to participate in an evaluation, parents are subjected to multiple interviews, perhaps psychological testing, and exposure of their conflicts to teachers, therapists, and other collateral professionals. Children are interviewed and observed in offices and often in their homes. This lengthy process will typically take 3 to 4 months to complete, will typically be expensive, and may yield a report that is both potentially insightful and potentially damaging to the family. With that in mind, a relevant question would be, "Why do courts order families to undergo child custody evaluations?"

In fact, there are numerous commentators in the professional literature who would argue that judges should not be sending families for child custody evaluations (see, e.g., Emery, Otto, & O'Donohue, 2005; R. Kelly & Ramsey, 2009; O'Donohue & Bradley, 1999). Parent groups have used the Internet to complain about child custody evaluators, judges, attorneys for children, Parent Coordinators, and others who work in the family law field. In the past 10 years, there has been a significant increase in licensing board complaints against mental health professionals who perform child custody evaluations and work as Parent Coordinators. This may lead to the relevant question, "Why would a mental health professional participate in and conduct a child custody evaluation?"

Additionally, many parents feel that an evaluation is intrusive and exposes the family to significant airing of the proverbial "dirty laundry." As noted previously, evaluations are costly and can add many months to the court and divorce process. Parents worry about the impact of the evaluation on their children, and often worry that an evaluator will make recommendations that limit their custodial rights and interfere with their relationships with their children. A relevant question for parents would be, "Why would any parent request or participate in a child custody evaluation?"

The answer to these questions lies in understanding how parents and courts benefit from an evaluation.

## How the Court Benefits From an Evaluation

Typically, a judge will order a child custody evaluation under a range of circumstances. In my experience, this can include those circumstances in which there are significant allegations such as drug and alcohol abuse, family violence, child abuse, significant mental health problems, and parental fitness. Oftentimes, a judge will have two parents in the courtroom who both appear to be good enough at parenting, and at other times, one or both parents appear to have significant problems. Increasingly, judges look to the mental health expert to assist in understanding complex psychological questions of attachment between the child and her parents, sibling relationships, and the developmental needs of children.

In a mobile society, one parent may wish to relocate with the children for a variety of reasons, such as employment, economics, new relationship opportunities, and more. In many jurisdictions, a judge will find it helpful to request a child custody evaluation to address the relevant psychological factors associated with the relocation question. My experience in California is that a judge will quite frequently request the assistance of an evaluator in a relocation case in order to provide information to the court about the relevant psychological issues described in the *LaMusga* decision (*In re Marriage of LaMusga*, 2004).

While judges are guided by the law in making decisions regarding the best interests of children, they may look to the neutrally appointed child custody evaluator to assist in understanding the complexity of the family dynamics and the relevant psychological factors that can lead to a determination of the child's best interests. Ultimately, in many ways, the neutrally appointed child custody evaluator serves as a quasi-consultant to the judge, providing critical data about the family for a better understanding of the family dynamics and the needs of the children.

> A key role for the child custody evaluator is to be helpful to judges. Evaluators help judges by providing data and analysis to understand complex family dynamics associated with best-interests factors in the law.

## How the Family Benefits From an Evaluation

The majority of parents going through a divorce will reach an agreement on their own about the parenting plan. Such low- or medium-conflict parents will agree on important decisions about their child, such as where he will go to school, what extracurricular activities he will participate in, and what nonemergency medical procedures to consider (e.g., orthodontia). They will agree on a parenting plan that will delineate the times that their child is with his mother and the times that he is with his father. They may have used mediation or resolved these issues on their own. Obviously, these parents do not need an evaluation, nor would the court order one.

On the other hand, some families, perhaps as many as 20%, are high-conflict families. They cannot agree on the parenting plan, how to make decisions for their child, nor are they able to focus on their child's needs because of their mutual differences. As noted earlier, with many of these families there are allegations of family violence, high conflict, significant mental health problems, concerns about the other parent's new romantic partner, substance abuse, and the alienation or estrangement of children. The primary benefit of an evaluation to families in these circumstances is that the evaluation will provide an opportunity for parents to voice their concerns to an expert in child development and mental health so that they are truly heard by someone. Many parents going through the divorce process feel that no one, sometimes not even their attorney, hears them. Many parents believe that no one cares about their child. In court, they may have been given little, if any, time to speak to the judge, who is often overwhelmed with a busy calendar with many cases to be heard. A neutrally appointed child custody evaluator will spend considerable time with each parent trying to understand individual concerns and perceptions of their child's needs. This can be comforting to parents who have a need to be heard about these concerns.

By listening to children, evaluators can also help identify when children are truly caught in the middle of a loyalty conflict between their parents and can describe the impact of that exposure to conflict. It is common for children's voices to be absent in the courts in the United States, and participation in a child custody evaluation will help children voice their concerns, share their wishes, and explore their feelings. While the child custody evaluator is not serving in the role of a therapist, the evaluation process may be therapeutic to children going through the evaluation. If the evaluator finds that the child is experiencing significant problems, she can refer the child for therapy and help the parents understand their child's developmental needs. In these ways, not only does the evaluator serve the opportunity to hear the child's voice, but she can also be a child advocate, advocating to the court and to the parents to meet the child's psychological and developmental needs.

A third potential benefit for the family comes from the fact that the same mental health expert is observing all family members. In the midst of a bitter divorce, therapeutic services are often fragmented, with each parent having his or her own therapist, attorney advocate, and sometimes even family friends become fragmented between parents. Many children are seeing their own therapist, as well. Each helping professional has a specific role, that is, to advocate for his or her respective clients' psychological or legal needs. Such professionals do not have critical information about the other family members. While their advice might be helpful and appropriate to their client, it may not be in the children's best interests. By having a neutrally appointed child custody evaluator listen to and observe all family members, talk to the relevant collateral witnesses on both sides, and consider everyone's input before reaching conclusions about the children's best interests, fragmentation disappears. If the evaluation is done correctly and thoroughly, all data collected and any recommendations offered will be addressed in a comprehensive manner for all concerned.

At the end of the evaluation process, when an evaluator writes a complete and comprehensive report, parents benefit from the report by learning about their child's needs and how the parents can work together to meet those needs. The evaluation report can help parents focus on the child rather than on their conflicts with one another and be a teaching tool to help them learn ways to resolve their conflicts and serve their child's needs. Furthermore, because a good evaluator will be up-to-date on current research in the field, the evaluator can help parents understand relevant issues such as overnights with their young child, the impact of conflict on children, the benefits of shared parenting in some circumstances, and the risks of shared parenting in other circumstances. This will enable the parents to be more effective as parents after the divorce.

Ultimately, an evaluation is most helpful to the family when the evaluator's report and conclusions can help reduce conflict, help parents reach a settlement without litigation, and keep parents focused on their child's needs and best interests. A well done evaluation may help parents recognize the need for solution and compromise and, while mediation was not successful prior to the evaluation, that settlement is much more likely after an evaluation. To the extent that settlement occurs, this will always benefit children, as it will allow for a reduction in conflict and provide an opportunity to move forward in a healthy way on behalf of the children.

> Evaluators help families and children by providing useful information that can help the family settle the custody dispute without court intervention.

## When Is an Evaluation Harmful?

Even with the preceding in mind, there are certainly times when an evaluation should not be performed. Certainly, if one or both parents are ambivalent about the divorce, marriage counseling may be much more appropriate. Second, except in those circumstances where the allegations are huge or when controlling domestic violence may preclude it, parents would always benefit from an effort at mediation before jumping into an evaluation. Research is clear (see, e.g., Emery, Sbarra, & Grover, 2005; J. Kelly, 1996) that parents are likely to have a greater sense of satisfaction and follow through positively when they have reached their own solution regarding their children. When mediation services are available, I almost always recommend that a family try mediation first, even in some circumstances in which there has been domestic violence.

Additionally, there may be times when one parent or the other will not cooperate with the evaluation. There may be times when, especially in a rural community with few experts, no one has the skill to provide a comprehensive child custody evaluation. At times, a child's therapist may be asked for input into the custody and access plan. In my opinion, a child's therapist should never provide input to the court about the parenting plan that is in a child's best interests, though she may discuss with parents her thoughts about various custodial options. In all of those instances, caution must be taken before conducting the evaluation, making sure that ethical boundaries are maintained and that appropriate practice standards have been met. These will be discussed later in this chapter.

## Who Is the Client/Consumer?

In my experience, child custody evaluations are almost always performed following a stipulation or court order identifying the particular mental health professional appointed to do the evaluation. Some evaluations are conducted by experts in private practice while others are conducted by experts in the public sector. Regardless of where one works, when appointed in this fashion, the child custody evaluator serves as an expert of the court. In California, for example, the evaluator is appointed as the court's expert under Section 730 of the Evidence Code, which defines the role of experts so appointed. As a result of that court appointment, the expert is likely to have quasi-judicial immunity from lawsuits. The court order will typically delineate who is responsible for the evaluator's fees, which are not going to be paid by health insurance because this evaluation is for a legal matter. Sometimes both parents share the cost of the evaluation equally, and at other times, there is a disproportionate sharing of costs, while in some instances, one parent pays the entire fee. The payor is not the client.

In my belief, the client is both the judge and the family. If the case goes to trial, the evaluator's report is designed to be helpful to the judge in reaching a sound decision on behalf of the best interests of the children. However, it is also clear that the majority of cases that go to evaluation are settled after the evaluation. In an overburdened legal system, judges are certainly looking to the parents and their attorneys to resolve their dispute at the conclusion of an evaluation. I believe that the ethical duty of evaluators is to meet the needs of the family first and foremost, always focusing on the best interests of the child. As such, both the family and the judge serve as the consumer of the evaluation, with a focus always being on the best interests of the child. In that regard, no matter who is paying for the evaluation, in what context and for what reasons it is ordered, or whether the end result is a settlement or a trial, the children of divorce become the primary focus of the evaluation and their needs must be served first.

## Practice Standards and Ethical Issues

In recent years there has been a shift in the thinking about child custody evaluation guidelines and standards (Kirkpatrick, 2004). The Association of Family and Conciliation Courts (AFCC; 2006) and the American Psychological

Association (2009) have updated their previously published *Model Standards of Practice for Child Custody Evaluation* (AFCC) and *Guidelines for Child Custody Evaluations* (American Psychological Association). As stated in the Introduction to the AFCC *Model Standards,* "These *Model Standards for Child Custody Evaluation* are designed to promote good practice; to provide information to those who utilize the services of custody evaluators; and to increase public confidence in the work done by custody evaluators." In addition, California Rule of Court 5.220 provides direction and guidance to evaluators in the courts of what to expect in the child custody evaluation process. The rationale for such *Model Standards, Guidelines,* and Court Rules is clear: to raise the bar and promote good practice by psychologists and other mental health professionals conducting evaluations, and to increase the likelihood of uniformity within the evaluation process. Kirkpatrick (2004) describes this baseline as the "floor," not the "ceiling" for our work.

These *Model Standards, Guidelines,* and *Rules of Court* address issues such as evaluator qualifications, training and experience, proper procedures, ethical issues, bias, assessment techniques, and other critical issues for evaluators. They may define the scope of the evaluator's work, discuss issues surrounding confidentiality and the lack thereof, clarify the importance of understanding the law and the court culture in one's community, address issues in record-keeping and the disclosure of records, address the importance of informed consent, and focus on testimony and report writing. The *Model Standards* and the *Guidelines* are aspirational in nature. The *Rules of Court* in California, on the other hand, are specific and have language that the evaluator "shall" comply with those rules.

For example, while the AFCC *Model Standards* suggest that evaluators have at least a master's degree in a mental health field that includes formal education and training, and recommend ongoing continuing education in a range of areas relevant to family law, California Rule 5.220 requires an evaluator to have that minimum master's degree, be licensed by the state, and have an initial minimum 40 hours of general continuing education and 16 hours of domestic violence continuing education before conducting any evaluations, plus an additional 8 hours of general continuing education and 4 hours of domestic violence continuing education annually in order to continue doing child custody evaluations. California Rule of Court 5.225 addresses these training and experience requirements directly. It is a requirement of the California Rule that an evaluator sign a document under penalty of perjury that he or she has met the training and experience requirements of the Rule before conducting an evaluation.

The purpose of the California Rule is to ensure that all evaluators have the requisite training to conduct these evaluations. It is critical to know the education and training requirements in your particular jurisdiction.

Another critical issue often referred to in these practice standards has to do with the issue of confidentiality and informed consent. For example, the California Rule states that all evaluations must include "a written explanation of the process that clearly describes" a number of things, including the purpose of the evaluation, the scope and distribution of the evaluation report, limitations on the confidentiality of the process, and cost and payment responsibility for the evaluation. This is akin to informed consent. There is also a requirement for the evaluator to "include in the initial meeting with each child an age-appropriate explanation of the evaluation process, including limitations on the confidentiality of the process." While there is no informed consent with children, this would be akin to an informed assent process. Additionally, recognizing that collateral witnesses also need to be informed about the process and their role in the custody evaluation process, the AFCC *Model Standards* suggest that evaluators take steps to ensure that collaterals know and understand the potential uses of the information that they are providing. These Standards recommended that this disclosure to collaterals be made in writing. In my opinion, these requirements regarding informed consent and assent are appropriate regardless of where you practice.

Another critical issue is ex parte communication within the evaluation process. Ex parte communication is communication with only one side and is generally prohibited in child custody work. The *Model Standards* state that "child custody evaluators shall not have substantive ex parte communications about a case with the Court or with the attorneys representing the parties." The California Rule requires counties to address ex parte communication in their orders, and court orders typically will prohibit such communication between one side and the evaluator. In most orders appointing me as an evaluator, it is required that any materials sent to the evaluator be copied to the other side, thus prohibiting one-sided communication with me. In Solano County, California, the standard court order requires permission by both sides before any documents can be sent to the evaluator. In the event of a dispute about what the evaluator should receive, the court will make a determination of what documents the evaluator should get. Finally, a different California Rule—Rule of Court 5.235—prohibits the custody evaluator from having ex parte communication with someone appointed as minor's counsel without the court's prior authorization, though in other jurisdictions it is acceptable to have ex parte communication with an attorney for the child, considering that professional to be a collateral witness. Again, it is important to know the standard regarding ex parte communication in your jurisdiction.

Another critical issue addressed in the Rules of Court and the *Model Standards* is the child custody evaluation report. Among other things, the Rule requires the evaluator to discuss with parents the relevant distribution of the report. I make it clear to all participants that the report will be sent to the judge, to the attorneys, and, in some counties, to the parents themselves. If a parent is self-represented and does not have an attorney, local county rules typically determine how that parent gets to read the report and whether or not parents, in general, have access to the report and receive a copy of the report.

In addition to the distribution of the report, the *Model Standards* and the Rule discuss the nature of the evaluator's findings and how to present them. For example, the California Rule states,

> In any presentation of findings, the evaluator must . . . Summarize data gathering procedures, information sources, and time spent, and present all relevant information, *including information that does not support the conclusions reached* (emphasis added) . . . describe any limitations in the evaluation that result from unobtainable information, failure of a party to cooperate, or the circumstances of particular interviews . . . only make a custody or visitation recommendation for a party who has been evaluated [and] . . . provide clear, detailed recommendations that are consistent with the health, safety, welfare, and best interests of the child if making any recommendations to the court regarding a parenting plan. (Rule of Court 5.220, (e) 3 A–D)

The *Model Standards* (2006) state, "[C]hild custody evaluators shall strive to be accurate, objective, fair and independent in their work and are strongly encouraged to utilize peer-reviewed published research in their reports." In my opinion, these requirements are appropriate regardless of where you practice.

Another area in which both the *Model Standards* and the California Rule provide direction is that the evaluator needs to maintain objectivity, use multiple methods of data gathering, and maintain relatively balanced procedures. In a typical child custody evaluation, the evaluator will have several interviews with each parent; several interviews with the child; observations of children and parents together, possibly including home visits, the use of psychological testing and other parenting-related instruments; collateral record review; and collateral phone calls to a variety of relevant people. These procedures will be discussed in Part II. Rule of Court 5.220 and the *Model Standards* recognize that procedures cannot always be balanced. For example, in a recent international relocation evaluation, I spent several days in the international country and several hours with the family to see where the parent wanted the child to live. I did not spend the same amount of time in the local city because I already knew about that city, as did the court. However, I made it clear that, while the procedures might not have looked balanced (and they were not) there was a reason for the unbalanced time spent on each side and focused on the importance of maintaining my neutrality in the case. I urge evaluators to explain themselves when an evaluation lacks balance. This will allow the court and other readers of the report to recognize the legitimacy of unbalanced procedures so that the report remains objective and does not appear biased. It is always critical for the evaluator to be neutral in data gathering as well as data reporting.

In order to avoid the appearance of bias, it is always important to disclose any potential conflicts of interest. In my experience, there are obvious potential conflicts of interest, such as when one of the attorneys, the judge, or a family member is a friend of yours or has been a therapy client of yours. However, there can also be more subtle potential conflicts of interest. A conflict could be perceived when I have published an article or spoken on a panel at a conference with one of the attorneys, if I have been a consultant to the attorney on one side of the case, or even if one of the therapists involved in the case is a close friend of mine. Because I serve as a consultant to many attorneys in my community, my appointment is rarely a problem when both attorneys have previously been in that role. In another example, my wife used to work as an occupational therapist in the schools, and I have been referred cases where one of the children is a special education student at my wife's school. I disclose this potential conflict of interest. In a recent potential case, I was asked to do an evaluation in a city where I do not have an office. I had planned to use the office of a colleague, and one of the parents was concerned that I would be biased because the colleague had done a previous evaluation that was critical of that parent. As a result, I declined acceptance of the referral. Regardless of the potential source of conflict, I believe it is critical to inform parents and attorneys of potential conflicts of interest in any case, preferably before work on the case has begun. However, there could be times when you do not even recognize the connection until receiving the list of collateral witnesses, one of whom might be a friend or close colleague. It is always important to disclose the potential conflict so as to avoid the appearance of bias later in the process. Remember, your licensing board may consider the appearance of your potential conflict a serious offense if one parent files a complaint and you had not taken steps to disclose or rectify the potential conflict as soon as you became aware of it.

In a similar vein, it is not uncommon, especially in small communities, for someone who has had a prior professional role (e.g., mediator, couple's therapist, child therapist, etc.) with one or more family members to conduct the evaluation. In my opinion, and typically in the opinion of licensing boards, it is always wise to turn down a child custody evaluation referral when one has been in a prior role with any family member. In the rare event that you are in such a small community that you are the only person who could do the custody evaluation, it is critical to inform all participants of the risks inherent in switching roles and in becoming the court-appointed child custody evaluator. If you were a therapist for the child or one of the parents, it is difficult to remain neutral and objective because you have been given generally one-sided information. If you were a mediator, you have been provided information that was meant to be confidential and used for settlement purposes and will now potentially be used against a parent in a custody evaluation. Even if you are a child's therapist, your role was a therapeutic one to the child and you gathered information while engaged in that role. Changing to the evaluator role would preclude returning to the therapeutic one. Furthermore, because you gained information that is confidential when you were a therapist, you would now need to disclose that information in your report as the evaluator. For these reasons, I believe it is never wise to change roles, even though the

American Psychological Association's *Ethical Principles for Psychologists* (2002) do allow for dual relationships if they are not being performed at the same time. More on the issue of dual roles and multiple relationships will be discussed in Chapter 2.

It may be appropriate if you have done the original evaluation to be the expert appointed to do an updated evaluation. In that circumstance, the evaluator is not switching roles but has the knowledge gained from the original evaluation to help in the update. At times, it is preferable to recuse yourself from performing the update if one or the other parent might believe that your prior role and conclusions would make you subject to bias. As always, the appearance of bias is just as important as the bias itself.

As noted previously, California Rule 5.220 states that the evaluator must include information in her report that "does not support the conclusions" even while including information that "does support the conclusions." In a similar vein, the *Model Standards* state, "[O]pinions expressed by child custody evaluators shall be based on information and data obtained through the application of reliable principles and methods. Evaluators shall differentiate among the information gathered, observations made, data collected, inferences made, and opinions formulated." The *Model Standards* go on to state, "[T]here shall be a clear correspondence between the opinions offered and the data contained in both the forensic report and the case file." In my opinion, one of the most glaring deficiencies in many child custody evaluation reports is the lack of clarity about the source of conclusions and inferences made by the evaluator. This will be discussed in greater detail in Chapter 10, focusing on the evaluation report.

Finally, in addition to items noted already, California Rule 5.220 has a lengthy section on ethics, stating that the evaluator must

> maintain objectivity, provide and gather balanced information for both parties, and control for bias . . . protect that confidentiality of the parties and children in collateral contacts and not release any information about the case to any individual except as authorized by the court or statute . . . not offer any recommendation about a party unless that party has been evaluated directly or in consultation with another qualified neutral professional . . . strive to maintain a confidential relationship between the child who is the subject of an evaluation and his or her treating psychotherapist . . . operate within the limits of the evaluator's training and experience and disclose any limitations or bias that would affect the evaluator's ability to conduct the evaluation . . . not pressure children to state a custodial preference . . . not disclose any recommendation to the parties, their attorneys, or the attorney for the child before having gathered the information necessary to support the conclusion . . . [and] disclose to the court, parties, attorney for a party and attorney for the child conflicts of interest or dual relationships, and not accept any appointments except by court order or the parties' stipulation. (Rule of Court 5.220, (h) 1–10)

In my opinion, these ethical principles for child custody evaluations are stated well by the California Rule and should be followed by all child custody evaluators.

Though providing fewer specific practice guidelines or standards, the 2009 American Psychological Association (APA) *Guidelines* provide some very good Orienting Guidelines, such as "the purpose of the evaluation is to assist in determining the psychological best interests of the child," "the child's welfare is paramount," and that the evaluation "focuses upon parental attributes, the child's psychological needs, and the resulting fit." Like the AFCC *Model Standards,* the APA *Guidelines* encourage evaluators to strive to "gain and maintain specialized competence," "function as impartial evaluators," "engage in culturally informed, nondiscriminatory evaluation practices," and "avoid conflicts of interest and multiple relationships in conducting evaluations." Additionally, the *Guidelines* provide certain procedural direction, suggesting that psychologists strive to "obtain appropriately informed consent," "employ multiple methods of data gathering," "interpret assessment data in a manner consistent with the context of the evaluation," "complement the evaluation with the appropriate combination of examinations," "base their recommendations, if any, upon the psychological best interests of the child," and "create and maintain professional records in accordance with ethical and legal obligations."

> Following *Ethical Principles, Model Standards, Evaluation Guidelines,* and Rules of Court can help ensure that the evaluation procedures are appropriate.

## Evaluator Biases

Much has been written about the potential for bias in child custody evaluations (see, e.g., Gutheil & Simon, 2004; Martindale, 2005; P. Stahl, 2006). While it is beyond the scope of this chapter to go into depth about potential evaluator biases, I will focus on a handful of potential biases and ways to avoid them. The material presented here was adapted from an article I wrote on avoiding bias in relocation cases (P. Stahl, 2006).

Gutheil and Simon (2004) list several types of bias that may affect an expert's work as a way of helping to avoid the impact of those sources of bias. While all sources of bias are relevant in any family law or forensic matter, I will focus on some potential sources of bias and the risk that each has in deciding a particular relocation case.

### Gender Bias

Gender bias is one of the more classic biases in family law, as custody evaluators, family mediators, and judges are frequently accused of gender bias and of treating women and men differently in the system. Politically, there are mother's-rights advocates and father's-rights advocates who, by their very nature, take advocacy positions on a variety of issues. I believe that the research that focuses on "the psychological parent" (see, e.g., Goldstein, Freud, & Solnit, 1984) tends to support and favor mothers over fathers. Other observers interpret the growing research data on fathers and their involvement with children (see, e.g., Lamb, Sternberg, & Thompson, 1997) as supporting a father's-rights bias. It is critical for judges and evaluators to avoid gender bias in their work.

## Cultural Bias

This refers to the potential for a judge or custody evaluator to make decisions based on aspects of the culture of one or both of the parties being served. One way this may surface in relocation cases is when one of the parents wants to move children to a country that has very different cultural experiences or to a country that has not adopted the Hague Convention on the Civil Aspects of International Child Abduction. While the cultural issues may be important, especially in a long-distance relocation, it is only one factor and might not be the only relevant issue to be considered. I have seen a situation in which an evaluator highlighted the distance to a South American country and the need for the child to adjust to a new culture as being more important than all of the other issues in a particular case, including the child's special education needs and the relative attachment differences, when making a recommendation against the move.

## Primacy or Recency Bias

Primacy bias refers to the tendency to rely on the first pieces of information that an evaluator hears, whereas recency bias refers to an evaluator relying on the last pieces of information that the evaluator hears (Gutheil & Simon, 2004). These potential biases are a significant risk in all child custody evaluations. For example, if the evaluator hears early in the evaluation from one parent that the other parent who wants to move has often interfered with access, the hypothesis of the interference may take precedent over conducting a complete evaluation focusing on many factors. A similar risk occurs when an evaluator hears from a collateral witness toward the end of an evaluation that one parent has not attended any parent–teacher conferences. While this might be important data, the risk of bias occurs when the evaluator stops gathering more data because she believes that this last piece of data puts the proverbial nail in the coffin and stops gathering data that might be critical in reaching a conclusion.

## Confirmatory Bias

Like the bias associated with primacy or recency effects, confirmatory bias is the tendency for a custody evaluator to look for certain data or evidence that supports a particular position and then try to make all of the other data fit that position. This is also called anchoring bias: The evaluator anchors herself to particular data and does not consider other data that might support a different conclusion. Hence, the evaluator is looking for data to support the position that the evaluator holds or believes. This is a significant risk in many types of evaluations. For example, it is a risk in relocation cases if the evaluator believes that moves are either generally a good thing or generally a bad thing. Confirmatory bias is a risk when considering different parenting plans if the evaluator believes that children need a 50–50 arrangement, or that such an arrangement is harmful to children. Confirmatory bias interferes with the evaluator's ability to look for data or evidence that does not support the conclusion reached. In order to reduce the risk of confirmatory bias, the evaluator must consider multiple hypotheses and continue gathering all relevant data before reaching any conclusions on the case.

## Bias From Psychological Test Data

Psychologists who are prone to view cases a certain way are at risk for interpreting psychological test data to support a particular position rather than using it to generate hypotheses. While there is significant risk for the misapplication of psychological test data in any child custody evaluation (see Chapter 8 for more on psychological testing), it is my opinion that there is great risk for this misapplication of test data to support a particular conclusion in a relocation case. For example, if a parent in a relocation case tests as defensive and presents herself in a favorable light on an Minnesota Multiphasic Personality Inventory (MMPI-2), as many custody litigants do (see, e.g., Bathurst, Gottfried, & Gottfried, 1997), a psychologist who is reluctant to recommend in favor of a move might use that data, and that data alone, to suggest that she cannot be trusted to support the child's relationship with the other parent after she moves. Similarly, a psychologist might suggest that a parent who scores as narcissistic on the Millon Clinical Multiaxial Inventory-III (MCMI-III) and the Rorschach Inkblot Test might not be sufficiently child-focused to be the primary parent and recommend that the other parent be able to move with the child. The problem with both of these situations is that psychological tests should be used only to generate hypotheses about people's personality traits and should never be used to generate recommendations (Gould, 1998; P. Stahl, 1999).

## "Truth Lies Somewhere in the Middle" Bias

I have identified a few potential sources of bias that are not mentioned elsewhere in the literature. One example is what I call the "truth lies somewhere in the middle" bias. Many evaluators, in particular those who are at risk for burnout because they have worked in the system for a long time, are at risk for exhibiting this bias. There is a tendency to perceive that a couple engaged in conflict contributes equally to this conflict. While that is potentially true in any divorce, there are other instances in which one parent drives most of the conflict and the other parent tends to be more reactive to that conflict. This "truth lies somewhere in the middle" bias prevents evaluators from recognizing the unique contributions of each parent to the conflict. However, these unique contributions to the conflict are likely to be an important and relevant factor to consider. Assigning equal blame to both parents when the responsibility for different levels and components of the conflict are more likely caused by one parent rather than the other parent is a mistake.

## "Attila the Hun Doesn't Marry Mother Theresa" Bias

Another potential bias that is not described elsewhere is what Rotman called the "Attila the Hun doesn't marry Mother Theresa" bias (A. Rotman, personal communication, 2000). Many experienced evaluators have long recognized that, in most families, parents are relatively equal in their parenting ability. Like the "truth lies somewhere in the middle" bias, this bias presupposes that a healthy parent is not likely to marry a non-functional parent. While that frequently may be the case, it is not necessarily the case. When looking at individual family members, there are many instances in which one parent or the other is clearly psychologically healthier than the other, has a healthier attachment with the child, and/or has a parenting style that is more consistent with a particular child's temperament and needs.

## "For the Move" or "Against the Move" Bias

All of this leads to my concern that many evaluators have a bias that moves are either a good thing or a bad thing for children. Those who tend to be pro-move take the position that a custodial parent who wishes to move should generally be allowed to move as long as the custodial parent has a legitimate reason for moving and/or is not attempting to interfere with the access rights of the other parent. They might bring a unitary approach to relocation cases in which, once they determine that one or the other parent is "the psychological parent," and once they determine that there is a legitimate reason for moving or that there is no evidence of interference with the other parent's access, the expected outcome is that this parent can move with the child. Jurisdictionally, there are many states in which case or statutory law supports such a presumption in favor of moving, but there is no evidence in the literature to suggest that psychologists should have such a presumptive belief in relocation cases.

Similarly, there are many custody evaluators who perceive that it is a parent's responsibility to stay near the other parent in order to preserve the child's access to the other parent and the involvement of both parents in her life. I believe that, while there is research data to support the belief that children benefit from both parents' active involvement in their life (J. Kelly & Emery, 2003), extrapolating that data to support a presumption against moves confounds the issue. Clearly, there are many circumstances in which a move is both legitimate and justified, whether for academic, economic, or other personal/family reasons. In those cases, one parent or the other is going to move. It is incumbent on evaluators and judges not to confuse the preference for shared co-parenting that may exist in some of the research and some statutory laws with a presumption that moves will harm children. Rather than having a presumption against the move, it is my view that evaluators and judges must consider and weigh the relative risks and benefits of having the child move with one parent as opposed to having the child not move and remain primarily with the other parent. Those observers who encourage "conditional change of custody orders" to try to prevent some parents from moving (e.g., Braver, Ellman, & Fabricius, 2003) run the risk of using an "against the move" bias as a way to keep both parents in the same geographic location.

> Biases are potentially insidious and can interfere with a neutral analysis of data. Ethics require awareness of biases to reduce their impact.

## Reducing the Risk of Bias

One of the ways to reduce the risk of bias affecting a person's conclusions is to recognize clearly that biases exist and that we are all at risk of being affected by our biases. Once they consider this fact, evaluators can examine their conclusions and decisions and look for trends or evidence of such bias. For example, some evaluators have rarely recommended in favor of a move. Other evaluators typically recommend joint physical custody. Still others might never recommend shared parenting with the belief that children feel like Ping-Pong balls going back and forth between their parents' homes. Some have taken the position that overnights with the noncustodial parent are never a good idea until a child reaches at least 3 years of age, while others posit that infants can adjust well with any schedule that encourages both parents' active involvement. All of this is based on bias and not the particulars of the case. If these evaluators do not examine the reasons for their beliefs, they can never determine whether they are based on some type of bias or not.

Suppose you have discovered that you are at risk of letting your bias contribute to your decision-making. Once you recognize that bias exists, the next step you can take is to participate in peer consultation. Discuss your challenging cases (and most relocation cases and infant cases are challenging) with several peers, especially those whom you know to be more experienced in these matters. I suggest that you use that consultation to challenge your thinking, so it is helpful to choose colleagues who might not always see things the same way as you. Encourage your colleague to play devil's advocate with you, to force you to make a less biased analysis.

Along the same lines, play devil's advocate for yourself. Challenge your reasoning. Ask yourself if you have considered all of your data or if you have showed evidence of confirmatory, recency, primacy, or anchoring bias in your report. If you have used multiple methods to gather data (which is expected) and maintained multiple hypotheses at each stage of the case, and if you have considered and integrated all data before reaching conclusions, you will be at less risk of having a bias affect the outcome of a particular case.

Another excellent way to reduce the risk of bias is to take, and teach, continuing education courses in all areas of assessment and family law. Evaluators need to stay up to date on all of the relevant research in the areas of family law, including relocation, domestic violence, issues of abuse, child development and attachment theory, alienation, the effects of divorce and high conflict on children, and ways to ameliorate the negative effects of divorce. In so doing, they can reduce the likelihood that biases like the ones discussed in this chapter will contribute to their conclusions.

## THE BOTTOM LINE

- The AFCC *Model Standards,* the American Psychological Association *Guidelines,* and the Rules of Court exist to help guide evaluators toward optimal practice. Even if you do not live and work in a jurisdiction with Rules of Court guiding your practice, or even if you are not a psychologist or AFCC member, these *Model Standards, Guidelines,* and Rules of Court provide sound guidance to any child custody evaluator.
- Important tips include:
  o Always get a court order before conducting the evaluation
  o Obtain informed consent before conducting your evaluation and disclose the limits of confidentiality of the process to all participants (parents, children, and collateral witnesses)
  o Avoid ex parte communication with the judge or an attorney for one side
  o Use multiple methods of data gathering in conducting your evaluation
  o In your report and your testimony, present all of your data, including data that do not support your conclusions
- Child custody evaluations are for the court and the family, with the focus being on the best interests of the child. Reports should always be written with that in mind.
- The potential for bias exists for all of us. Examine your practice and look for sources of bias. Maintain peer consultation and take (and teach) continuing education in many child custody and divorce areas.

# 2

# The Mental Health Expert's Many Possible Roles[1]

As suggested in Chapter 1, the mental health expert is brought in under many different circumstances when working with families of divorce. Each possible role is unique and requires the mental health expert to provide a different service to the individual or family in need. Oftentimes, the mental health practitioner is asked by the family to engage in more than one role. As noted in Chapter 1, the complications and risks of blending or changing roles far outweigh any possible benefit to the family. In this brief chapter, I will outline the various roles that mental health practitioners may experience, suggesting styles of practice that work for each role. The chapter will end with a continued discussion of the risks associated with dual relationships, especially those related to custody evaluations.

Some mental health roles are therapeutic in nature and some are forensic in nature. S. Greenberg and Shuman (1997) wrote about the "irreconcilable differences" between forensic and therapeutic roles. They identified the differences along many dimensions, including but not limited to the differences in understanding who the client is, differences in dealing with confidentiality, differences in competency required by the professional, differences in the nature of hypotheses to be tested in the role, differences in the nature and degree of "adversarialness" in the relationship, differences in the goal of the professional in each type of relationship, and differences in the impact of the professional's judgment on the relationship. I urge anyone who has not read this article to find and read it, as it remains the clearest and most comprehensive article on the topic ever written, in my opinion.

## Therapists

Traditionally, a therapist for an individual will see her role as being that of an advocate for the mental health needs of that individual. The therapist gets to know the inner thoughts and feelings of her client, understands her client's many conflicts, and truly understands her client's strengths and weaknesses as an individual. The therapist will often hear about other family members through the eyes of her client, and will learn about her client's perceptions of the relationships the client has with his with spouse and children. A therapist gathers this information to understand her client's perceptions to help him with the problems he experiences in his life. Therapists recognize that the things the client says are a function of his perceptions, and not always the "truth." In our role as therapists, truth may not matter as much as perception, because the client's perceptions are of paramount importance as we try to help him with his internal and relationship conflicts throughout his life.

As noted in Chapter 1, an individual therapist would never make a recommendation regarding custody to the court because the individual therapist has not met all of the parties, has not evaluated relationships, does not know objectively the strengths and weaknesses of both parents, and cannot know what is in the child's best interests. Additionally, therapy is typically seen as a confidential relationship, and if a therapist were to make such a recommendation, even with the authorization of her client, it could open up the therapy to complete disclosure to the other side and to the court. Based on my experience and based on a standard of care informed by the Association of Family and Conciliation Courts' (AFCC) *Model Standards of Practice for Child Custody Evaluation* (2006), the American Psychological Association's (APA) *Guidelines for Child Custody Evaluations* (2009), and the *California Rules of Court* (2009), I suspect that such an action would invite a complaint from the therapist's licensing board. Always check with your malpractice carrier before writing such a letter to the court.

> A person who has been a therapist for any member of a family should avoid becoming a child custody evaluator.

As a child's therapist, we may be trying to help the child with specific behavioral problems, or, during a particularly messy divorce, we may be helping the child find refuge from the tensions in her life. We need to be very careful when asked to be a child's therapist if the parents are divorced or in the midst of an ongoing divorce battle. It is important to ascertain that we have the permission of *both* parents, and we need to be clear that we will be providing treatment to the child, not providing information to be used in a custody dispute. It may be best to have a court order to provide the therapy so that neither parent can terminate the therapy without getting a new court order.

A child going through the divorce of her parents often needs the assistance of a therapist to help sort out her feelings, not a therapist who is caught in the advocacy of her parents. She may need the therapist to be an advocate in communicating with her parents about her fears, feelings, and more, but not participate in the acrimonious battle between the parents. When she works with her client's parents, the child's therapist is an advocate for the child, and assists the parents in issues of parenting and improving the communication and relationship between the child and her parents. Again, the child's therapist is an advocate for a single member of the family, and she recognizes that her information is the result of the child's perceptions, not always a complete measure of the truth. In fact, many children, when they perceive the therapist to be in the middle of her parents' custody disputes, are unwilling to trust in the therapeutic alliance any longer.

A growing form of child therapy is referred to as "safe haven" therapy. In such therapy, which is almost always court ordered, the therapy is guaranteed to be kept from the court litigation. In high-conflict families, the court will order a child taken to therapy, and order that neither parent can try to influence the therapy or bring information from the therapy to court. Such a therapist would be unable to speak as a collateral witness to a child custody evaluator or Parent Coordinator (see later this chapter) without court authorization, because the therapy is protected. If appointed to this role, you will need to understand critical issues involved with high-conflict families of divorce.

Just like an individual adult therapist, the child therapist should never write a letter to the court recommending a particular custody plan. In an ongoing informal survey of judges,[2] judges have expressed almost universal frustration over getting such letters, even though regular family law judges may get several of those letters in a month. Again, I would urge anyone considering writing such a letter to consult with one's malpractice carrier, regardless of whether or not one or both parents have asked for such a letter.

> Therapists must avoid writing letters to the judge with custody recommendations, even if urged to do so by their client or a parent.

A family therapist, while aware of more of the family's "truths" because she sees the entire family together, also has a primary focus. That focus is clearly to assist the family system to improve its functioning, with more open communication and often less overdependence between family members. The goals of the family therapist are usually to bring about change within the family dynamics and to help members function more autonomously, while simultaneously improving unity and communication and encouraging more functional dynamics for the family. Often the family therapist is trying to help the family to stay together and, as such, is unprepared to tackle the complex issues of the divorce and recommend for "the best interests of the child."

A couples' therapist focuses on the marital relationship, trying to help spouses learn to communicate better, and assist the individual adults to work toward an improved marital relationship. While the therapist may have talked about the children, she usually does not really know too much about each of the children and their individual needs. Clearly, she knows a lot about the marital partners, how they communicate, and what their issues have been. Yet, she, too, is not in a position to make recommendations about custody/access because there are too many gaps in her knowledge. Again, if you are in that role, even if both parents want you to do so, consult with your malpractice carrier before writing such a letter to the court.

Finally, it is important to recognize that, as with custody evaluators and other professionals, there are good therapists and therapists who contribute to the family's problems. It is important for the court to be aware of the impact of the child and adult therapy on the overall family dynamics. If necessary, the court (and the evaluator in her recommendations) might want to consider removing a therapist who is causing more problems than being helpful in a given case. For more information on this topic, see the article by L. Greenberg, Gould, Gould-Saltmann, and Stahl (2003).

# Therapeutic Reunification

When there has been a long history of little or no contact between a parent and a child, the court may appoint a reunification therapist to build, or rebuild, the relationship between the parent and child (see, e.g., Deutsch, 2008). Perhaps there has been a period of no contact due to allegations of abuse. If the abuse allegation has been ruled against by the court, the court will typically order contact to resume. However, the judge may want to rebuild the relationship slowly and with the help of a therapist. Similarly, when there has been limited contact between a parent and child due to the estrangement or alienation of the child, therapeutic reunification may be ordered to start the process of reconnecting parent and child. The therapist can work with both parent and child, usually with a combination of individual and conjoint work, to help rebuild the relationship.

Similarly, it would not be uncommon if there has been no contact between a parent and child for a therapist to be appointed to help build the attachment. This might be done in paternity cases where there has been no contact for several years, and then the biological father petitions for contact. When this happens, the therapist is needed to help the child and the parent to get to know one another. After some time, the parent and child can begin the process of increasing time together and taking the relationship outside the therapist's office.

Just as other therapists should avoid getting involved in the decision of when and how much parenting time each parent should have (i.e., custody and access decisions of the court), reunification therapists should resist the request of the court to "decide" when there should be an increase in the estranged parent's parenting time. Perhaps the best situation is to have a collateral role with a court-appointed Parent Coordinator (discussed later) in which the therapist informs the Parent Coordinator how the therapy is progressing and then lets the Parent Coordinator make a decision or a recommendation to the court. Otherwise, if the child or either of the parents is not happy with the recommendation of the therapist, it could sabotage the therapeutic efforts.

# Collaborative Law Coach

According to Tesler (2004), collaborative law is a

> dispute resolution model in which both parties to the dispute retain separate, specially-trained lawyers whose only job is to help them settle the dispute. If the lawyers do not succeed in helping the clients resolve the problem, the lawyers are out of a job and can never represent either client against the other again. All participants agree to work together respectfully, honestly, and in good faith to try to find "win-win" solutions to the legitimate needs of both parties. No one may go to court, or even threaten to do so, and if that should occur, the Collaborative Law process terminates and both lawyers are disqualified from any further involvement in the case.

Mental health professionals get involved with collaborative law in the role of a collaborative law coach. Coaching is a form of consultation. Oftentimes, the adults in collaborative law will have their own coaches, and it is not uncommon for parents to work together with a different child coach. The adult coach helps the client reduce the stress associated with divorce, stay focused on the conflict-resolution process by identifying and prioritizing goals, maximize communication with the spouse and attorneys, and assist in negotiation, and also supports the client through the divorce process in a less adversarial and more productive way, with less reaction to emotions. The child coach helps parents understand the child and her developmental, social, academic, and psychological needs; develop a functional parenting plan; remain focused on the child and improve communication about her needs; and learn to work together in a productive parenting manner.

Collaborative law coaches will never write a report to the court or make recommendations to the judge, though coaches may write letters to the collaborative attorneys or participate in collaborative meetings with the attorneys if that will benefit the adults or child client whom they serve.

# Psychologist Evaluator/ Psychiatrist/Vocational Evaluator

In a recent child custody evaluation, one of the parents had undergone an Independent Medical Examination (IME) by a psychiatrist to help understand a history of significant emotional and potentially suicidal feelings. In a different evaluation, the parent who wanted to move underwent a vocational assessment to help in understanding her earning capacity in both her current and proposed locations. In a third evaluation, the child had undergone an assessment for her Individual Educational Plan (IEP) and to understand her special education needs for school. Each of these unique assessments had an important role within the family, but would not be used instead of a child custody evaluation to help in understanding custody and access decisions for the court.

For a variety of reasons, an individual may have undergone a psychological or other type of evaluation. Other examples could include the child, who may be evaluated because of school or behavioral problems, or as part of an overall diagnostic assessment prior to beginning therapy; or the adolescent or adult with drug or alcohol problems who has participated in a psychological assessment as part of the initial determination of appropriate treatment planning for her substance abuse. Similarly, an adult who has been hospitalized for an acute depressive reaction may have completed a psychological evaluation in order to assess his psychological condition, or a woman with a chronic mental illness may have had several psychological evaluations over time in order to assess any change in her functioning as part of ongoing treatment plans. As with the previously described therapist role, the goal of these psychological evaluations is clear: to assess an individual's cognitive and/or emotional functioning, usually for the purpose of assisting in the development of appropriate interventions. Although the client is usually part of a family, the individual psychological evaluation is not related to family functioning in any comprehensive way. The evaluation is an analysis of the individual, not within the context of the family. As such, the psychologist evaluator is not in a position to make an assessment of the complex issues of custody and/or access.

At the same time, this psychologist will often be a collateral witness in the evaluation. Either the child custody evaluator will want to talk with the psychologist who performed the individual assessment as a collateral witness, or at the very least, she will want to use the report for adjunct collateral information in the context of the overall custody evaluation.

# Mediator

A mediator is directly involved in the divorce process, either court-connected or in private practice, to assist the divorcing couple to settle their many disputes and reach solutions that assist in conflict reduction during the divorce process. In most states, the mediation process is confidential, which prevents the mediator from participating in the adversarial court process. This confidentiality enables the mediator and the couple to work more effectively in trying to resolve conflict, without fear that things said in mediation can be used against the other person in litigation. Many mediators view such confidentiality to be essential for mediation to result in a successful outcome. California has a unique family court system in which mediation may not be confidential and may result in a recommendation for a custody and access plan. While I recognize the need to get relevant information to the court in these circumstances, I am concerned that these recommendations may yield a recommendation made on the basis of very limited information.

Regardless of the confidentiality, a mediator's primary objectives are to help the couple reduce conflict while reaching solutions about the many issues on which they disagree. More often than not, mediation focuses on the custody disputes, and the mediator will try to use her knowledge and negotiation skills to assist a couple in coming up with their own parenting plan. Whether such mediation takes place in a private mediator's office or in a court-connected setting, the goal of mediation is to assist the couple in developing their own parenting plan for the children, without any recommendation from the mediator. In the event that the couple cannot reach an agreement, local court rules may allow the mediator to provide information regarding the family dynamics so that the judge can make an order regarding the custodial arrangement. Regardless, because the mediator will have had prior contact with the parents, the mediator is not an appropriate resource for evaluating the family. As such, the mediator should decline any referral to be the court-appointed child custody evaluator. The mediator, like most of the other persons listed in this chapter, is likely to be a collateral witness for the child custody evaluator, unless confidentiality precludes such involvement by the mediator.

# Consultant to Attorney/Expert Witness

A family law attorney and a mental health practitioner may develop a working relationship in which they periodically consult with one another on more complex cases. I have been asked by attorneys to review custody evaluations, not necessarily to critique the evaluation, but to help the attorney understand some of the dynamics involved in a particular family matter. I have also been asked for my perception of the risk to children based upon limited information, to see if a custody evaluation might be in order. There is a growing use of experienced custody evaluators to critique the custody evaluation or other work product of a neutrally appointed evaluator to assess its thoroughness and to determine whether the recommendations made by the evaluator are consistent with the data collected in the evaluation. This is a unique field and is increasingly being used in cases that go to trial rather than settle after mediation or the completion of a child custody evaluation.

Similarly, during litigation, the court may require the expert testimony of a psychologist or other mental health professional to assist in understanding certain factual information in the case. In this situation, I am referring to testimony not derived from the completion of a custody evaluation, but simply connected to one's knowledge of problems of divorce, general psychological principles, child development, or some specific divorce-related matter, such as relocation. I have seen psychologists provide testimony to the court to assist in determining whether or not a custody evaluation is necessary. On other occasions, I have known psychologists to provide expert testimony associated with some aspect of child development that is quite complicated, and therefore a significant issue for the court's understanding. In such instances, the mental health expert is providing a specific function to the court in the absence of direct knowledge of a particular case. The consultant may be asked to provide expert witness testimony about issues in front of the court, such as relocation, child development and overnights with young children, domestic violence, or alienation. This expert would avoid making specific recommendations about the best interests of a child she has not evaluated, though it may be appropriate to discuss relevant risks and benefits of various custodial options based on hypothetical questions posed by the attorneys. As with the other roles, this expert will not be able to provide the complete neutrality that is necessary in custody evaluations, should the case be referred for one.

Although many mental health experts will not engage in unilateral assistance of one attorney, there are occasions where it may be very appropriate, as long as the consultant does not make specific recommendations regarding custody or access. The goals for such consultation will be to assist the attorney in understanding the aspects of family dynamics while providing suggestions to the attorney about how to proceed in her case. While colleagues express a certain degree of risk in such consultation, I have found that, as long as the psychologist adheres to her ethical principles, she can provide consultation to the attorney that is ultimately useful for all members of the family, not just the attorney and her client. This role will be discussed in greater length in Chapter 16.

# Parent Coordinator

In growing numbers, mental health professionals are being asked to take on the role of Parent Coordinator. Their tasks are generally the same, though different jurisdictions identify these individuals in different ways. For purposes of this section, my use of the term *Parent Coordinator* will also refer to terms that some states use or have used, such as Special Master (California), Mediation/Arbitrator (Colorado), Family Court Advisor (Arizona), or Wise Person (New Mexico). AFCC (2005) has also promulgated *Guidelines for Parenting Coordination.*

Often, the Parent Coordinator is appointed following the completion of a custody evaluation when the evaluator recognizes that the parents will need someone outside of the court to continue in an ongoing way to monitor or settle issues between them. In some states, the role of Parent Coordinator is defined by statute, and refers to the quasi-judicial task of hearing all sides to a dispute and making binding decisions upon the parties. In many instances, the task of the Parent Coordinator is narrowly defined, such as to address issues of transportation and monitoring the dropping off/picking up of the children. In other situations, the role of the Parent Coordinator is broadly defined, such as to address all outstanding disputes between the parents, help them to settle, and if they cannot, to order binding decisions upon them. California and most other jurisdictions do not allow a judge to "order" a couple to hire a Parent Coordinator to assume judicial authority, instead only allowing for the Parent Coordinator to be appointed by stipulation of both parents. In practice, the best method may be to stipulate that the Parent Coordinator's order will become binding unless appealed by either party within a defined reasonable period of time (e.g., 20 days).

> The Parent Coordinator can be invaluable in helping parents learn to reduce conflict and work toward resolving their disputes, and in keeping children out of the middle of the conflict.

In my experience, the Parent Coordinator's actual task is complex and involves the skills of detective, evaluator, therapist, educator, teacher, parent, mediator, and judge, depending on the issues that need settlement. In my various appointments over the years, I have helped parents with the following tasks:

- Choosing a child's school
- Determining a child's involvement in extracurricular activities (where, what activities, when)
- Adjusting the parenting time schedule when one parent had a variable work schedule and they were trying to maintain a relatively equal parenting plan
- Determining whether a child would see a therapist and who the therapist would be
- Helping the parents learn to communicate with one another in a civil manner

- Helping parents see when their communications were hostile and inappropriate
- Ensuring that the nonresidential parent received all of her parenting time, and making sure that appropriate makeup time was enforced if the regular time was missed
- Generally resolving issues so that parents stayed out of court

My experience with other Parent Coordinator appointments included the following tasks:

- Monitoring drug/alcohol tests and ensuring that the testing protocol was appropriately followed
- Monitoring compliance with other court orders
- Making necessary decisions to help children's lives move seamlessly forward

Because the Parent Coordinator's authority extends only as far as the parents are willing to agree, the Parent Coordinator needs to use all of her skills to keep the family out of court and focused on the needs of their children. In my experience, the stipulation and appointment of a Parent Coordinator, especially when the role is carefully defined, is a useful way for encouraging some of the more litigious clients to learn more cooperative ways of co-parenting or parallel parenting, stay out of court, and lower the economic and emotional costs of their divorce. Finally, although the Parent Coordinator cannot become an evaluator because of the need for complete neutrality, when a subsequent evaluation is needed, the Parent Coordinator's input as a collateral witness would be valuable. For more information on the role of the Parent Coordinator, see P. Stahl (1995), Coates et al. (2003), Sullivan and Kelly (2001), and the Special Issue on Parenting Coordination of the *Journal of Child Custody* (Vol. 5, Nos. 1–2, July 2008).

## The Custody Evaluator

When a mental health professional is given the task of completing a custody evaluation, that evaluator must come into the process completely neutral, without hidden bias, and with no prior contact with any member of the family. Such an ethical position would preclude anyone who has been a therapist, mediator, consultant, expert witness, psychologist evaluator, or Parent Coordinator to anyone in the family from being the neutral, court-appointed evaluator. Unlike the other professional roles outlined, it is the task of the evaluator to assess the entire family objectively, focusing on the dynamics of the family, the individual strengths and weaknesses of each parent, and the functioning of the children, while making recommendations to the court regarding the best interests of the child. It is a unique role, and must, in my opinion, be kept separate from the other roles outlined.

# Dual Relationships

As noted in Chapter 1, there are now several professional associations that have ethical rules regarding custody evaluations. For many evaluators, the simple rule is "never conduct a custody evaluation when the evaluator has had a prior relationship of any kind with any member of the family." Thus, if the evaluator has given expert testimony to the judge related to a particular family's dynamics, or if he has been a therapist to any member of the family, or a mediator, or a consultant to one of the attorneys for this family, it is inappropriate to conduct a custody evaluation. As mentioned in Chapter 1, a custody evaluation must be completed by a neutral, impartial mental health expert who gathers facts about the family and its individual members in order to make a recommendation for the custody and access plans of the family. Prior knowledge of any family member would make such neutrality impossible.

In many situations, it may be perfectly helpful for the other mental health expert, usually a therapist or mediator, to talk with the child custody evaluator, and provide her input to the evaluation process as a collateral witness. In such circumstances, the evaluator will need to gather such information as an adjunct to the rest of the facts of the case.

There may also be times when the other mental health professional may not want to talk with the evaluator. In those circumstances, the other mental health professional may compromise himself and could possibly violate his client's rights if he is not careful. There are at least two such instances that come to mind. One is the mediator who has ensured the confidentiality of the mediation process from the litigation. Even if both parents sign a release of information authorizing the evaluator to speak with the mediator, the mediator is likely to claim confidentiality, as her knowledge was gained with confidentiality in mind. Providing information to the evaluator while knowing that the evaluation could ultimately end up in litigation could therefore be a mistake. In addition, if, following the evaluation, the couple were to go back to mediation, it would be difficult to trust the mediator in the future if confidential material had been disclosed.

A second instance where this is critical is with the child's therapist. As noted earlier, some children's therapists are appointed to perform "safe-haven therapy" and will have the confidentiality confirmed by court order. At other times, however, the therapist is working with a child whose parents are in the midst of a heated custody dispute and the primary task of the therapy is to provide a safe place for the child to express herself. Even if this therapy is not court-ordered as safe-haven therapy, the therapist in such a case will most likely want to ensure the child's confidentiality in order to protect the child's emerging thoughts and feelings. Even though parents may authorize the release of information, there are times when maintaining our silence is critical so we can assist the child in staying out of the middle of the parental dispute. If the child fears that her communications could end up being divulged to the evaluator, or to her parents, this child is likely to hold back from sharing necessary feelings and thoughts with her therapist. By ensuring confidentiality, and maintaining it even when an evaluation is in progress, we are providing a place of safety for the child. Obviously, there may be times when it is critical for the therapist to talk with the evaluator, such as when she feels that there is a degree of risk for the child in relation to one of his parents. Clearly, the therapist must balance the child's right to privacy and need to stay out of the middle of the conflict with the need for the evaluator to have crucial information about the child and his relationships. As noted in Chapter 1, California Rule of Court 5.220 addresses this issue by requiring court-appointed child custody evaluators to ensure the confidentiality of communications between the therapist and the child.

To safeguard the need for confidentiality of the child's therapy, in many jurisdictions the court will become the holder of the child's psychotherapeutic privilege. Then, when a dispute arises regarding this question, the judge will make a decision about confidentiality and the extent to which the child's therapist should provide information to the evaluator, and whether this information should be safeguarded, sealed by the court, and kept out of the report and the legal proceedings.

Similarly, the individual therapist of an adult client may wish to maintain confidentiality from the evaluator. A therapist may feel that he cannot divulge confidential information, even when a release was signed, because it would interfere with his ability to be a therapeutic advocate for his client. At all times, the evaluator needs to be sensitive to the ongoing goals and needs of the other mental health experts when consulting with or seeking information about the family or an individual member of the family.

Another possible source of controversy among evaluators is the blending of the roles of evaluator and mediator. On occasion, especially in California where recommending mediation is common, after being appointed to conduct the evaluation, an evaluator who also does mediation may find that a particular couple may not be that far apart and could benefit from mediation rather than going through the evaluation process. Many attorneys and court personnel would suggest that the evaluator could easily shift roles and try to mediate the issues between the parents. After all, a working alliance is being established, and some would argue that the evaluator would be the best person to attempt such mediation.

While I agree that the timing may make sense, it is my belief that if a mental health professional is appointed by the court to do a custody evaluation and the evaluator senses that mediation would be more appropriate, she should suspend her evaluation and refer the couple to a willing mediator and assist that mediator in understanding the dynamics that suggested that such mediation could be successful. The primary reason that I am opposed to changing roles in the middle is that should mediation efforts fail, it will be difficult for the evaluator to reestablish the necessary impartiality to complete the evaluation. It is my belief that once we blend roles, we lose effectiveness in whatever role we end up taking. By maintaining the integrity of a single role from beginning to end, we can assure the family that we are undertaking that role to the best of our ability, with no other agenda in mind. When objectivity and neutral impartiality are required, it is easy for the evaluator to *always* maintain it, as long as she never changes roles during the evaluation process.

At the same time, it has been argued (Barsky, 2007) that there is a place for the blending of mediation and evaluation. Barsky refers to the process as "mediative evaluation" and suggests that if an evaluator were to offer the role, it should be defined as distinct from either mediation or evaluation and provide clear and distinct informed consent of the process at the outset. He adds that it is a potentially dual role and should be offered only if all the parties recognize the inherent risks involved, and if there is both a grievance procedure and a method for terminating the process. While believing that the role is a valid one, and not automatically a dual role, Barsky does recommend referral to others, especially in those situations where the mediative evaluator is concerned about risk.

Finally, after completing my evaluation, I have often been asked to follow my evaluation role and become a mediator, therapist, or a Parent Coordinator. While I recognize that a certain degree of flexibility is in order once the evaluation has been completed, I have come to the conclusion that it is best for me not to mix roles even after the completion of an evaluation. Oftentimes I am asked to complete an updated evaluation at a later date, and again, if I have shifted roles after the completion of an evaluation, I can no longer maintain the necessary neutral impartiality. Similarly, I have seen many cases go to trial as long as a year to 18 months after the completion of an evaluation. If I have taken on another role in that time, and my testimony related to the evaluation is necessary, it is likely that this testimony will be compromised by my new role in the case. The more I see the possible complications of blending roles, the more I am convinced that it is safest to maintain rigid boundaries after completing the evaluation. The only time I would recommend that an evaluator shift roles after an evaluation has been completed is in those geographic areas where there are few experts, and where the shifting of roles may be necessary in order to provide the necessary therapeutic, mediation, or other dispute resolution assistance after an evaluation has been completed. Even in such circumstances, it would be wise to caution the family and to seek the advice of the court prior to undertaking such a shift in roles.

It is my firm belief that, as mental health professionals, we must keep separate our many possible roles when working with divorcing families. During the course of an evaluation, we seek information from other professionals who have worked with various family members, and confidentiality may be more important than assisting an evaluator with her assessment. Once we have begun an evaluation, it is my belief that as evaluators we must not change roles, though a suspension of the evaluation might be in order if efforts toward mediation could become successful. Finally, except in rare circumstances, it is best if an evaluator does not change roles even after the evaluation so that he can maintain his evaluator integrity in case there is a need for updated evaluations or future testimony associated with the prior evaluation.

## THE BOTTOM LINE

- Psychologists and other mental health professionals have a variety of roles that they can participate in with families of divorce.
- There are substantial differences between therapeutic and forensic roles, differences that lead to the structure and process of each type of role.
- These roles should rarely, if ever, be blended or mixed, and professionals should avoid switching roles unless absolutely necessary.
- There is a significant risk of licensing board complaints if a person in one role switches roles inappropriately.
- It would be considered a switch of roles if a child's therapist were to provide a custody recommendation to the court. Not only might this violate confidentiality, but it would reflect the professional's mixing of therapeutic and forensic roles.

## Notes

1. Much of the information in this chapter has been taken from P. Stahl (1994).

2. When teaching judges in the National Judicial College courses related to family law, I commonly ask judges whether they get letters from therapists and their perception of the value of those letters. Over the 10 years of doing this informal survey, I have yet to hear a judge say that she has found them helpful. On the contrary, all of the judges describe that they interfere with the judicial process; many judges state that such letters have led them to remove the child's therapist from that role.

# 3 Fundamental Questions in Most Custody Evaluations

As indicated earlier, custody evaluations are usually requested by the courts or the attorneys in order to address some specific question or questions about the divorce of the parents, usually as it relates to the parenting plan for the children, referred to in many states as "custody and access." These questions can be rather narrow or they may be complex. In this chapter, I will focus on the fundamental questions involved in nearly all custody evaluations. Essentially, there are five main topics that I will focus on. These include (1) "the best interests of the child"; (2) the bond between the child and his parents or siblings; (3) psychological dysfunction, the capacity to parent, and the strengths and weaknesses associated with each parent's ability to parent, nurture, and understand the children and their needs; (4) the nature of the co-parental relationship; and (5) recommendations for how the parents can share the time with their children, that is, the parenting plan. While more complex evaluations will often necessitate additional recommendations, almost all evaluations, by their very nature, will end with some type of recommendation related to this parenting plan. This chapter will focus globally on these five questions. More details about these issues will emerge later in the book.

## The Best Interests of the Child

Just what are "the best interests of the child"? Since abandoning the tender years doctrine in the 1970s and 1980s, all states now focus on the best interests of the child, which were first described by a judge in the early 20th century. While the tender years doctrine usually led to the placement of children with their mother, the best interests of the child has been seen as gender neutral. This, of course, has led to the politicalization of child custody, as mother's-rights groups and father's-rights groups argue about which gender is harmed by the "best interests" statutes. In a legalistic way, state laws define the best interests of the child around parameters such as nurturing, guidance, religious

> The best interests of the child can be specific and have many factors, or it can be vague and truly left to the interpretation of the court.

and economic issues, emotional attachments, stability, and the maintenance of a healthy relationship with both parents. Many states define or identify specific factors that are to be considered when determining the best interests of the child, while other laws may be more vague. Some states have what is referred to as a "friendly parent provision," in which the court is to consider which parent might be more likely to support the child's relationship with the other parent. In most states, the wishes of the parents are a consideration in a best-interests analysis as are the wishes of a mature child regarding her placement.

One of the states with a very comprehensive best interests statute is Michigan. The definition of *best interests* in the Michigan statute includes the following factors:

(a) The love, affection, and other emotional ties existing between the parties involved and the child

(b) The capacity and disposition of the parties involved to give the child love, affection, and guidance and to continue the education and raising of the child in his or her religion or creed, if any

(c) The capacity and disposition of the parties involved to provide the child with food, clothing, medical care, or other remedial care recognized and permitted under the laws of this state in place of medical care, and other material needs

(d) The length of time the child has lived in a stable, satisfactory environment, and the desirability of maintaining continuity

(e) The permanence, as a family unit, of the existing or proposed custodial home or homes

(f) The moral fitness of the parties involved

(g) The mental and physical health of the parties involved

(h) The home, school, and community record of the child

(i) The reasonable preference of the child, if the court considers the child to be of sufficient age to express preference

(j) The willingness and ability of each of the parties to facilitate and encourage a close and continuing parent–child relationship between the child and the other parent or the child and the parents

(k) Domestic violence, regardless of whether the violence was directed against or witnessed by the child

(l) Any other factor considered by the court to be relevant to a particular child custody dispute

In other states, there is considerable vagueness about the issues that are at the core of the question of the best interests of the child. Some would argue that this is purposely vague to allow the courts broad discretion, given the unique facts of each family. The American Law Institute (ALI; 2002) has identified that the best-interests statute in most states is problematic because it is indeterminate and that the vagueness in the statute creates conflict for many parents. The ALI developed what it referred to as the "approximation principle," in which child custody and the parenting plan would be based on an approximation of what the parents had done previous to the separation. However, this could be just as problematic, as parents would be in conflict over what the history was and about the changes that would take place once the divorce is final.

A third option, increasingly used in some states, is for states to focus on both the rights and responsibilities of parenting. For example, in Florida's recently revised § 61.13, there is no longer a mention of custody, but the statute instead focuses on how parents are to develop a plan to share residential responsibilities; that is, with one parent as primary and the other as nonresidential or via rotating or shared residence. The statute also focuses on how parents are to develop a parenting plan in which they outline how they will share decision-making responsibilities; that is, whether or not parents share in making decisions or one parent makes the majority of decisions in the child's life. In some families, the decision-making is split, with one parent making some decisions on behalf of the child, for example, the medical decisions, and the other parent making different decisions on behalf of the child, such as the extracurricular decisions. In this recently revised statute (Florida Statute 61.13, 2009), there is no mention of custody and access.

Ultimately, parents end up in a child custody evaluation when they disagree about the best interests of their child. Increasingly, fathers are seeking an equal time-share and custody of their children, which results in an increase in the use of psychologists and other mental health professionals to assist the courts in determining the best interests of the child. However, while mental health professionals can address the psychological components of best interests, they have a difficult time addressing other ones, such as "moral fitness of the parents." Most parents do not care what the statute says, but instead are focused on what they believe to be best for their child.

When doing a custody evaluation, we are often faced with specific questions in the midst of complex family issues. Rarely is it a simple process to evaluate both parents and the child and develop a parenting plan that is clearly in the best interests of the child. Instead, we are often faced with many complex and competing needs of children and their parents. While the needs of the children must come first, it is often necessary to set up these needs in a hierarchical pattern in order to reach a solution.

For example, if an adolescent child wishes to leave her primary residence with her mother to live primarily with her father, and she has two younger siblings who are going to remain with the mother, we must not only look at the best interests of this adolescent child, but at those of her siblings as well. Focus must not only be on the needs of the older child vis-à-vis her relationships with each of her parents, but the needs of both her and her siblings and their relationships with one another.

This can get quite complex. For example, in one of my previous evaluations, the family had a preexisting custody arrangement in which the older adolescent boy lived primarily with his father and the younger preadolescent boy lived primarily with his mother. The boys saw each other during the week and visited each other's homes every other weekend. This provided regular contact for the brothers and fairly regular contact with the noncustodial parent. The evaluation questions focused on whether or not the younger brother should move to a different state with the mother and stepfather, who was transferred because of his job. Because his mother and stepfather were definitely moving (they had been married approximately 7 years and the stepfather had known the younger boy most of his life), the issues were clear. Does the younger boy stay with his mother as primary custodial parent and continue a visiting relationship with his father, but risk a significant change in his relationship with his father and brother because he would see them only at holidays and for extended periods of time over the summer? Or, should he stay with his brother and father, have a significant change in his day-to-day lifestyle, miss his mother and stepfather a great deal, and visit them along with his brother during holidays and vacations. As the evaluation progressed, it was clear that there was no perfect solution for *his* best interests short of the stepfather having good employment in his original community. Given economic circumstances at the time, that was an impossibility. While many different solutions could be in the best interests of this child, it appeared in this particular family that it would be "best" for the boy to move with his mother and stepfather to a different state, even though it took him from his father and his brother.

I recently completed an evaluation in which parents were sharing custody of their son in a week–week schedule. This had been going on for 4 years since the parents' initial separation. Both parents had remarried. The father had a new child and was being transferred by his employer to another state. Each parent wanted to keep the child during the school year, allowing for extensive access during the non-school time. The child, who was 8 years old, loved both of his parents and was involved in many activities in his community with his mother and did not want to leave them. Yet, he also did not want to leave his little brother who would be moving with his dad. Ultimately, I did not make an actual recommendation because the best-interests choice was between staying in his mother's community with his friends and school and activities versus moving to his father's new community with his younger half-brother. In this case, the judge kept the child with his mother for the first 2 years, and then, after the child missed his younger brother more than expected, and also missed his father, a subsequent updated evaluation led to the change of primary custody to his father in the new state.

Over the years that I have done evaluations, based on research and experience I have reached the conclusion that a few fundamental issues pertain to the best interests of the child. First, the best parenting is achieved with two psychologically healthy and available parents, with each parent remaining actively involved in as much of the child's daily life as possible (see, e.g., J. Kelly & Emery, 2003; Lamb, Sternberg, & Thompson, 1997). It is also best when both parents take an active interest and participation in the child's school life, social life, activities, and the like. While this need not be a 50–50 parenting plan, it does require both parents' active involvement in a wide range of the child's life experiences as long as the time is distributed well (M. Lamb, personal communication, May 6, 2002).

Second, nearly all of the research on children's adjustment to divorce makes it clear that children need their parents to develop a postdivorce relationship that is relatively free of hostility and conflict and in which the relationship with the other parent is promoted to the child (see, e.g., Ahrons, 2001, 2004; J. Kelly & Emery, 2003).

A third need for children is that they share time with each parent in a way that is developmentally appropriate. That means that for younger children, there might be more transitions than would be typical for older children (see, e.g., J. Kelly & Lamb, 2000) and that for older children, there would be fewer rather than more transitions over a short period of time, and that the transitions flow naturally in the child's life. At the very least, these transitions must make sense to the child and the way she lives her life, such as around school times or days, parents' work schedules, and so forth.

Fourth, it is important that the parenting plan makes sense developmentally, according to the age and abilities of the child (see Chapter 5). Fifth, it is important that, when there is significant conflict between the parents or between a particular child and his parents, there be a mechanism under which the conflicts can be managed and reduced. Sixth, if one of the parents is dysfunctional or abusive, or is engaged in a relationship that is physically destructive or emotionally toxic to a child, the child's needs for safety must always come first; see, for example, California Family Code § 3020, which states,

> The Legislature finds and declares that it is the public policy of this state to assure that the health, safety, and welfare of children shall be the court's primary concern in determining the best interest of children when making any orders regarding the custody or visitation of children. The Legislature further finds and declares that the perpetration of child abuse or domestic violence in a household where a child resides is detrimental to the child.

Ultimately, to the extent possible, if a postdivorce relationship between a child and her parents can stay either similar to or become healthier and more positive than the predivorce relationship, I am succeeding in developing an arrangement that will truly be "in the best interests of the child."

## The Family's Relationships

When conducting a child custody evaluation, the evaluator is focused on two types of relationships within the family. I refer to the first type as the "vertical relationships," that is, the relationship between the parents and

> Two types of relationships need to be evaluated: the vertical relationships between parents and their children, and the horizontal relationships between the co-parents.

their children. The evaluator has to identify whether or not parents and their children have a healthy and secure bond and attachment and whether or not parents are capable of meeting their child's day-to-day developmental needs. Within this area, custody evaluators are looking at each parent's style of parenting and whether or not that style of parenting is a good fit with the needs and functioning of their children.

There is a great deal in the psychological literature about attachment and bonding between parent and child (see, e.g., the custody and attachment literature identified in the Attachment and Child Custody [2009] special issue of *Journal of Child Custody*). One of the most important factors for the child custody evaluator to evaluate is the relationship between the child and his parents, and whether or not there is a difference in the bond between the child and his mother or his father. In previous years, there was a great deal written about the child and his "psychological parents," and the belief that mothers, as a whole, were more nurturing and important to children than were fathers (see, e.g., Goldstein, Freud, & Solnit, 1984). In more recent years, there is considerable growing evidence that the child develops an attachment with both of his parents, and has a need to maintain and grow in his relationship with them both (see, e.g., J. Kelly & Lamb, 2000; Ludolph, 2009). As such, I need to assess the current state of that relationship in order to promote continued growth in the attachment over time.

Some parents are under considerable stress when they separate and parenting skills suffer at the time of divorce. Other parents continue to parent in a healthy way even after the separation. Once free of the emotional constraints of a tension-filled marriage, some parents become healthier and more nurturing in their parental role. By attempting to understand the nature of the relationships between a child and her parents, and by attempting to understand the psychological functioning of the parents, I will be able to provide recommendations that I hope will lead to an enhancement and growth of that relationship with both parents.

While assessing this bond and attachment, I am looking not only at the relationship between the parents and the child, but at the ability of each parent to promote and encourage the growing attachment and bond of the child to the other parent. Evaluators need to understand the conscious and unconscious behaviors that promote such a bond and that can lead to a sense of security for the child. Because this security comes from the formation of and development of a healthy bond with nurturing parents, it will be very important in doing the evaluation to assess each parent's ability to parent and each parent's ability to promote the bond between the child and the other parent. In order to allow for that, it is important to understand how each parent is able to let go of the "couple's issues" and shift to a co-parenting role for the benefit of the child.

# Parenting Strengths and Weaknesses

The third global issue that is a part of every custody evaluation relates to gaining an understanding of each parent's relative strengths and weaknesses, and their relative ability to understand and meet the needs of their child. Listening to parents during the evaluation process, we often hear of the many ways that each parent believes that he or she is "better" than the other parent. The strengths that we are looking for include their ability to focus on their child's emotional needs; understand issues of psychological growth and development; provide stability, nurturance, and guidance to their child; promote a positive relationship with the other parent; and promote a well-rounded, stimulated life for their child.

Some parents are extremely vague and seem able to focus only on their perceptions of the shortcomings of the other parent. These parents, many of whom have significant psychological dysfunctions, have a very difficult time talking about what they have to offer in the way of positively parenting their child. As in a nastily run political campaign, many parents can focus only on the "negative" about the other parent.

In order to understand all of this fully, we need to use several ways to develop an understanding of each parent's capacity to parent and psychological fitness. By using multiple interviews, with direct observation of parents and children together, with a review of collateral information and contacts with objective and neutral collateral sources, and with structured questions that are designed to understand this issue, we can hope to come to an understanding of each parent's capacity to parent over a broad spectrum. In more complex evaluations, we might need to assess drug and/or alcohol use, severe psychological dysfunction or personality disorders, or other features that may significantly impact a person's ability to meet his or her child's needs. We might need to use psychological tests and/or drug testing for a better understanding of these issues.

The evaluator will focus on the styles of parenting, and whether or not parents are utilizing authoritarian, permissive, or authoritative styles of parenting. Research consistently shows that the authoritative style of parenting is likely to be the healthiest style for the development of psychologically healthy children (see, e.g., Baumrind, 1996).

No matter what, it is critical in every evaluation to understand each parent's personality as it relates to the issues of parenting and reducing postdivorce parental conflicts. It is important to recognize that a parent is not "all good" or "all bad," and to focus on each parent's specific strengths and weaknesses. This is a vertical dimension that focuses on the actual parenting of the child.

> Authoritative parenting, in which parents are sensitive to the child and her emotions, while providing routine and structure, is the healthiest style of parenting.

Specific skills that parents of divorce need to develop include, but are not limited to, the following:

- Not putting the children in the middle of parental conflict and not asking children to carry messages between the parents

- Not saying derogatory things about the other parent
- Not talking with the children about the issues of the divorce
- Not asking the children about the other parent's activities
- Not inducing guilt over loneliness when the child is with the other parent
- Not arguing with the other parent when dropping off/picking up the children

In addition to avoiding these negative parenting qualities, divorced parents need to:

- Parent authoritatively (Baumrind, 1996), that is, with warmth, structure, guidance, and sensitivity to the child's emotions
- Provide information to the other parent about the child
- Be flexible in making plans for the children
- Encourage the child to enjoy her relationship with the other parent and that parent's family members
- Take care of themselves so they can increasingly take care of their children

By asking questions of each parent and the children about these issues, and by understanding how the parents deal with these critical issues, we can better understand the strengths and weaknesses of each parent regarding the divorce.

# The Co-Parental Relationship

While the quality of parenting is a vertical dimension to understand in custody evaluations, the co-parent relationship is a horizontal dimension that also needs to be understood. Because most custody evaluations result in a recommendation for sharing the job of parenting, even when we recommend one primary residential parent and one nonresidential parent, we need to understand the nature of the co-parenting relationship when evaluating the family. The primary task of co-parenting is to cooperate with the other parent in raising the children regardless of how one parent feels about the other parent. In order to co-parent, one must be able to separate one's "couple's issues" from the children's needs. A good co-parent is able to keep the children out of the middle of the divorce issues, and avoids the pitfalls noted in the previous section. Parents need to communicate with each other, not through the children, about school, religion, activities, health, and other areas of importance to the children. The best co-parents can do this in a business-like, neutral way, without emotional entanglement.

Research identifies four types of postdivorce relationships: Parenting Pals, Cooperative Colleagues, Angry Associates, and Fiery Foes (Ahrons, 2004).

Children of divorce do best when their parents cooperate in parenting and they do worst when their parents remain in conflict.

Children function reasonably well when their parents are disengaged from conflict. One task of the recommendations is to encourage conflicted parents to become disengaged, and then to help disengaged parents to cooperate and communicate with one another. By understanding the co-parental relationship, and whether it is cooperative, hostile, or disengaged, we can recommend ways to help the parents improve the situation for their children. The co-parent relationship and issues of conflict will be discussed more thoroughly in Chapter 11.

## Time-Sharing Recommendations

As evaluators, it is our job to take these broad issues—best interests of the child, the vertical relationships between the child and her parents, each parent's strengths and weaknesses and their relative capacity to parent, and the horizontal co-parent relationship—and put them together to formulate a plan for sharing the time between the parents. Some time-sharing plans are quite specific, such as every other week with each parent, or primary residence with one parent with every other weekend with the other parent. Many plans specify how the parents will share or alternate holidays and school vacations. Other time-sharing plans are quite vague and may simply state that primary residence is with one parent and there is "reasonable" parenting time with the other. In my experience, there is less room for ongoing conflict between the parents when the schedule is specifically defined, and there is benefit to the children (especially older ones) if there is some flexibility in the structure (especially at the child's request). Balancing these needs is one of the evaluator's tasks.

Even in relatively dysfunctional situations, it is likely that each parent will spend some time with the child, even if parenting time is supervised with a disturbed or abusive parent. Evaluators need to be as creative as possible in the development of a time-sharing plan that maximizes the strengths of each parent, provides for the stability necessary for the child, and, when possible, meets the parents' needs as well. It is important to understand each parent's needs in doing the evaluation, because, to the extent that they can complement the needs of the child, this is an added plus.

Finally, it is critical for the evaluator, in her written report, to help each parent understand the reasons for the recommendations so that each parent can accept, promote, and implement the plan. Over the years that I have been doing evaluations, I have found that the best recommendations take into account the relationships among the child, siblings, and both parents, as well as the ability of each parent to understand and meet the child's many needs. Once that is done, I can formulate a plan that hierarchically addresses the competing and varying needs of the child. Then, I hope to enlist the parents' mutual support in following the recommended parenting plan. Sometimes I may try to help each parent feel that he or she has "won" something, but this

> There is no best parenting plan arrangement. The ideal plan for a given family will take into account the child's relationship with each parent, the child's developmental needs, the parenting styles and strengths and weaknesses of each parent, the co-parental relationship, and the logistics of work schedules and how close the parents live to one another.

is best accomplished when each parent understands that the recommendations are in the best interests of the child. If either parent feels that he or she has significantly lost, and cannot understand how the recommendations are beneficial to the child, it will be very difficult for that parent to support the parenting plan and work to make it succeed.

This chapter has focused on the broad issues related to typical custody evaluations. As described, each of these issues is fundamentally connected to each of the other special issues that are frequently addressed in most custody evaluations. Whether we look at narrower issues of sexual, physical, or emotional abuse; spouse abuse and domestic violence; the child's specific special needs; drug and/or alcohol addictions; severe mental illness; criminality; parental alienation; relocation issues; or others, we need to understand them in relation to each of these broad questions.

Even drug-abusing, violent, and alienating parents are likely to have certain strengths, and, though we may recommend limited or supervised visitation until the parent is free from the influence of drugs, stops the violence, or stops the alienation, we still need to understand how to enhance relationships between the child and *both* parents. We do this by delineating both the strengths and weaknesses of each parent, as well as by describing the nature of the bond between each parent and the child. As noted previously, this will be described in further detail throughout the book.

## THE BOTTOM LINE

In all child custody evaluations, the evaluator will be focusing on the following:

- The "best interests of the child" (as defined in the state in which the evaluation is being conducted)
- The nature of the child's relationships with each parent (the vertical relationships)
- The strengths and weaknesses of each parent as these relate to parenting and the resulting fit between each parent's parenting and the child and her needs
- The co-parental relationship and the amount of conflict between the parents (the horizontal relationships)
- The way in which these factors integrate into the parenting plan

# 4

# General Divorce-Related Research and Basic Statutory and Case Law

Since the late 1970s there has been considerable research on all aspects of divorce, ranging from the impact on adults and children, what causes divorce, how children are potentially harmed by divorce, and the mitigating factors that might reduce that harm. In this chapter I will outline some of the general research that will apply to all of the families that are seen in child custody evaluations. The research has been conducted throughout North America and in Europe, Australia, and New Zealand. In this chapter I will focus on the general divorce-related research rather than the specific research associated with other complex issues, such as high conflict, domestic violence, alienated children, and relocation, which will be discussed more thoroughly in chapters devoted to/focusing on those issues: Chapters 11, 12, 13, and 14, respectively. I will be discussing research associated with child development issues in Chapter 5. The research outlined in this chapter will likely apply to situations in all divorces.

## A Quick Primer on Research

Before focusing on the research itself, it is important to discuss relevant issues associated with such research. It is always important to remember that there is good research and not as good research. This will always depend on the sample group, the sample size, the interpretations made by the researchers, the generalizability of the research, and other such issues (Emery, 1999).

In addition, it is also important to know that there are four types of research. First, there is cross-sectional research, which looks at two factors such as children's inclusion in the mediation process and child-focused mediation and compares how those factors might affect another factor, such as children's well-being or parental cooperation with the mediated agreement (see, e.g., McIntosh, Wells, Smyth, & Long, 2008). This type of research looks at a particular sample of children and families, at a particular point in time, and attempts to increase our understanding of that particular issue.

A second type of research is longitudinal, in which researchers follow a particular group of people to understand the impact of a particular variable on a sample of people being followed. An example of this is the long-running research conducted by Wallerstein and others, who have followed the same group of Marin County children since the late 1970s to understand the impact of divorce on those children, who are now adults (Wallerstein, Lewis, & Blakeslee, 2000).

A third type of research is retrospective. In retrospective research, a sample of participants, often college-aged students, is studied to understand how they recall being affected by a particular variable. For example, Fabricius and Braver (2006) have studied college students to understand their recollection of the impact of relocation on them when they were children. In that particular study, there was a cross-sectional component as well, as the study looked at the impact of the relocation on students' current functioning.

The final type of research is a meta-analysis. In a meta-analysis, researchers look at the data from multiple studies and combine them to see whether there are particular findings that are consistent across samples. In one such study, Bauserman (2002) reviewed all of the studies related to joint physical custody in order to identify whether children function better and adjust better to their parents' divorce when they experience shared custody with their parents.

Each of these different types of studies has important contributions for understanding the impact of divorce on children. In the rest of this chapter, I will identify several findings that seem fairly consistent across different types of research and over time.

# Risks of Divorce to Children

By and large, children of divorce are at higher risk of significant problems, both short term and long term, compared with children who are not from families of divorce. These risks are in the areas of self-esteem, depression and other mental health problems, insecurity, school behavioral problems and lowered school performance, delinquency, relationship problems, peer relationship problems, and an increased likelihood of later getting divorced themselves (J. Kelly & Emery, 2003). Wallerstein et al. (2000) identified that young adults who come from divorced families hold onto the sadness and feelings of loss associated with their parents' divorce when they were children. Some problems are considered more short term, while others have a tendency to last for a longer period of time.

More recently, Amato and Hohmann-Marriott (2007) identified that even with healthy divorces, that is, ones in which there is low conflict and high communication between the parents and in which children see both parents on a regular basis, children are at higher risk of problems educationally and relationally, suicide, early age for birth of their children, poor self-esteem, and other problems that are typically seen to be a greater risk from problematic divorce.

## Risk Versus Resilience

At the same time, while these risks are very real, there is no one-to-one correlation between divorce and problems in any of these domains (see, e.g., J. Kelly, 1996). What is clear is that not all children of divorce have such problems, and many children of divorce seem to have little or no long-term adjustment problems whatsoever. As far as the numbers are concerned, research suggests that approximately 15% of children in non-divorced families have significant emotional and adjustment problems in their life. Similarly, approximately 25% of children in divorced families have similar emotional and adjustment problems later in their life. While divorce results in a greater likelihood of risk for children, it also suggests that perhaps as many as 75% of children in divorced families have reduced risks over time. According to Kelly, resilience rather than risk is the norm for children of divorce.

With that in mind, there are some research findings that clearly show increase in the risks for children (Emery, 1999). These items include economic factors (poverty is a risk factor for children of divorce); poor parenting (poor parenting is a risk factor for all children, but especially children of divorce, and especially in the first year of divorce); high conflict between the parents, especially conflict that children are exposed to and enmeshed in; the absence of a parent; and potentially relocation (this is a mixed issue). When any of these factors exist, there is a much greater risk of a poorer adjustment to the divorce.

## Mitigating Factors

Whenever there are risk factors, there are also mitigating factors that reduce the likelihood of such risks. For children of divorce, these mitigating factors seem to include:

- Active involvement of both parents in a wide range of the child's life experiences and activities, and with both parents involved on a regular and frequent basis in which the time with both parents is distributed well (Lamb, Sternberg, & Thompson, 1997)
- A healthy temperament
- The ability to ignore pressures from one or both parents
- Parents who engage in low conflict and high communication regarding the children and their needs
- Parents who maintain appropriate expectations, consistency, stability, and predictability

> Poverty, conflict, the absence of a parent, and poor parenting are significant risk factors in children's adjustment to divorce, while the active involvement of both parents in the child's life and healthy, authoritative parenting are mitigating factors in the child's adjustment to her parents' divorce.

Additionally, children do best when parents use authoritative parenting (Baumrind, 1996), that is, who provide healthy guidance and structure and promote appropriate maturity demands while being emotionally attentive and sensitive to their child's needs

## Research on Parents' Relationships After Divorce

Another area of general research is related to the way in which parents relate to each other after they divorce. Although the numbers are not absolute, because the research is variable, it appears that about 20% of parents engage in a fairly healthy, positive relationship in which they act like "Parenting Pals" (Ahrons, 2004). Parenting pals are friendly, are cooperative, engage in low conflict, and support each other with their children. Another 30% of parents are considered "Cooperative Colleagues" in that they act in a business-like manner with low to medium conflict. They can be with one another in public, but often need help in communicating and making decisions on behalf of their children. Many cooperative colleague parents use mediation to help resolve difficulties. Others tend to disengage (Maccoby & Mnookin, 1992) and avoid communicating.

A third group of postdivorce parents are considered "Angry Associates" (Ahrons, 2004). Angry associates often need specialized parent education programs to help them learn skills to reduce their conflict. They often benefit from co-parent counseling and may truly need some type of parallel parenting. For more information on parallel parenting, see Chapter 11, "Nonviolent High-Conflict Families."

The final group of postdivorce parents is considered to be "Fiery Foes" (Ahrons, 2004). Fiery foes are the frequent fliers of the courts, in that they repeatedly return to court to argue over almost anything. They tend to be low communication and high conflict. They often misinterpret court orders in a way that is highly problematic. Increasingly, jurisdictions are using Parent Coordinators to help fiery foes manage their co-parenting relationship. Again, there is more information on these parents and the best way to manage them in Chapter 11.

> Parents range in their postdivorce relationship between parenting pals, cooperative colleagues, angry associates, and fiery foes. Some parents simply disengage and have no relationship. The family's postdivorce relationship must be understood by the child custody evaluator.

## Basic Statutory and Case Law

As noted in Chapter 1, it is critical for child custody evaluators to understand the law. While we are not attorneys, we are expected to have a basic understanding of the law, at state and federal levels, as well as a basic understanding of local court rules and procedures (Association of Family and Conciliation Courts [AFCC], 2006). These laws can easily be found on the

Internet or through consultation with a local attorney colleague. In this chapter, I will describe three federal laws (two statutory laws and one case law decision) that help guide the work of the evaluator. I will also discuss the 1980 Hague Convention on the Civil Aspects of International Child Abduction (*Hague Convention,* 2010), which guides the courts in international cases. I will then use the state of California as an example of the statutory and case law decisions that help guide our work. All of this discussion will be rather limited, and the reader is encouraged to go to the Internet or other sources to learn more about the cases and statutes described.

# Uniform Child Custody
## Jurisdiction and Enforcement Act (1997)

The Uniform Child Custody Jurisdiction and Enforcement Act (UCCJEA), which has been adopted by 46 states, was drafted by the National Conference of Commissioners of Uniform State Laws in 1997. According to the Wikipedia article (see Uniform Child Custody Jurisdiction and Enforcement Act, 2010), the act creates the rules by which the child's home state, which is defined as the state where a child has lived with a parent for 6 consecutive months, has jurisdiction over the custody case. In the event that there are two (or more) states that have such home state jurisdictions, the courts in those states must communicate with one another in order to determine which state will hear the dispute:

> A court which has made a child-custody determination consistent with UCCJEA has exclusive, continuing jurisdiction over the determination until that court determines that neither the child, the child's parents, and any person acting as a parent do not have a significant connection with the State that made the original order and that substantial evidence is no longer available in the State concerning the child's care, protection, training, and personal relationships; or that court or a court of another State determines that the child, the child's parents, and any person acting as a parent do not presently reside in the State that initially made the child custody order.

The UCCJEA also has a uniform procedure to allow persons to register and enforce custody orders across state lines.

# Parental Kidnapping Prevention Act

The Parental Kidnapping Prevention Act (PKPA), signed by Congress in 1980, is designed to establish national standards regarding child custody jurisdiction throughout the United States. As long as the state that initially asserts jurisdiction follows the correct rules, its orders will result in a finding of "full faith and credit" in other states. This means that other states will abide by the order of the first state (Parental Kidnapping Prevention Act, 2008). The PKPA also prohibits one state from modifying the custody decree of another state without complying with the terms of the PKPA. The PKPA was amended in 1999 to include visitation rights in the definition of custody rights outlined in the original bill.

## *Troxel v. Granville* (2000)

Prior to this case coming before the U.S. Supreme Court, many states, including the state of Washington, had increasingly allowed for third-party custody and visitation rights, often for grandparents, that increasingly allowed "any person" to petition for visitation rights "at any time" whenever such visitation may be in the child's best interests. In this particular case, at the trial court level, the custodial mother (Granville) had agreed to some visitation between her children and their paternal grandparents (the Troxels) after the death of the children's father. However, the Troxels wanted more visitation and the trial court ordered more visitation than Granville wanted them to have. She appealed, and the state court of appeals reversed the trial court's decision. This reversal was later upheld by the state Supreme Court. In affirming, the Washington Supreme Court held that the Washington statute (§26.10.160(3)) constitutionally infringes on parents' fundamental right to rear their children, reasoning that the federal Constitution, in particular the Fourteenth Amendment, prohibits a state from infringing on a parent's right to parent as she sees fit unless there is risk of harm or potential harm to the child. Because the Washington statute broadly permitted anyone at any time to petition to such visitation rights, the court found the statute to be unconstitutional. When the case was accepted by the U.S. Supreme Court, the Court affirmed the state Supreme Court's decision. The facts of the case were that no one had determined the mother to be an unfit mother, and as such, there was no risk of potential harm from allowing her to parent as she saw fit. This case reaffirmed a parent's fundamental right to parent. Because child custody evaluators sometimes are appointed to look into third-party visitation rights cases, understanding the *Troxel v. Granville* decision is important.

## Hague Convention on the Civil Aspects of International Child Abduction

This treaty was drafted to "insure the prompt return of children who have been abducted from their country of habitual residence or wrongfully retained in a contracting state not their country of habitual residence"

(Hague Convention preamble). The primary purpose is to "preserve whatever status quo child custody arrangement existed immediately before an alleged wrongful removal or retention thereby deterring a parent from crossing international boundaries in search of a more sympathetic court" (*Hague Convention*, 2010).

The Hague Convention applies in cases where both the country of the child's habitual residence and the country to which the child was taken have signed onto the Convention, when the child is younger than 16 years old, and when the child has been "wrongfully removed" in violation of custody rights of the law of the state of the child's habitual residence. The Hague Convention has been signed and ratified by approximately 70 countries, including the United States, United Kingdom, South Africa, Australia, and New Zealand. It has not been ratified or signed by most countries in Africa, most countries in the Middle East, and most Asian countries. For a complete listing of Hague Convention countries, see U.S. Department of State (2009). From there, you can search the compliance statistics and see which countries are signers to the Convention. Additionally, even some countries that are signers to the Convention are not in compliance, according to the U.S. State Department. In 2009, Honduras was considered to be a noncompliant country, and Brazil, Chile, Greece, Mexico, Slovakia, Switzerland, and Venezuela were listed as countries demonstrating patterns of noncompliance. While it is rare to get an international child custody evaluation, it is always important to understand these issues and know where to find information if one occurs.

> It is critical to understand not only the divorce and child custody research, but also statutory and case law, and local court rules, in the state in which you practice.

## California Statutes

The state of California has a number of statutes related to family law matters. Family Code § 3111 is the statute that defines the best interests of the child. Compared with other states (e.g., Michigan; see Chapter 3, this volume), the California statute is relatively vague, focusing on the need for the court always to consider the health, safety, and welfare of the child; any history of abuse; the nature of contact with each parent; and the habitual or continued illegal use of substances. Family Code § 3020 relates to the legislative public policies regarding divorce. Essentially, § 3020 states that it is public policy to ensure that the "health, safety, and welfare of the child" is the court's primary concern in determining the best interests of the child, and it is public policy to "ensure that children have frequent and continuing contact with both parents" and to encourage parents to share the rights and responsibilities of child rearing, "except where the contact would not be in the best interests of the child." This section concludes with the statement, "Where the policies set forth in subdivisions (a) and (b) of this section are in conflict, any court's order regarding custody or visitation shall be made in a manner that ensures the health, safety, and welfare of the child and the safety of all family members." In other words, health, safety, and welfare trump frequent and continuing contact.

Family Code § 3040 defines that child custody should be granted in the following order of preference according to the best interests of the child as provided in Family Code § 3011 and 3020:

(1) To both parents jointly pursuant to Chapter 4 (commencing with Section 3080) or to either parent. In making an order granting custody to either parent, the court shall consider, among other factors, which parent is more likely to allow the child frequent and continuing contact with the noncustodial parent, consistent with Section 3011 and 3020, and shall not prefer a parent as custodian because of that parent's sex. The court, in its discretion, may require the parents to submit to the court a plan for the implementation of the custody order.

(2) If to neither parent, to the person or persons in whose home the child has been living in a wholesome and stable environment.

(3) To any other person or persons deemed by the court to be suitable and able to provide adequate and proper care and guidance for the child.

The statute concludes by stating,

This section establishes neither a preference nor a presumption for or against joint legal custody, joint physical custody, or sole custody, but allows the court and the family the widest discretion to choose a parenting plan that is in the best interest of the child.

Family Code § 3044 is the statute regarding domestic violence. Essentially, it is a rebuttable presumption that states that a perpetrator of domestic violence shall not have joint or sole physical or legal custody of one's child absent a showing that rebuts the presumption. It also defines the rebuttable factors and states that the presumption may be rebutted only by a preponderance of the evidence. Family Code § 3044 also references other statutes related to the definitions of domestic violence, which are found elsewhere in the penal code.

Finally, there are two other statutes that are also important for custody evaluators. Family Code § 3041 is the statute related to third-party custody without the consent of the parents. As would be expected under *Troxel v. Granville* (2000), the statute specifically refers courts to make a finding that granting custody to a parent is detrimental to the child and that granting custody to a nonparent is required to serve the best interests of the child. Additionally, Family Code § 3042 is the statute that defines the role of a child's wishes. It states,

If a child is of sufficient age and capacity to reason so as to form an intelligent preference as to custody, the court shall consider and give due weight to the wishes of the child in making an order granting or modifying custody.

Child custody evaluators may certainly provide testimony (in their report or in live testimony) regarding whether or not the child is of sufficient age and capacity to reason so as to form an intelligent preference as to custody.

# California Case Law

Over the nearly 25 years I have been doing child custody evaluations in California, there have been numerous appellate decisions made by various state courts of appeal and the State Supreme Court. Again, while I am not an attorney, I always believe it is important to understand relevant case law so I can integrate my work into the expectations of the court. As indicated in Chapter 1, the child custody evaluator's task is to be helpful to the court. When appellate courts direct trial court judges to consider certain factors, or approach cases in a certain way, it is important for the child custody evaluator to understand those expectations.

For example, in *Montenegro v. Diaz* (2001), the California Supreme Court stated that courts must decide whether or not a previous court decision was a final decision or one to be considered temporary. The standard to be applied if the order is temporary is different from the standard to be applied if it is a permanent order. A temporary order can be changed for nearly any reason, whereas a permanent order can be changed only if there is a substantial change of circumstances since the previous order. As an evaluator, I have been asked by the court to address whether or not there is a change of circumstances. If I did not understand the *Montenegro* decision, it would be hard to address this issue and be helpful to the court.

In *In re Marriage of Seagondollar* (2006), the appellate court admonished judges and evaluators to follow the Rules of Court. The court listed several reasons why the trial court's procedural errors deprived the father of a fair hearing in a relocation case. These errors included:

- Mother's failure to file a response to Father's Order to Show Cause (OSC)
- Lack of good cause to hear Mother's OSC on Shortened Notice
- Refusing to hear Father's Motion to Quash before hearing Mother's OSC
- Refusal to continue the hearing ("a mere 3 days") to permit Father's expert to testify
- An inadequate order defining the purpose and scope of the Evidence Code § 730 evaluation

California evaluators need to understand *Seagondollar* not only for the procedural issues involved in the case, but also because the court of appeals criticized both the trial court and the evaluator regarding the scope of the evaluation. In this case, there had been nothing in front of the court related to the relocation question. Nonetheless, the evaluator did an evaluation focused largely on the issue of relocation. On this issue, the court of appeals stated,

> The trial court's failure to continue the hearing to permit Timothy to present his expert witness becomes more striking when considered in light of the errors committed in appointing Dr. Adam to conduct an Evidence Code section 730 evaluation. Timothy argues a "detailed order" defining the purpose and scope of the evaluation was not in place before Dr. Adam performed his evaluation. California Rules of Court, rule 5.220(d)(1)(B) states each court must "[g]ive the evaluator, before the evaluation begins, a copy of the court order that specifies: [¶] (i) The appointment of the evaluator under Evidence Code section 730, Family Code section 3110, or Code of Civil Procedure 2032; and [¶] (ii) The purpose and scope of the evaluation." The minute order in this case stated, "[t]he court appointed Dr. Stephen Adams [*sic*] to conduct a limited [Evidence Code section] 730 evaluation. The cost of the evaluation shall be divided equally between the parties, subject to reallocation." That's it. The order specifies the evaluator's appointment, but fails to specify the purpose and scope of the evaluation.
>
> In response, Melinda argues: "The facts actually support a clearly defined purpose and scope that was known to counsel, to Dr. Adam, and to both parties. Dr. Adam's November 1, 2004 testimony described the purpose and scope of the evaluation, *as he understood it*. His testimony also provided that at the time of his first meeting, both Melinda and Timothy were advised of the purpose and scope and the process that he would use in his evaluation." [Italics added.] In other words, Melinda all but concedes the scope of the evaluation was based on Dr. Adam's interpretation of the unspecific order issued by the trial court—an order issued when the trial court acknowledged this was not a move-away case.
>
> Defining the purpose and scope of Dr. Adam's evaluation was more than an academic exercise. When Dr. Adam was appointed, Melinda's move-away was not in issue: She had not requested a modification of custody by responsive pleading or her own OSC. Her counsel had represented that Melinda did not intend to relocate until after the hearing on Timothy's March OSC (then set for July). The trial court had stated this was not a move-away case. Yet, Dr. Adam evaluated the issue of Melinda moving to Virginia with the children and concluded she should be given primary custody.
>
> We need not decide the level of detail with which an order appointing an Evidence Code section 730 evaluator in a family law matter

should define the purpose and scope of the evaluation. In this case, the order was woefully inadequate because it failed to define the purpose and scope of the evaluation *at all*. Compounding the problem here was that the trial court ordered an Evidence Code section 730 evaluation before Melinda had filed a response to the March OSC. Because the order appointing the evaluator was made before Melinda had filed a response framing the issues for trial, the order gave the evaluator carte blanche to define those issues, as well as the purpose and scope of the evaluation. That result demonstrates why, in family law matters such as this, a child custody evaluator usually should not be appointed until a responsive declaration or pleading is filed.

As Timothy points out, Dr. Adam had an opportunity to correct the trial court's error by supplying the parties a written protocol describing the purpose of the evaluation and explaining the procedures he intended to follow, as required by California Rules of Court, rule 5.220(e)(1)(A). Dr. Adam did not prepare such a written protocol. He could not satisfy his obligation to supply a *written* protocol by discussing the evaluation orally with the parties at his initial meeting with them.

This level of detail is being included to inform readers that case law decisions can have serious impact on the manner in which evaluators conduct themselves. As such, evaluators are always encouraged to understand relevant case law in their respective jurisdictions.

Finally, there are a number of decisions associated with relocation law in California. To be sure, the U.S. Supreme Court has extended the right for adults in our society to live wherever they want. What puts this in conflict is that the family court determines where children will live and in what custodial arrangement if two parents live far from one another. While California Family Code § 7501 defines that a custodial parent has a presumptive right to move absent a showing of harm to the children, various case law decisions have added to that. In 1996, *In re Marriage of Burgess* allowed a parent who had only a bit more custodial time than the other parent to move 40 miles away. This set a precedent for the next 10 years in which custodial parents typically had a right to move anywhere, for any reason. A few years later, the court of appeals (*In re Marriage of Edlund v. Hales,* 1998) as a part of their decision allowing the move of a very young child, stated that neither an evaluator nor a judge may ask the moving parent what she might do if the court decides against the relocation of the child. The rationale is that this would put the moving parent in the bind of having to appear as if she's choosing between her desires for change (i.e., the move) and caring for her child. The court determined that decisions have to be made on the basis of the best interests of the child, as if the parent is moving. *In re Marriage of Condon* (1998) set ground rules for international relocation cases and allowed judges to set bonds to ensure that the relocating parent abides by court orders for ongoing visitation and decision-making. More recently, in *In re Marriage of LaMusga* (2004), the California Supreme Court returned to the issue of relocation and reminded the state trial courts that the presumptive right to move was limited to potential harm to the child. It set out eight factors for the court to consider in relocation cases, while simultaneously reaffirming that in joint custody cases, a best-interests analysis of mother-custody in one location versus father custody in the other location would apply.

## THE BOTTOM LINE

The cumulative evidence suggests that children are at risk of greater problems adjusting to their parents' divorce with exposure to high conflict, poor parenting, and the limited involvement of one parent. The cumulative evidence suggests that children are at lowered risk when parents are psychologically healthy, engage in healthy and authoritative parenting, are in low conflict, and are involved in the child's life on a regular and frequent basis in a way that is distributed well.

The task of the child custody evaluator is to integrate this research into the specific findings of the family. The evaluator will examine the following:

- The psychological health of the parents
- Parenting styles (authoritative vs. authoritarian or permissive parenting)
- The temperament of the child
- The conflict between the parents and the extent to which the children are exposed to the conflict
- The emotional and practical availability of both parents
- Any particular allegations being made by each parent

By assessing these global issues (and any other specific issues relevant to the family), and by understanding the divorce and custody research, the evaluator will be prepared to make recommendations to improve resiliency for the child in adjusting to the divorce.

Finally, by understanding the laws (both statutory laws and case laws) in your jurisdiction, you can be certain that you are acting professionally and competently within the jurisdiction in which you practice.

# 5

# Children's Developmental Needs

As cited earlier in this book, custody evaluations are about the children. Whether the focus is on parental alienation, domestic violence, relocation, or high conflict between the parents, custody evaluations are about the needs of children. The task for a child custody evaluator is to integrate the diverse data parents present to formulate recommendations which best address the needs of the children and the ability of each parent to meet those needs.

In general, these needs will be impacted by developmental criteria, the temperament and emotional functioning of the child, the relationships that the child has with each parent, the degree to which the child is both directly and indirectly impacted by the parental conflict, and the child's wishes (greater weight is given as the child gets older and more mature). In families with several children, each child may have different developmental needs. It is not uncommon for siblings of different ages to have varying quality relationships with each parent. Within each child, there are potentially competing needs. One example is the need to develop secure attachments with both parents in infancy, the need for frequent and continuing contact with both parents, and the need to limit the number of transitions between homes. In this chapter, I will focus on developmental needs, children's reactions to parental conflict, the importance of listening to children while protecting their privacy, and the competing needs between siblings and within the individual.

## A Developmental Framework

Wallerstein and Kelly (1980), Goldstein, Freud, and Solnit (1984), and Hodges (1986) were among the first to comment on the differing needs that children of different ages have following a divorce. Bray (1991) refined this issue, integrating a developmental approach to understanding the child's adjustment to divorce. Bray said, "[D]ivorce is not necessarily worse for children at certain ages; rather children at various ages tend to have different reactions and symptom patterns." He added, "Given developmental differences and issues, visitation and access may need to vary depending on the age of the child." Others, including McKinnon and Wallerstein (1987); Kalter (1990); Johnston (1995); Johnston, Roseby, and Kuehnle (2009); Whiteside (1996); Solomon and George (1996); and Ludolph and Viro (1998), focused on the developmental needs of children of divorce. Throughout, the question of overnights for very young children, usually defined as aged 0–3 years, has been the most controversial.

Subsequent to publication of my second book, *Complex Issues in Child Custody Evaluations,* there has been considerable research and thinking on this matter. J. Kelly and Lamb (2000); Warshak (2000a); Solomon and Biringen (2001); Gould and Stahl (2001); Pruett, Insabella, and Gustafson (2005); Ludolph (2009); and others have weighed in on the issues of children's attachments and the question of overnights for infants and young children. What follows is a brief description of this research, normative developmental tasks for children, and how divorce impacts development. I urge child custody evaluators to become familiar with this literature before doing any evaluations involving very young children.

# Infants and Toddlers (0–3 Years)

During this stage, the foundations of basic trust and relationships are formed. In the first year of life, children develop initial attachments, a necessary precursor for the development of basic trust. According to attachment researchers, children begin the process of attachment to both parents at about the age of 6–7 months, usually at the same time. By the end of the first year, receptive language skills are developing and the infant's personality is starting to form. Ideally, by that time, children have developed a healthy, secure attachment with both parents. However, in paternity cases, some children do not even know their father until after that age, and they have an attachment to only one primary parent.

Attachment research defines that there are different types of attachment (Ludolph, 2009). Children can establish a secure relationship, an insecure attachment, or a disorganized attachment. Obviously, it is hoped that a child's attachment will be secure, which tends to happen when the parent(s) are emotionally warm, sensitive to the child's emotions and physical needs, and sufficiently responsive to those needs. However, when a very young child is raised by parents who are unresponsive to his needs or, by parents who are abusing substances, when the child is exposed to significant conflict, or when the child is exposed to domestic violence, there is a significant risk that the child will form an insecure or disorganized attachment.

> Very young children, while being able to tolerate and benefit from overnights with each parent, require stability and consistency of routine, and require the parents to be able to communicate about the child and her needs.

Once a predictable, secure relationship with attachment figure(s) has been secured, the infant begins to separate from that primary parent to form his or her own personality. This process is often referred to as "separation-individuation." During the toddler years, children begin developing auton-omy and experimenting with separation, starting to assert themselves. Their emotions are quite volatile. By age 3, if all goes well, emotions settle down, language skills are intact, and they are likely to be toilet trained. They are ready for a burst of psychological growth that will take place over the next 3 years. Recent findings suggest that, while attachment is generally formed by age 3, it is not completely consolidated until approximately age 4 (see, e.g., Marvin, Cooper, Hoffman, & Powell, 2002; Marvin & Schutz, 2009).

Children in this 0–3 year age group require predictability, consistency, and routine. When parents have never married and have separated or a divorce occurs during this time, there is a loss that the child cannot understand. This can be more pronounced if there is a major disruption in the consistency of the existing primary attachment relationship(s). Symptoms of regression may include problems with feeding, sleeping, self-soothing, and irritability. Some children become depressed and withdrawn, especially because they cannot express their loss in words. Separation anxiety for children in this age group can become exaggerated. If one or both parents become depressed, which is quite common, basic care may be diminished.

Children at this age are at risk for more serious regression or developmen-tal delays if the basic care giving is lacking due to depressed or disturbed parents. It is not uncommon for young, possibly immature adults (aged 18–25) to have babies. Sometimes they never lived together, or they may have separated during the first 2 years of the child's life. The developmental needs of the children may become impacted by the maturity level of the parents. Ultimately, the factors that increase the risk of insecure attachments include poverty, family violence, intense marital conflict, poor parenting styles, abuse and neglect, and major life changes, such as separation.

The evaluator must pay attention to the quality of the attachments in the child's relationships. Rather than the idea of "one psychological parent," or a "primary parent," research supports that children develop multiple attachments to both parents, as noted above. While both parents are important, this does not mean that the child does not have preferences for one parent over the other. Some children have one parent that has attended to the majority of day-to-day needs. Other children may have two or three adults (two parents and a relative or other day-care provider) who have attended to day-to-day needs. The task for the evaluator is to assess the nature of the child's relationship with each parent and the ability of the parents to communicate about the child. Once that is done, it is important to recommend a parenting plan reflecting the following:

- The child's relationship with parents to whom the child is attached is of major importance during these first 3 years of life.
- A child can develop within normal limits when separated from one parent to whom the child is attached to be with the other parent to whom the child is attached (Warshak, 2000a). This will be affected by the extent to which each parent has been directly involved in the child's life.

- The attachment(s), parenting skills of the parents, and environment the child is exposed to are critical for the child.
- More frequent, shorter contact with each parent may be ideal so that the child is not away from either parent to whom she is attached for more than 3 days (J. Kelly & Lamb, 2000).
- The major role of caregivers is to provide a secure base, firm support, flexible self-control; to support communication; and to help with gender identity and sex role development.
- With increased capacity for memory and cognition, many children in the group from 18 to 36 months who have had one primary attachment may begin to tolerate and benefit from overnight time with the other parent.
- There is no evidence that overnights with the noncustodial parent cause children of this age harm (Ludolph, 2009; Pruett et al., 2005).
- It may be difficult to develop a relatively equal parenting plan for children in this age group because there may be too many transitions and disruptions to the primary attachments. Additionally, it is likely that children will be harmed if parents are contentious and in high conflict if there is an equal parenting plan that is not agreed to by both parents. Children at this young age need parents who are in high communication and low conflict if they are going to have successful shared physical custody (McIntosh, 2009).
- Children who have disorganized or anxious and insecure attachments may need one primary parent. Other key factors that may help these children are similar routines in each household, relative stability of the transitions, and parents who can communicate about the child and his or her developmental, medical, and emotional needs.
- This communication must allow the parents to be sufficiently responsive to the child and his or her needs. Parents with infants and young children, regardless of the parenting plan, need to have the capacity to help each other understand the infant, work together to develop routines that are familiar to the infant, collaborate on soothing techniques, help each other as language emerges, and reassure each other in their respective parenting techniques. It is best if such parents are flexible in their response to the child's changing needs. Such a pattern is used in healthy intact families, and if it is used in a separated family, the shared parenting plan will be natural for the child and his or her development.
- When parents are in significantly high conflict, very young children appear to benefit the most from schedules that resemble their preseparation patterns of contact with each parent. While neither parent needs to be considered the primary parent, the child needs predictability in his or her environment until the conflict can settle down.
- Additionally, when conflict is high, it is helpful to have transitions at neutral sites like day care when parents use babysitters or extended family

members to help in the parenting, when the parenting plan is highly structured so it provides predictability to the child, and when parents use a mediator or Parent Coordinator to help resolve differences and communicate about their child and his or her needs with daily journals.

The major task for the evaluator is to find a way to balance the child's attachments with each parent so that the child's need for stability, predictability, peace, and security are met. The evaluator must also pay close attention to the ability of the parents to meet the child's changing moods and needs. Evaluating the emotional functioning of each parent is critical in this regard. The child's temperament is also a critical variable that needs to be understood by the evaluator. While the rights of each parent are important during this time, the developmental needs of the child must come first. This might lead to situations that seem to one parent to be unfair. Because most state laws are focused on the best interests of the child, it is critical to describe the child's needs in our reports and use that description to help parents understand when our recommendations do not make sense to them. More on report writing will be discussed in Chapter 10.

## Never Paint by the Numbers

In 2001, Gould and Stahl described the critical task for the evaluator with regard to the question of overnights. Recognizing that there continues to be controversy about overnights, they suggested that the evaluator consider the following factors when deciding whether or not a particular very young child should have overnights with the nonresidential parent:

- The history of caregiving done by each of the parents: If the child has had a history of joint care taking and has shown little, if any, difficulty being parented and cared for by each parent while the family was intact, then one might look closely at continuing the parenting arrangement that existed prior to the separation.
- If both parents were actively involved in the infant and toddler's daily care and nighttime rituals, it might be developmentally appropriate to continue to foster the relationship between the young child and each parent by including overnight parenting time with each parent.
- If there has been one primary parent, and that parent has done the majority of care giving, it might be more appropriate to continue the primary relationship while gradually encouraging the other parent to increase his or her involvement with and parenting of the child.
- The skills of each parent to assess might include both daytime parenting and caretaking behaviors as distinct and separate from nighttime parenting and caretaking rituals. Evaluators should recognize that

parents have different strengths and weaknesses. When living together, many parents tend to complement each other in various ways.

- The evaluator's analysis of skills may determine that mother is competent in one area in which the father is less skilled while father is more competent in some areas in which mother is less skilled. When living apart, there is no complementary relationship for the child. When each parent is asked to fulfill the responsibilities of both parents during the time that their child is in their individual care, it is important to understand how each parent manages this. A competent evaluator needs to critically examine the complementary fit that existed during the marriage in order to understand the advantages and disadvantages each parent brings to the infant or toddler when parenting the child alone.

- When there are significant differences in competence, the evaluator works to craft parenting recommendations that allow each parent to have care of his or her young child in a way to maximize the strengths and minimize the weaknesses of each parent and parent–child interactions.

- Another dimension to be evaluated is the question of the child's temperament. Some children, regardless of the parents' relative strengths and weaknesses, may have a temperament which requires more stability and consistency, and a routine that is primarily with one parent. Other children, who are more flexible and easygoing, will be able to move more easily between households, as long as both parents are relatively equal in their daytime and nighttime parenting abilities.

- As noted earlier, a very critical dimension to consider is the nature of the communication between the parents about their child. Parents who share information about a wide array of developmental issues are usually more successful in sharing their child than parents who cannot. When there are problems in communication, evaluators can recommend ways to enhance the communication about the child, regardless of overnight access.

- Finally, Gould and Stahl suggested that evaluators also consider the care being given by other caregivers, such as nannies, grandparents, and others. If parents use a nanny to go back and forth between each parent's home with the child, and if parenting competencies are relatively equal, it is more likely that the child can successfully spend relatively equal time with both parents. Since children potentially develop multiple attachments with multiple caregivers, an analysis along this dimension will help the evaluator when considering access and residential arrangements.

- Gould and Stahl (2001) said,

> Regardless of whether one agrees with the position that infants and toddlers are able to accommodate overnight parenting arrangements with each parent or need a single, stable overnight placement, the art of child custody evaluations is applying the results from aggregate research results to the specific, ideographic (and idiosyncratic) needs of a particular family. Research results are important in their ability to

guide our thinking about how specific results might be relevant to a particular family system. There is never any substitute for exploring the parenting history and relevant dynamics of a particular family and then integrating that data with current research. Of course, evaluators will include collateral contacts along with interviews and direct observations in evaluating the above dimensions. (pp. 374–375)

- Ultimately, they concluded, "Evaluators never paint by the numbers. We always need to consider the best application for each family we assess, integrating all of the research into our understanding of the particular family and the particular child's needs" (p. 375).

## Preschoolers (3–5 Years)

During the preschool stage, the child is developing a better ability to understand language, relationships, and feelings. Children of this age are making significant progress in their cognitive skills and peer relationships. Sex role identification is developing. If the separation-individuation process has been healthy and the child has a secure attachment with one or both parents, children of this age can be expected to expand their horizons, go to preschool, and develop friendships. These children are often delightful, learning to manage their feelings and being inquisitive about everything. If attachments and caregiving are secure, these children will be ready to venture off to kindergarten with good self-esteem and confidence.

On the other hand, preschoolers are at risk for fairly serious regression when attachments are anxious, and they do not understand the conflicts of their parents. They may become easily confused and do not understand what is occurring around them. Developmental delays and regression in toileting, sleeping, and feeding are common. They may experience irritability and clinging behavior. Some children become depressed and withdrawn. Nightmares may become more pronounced. Self-confidence may suffer, and there can be increases in aggressive and anxious behaviors. Many of the children in this age group worry about their parents and may try to act "perfect." They may do this out of fear or they may be unconsciously taking care of their parents. We may be seeing the early signs of parentified behavior, in which they care emotionally for their parents, ignoring their own needs. A certain amount of this behavior is normal during the early stages of divorce, but when such behaviors are many, or extend for more than a year, they could reflect a more serious adjustment problem for the child.

I encourage the evaluator to see these young children in home visits. This is the natural environment for such children and it will put them at ease. A home visit will give the evaluator an opportunity to evaluate the respective relationships to both mother and father. The evaluator will look for positive signs of warmth, affection, comfort, empathy, and limit-setting, as well as negative signs of rigidity, detachment, hostility, or controlling interactions between the child and parent. The evaluator will look for clues about the child's mood and adjustment with each parent. Talking to preschool teacher(s), babysitter(s), and the pediatrician will give the evaluator valuable information about how the divorce is affecting the child away from the home. (More on the evaluation and process and talking to collaterals will be discussed in Chapters 7 and 9.)

Once the evaluator understands the various dynamics of the family, he will be making recommendations consistent with the following:

- Continue to focus on predictability, routine, and structure for the child.
- Children aged 3 and older can certainly tolerate overnight contact with each parent.
- Discipline and routine need to be consistent within each parent's home.
- Parents continue to need to share daily information about the child and his or her eating, sleeping, toileting, medical, and social/emotional functioning.
- Children need freedom from direct exposure to parental conflict. Parents who continue to be in conflict might consider using neutral sites (e.g., school or day care) for transitions and neutral decision-makers.
- Children in this age group often benefit from longer blocks of time with each parent, which enables them to be settled in routines at each home. Many of these children do not do well with frequent transitions.
- With this age group, parents need to put their needs secondary to the child's. While the noncustodial parent may want longer blocks of time with his or her younger child, many children of this age still need a primary home. This is dependent on the quality of attachments, whether parents are consistent and relatively free of conflict, and whether the child is experiencing significant vulnerability and stress.
- There may be situations in which each parent has some pathology or parenting flaws, *but each offers the child something the other does not.* In those cases, the evaluator will want to recommend a parenting plan that maximizes each parent's strengths while minimizing the extent to which the child is exposed to the pathology.

The major tasks for the evaluator are to determine the degree of vulnerability and tension in the child and the ability of the parents to co-parent, relatively free of conflict. For those families in which the co-parenting relationship is relatively free of conflict and the children are adjusting well with relatively equal attachments with each parent, some form of shared residential arrangements can be workable. However, given the potential for regression and vulnerability in children of this age, when the child is exposed to conflict and is feeling stressed and vulnerable, or when the routines in each parent's home are quite different, the child may need a primary home, with a growing amount of time in the other parent's home. The evaluator will want to make recommendations to encourage cooperation of the parents. However, as described later in Chapter 11, when conflicts are intractable, the evaluator will want to structure the parenting plan in a way that removes the child from the conflicts and encourages parallel parenting. Just as with younger children, the developmental needs of preschool children must come before the rights of each parent, even if a sense of unfairness continues.

Finally, when conflict is high, children of this age continue to benefit when they are removed from the intensity of their parents' conflicts, when transitions are completed through day care or other neutral sites, when parents communicate via a daily journal, and when parents keep routines predictable and consistent between both homes. This is always a dimension to be understood for children of this age.

# School-Age Children (6–12 Years)

School-age children thrive on structure and routine. Peer relationships are growing, and they are learning to master social rules. Creativity continues to grow and these children are adept at making up games with unique rules. Rules are important because these children focus on fairness in their life. Socialization and being part of a group are important to children of this age. They are learning to understand and express their feelings better and to master cognitive and academic skills. They can be quite silly at times and still prefer to play much of the time. They are learning skills in such areas as academics, sports, music, dance, art, and so forth. Self-esteem grows when they function well in school, on the playground, and in the family. It is not uncommon for children of this age to have different relationships with each parent, preferring mom for some things and dad for others.

Divorce brings many challenges to children of this age. Younger school-age children tend to feel the loss of the family and may experience sadness and crying, often longing for the return of the family unit. Older children in this age range may be likely to experience anger and to struggle to mobilize self-esteem. Children of this age often feel directly responsible for the divorce, especially if they perceive that conflict focused on them. These children may exhibit multiple symptoms, including tantrums, regression, sleep problems, acting out, behavioral and academic problems in school, withdrawal or aggression with peers, and depression. This is a population that believes in fairness, and wants to please their parents. They feel overwhelmed by their parents' conflict and usually try to fix it, yet they are ill equipped to do so. When a parent is depressed, these children are at risk for parentified behavior in which they attempt to take emotional care of that parent.

In extreme high-conflict families, this population may present as asymptomatic on the surface, but feel overwhelmed and vulnerable underneath (see, e.g., Johnston et al., 2009). These children are at risk for emotional splitting in which one parent is described as "all good" and the other as "all bad," resulting in the child becoming alienated (see Chapter 13 for more on the alienated child). They often feel stuck due to loyalty conflicts and may become emotionally constricted, worrying about both of their parents. Alignments that were natural in the predivorce family become highlighted, increasing the children's risk of alienation. These children have difficulty maintaining a strong internalized self-image as a result of the conflict. They may become overwhelmed and disorganized, struggling with the different emotions and behaviors of each parent.

It is not uncommon for children to hear one parent blame the other or hear different explanations from each parent for things they experience. For example, when one parent says, "I don't know why your mother doesn't call you when you're here. She probably doesn't care much for you," and the other parent says, "I called you three times last night, why didn't you call back? Doesn't your dad give you the messages?" this is quite confusing to children, who do not know which parent to believe. The evaluator needs to understand how the child feels and what the child processes when the parents are derogatory to or about each other and the child is placed in such confusing situations.

The evaluator should be alert to the level of confusion, emotional constriction, and vulnerability within the child. The evaluator needs to understand the child's ability to differentiate his or her own feelings from the competing demands of the parents and express those feelings. It is important to understand how the child is managing his or her non-divorce life, such as school, extracurricular activities, and friendships. Children of this age feel stress and gather fragmented pieces of information from their parents. It is important to know how they manage this stress and what assumptions they are making about the fragmented details they receive from their parents.

> School-age children are at risk of becoming alienated or parentified. Parents must keep their children out of the middle of conflict and should not use their children as messengers. Evaluators should be alert to signs of these problems.

In evaluating parents with children of school age, the evaluator will be trying to recognize how each parent understands the developmental needs of his or her child, and how each parent envisions helping with those needs. I have found that the most important traits in parents are empathy, consistency, support for the other parent, maintaining good boundaries, and being able to articulate plans for setting limits and discipline. Authoritative parenting, in which parents have a fairly structured routine while being sensitive to the child's emotions and responsive to the child's needs, is important. The psychological health of each parent is also important, as it reduces the likelihood that the child may be put in a caregiving position.

Once the evaluator understands the various dynamics of the family, she will be making recommendations that encompass the following concepts:

- Suggest a structured and consistent time-share that ensures access to each parent, when indicated. Optimal parenting plans range from 35% to 65% of time with either parent (and thus a primary home), to shared physical residence in which the child is with each parent about half of the time. While children of this age often express a wish for equal time with each of their parents, this may simply be to keep things fair for their parents and not reflect their true feelings or the history of their relationships. It may or may not be in the child's best interests, depending on all of the other relevant factors.

- While shared residence may be best in a given situation, it requires a degree of consistency and willingness for the parents to resolve their conflicts away from the child. It also requires the parents to share all of the tasks of parenting and help the child and each other transfer the child's things (school supplies, athletic equipment, etc.) from one house to the other without conflict.
- The time-share needs to promote each parent's strengths, while giving each parent time alone to recover from the divorce on his or her own.
- Exchanges need to minimize the extent to which the child is exposed to the conflict. School or other neutral places are excellent transition places between mom's house and dad's house.
- The parents need a plan for conflict resolution that keeps the children out of the middle. Children should not be messengers or spies for their parents. Communication needs to be by and through the parents, with the aid of a neutral professional when required.
- To the extent the parents can do it, there should be a plan for co-parenting. For those parents who are in more extreme conflict, a pattern of parallel parenting and detachment from each other will be optimal. This will be discussed in greater detail in Chapter 11.

Thus, the major tasks for the evaluator are to determine the degree of emotional constriction and loyalty conflicts within the child and the ability of the parents to co-parent, support the child's relationship with the other parent, empathize with the child and his feelings, and promote the child's mastery of age-appropriate skills and tasks. For those families in which the co-parenting relationship is relatively free of conflict, the children have a strong attachment to each parent and are adjusting well, and both parents are relatively equal in their attachments, some form of relatively equal, shared residence custody may be ideal.

However, given the potential for children to be caught in the middle of the conflict between their parents, and given the risk of parentification and alienation in children of this age, such a plan will not always work. Instead, when the child is exposed to too much conflict, when the child is not managing his stress very well, when the routines in each parent's home are significantly different, or when one or both parents struggle to empathize with the child and maintain healthy parent–child boundaries, the child is likely to need a primary home, with blocks of time in the other parent's home to ensure continuity and growth of each parent–child relationship.

## Adolescents (13–17 Years)

The major task for the adolescent is developing greater independence and autonomy from the family. Their separation-individuation process is similar to that of the 2-year-old. There can be a tendency to act with oppositional and negative behaviors. Just as with the toddler, adolescents express some resistance and rebelliousness while forming their identity. Healthy adolescents function well in school, have self-confidence, and have strong peer relationships. They learn to talk with their parents about life goals, and they begin to plan for driving, working, and college or vocational school. As a group, adolescents tend to be somewhat moody and reactive in their emotions. They may feel overwhelmed by pressure from their peers, use poor judgment, and be socially insecure. Their ideas, values, and goals are in a state of turmoil and may change considerably over their middle school and high school years. However, these years can be exciting ones as teens grow into productive and idealistic individuals.

However, with this considerable internal adjustment, this is a population at potential risk. This is true for adolescents of intact families as well as for families of divorce. When children are this age when a divorce occurs, they worry about the loss of their family life. They tend to feel a blend of responsibility and guilt, and anger for the way it has affected them. Children of this age tend to be self-centered naturally, and the divorce becomes a disruption to them. They may avoid both of their parents, especially if the parents are burdening them with loyalty conflicts and adult problems. When there is a pattern of high conflict, children in this age group are at risk for persistent academic failure, depression, suicide, delinquency, promiscuity, or substance abuse. With their ability to see things more abstractly, they become much more aware of their parents' flaws. This may lead to a more rapid destruction of their idealized view of their parents, resulting in anxiety and anger. This anger may take a fairly self-righteous stance, and adolescents may resist contact with the parent whose flaws have been significantly exposed.

In interviewing adolescents, the child custody evaluator has several objectives. First, adolescents must be listened to. From the adolescents' perspective, and indeed in fact, it is "their" life, not the evaluator's, the judge's, or a parent's. The adolescent's maturity level needs to be evaluated, as some adolescents are rather mercenary, pitting one parent against the other in emotional (or material) blackmail. One of the primary tasks of the evaluator is to understand the degree of emotional risk that the teen is experiencing.

Some adolescents want little or nothing to do with one of their parents and the evaluator must understand what that desire is about. This must be explored completely, both with the adolescent and with the parents. Sometimes, it is the result of alienation by one parent; sometimes, it is the result of frustration with the conflict; sometimes it relates to the moral indignation over the parent's divorce-related behavior; and sometimes, it is the result of legitimate frustration that has built over a long relationship of frustration and pain. When an older adolescent (15–17) is adamant about how he wants the parenting plan to be, it is important for the evaluator to have a significant reason if the older adolescent's wishes are not followed. Courts do not want to set up a situation that may encourage an adolescent to rebel (any more than he would anyway).

At the same time, the evaluator must evaluate each parent's capacity for the following:

- Maintaining the parent role and providing structure and rules that adolescents need
- Dealing with the mood swings and emotional turmoil of the adolescent that may be aggravated by the stress of the divorce
- Supporting and understanding the adolescent's need for increasing independence and autonomy
- Avoiding the tendency to engage the child in being a confidante and seeking the teen's support for the adult's issues
- Communicating on relevant issues in the adolescent's life (e.g., school, driving, college plans, dating, working, and other activities)

Finally, the evaluator needs to understand each parent's view of the child's maturity, capacity for independence, and validity of the child's self-determined "voice."

Once the evaluator has accomplished these tasks, she can make recommendations that encompass the following:

- A time-share plan that incorporates a range of possibilities. Many adolescents prefer one primary home, in large part to avoid confusion for their friends. Many of these teens will want some weekends or evenings with the other parent. Some will prefer a balanced, 50–50 plan with their parents. Much of this will depend on the prior history of the relationships with each parent and the availability of the parents to meet their needs. At times, adolescents may want to use one parent's home to get a break from the other parent or from younger siblings. More than anything, adolescents will often want a say in the parenting plan.
- Adolescents may require a different schedule than younger siblings. If so, the evaluator will want to recommend specific times that the siblings can be together.
- A statement about the need for any possible support services such as therapy, substance abuse counseling, tutoring, or other such needs.
- To the extent this is relevant, statements about the need for the parents to manage their conflicts away from the teen and maintain healthier boundaries with their adolescent child. If one or both parents confide adult issues to the teen, this should be discouraged.
- In cases of severe high-conflict, the evaluator may want to encourage the teen's autonomy and detachment from both parents. In that case, helping the adolescent find other appropriate supportive adults may also be indicated. For those teens, recommending someone to monitor and assess the ongoing risks would also be important.

Thus, the major tasks for the evaluator are to understand the feelings, wishes, and thoughts of the adolescent and integrate those with the ability of the parents to meet the needs of that adolescent. When parents have relatively consistent parenting styles, and when the adolescent supports it, some form of shared physical custody can be workable. However, teens and their parents may need to develop a different parenting plan when the teen wants a primary home. It is critical for the evaluator to understand the degree of risk the child is being exposed to, whether it is the result of the conflict or of a lack of adequate parenting. The evaluator will recommend a parenting plan that the child is willing to accept and that provides the necessary parental structure, reduces the child's involvement in adult issues, and keeps the child free from the conflicts of the parents.

# Children's Reactions to Parental Conflict

Certainly, the extent of children's reactions is dependent on many variables, including the following:

- The age of the child
- The intensity and chronicity of the conflict
- The degree of violence or fear of violence associated with the conflict
- The degree and length of time during which the child has been exposed to the conflict or to just fragments of it
- The psychological health of the child

In general, a history of aggression and conflict in the family has been strongly and consistently associated with emotional, behavioral, and social problems in children. While children from these families have more adjustment problems than normally expected, the range for individuals is broad. Kline, Johnston, and Tschann (1991), Johnston (1994), and Hetherington and Kelly (2002) suggest that a good parent–child relationship can buffer children from interparental conflict. Individual characteristics of the child (e.g., a more adaptable temperament or better coping skills) may help the child be more resilient to the conflict. Johnston (1994) found that "an association between joint custody/frequent access and poorer child adjustment appears to be confined to divorces that are termed 'high-conflict.'"

Very young children may be partially protected from the negative effects of conflict because they do not fully appreciate the conflict experience, but even they are susceptible to emotional distress, somatic complaints, and regression in their development. Older preschool children may be more likely to understand the conflicts and the feelings of their parents. Their reactions may include regression, confusion, sadness, low self-esteem, and fear. They may avoid peer relationships and withdraw from their caregivers.

School-age children are much more likely to have a range of reactions, starting with guilt. Children of this age often feel responsible for the conflicts of their parents. They show a greater frequency of externalizing (aggressive or delinquent) and internalizing (withdrawn or anxious) behaviors. This is a group that is highly susceptible to school problems, regression, and poor self-esteem (Johnston, Kline, & Tschann, 1989). When violence is associated with the high conflict, boys in particular are at risk for delinquent acting out.

Adolescents who have been exposed to conflict and violence tend to be aggressive and have multiple behavior problems, including truancy, problems with authority, and revenge-seeking behaviors. They are at risk for drug abuse, promiscuity, social alienation, delinquency, and school failure. They may attach to destructive peer groups and gangs as a substitute for the family. Internalizing adolescents may feel suicidal, emotionally constricted, and numb to the pain that they feel.

Given the extent to which conflict seems to be a predictor of postdivorce adjustment, a critical element of all child custody evaluations is the degree of conflict associated with the divorce and the direct and indirect impact of the conflict on the child. As will be described in Chapter 11, recommendations should be made that reduce the extent to which parents can engage in their conflict and continue exposing the child to it.

# Giving Children a Voice Versus Protecting Their Privacy

One of the dilemmas facing child custody evaluators relates to the issue of confidentiality within the evaluation process. Typically, when children see a therapist, the information given to a therapist can be kept confidential and, in particular, shielded from their parents and any dispute. Unfortunately, that is not the case in a child custody evaluation in which the evaluator might have to disclose information provided by the children. The ethics of the American Psychological Association (2002) state that psychologists must discuss limits of confidentiality with their clients. In some jurisdictions, the court order appointing a child custody evaluation states that the evaluator must explain to children the limits of confidentiality in the custody evaluation process. The *Model Standards of Practice for Child Custody Evaluation* of the Association of Family Conciliation Courts (AFCC) also expect that evaluators will discuss the limits of confidentiality with all persons participating in the child custody evaluation, including the children who are the subject of the evaluation (AFCC, 2006). The purpose is to be clear with the child that the information provided by the child is likely to be divulged to parents, potentially setting up the child for conflict with that parent. While I have found that few younger children (under age 8) concern themselves with this issue, many preadolescents and adolescents are very aware of confidentiality issues and express concern that what is told to the evaluator is likely to be shared with the parents.

It is important for the evaluator to explain to the child, in an age-appropriate way, what information will be shared and what information can potentially be protected. I start by informing the child about reporting requirements and then tell the child that the evaluation is not confidential. However, if the child is hesitant to talk, I try to talk with the child about why she is reluctant to talk, and I then may say to the child,

> If there is anything that you want to share with me that you would rather I not tell your parents, I can leave that information out of my report or be rather vague about what I say in the report. However, I take notes of everything that you say and if your parents continue to argue about custody, and they go to trial, it is possible that they could find out anything that you have said to me because they may want to see my notes. Since that is the case, you should only share information that you would be comfortable having your parents know about.

When there is critical information that I must tell the judge, I inform the child that I must include such information for the judge and will encourage the court to restrict access to that information. It may be necessary to recommend that the court appoint a Guardian Ad Litem, Best Interests Attorney, or someone specific (depending on jurisdiction) to represent the best interests of the child and to address the question of what information can be shared with parents.

At the same time, however, many children wish to have a voice in the outcome of the evaluation. While most custody evaluators are trained not to ask children who they want to live with, it is important to provide an opportunity for a child to express his or her wishes about the custody outcome, *if the child has such wishes*. I find that this dilemma can be most easily solved by talking about the child's overall life, and, when asking the child about his or her relationships with each parent, saying to the child something such as,

> You know, one of the things about a custody evaluation is that it is about your life, not your parents', and not mine. You've told me about some of your feelings about your mother and your father, and I wonder if you've thought about how you would like to spend time with each of them. While the ultimate decision will either be made by your parents or the judge, if you have any thoughts about how you'd like to spend your time with each of your parents, and if you want to share those thoughts with me, I can use that information in making my recommendations. Just so you know, however, I don't make my recommendations simply based on what you tell me you'd like, but based on all of the issues that I think are important in your life. As we talk, if you have any questions about that, please let me know.

Thus, the child can be encouraged to share his feelings and wishes without being put on the spot to make a decision or choose between parents. What I generally find is that some children are quite articulate in explaining how and why they would like to spend time with each parent, having given it much thought. They may be comfortable with their parents knowing how they feel and are not concerned about confidentiality. Other children are avoidant of their feelings, reluctant to take a stand and be in the middle of the conflict. They not only tell me that they have no preference between their parents, but they even try not to think about how these issues affect them. It is important to gather the information necessary to help the judge understand not only the child's feelings and the basis of those feelings, but also the child's maturity and capacity to understand the potential impact of her wishes.

As indicated earlier in this chapter, children who experience significant conflict between their parents tend to be hypervigilant about how things affect their parents and are very reluctant to think about how things affect themselves. It is these children who look at me with blank stares when I express that it is about their life and not their parents'. Even if a child does not give concrete information about his wishes, this still helps explain how the conflict is affecting him. It is important for evaluators to remember that the content of what children say may be less relevant than the process in which they say it, as well as the fact that they may not say very much at all.

In my opinion, if evaluators are clear with children about the limits of confidentiality, provide children an opportunity to express their wishes and feelings in a neutral, non-forced way, try to understand the child's life outside the family and the divorce issues, and look for clues as to the impact of the conflict on the child, the evaluator can understand how much to protect the child and her feelings, or feel comfortable with sharing the child's observations of the family dynamics with the parents and the court.

> It is always important to clarify with children the limits of confidentiality. If a child has a preference for the parenting plan, she should be encouraged to share it. If she doesn't express a preference, don't push for one.

## Weighing the Needs of a Single Child Versus the Needs of a Sibling Group

One of the more complicating factors for child custody evaluators is the family with several children across developmental spans. There are many reasons to keep children together and on the same schedule with their parents, and quite often this is the most sensible choice. Siblings are a natural support group and may be a buffer against the conflict. Young children may use older children as a transitional object, easing their anxiety with overnight visits, for example. In fact, in a California relocation case with four children where the trial court recommended that the mother be allowed to move to another state with two of her children and the other two children were to remain in California with their father (*In re Marriage of Williams,* 2001), the court of appeals stated that children cannot be separated absent a showing by the court of how the separation of the children is in each child's best interests.

For a variety of reasons, it may be more appropriate to have children on different schedules with each of their parents. The evaluator needs to understand the individual needs of each child and integrate those needs with the needs of the sibling group.

For example, a 6-year-old and a 15-year-old each have different developmental needs. It is likely that each will have a different quality of relationship with each parent. The 6-year-old may have a different need for structure in the schedule than will the 15-year-old, who is beginning to develop a life more separated from her parents. Young school-age children often do very well in a structured schedule in which there is defined time with each parent and in which the child can gain from the strengths of each parent. In contrast, the 15-year-old may want or need a schedule that is looser and revolves around school, extracurricular activities, and a part-time job. Many teenagers prefer to be in one primary home, in large part so that friends know where to find them. For them, it may very well be appropriate to recommend different time-shares with each child, with overlaps at various points of the month.

For example, if the 6-year-old is on a schedule in which he is at his mother's every Monday and Tuesday, at his father's every Wednesday and Thursday, and then alternating weekends, while the 15-year-old is primarily at her mother's and with her father one night for dinner and every other weekend, it would make sense to schedule the 15-year-old to be with the father during her brother's time with her father. This recommendation provides maximum overlap at the father's house and gives each parent some time alone with each child individually.

While this major age difference makes it easy to identify the validity of sometimes separating children, it is not at all uncommon for children who are even closer in age to benefit from slightly different schedules. Certainly, young children aged 2 and 5 may have a need for different schedules, especially if the 2-year-old is experiencing greater signs of separation anxiety or insecurity soon after the parental separation. Paying close attention to the different developmental needs of each child increases the likelihood that a more appropriate schedule can be found for both children.

In addition to development, however, there can be differences in relationships. This may be because of mutually shared interests (e.g., one parent and child share an interest in athletics while the other parent and the other child share more of an interest in music) in which each child feels closer to a particular parent. Sometimes this is the result of personality styles where a child relates with and gets along better with one parent than the other. In this situation, the "goodness of fit" between each parent and each child is the critical issue to be understood. It may be that one parent is more attuned to the developmental functioning of an adolescent while the other parent may be more attuned to the needs and functioning of the school-age child. This might lead to a different schedule for each child.

A third reason to consider splitting children would be because of problems in the sibling relationship. When parents have been unable to manage their children's sibling conflicts, the children may need time away from one another to allow for a period of healing. In such circumstances, it may be appropriate to have one child living primarily with mom and another primarily with dad, with some overlap on weekends or once a week for dinner. If an older child consistently acts out anger toward a younger sibling, a period of separation may needed as well as interventions to try to understand the basis of that anger and efforts to improve things between the siblings.

While these examples have touched on only a few of the circumstances in which individual children may have different needs within a family, it is always important for the evaluator to pay attention to siblings' potentially differing needs. Even though it usually makes sense to keep siblings together, it is always important to consider the individual developmental needs of each child, discuss them with the parents, and formulate a parenting plan that maximizes the individual needs of each child.

# Balancing the Individual
## Child's Real Needs With the Ideal

Children have a variety of needs. If parents were fully committed to meeting their children's needs, they would use better conflict-resolution skills in their relationship and they would teach those skills to their children. Unfortunately, custody evaluators usually see families that do not function at that level. Custody evaluators consider a range of options in their recommendations, and it may be difficult to meet all of the children's needs. Instead, evaluators must consider the child's age and developmental needs, the emotional functioning of each parent, the respective strengths and weaknesses of each parent, the relative attachments of the child to each parent, the degree and intensity of the parental conflict, the child's emotional functioning, and the child's wishes in developing their recommendations. The fact that parents are in two different households may make this a difficult task. For some children, a long distance between the parents also may exacerbate or create these problems. One of the goals for the evaluator is to help parents meet the full range of their child's needs while living apart from each other.

For example, infants and toddlers have a need for healthy attachment relationships. This is critical for the formation of a healthy ego, separation, and the individuation of the young child. The young child who has healthy attachments can move on to preschool and other relationships in a fairly confident manner, secure that the world is a relatively safe place. If she encounters too much stress, inconsistency, and chaos in these young years, it will be difficult for her to manage later developmental tasks.

In order to foster these multiple attachments, the child needs to have frequent and continuing contact with each parent. This might result in some disruption in the child's routine. There could be a need for frequent exchanges between the parents. If there is much conflict between the parents, there may be a need for fewer exchanges rather than more frequent contact. If the attachments are insecure with one or both parents and long blocks of time with each parent are recommended, the child may not be able to develop secure and healthy attachments with either parent. Evaluators need to consider all factors when balancing the varying needs for the individual child.

A second situation in which insecure attachment frequently occurs is with relocation cases. It is impossible to have frequent and continuing contact with both parents when one parent lives several hundred miles or farther away from the other parent. Children may not tolerate frequent long-distance travel, either in a car or on a plane. Maintaining close ties with the faraway parent can be quite difficult. If the child is very young, it may be necessary to sacrifice one relationship for the sake of a healthy primary attachment and the development of a healthy separation-individuation. When weighing the various factors, I would encourage parents to find ways to help the child with his development and put aside their rights until the child's attachment is secure.

I believe that evaluators should make recommendations that promote healthy child development first and the interests of the parents second. This might mean delaying a move until the child has reached the age of 4 or 5, when object constancy is intact and the attachment with both parents is secure. If a move must take place at an earlier age, I would encourage the noncustodial parent to do more of the travel to see the child in the *child's* environment rather than expect the child to be disrupted by frequent travel. These relocation issues are discussed in greater detail in Chapter 14.

An evaluator may find that each parent has different strengths; for example, one parent may be very good at dealing with the structure and routine of the child's educational needs while the other parent is more emotionally bonded and attuned to the child's feelings. Developing a parenting plan that balances all of the child's needs for emotional and academic development can be tricky.

In conclusion, I believe that the evaluator's key task is to recognize that children have a multitude of emotional, physical, relationship, developmental, and academic needs and to integrate them into a hierarchy of importance. While this will be subject to the particular realities of each family, keep in mind that younger children have a need for stability and security; school-age children have a need for routine, structure, and support for their education, peer relationships, extracurricular interests, and self-esteem; and adolescents have a need for structure and growing autonomy, along with preparing for adulthood. It is my position that evaluators first must understand the child's needs along this hierarchy, and then understand each parent's ability to meet those various needs. By looking at the strengths and weaknesses of each parent and the level of conflict between the parents, evaluators can draft recommendations that meet the majority of the child's important needs, while secondarily meeting the rest.

## THE BOTTOM LINE

A developmental perspective is critical when evaluating families. Remember that:

- Infants and toddlers typically develop attachments with both of their parents. While divorce and the separation of never-married parents can be stressful, the stress can be reduced by regular communication between the parents and regular access to both parents. Such access may result in more frequent transitions than is typical for older children.
- Preschool children typically have regular parenting time with each parent. The goal is to promote continued healthy and secure attachments, support the child's exploration outside of the family, and assist the child's growth in self-esteem and confidence.
- School-age children benefit from the active participation of both parents (when healthy and available) in a wide array of the child's life experiences and activities. While they do not require an equal time-share with parents, these children do benefit from substantial time with both parents, as long as the time is distributed well.
- Adolescents often want a say in the parenting plan. They may want a primary home so that their friends know where to find them. It may be important to balance the child's need for relationships with both parents and his need for maintaining his school, social, and work life.
- These developmental needs may be affected by other factors, such as the level of family conflict and the child's exposure to that conflict; the family logistics, including how far the parents live from one another; the psychological functioning and parenting ability of each parent; and the range in age of siblings in the family. Balancing these issues is a key task for the evaluator.

# PART II

## Conducting the Child Custody Evaluation

# 6

# Conducting the Custody Evaluation

## Part I. Observations and Techniques With Adults

The earlier chapters set the stage for understanding many of the dynamics of child development, the major issues of most evaluations, and the various roles that a mental health professional may play in doing evaluations. These next five chapters are designed to outline the steps of doing the custody evaluation. By understanding the evaluation process, and ensuring that we follow a similar process under most evaluation circumstances, we can conduct a custody evaluation that is more valid and consistent. This will satisfy the forensic requirement that child custody evaluations follow a standard protocol, increasing the scientific reliability of the process. As evaluators, we are obligated to maintain multiple avenues of data gathering (Association of Family and Conciliation Courts, 2006). These include interviews, with parents and children, observations of family members, gathering and reviewing collateral information, and possibly psychological testing. This chapter will focus on the issues related to the start of the evaluation, and the evaluation process with the adults. Chapter 7 will address the issues involved in understanding and evaluating the children, and the various techniques in working with them. Chapter 8 will address psychological testing. Chapter 9 will discuss the issues associated with collateral data. Finally, Chapter 10 will focus on the report and the way in which evaluators share the results of the evaluation.

## The Court Order and Initial Contact With Attorneys

There are several steps that are best to take before actually beginning the custody evaluation. The first steps include the initial phone call and review of the court order. Typically, I do not start any work until I have received a copy of the order from the court that has appointed me to conduct the evaluation.

Receiving the order is a required first step in California before beginning the process, because California evaluators must file a form, under penalty of perjury, with the court that the evaluator is eligible to perform the evaluation, based on the evaluator's training and experience. As noted in Chapter 1, this critical first step is also important to help reduce (but not completely eliminate) the risk of lawsuits farther down the road. In my experience in both California and Arizona, the court order names the evaluator and provides the scope of the evaluation. While some evaluators suggest that the court order should list specific referral questions, my experience is that some courts will do so and others will not. However, typically the order will identify the gross parameters of the referral, such as whether the evaluation is to be a full evaluation, a relocation evaluation, a general best-interests evaluation, or a more limited, focused evaluation. The court order will also address the issue of who is responsible for payment of the evaluator's fees, identify any specific issues associated with collateral record data (e.g., in Solano County, California, there is a requirement that attorneys must agree on what information will be sent to the evaluator before anything is sent, and, in the event that they cannot agree, the court will determine what information will be sent), and address issues about the lack of confidentiality in the evaluation process, when the report is to be completed, and who the report will be sent to when it is completed. You will always look to the court order as the first indicator of your role in the case.

Either before the attorneys have agreed to my appointment as the evaluator or soon after receipt of the court order, I typically have a joint conference call with the attorneys to have them explain further the reasons for the evaluation, gather relevant family information (everyone's name, names and ages of children, where people live, etc.), and to discuss my process. I tell them about fees and my informed consent process. I let them know when it is likely that I can start the evaluation process and how long it will take. I encourage them to identify what collateral record information they plan to send to me and remind them that anything they send to me must be simultaneously sent to the other side. I encourage them to try to agree on what information I will receive and have it sent to me only once. I then instruct the attorneys to have their clients contact me by phone in order to set up the initial appointments.

If I am working with attorneys who are unfamiliar with me as an evaluator, I will ask if they have any questions about me as an evaluator and try to answer those questions clearly and promptly. As always, I believe in complete transparency and openness in answering those questions and in making sure that attorneys are comfortable with my role in their case. Once those phone call is complete and I have the court order, I await the phone calls from the parents.

# The Initial Phone Call and Contacts With Parents

It is very important to talk to both parents before scheduling appointments in order to make certain that they both plan to follow the court order and participate in the evaluation. All too often, I find that one parent is in agreement with the evaluation and the other parent is not. When that happens, I recontact the attorneys to get clarification on what to do, and sometimes inform the court that the parents are not in agreement and ask the court for direction. Of course, in any such communication with the court, all attorneys are copied on the communication. At other times, both parents are in agreement with the evaluation and are willing to participate. In each such phone call, I briefly explain the evaluation process and schedule the first appointments. As with the attorneys, I ask if there are any questions about me as an evaluator, I ask for basic identifying information, and I inform the parents that I will send my retainer agreement and informed consent document, along with my intake form, to them and their attorneys. I usually send these forms via e-mail.

During that initial phone call, I briefly explain my evaluation process and answer any questions about my credentials, experience, inherent biases, and other professionally related questions that a parent might have. By answering such questions, I try to assure the parents that I will be doing an evaluation that focuses on their children's needs and will work toward understanding and making recommendations related to their disputes. I inform the parents that I will recommend a parenting plan that is in their child's best interest. Even with a reluctant parent, I try to use the initial phone call to answer questions and ease that parent's resistance and answer concerns about participation in the evaluation. I also make it clear that if they have any questions about the informed consent document, they can raise those questions with their attorney. For parents who are self-represented, I inform them that such questions might have to be answered in a conference call with the other attorney. This is to maintain balance in the communication with both sides and avoid ex parte communication with one side.

By explaining the evaluation procedure, I try to reduce each parent's initial anxiety about the evaluation. Such anxiety is quite common for people involved in court proceedings. It is important for the evaluator to remember that most people involved in a custody dispute have been in constant warfare, and often receive little information about what they can expect through the court process. If the evaluator thoroughly explains the evaluation process and answers all of either parent's questions, she can assist each parent in reducing anxiety, and encourage both parents to feel better about the process.

In addition to all of that, it is important for the evaluator to understand what the parents are looking for from the evaluation. Frequently, there are stepparents, step-siblings, grandparents, and significant others that the parents wish to be seen as part of the evaluation. There may be many people that the parents want me to talk with in order to get historical or other information. It is very important in this initial phone call to elicit from the parents their understanding of the components of a complete custody evaluation and what they want me to do. Often, parents are worried about the effect of the evaluation process on their children, and they have questions about how I intend to see the kids. If there are siblings, they may want to know if I plan to see their children together or separately, and they may have a reason for their preference. By answering parents' questions and eliciting their assistance in their evaluation, I can ensure that the parents become participants who are actively involved in the decision-making regarding their children.

# The Initial Contract

After completing my joint phone call with attorneys and speaking with each parent, I send my informed consent document to each parent, with copies to the attorneys. This document, required by the California Rules of Court (5.220) and also by the *Ethical Principles of the American Psychological Association* (2002), informs parents about the process of the child custody evaluation, outlines my job, and informs them of their responsibilities during the process.

This document has four primary sections. First, I discuss the procedures, including the multi-method approach that I take. I inform parents that I will have several interviews with each of them, interviews with their children, observe them with their children, perhaps perform some psychological testing and give them some parenting questionnaires, and review all collateral information given to me. I inform parents that I will be calling some collateral witnesses, usually professional rather than friends or family members. I then inform parents that I will be writing a report at the end of the process, which is sent to the court, attorneys, and any self-represented parent.

Another section of the document is focused on the limits of confidentiality. It is critical to inform parents that there is no confidentiality in the process and that I will be asking each of them, and their children, about critical issues. Third, I talk about my fees, informing them that the fees are just for the evaluation, and that, if the case goes to trial, there will be additional fees. Finally, I explain to parents the nature of recommendations that I might be making and the limits of those recommendations.

A sample contract is included in Appendix B.

# The First Conjoint Appointment

Over the years, I have found that the easiest way to begin an evaluation is to meet face to face with both parents for the start of the first session. Because I include psychological testing in nearly all evaluations that I do, the logistics of this first appointment are very easy. I meet with the parents together for 20 to 30 minutes, and during that time, I am able to answer their questions, discuss their initial anxiety, provide more information about the direction of the evaluation, establish my neutrality, and focus on the primary issues of the evaluation. This is the time to ensure that the parents understand their court order, and I encourage parents to ask me any questions about myself, my experience, and my biases. I talk openly with parents about my general belief that it is best for children when both parents share in the postdivorce parenting unless circumstances do not support this. I try to help them know that if they can agree on a custody plan, it is better for their children than if they remain in conflict with one another. I tell parents that it is my hope that the evaluation will help them find a solution to their conflicts over custody, and that research shows that children can tolerate almost any solution that settles the conflict better than the ongoing conflicts that some parents continue. I try to answer any questions parents may have about such issues when both of them are together as a way to explain the importance of their cooperation when the evaluation process is complete.

The first interview is also the time to talk with them about how to talk to their children about the evaluation, taking into account the age of the children. For preschool-age children, I encourage parents to explain that I am someone who wants to meet them and see them with each parent so that I can help them with their parents' divorce. For older children, if the evaluation is at the beginning of the divorce, I encourage parents to explain to their children that they are in disagreement about how to share the job of parenting now that they are getting divorced, and I will be talking with them, the children, to understand their thoughts, fears, wishes, and feelings about their parents and their parents' divorce. If the evaluation is significantly postdivorce, I encourage parents to talk openly, but without emotion, about the realities of the conflict, and I tell the children that I am there to help the parents settle the conflict. At all times, I tell parents to encourage their children to express any feelings they may want, and that I am there to listen to them and help them understand and express feelings about the divorce, and both good and bad feelings about each of the parents.

This appointment is also my best opportunity to see firsthand the nature of the interaction between the parents. During this time, I can see which parent acts more compliant, seems more angry, feels more controlled, feels more powerless, and so forth, and begin to get an idea of the interaction that leads to this. I can begin the process of understanding the ways in which the couple's conflict is contributing to the custody dispute and the way that the parents can, or cannot, communicate about their child. This is very important information as I begin thinking about the kind of parenting plan that will be most useful for the parents and their children.

Because I use psychological tests in most custody evaluations, it is then quite natural to split the parents, one doing some psychological tests alone in one room while I interview the other parent in the interviewing room.

On the other hand, there may be times where logistics or other issues preclude seeing parents together at the beginning. Certainly, when there is a domestic violence restraining order in place, I will not see them together at any time throughout the evaluation. I would never want to be in a position of encouraging either parent to violate the terms of the restraining order or put herself or himself at risk in my office (or in the parking lot). Another reason for not seeing parents together at the beginning would be when one parent prefers not to meet with the other parent. I believe it is better to support a parent's request to meet alone than to force people to meet together when one of them does not want to. A third reason for not meeting together could be logistical. I do many evaluations with one parent living in one community and the other parent in another location. Obviously, in those cases, parents cannot meet together. Additionally, with people's complex and busy schedules, I have found that it can be hard to get two parents to agree to meet together at the same time. Rather than delay the start of the evaluation until people can make a conjoint appointment, I have found it best to start the evaluation in a timely way, especially because courts expect a report to be completed by a deadline. With that in mind, I will start the evaluation as quickly as possible, even if it means that there is not going to be an initial conjoint appointment.

> Many child custody evaluators have a joint session with both parents. This conjoint session can help the evaluator directly see the interaction between the parents. Avoid conjoint sessions when there is a restraining order which would prohibit it.

## The Initial Individual Appointment

Regardless of whether or not I meet with parents conjointly before the first individual appointment, my first individual appointment is focused on getting information that the parent wants to share with me. I usually have two to four individual appointments with each parent, and within those appointments, there are several things that I am looking for. My first question to parents is always, "Why are we here?" This gives each parent an opportunity to tell his or her story. Rarely, until the couple gets to a custody evaluation, has either parent been truly able to tell his or her story to someone who will listen. Attorneys are advocates for their clients, and while they often provide a quasi-counseling role when they listen to their clients, their primary task is to focus on the legal issues involved in the divorce. In the courtroom there is precious little time, and almost no opportunity, for the parents to talk to the judge about their children or the marital problems. If the couple has been to mediation, they are so focused on solving the problems that there is little opportunity for telling the history or the pain the parents have experienced. Sometimes, this one question takes up most of the entire first interview, as I get to hear the information that the parent needs to tell me.

It is my belief that, in an effective custody evaluation, I will spend a considerable part of the interviewing time listening to the parents talking about their story. If I understand their pain, the sources of the conflict through their eyes, and the nature of their fears and beliefs about the other parent, it will assist me in the overall evaluation of the family. Through these interviews, I can hope to get a snapshot of the family and the family dynamics that will enable me to see how best to intervene to solve the custody issues. This is very important psychologically, because if parents feel heard, they may be more likely to go along with the evaluation's recommendations even if they do not agree with them.

In addition to listening to the story of the parents, there is a great deal of other information that I want to focus on during the evaluation. I want to ask questions that allow me to understand each parent's views of his or her strengths and weaknesses as a parent, as well as each parent's perception of the other parent's strengths and weaknesses as a parent. I need to talk about emotional attunement, discipline, structure, guidance, and the other factors that are often related to the question of the "best interests of the child." In many cases I need to understand what each parent's childhood was like, and the extent to which each parent's own childhood experiences are affecting the current custody dispute. I want to look for clues that parents are idealizing their own histories, as this is a sign that they might be idealizing their own parenting abilities. Obviously, I need to understand each parent's view of the child's functioning and needs and the child's need for a relationship with the other parent. I am also looking to understand how each parent will support the child's relationship with the other parent. When relevant, I need to understand critical issues related to the history of family conflict (Chapter 11), allegations of violence and abuse (Chapter 12), concerns about alienated or estranged children (Chapter 13), and relevant issues of a proposed relocation (Chapter 14). While those chapters will provide much more information about those particular topics, Appendix E lists the many kinds of questions that I typically ask in any best-interests custody evaluation.

Finally, I always want to focus on the affect of the client and the client's psychological functioning. I want to understand whether or not the parent can stay focused on the issues at hand, or whether the parent rambles a great deal. Of significant importance is how much the parent can look at himself or herself and try to understand his or her role in the nature of the problems. Most parents come to evaluations blaming each other, and may have considerable difficulty seeing any way in which they contribute to the problems. It is very important for me to understand the extent of projection, externalization of blame, denial, and so forth, that each parent brings to the evaluation. While these psychological traits might not preclude a parent from having reasonable time with or custody of the children (especially when both parents tend to externalize blame), they will go a long way toward understanding all of the recommendations I might need to make. In this way, I gather relevant data that will help me understand the psychological issues associated with the interaction between the parents and the way in which each parent manages his or her emotions. All of these factors are the essential ingredients of the clinical interviews with the parents.

One final important area of focus needs to be on "why the parents cannot agree." I look at the interactive dynamics between the parents, in addition to the individual dynamics of each parent: issues of power and control, anger and hostility, the history of the couple's conflicts, as well as the individual issues noted earlier (blaming, projection, and denial) that contribute in some way toward the inability of parents to reach a mutually acceptable solution for their children. It is common when seeing a family for a child custody evaluation that the parents

> Understanding each parent's version of the truth is an important first step before deciding on your interpretation of the truth. Some parents lie, some distort the truth, and some speak truthfully while leaving out important contradictory information.

cannot agree on many issues related to parenting their children. Therefore, it is critical that I understand through these interviews why this breakdown has occurred. Frequently, parents do not even talk to one another, and an agreement cannot be reached because of that. Many parents continue to harbor tremendous bitterness and resentment over the failed marriage, which also leads to an inability to cooperate for their children. By understanding these problems, I can better use this information in my recommendations and parenting plan.

## The Second Interview and Beyond

After the first interview, it is critical to balance the gathering of information that the parent wants me to know with the information I want to know. I use the second and third interviews to ask multiple questions about the relevant allegations, to ask each parent about the negative things I have heard from the other parent, and ultimately, to talk about the children. It is very important to ask each parent about the relevant allegations made by the other parent. If the mother talks about her concerns that the father is violent and abusive, or has a difficult temper, I want to understand the father's perception of the same thing. It is also important to get each parent to explain more details about their allegations. One of the things that can help me sort through the allegations is the lack of details a parent can give about the allegations. I keep asking questions of each parent until I fully understand each parent's complete perceptions of the allegations and each parent's responses to those allegations. When I critique other evaluators' evaluations, I often find that parents are most frustrated when the evaluator simply believes what the other parent has said without giving either parent the opportunity to respond to allegations. This leads to a concern that an evaluator was biased (more on this in Chapter 16).

The final issue that must be discussed with each parent is the children. I have always found it amazing that parents who claim to want the best for their children do not even talk about the children until prompted to do so by my questions. I ask questions to help me understand how each parent understands the child's life, feelings, and needs. I try to understand how each parent believes the child is functioning academically, psychologically, emotionally, and with their peers. I try to understand the routine in each parent's home and how similar or disparate those routines are. As my last interview with each parent is winding down, my final question nearly always is, "What do your children need?" With that question, I am trying to understand each parent's ability to focus on his or her children as opposed to staying focused on the allegations and issues with the other parent. I am also trying to understand the extent to which and the manner in which each parent can put aside his or her differences with the other parent and talk reasonably about the children. I wonder how each parent can include the other parent in the needs of the children and how each might plan to encourage and support the other parent's relationship with the children. I inquire about each parent's view of the child's feelings if the parent has not talked about that yet.

Ultimately, by the end of the multiple interviews, I hope to have gathered information about all of these critical issues and also each parent's views of the children and their needs. Use the sample questions in Appendix E to ensure that you ask each parent all of the important questions to get the information that you need.

## What to Believe?

One of the important issues confronting us is determining what to believe. We do not get the "truth" by reading court affidavits; they simply measure the "temperature" of the case. Our task is to gather all of the family's "truths" because there is never a single truth for the family. Quite frequently, parents tell completely different stories. They both believe that they are telling the truth, and are insistent about the events that they describe. Certainly, in situations where abuse/neglect or substance abuse is an alleged issue, we hear quite conflicting sides. But even in the evaluations in which parents are generally positive about each other's parenting, we hear different stories. In such families, we might hear mothers talk about the lack of involvement by fathers in the child's day-to-day life, and the father then comes and talks about how he is the baseball coach and is home helping with the homework several evenings a week. Determining truth can be very difficult and yet is one of the most necessary tasks in the evaluation.

I have learned that truth is clearly in the eye of the beholder. Sometimes one or both parents are clearly lying or trying to deceive the evaluator. Sometimes both parents are telling the truth, but simply focusing on different aspects of the same experiences. There is a continuum that ranges from parents who are lying or actively deceiving the evaluator to other parents who simply have different perceptions of the same situation. A deceptive parent may lie about the amount of time that each parent helped with homework, while misperceiving parents do not actually lie but tend to distort based on their feelings. They process experiences with "emotional facts," in which their emotions lead to distortions of the events as they actually occurred. For example, a mother who is angry that her husband was not there for her emotionally remembers that the father was only limitedly involved in the child's life, having missed birthday parties and school events. She remembers the number of evenings home alone with the children while the father was at work or with other activities. Her picture is one of having been left with the responsibilities of single parenting even when married, as she remembers the many times that the father failed to participate and expected her to do it all. Her memory is affected by her anger and history of abandonment feelings in the marriage.

In contrast, the workaholic father who was very self-centered during the marriage might not remember those events, but focuses largely on the times that he helped with big homework projects, coached Little League, and helped with Cub Scout projects for his child. Because he wants to view himself as a capable and involved father, he is looking at the picture that tells *that* side of the story. His memory is affected by his need to see himself in a favorable light.

In reality, neither one is "lying," but rather they are both looking at a different piece of the whole picture and creating emotional facts in which they see things through the eyes of their emotions and needs. My task as the evaluator is to understand the extent to which a parent may be deceptive and lying, defensive, narrowly focused in this small picture, or creating facts based on his or her emotions. The more disparate the perceptions of each parent, the more critical this determination is.

There are three interview techniques that I believe are extremely useful for understanding the truth of the family. The first technique is through confrontation and observation. By confronting the story that is presented by each of the parents, I can see whether or not the stories make sense, change, and so forth. By observing the affect of the parents through this process, I can help identify defensiveness and projection as opposed to openness and looking at one's self and one's real strengths and weaknesses. If, for example, every time I confront the father about the question of his minimal involvement, he blames the mother rather than answer the question, we can suspect that at the very least the father is defensive and avoidant, and possibly lying, as well. If when confronted, however, the father acknowledges that he wishes he had done more and was pleased to be involved in some activities, and if his affect is warm as he talks about the activities with this child, I can assume that at least he is telling the truth. Similarly, when I ask the mother about activities the father *did* participate in, and she continues to focus on "what a jerk he is" and how he was never around when she or the children needed him, I can assume that her anger at him for not being around when she needed him is coloring her view of the whole picture. Thus, with confrontation and observation, clues begin to emerge as to the real picture and the extent to which each parent is distorting or minimizing the issues.

The second technique that I find quite useful in determining truth is for the evaluator to play "the wise fool." I suggest that the skilled evaluator ask many innocent questions to understand the picture that the parent is trying to present. In a way, I lull parents into telling me things I need to hear so that I can truly learn the larger picture. Over the years, I have found that parents will frequently tell me what I need even when it goes against their main story. By "acting dumb" I can often elicit from parents the information necessary to get a truer picture of each parent's "real involvement" with the children and with the problems at hand.

A good way to draw parents in is by repeating to parents what they have been telling us, continually clarifying and supporting their statements. When they talk of helping with the homework, coaching, putting their kids to bed, and other such things, listen attentively and supportively. Then, just when a parent thinks I completely understand and agree, I use a form of confrontation to elicit specific examples of his or her parenting or to ask about something that the other parent or the children have been saying. For example, in a recent evaluation, a father was telling me how much his son wanted to come over more than he was allowed by the mother. I kept listening to him, trying to understand him better. Then, just when he thought I understood, I queried him about his son's statements that he was angry at his father for leaving his mother. I suggested that his son did miss him, but that did not mean that he wanted to visit more. Rather, it may have meant that he missed the family unit. Through the confrontation, the father was able to see how he misinterpreted his son's statements to validate his own wish to see his son more often.

The third technique that I find most useful is to talk with the children. Certainly, children see and hear a tremendous amount from their parents, and through their eyes and ears I can learn more of the truth, as well. In several recent evaluations, the adult children told of a long history of physical and emotional abuse from their father that he had denied. Younger children will frequently talk about the feelings they have when their parents say derogatory things in front of them about the other parent, even when the parents are adamant that they never talk about the other parent in front of the children. While I do not advocate acting like a detective with children and giving them "the third degree," with skillful questioning I can get information in the child interviews to develop a better sense of the parents' "truth." It is these techniques that are primarily useful during the interviews and that enable a skilled evaluator to understand the "truth" and the whole picture that is necessary when assessing a family of divorce. Of course, it will always be important to keep in mind that children may be telling me things that are not true, either because they have some motive for it or because of some suggestibility issues. This will be discussed in greater detail in the next chapter.

## Collateral Information

As noted previously, interviewing techniques, while useful, are not sufficient to understand the history of the family and the facts of the case. They must be interwoven with the information gathered from psychological tests (to be described shortly and in Chapter 8) and various collateral sources (to be discussed more fully in Chapter 9) who know the family in order to completely understand the real truth. I try to avoid talking with family friends and relatives, many of whom either feel in the middle of the divorce and do not like to choose sides between the parents, or who are clearly interested in choosing sides and are just as caught up as the parents in the battle between the parents. While I do not like to exclude anyone's information, I do not call people who may have limited useful information to provide. Instead, I tell parents at the beginning of the evaluation that they can have family members or friends send me letters, which I will gladly review and will follow up on if necessary. In this way, clients have control by guaranteeing they can provide me with any information they want me to have, while I simultaneously reduce the number of phone calls I need to make in an evaluation.

I find the most reliable collateral sources to be other professionals who have worked with the family, such as teachers, school principals, physicians, therapists, attorneys, day-care personnel, and others who have a professional relationship with one or more family members. Mediators who are not obligated to maintain confidentiality are also a good source of information. From these professionals, I can get an objective view of the family struggle and the ways in which each parent participates in it. I might learn from the teachers which parent has been active in parent–teacher meetings. If the parents are currently sharing custody, I might hear that a child is consistently unprepared and/or late to school when she is with a particular parent. I can see from the therapists which parent is more receptive to understanding the child's feelings, and I can hear from the day-care personnel about the battles they have personally witnessed at the pick-up/drop-off site. In this way, the information I gather from the collateral sources becomes a useful adjunct for rounding out the overall information I receive in the evaluation.

Through the years, I have found that it works best for me to delay the gathering of collateral information until I have formulated my initial hypotheses and have sufficient questions to ask these people. If I try to talk to them too soon, it is much more difficult to integrate their information with my questions, and if I am not careful, their perceptions may preempt my formulation of hypotheses regarding these complex issues. It is very important that the end result of an evaluation be the opinion of the evaluator, and not the restating of an opinion from one or more of the collateral sources. Should the parents not be able to agree even after an evaluation, and a trial is necessary, an evaluator will need to show that her opinion was derived from all of the material, and not from collateral sources alone. By waiting until I have specific questions and have begun to formulate my own opinion, I can safeguard against this concern.

# The Use of Psychological Tests

The issue of psychological testing will be discussed in more detail in Chapter 8, but for purposes of this chapter it is important to point out that psychological testing data may also help in understanding some of the issues related to the

truth of the family. Though most custody litigants tend to be defensive and try to portray
themselves positively (see e.g., Bathurst,
Gottfried, & Gottfried, 1997), psychological
testing may help to differentiate between the

> Collateral interviews and record reviews
> and psychological testing may help sort
> out the truth of each parent's story.

parents who are emotionally overreacting and those who have problems with
reality or who lie. Psychological testing may help to differentiate some of the
issues relevant to sorting out the truth of the family and its history.

## THE BOTTOM LINE

Interviews with parents are a critical step in understanding each parent's perception of the family
issues, the strengths and weaknesses of each parent, each parent's understanding of the children and
their needs, and the relevant issues pertaining to allegations or to relocation issues for the family. By
engaging in multiple interviews, gathering collateral information, talking with children and observing
children and parents together, and potentially using psychological testing and parenting questionnaires, I can hope to learn all I need to know about each parent and his or her parenting strengths
and weakness and his or her views about the children and their developmental, psychological, academic, and social needs. Ultimately, this will help me understand the critical allegations and issues in the
evaluation and gather data relevant to the best interests of the children.

It is important to point out that, no matter how hard I try, I may not be able to discern the actual truths
in the family. Some parents are good at deception, some children are very reluctant to share significant
information, and psychological tests do not always reveal whether one parent is more defensive or deceptive than the other. Trusted collateral sources may tell me different facts that also make it difficult to sort
out the truths. It may very well be that the truth lies somewhere in the middle of what each parent is saying, and it may also be that one parent is much more accurate in reporting than the other. When an evaluator is clear on the facts of the case, he should say so. In other circumstances, when the evaluator still
does not know what to believe, it is important to state specifically in the report that there is not enough
evidence to determine the truth, and then clearly outline what the evaluator knows, what the evaluator
believes (and what facts support that belief), and what the evaluator does not know. This will help the
judge in understanding whether or not the recommendations, which will be based on the best interpretation of the information gathered, are appropriate for the family being evaluated. This is because the judge
may have reached different conclusions about the family's truths based on evidence gathered at trial.
Writing the report and developing conclusions will be discussed more fully in Chapter 10.

# 7

# Conducting the Custody Evaluation

## Part II. Observations and Techniques With Children

The interviews with the children are a crucial part of understanding both the family dynamics and the relationship between the child and his parents. Many evaluators are used to conducting interviews with adults, yet have little or no experience in working with children. This is because a large percentage of mental health professionals never gain much experience in working with children during their training or professional careers. This chapter will begin by focusing on the types of information needed from our interviews with the children, and then focus on how to get such information from children at various ages. Issues such as seeing children and parents together, seeing siblings together, the role of children's preference, home visits, and other techniques will all be discussed.

At the outset, we must recognize two important things. First, it is very easy for an evaluator to inadvertently add to the distress that a child feels. A major goal when working with children during a custody evaluation is to help ease the child's anxiety about the evaluation experience and assist the child in feeling more secure talking about his relationship with *both* of his parents. To help with this, the discussion with children at the beginning of the evaluation interviews is critical. I have several goals for the first few minutes of my interviews with children. I talk with them about my role, their parents' divorce, and my recognition that they do not like to choose between their parents. I encourage children to talk openly about their feelings about both parents and make it clear that I am there to listen to them and their feelings more than the thoughts and feelings of their parents.

Second, we must also recognize that children's language skills are not the same as our own, and we must develop a good feel for the language of children when we do our evaluations. This is hard to come by without practice, but it is important for evaluators to know that children often do not understand the things that we may ask, yet they may respond as if they do understand. As such, I will ask children to repeat or to explain what I have said so that I can be more certain that we understand what each other is conveying. If we pay attention to children's words and ask them questions in a way that they can comprehend, we are more likely to be clear about their feelings, fears, and wishes.

# Significant Issues in the Assessment of Children/Gaining Rapport at the Beginning of the First Interview

In evaluating children, there are a few things to pay attention to even before the child comes to the office. First, evaluators want to understand children's thoughts and feelings and learn how the children comprehend their parents' behaviors and the issues of the divorce. Many young children do not even know what a divorce is; all they know is that their parents fight all of the time and dad recently moved out. Children are often told little or nothing about the changes in their family life (Dunn, Davies, O'Connor, & Sturgess, 2001). As a result, the evaluator will always want to understand what the child has and hasn't been told about the divorce and the family relationships, and who told the child what she knows. It is also important for the evaluator to recognize that children may be reluctant to share their feelings with a total stranger, and other times, they have been primed by one or both parents to "tell the examiner" everything. In the best of worlds, the children have been told that they are coming to the evaluation so that the evaluator can help the parents understand them and their feelings and work with the parents to improve the relationships and reduce the fighting. If children know that we are *their* allies, and our purpose is to understand the parents' divorce through *their* eyes, they can be more relaxed and reassured at the beginning of the evaluation.

I start all interviews with children by telling them the truth about my role. This is consistent with the language of the American Psychological Association (2009) *Guidelines for Child Custody Evaluations in Family Law Proceedings*, which state,

> If the examinee is legally incapable of providing informed consent, psychologists provide an appropriate explanation, seek the examinee's assent, consider the preferences and best interests of the examinee, and obtain appropriate permission from a legally authorized person (Ethics Code 3.10, 9.03). Psychologists are encouraged to disclose the potential uses of the data obtained, and to inform parties that consent enables disclosure of the evaluation's findings in the context of the forthcoming litigation and in any related proceedings deemed necessary by the court. (Guideline 9)

With this principle in mind, I inform children that I am a psychologist and ask if they know what a psychologist is or what a psychologist does. My role is to do an evalu-

> Always explain your role and the limits of confidentiality to children.

ation to help understand what is best for them regarding their parents' divorce. My goal is to help their parents reach an agreement on how to manage their divorce, in particular how to arrange the time that children spend in each parent's home. I then tell children that if their parents cannot reach an agreement after completing the evaluation, a judge will make a decision that is in their best interests. Children need to know about the difference between what people want and what is best for them. I try to use analogies appropriate for their age when having this discussion.

Second, the evaluator must help children understand the issue of confidentiality. Children usually do not know what confidentiality means, but they know they are sometimes scared to say things that will be told to their parents. Some children are afraid of having me talk to their parents about what they have said, and other children do not care how much of what they say gets shared with their parents. I believe it is critical to talk with children about the limits of confidentiality in the evaluation process. For psychologists, Ethical Code Principle 4.02 states,

> (a) Psychologists discuss with persons (including, to the extent feasible, persons who are legally incapable of giving informed consent and their legal representatives) and organizations with whom they establish a scientific or professional relationship (1) the relevant limits of confidentiality and (2) the foreseeable uses of the information generated through their psychological activities. (American Psychological Association, 2002)

In addition to complying with the Ethics Code, I am often directed by court order to inform children of the limits of confidentiality. You will want to check your court orders and ethics code before proceeding (see Chapter 1), but I always encourage evaluators to explain the limits of confidentiality to children.

With that in mind, after telling children of my role, I inform them that I will be writing a report when I am done with my evaluation and that their mother, their father, their parents' attorneys, and the judge will be reading my report. I tell children that I will be including things that we talk about in my report. I suggest that if there are things they do not want their parents to know, it may be best not to tell me. I tell them that if they do want to tell me things that they do not want their parents to find out about, I might be able to keep these from my report, but what they have told me will likely appear in my notes and their parents and their parents' attorneys may be able to see what is in my notes. I explain briefly that attorneys sometimes ask to get a copy of my file and that my notes will be in the file. This gives children control over what they want to tell me and keeps them fully informed of the limitations of confidentiality regarding this information. Children need to know that I can make an effort to protect their words (and will do so in the report), but they must also know that there will be times when I will need to discuss with a parent something that a child says during our interviews. By explaining all of this at the very beginning stage of my interviews with children, I can help the children feel safe, reduce their anxiety, and hope to get a clearer understanding of children's conceptualization of the issues, the children's feelings, and the children's true wishes regarding their future relationship with their parents.

A third issue that is important in gaining rapport is to discuss the evaluation "rules." I make it clear to children that my job is to ask some relevant questions to try to understand their feelings and thoughts about their life. Their job is to answer the questions if they want to, or choose not to answer those questions. With younger children, I explore their understanding of the difference between the truth and a non-truth and try and gain a commitment to always tell the truth. I tell children that they can decide what questions to answer and what questions not to answer. I let them know that I may ask a question a second time at a different interview, and that such a question does not mean that I did not hear or believe the answer, but rather I am wondering if they have any more to tell me about the question. I make it clear to children that there are no right or wrong answers to any of my questions; rather, I am trying to understand their feelings and their thoughts. I also inform children that we will have multiple interviews, so we have plenty of time to talk about all of the important issues in their life. Finally, I inform children that if they ever need a break, let me know about it. Children should never believe that they are stuck in my office if they want to stop or simply need to a break to use the toilet. I then ask if the child understands all of this, often encouraging the child to repeat the rules so that I can be sure that the child understands them.

The next important issue centers on finding a way to get the necessary information from the children without acting like an interrogator and adding to the children's anxiety, tension, and loyalty conflicts. Upon first meeting children, for example, I might try to reduce their anxiety by trying to understand who "they" are, just as I did with the parents. I try to talk openly about their potential anxiety, empathizing with how they might be feeling. I begin by asking about their friends, their hobbies and interests, their school, the music they listen to, their likes and dislikes, and other more benign items, as a way of building rapport and trust in the evaluation process. I use this information to then begin talking about their parents and their feelings about each of them. For example, if I find that the girl I am evaluating loves a certain kind of music and enjoys playing in the school band, and then I find that her father discourages her musical talent because he wants her to be an "A" student and be more focused on athletics, it tells me something about the father–daughter relationship. When I learn that she loves sports and then find that her father encourages and coaches her in a positive way, while also supporting her in school, it tells me something different about their relationship.

Finally, most evaluators discourage asking children "where" they want to live because most children do not want their parents to divorce or do not want to be in a loyalty bind between their parents. Children in most divorces wish to spend considerable time with both of their parents, absent critical issues such as domestic violence or alienation. Once children tell me that they love each of their parents, I tell the children that I do not plan to ask them where they want to live or who they want to live with. I say most children who love both of their parents say that they want to spend some time with each parent. This gives me an opportunity to hear a child's response, which may include a statement about living preferences. I also like to talk with children about their likes and dislikes regarding each parent, just as we did when talking about their friends. In this way, I try to gather the necessary information without putting the child at risk for increased anxiety. I am alert to the possibility that some children clearly have a preference about how they spend time with each of their parents and how they feel about going back and forth between two homes. This is a tough balancing act and requires that the evaluator avoids directly asking children where they want to live, while listening to what children say about where they want to live. I will discuss the issue of assessing the child's wishes for a particular plan later in the chapter.

## Children and the Potential for Suggestibility

Research in the last 20 years on interviewing children indicates that there are considerable risks associated with interviewing children, especially in relation to allegations of abuse. In this section, I will briefly identify some of this research and clarify the types of questions that reduce the risk of problems.

For purposes of this section, *suggestibility* is defined as the potential that a child's memory is affected by the child's emotions and the nature of an interviewer's questions (see, e.g., Ceci & Bruck, 1993). In research with young children to understand their memory and their potential for suggestibility (see, e.g., Ceci & Bruck, 1995; Goodman & Reed, 1986; Lyon, 1999; Ornstein & Haden, 2001; Poole & Lamb, 1998; Saywitz, 1994; Saywitz & Lyon, 2002; Sternberg, Lamb, Esplin, Orbach, & Hershkowitz, 2002), there is a lack of certainty about whether or not children are potentially suggestible and, to the extent children are potentially suggestible, what

> Debate exists about the extent of risk regarding child suggestibility, but evaluators are urged to understand this literature (on both sides) in order to reduce that risk in their evaluations.

causes children's memories to be affected in this way. While the research results remain variable, there are certain factors that seem to increase the risk of suggestibility, especially in children under age 5.

One possible source of suggestibility is the nature of the child's emotions (Poole & Lamb, 1998). It is likely that children who are emotionally aroused, usually because of fear, sadness, anger, and even happiness, may be at increased risk of suggestibility. These emotions may enter into the interview process. If the child is scared, feels she is pleasing the interviewer, or is emotionally aroused in some other way, there is a greater risk of suggestibility and that the child may make statements that are not completely accurate.

Another source of suggestibility lies in the nature of the interviewer's questions. Research suggests that leading questions, repeated questions, and forced-choice questions all increase that risk (Ceci & Bruck, 1995). Sometimes questions can contain the suggestion of what the answer should be. All of this is potentially a risk for suggestibility. For the child custody evaluator, it is important to avoid leading questions and to use the concept of elaboration and clarification in an open-ended way to better understand the child's experiences (Lamb, Orbach, Hershkowitz, Esplin, & Horowitz, 2007). When the child presents inconsistencies, query the child about the inconsistencies. For example, if you have heard different things from the child over the course of multiple interviews, it is important to ask the child something like, "When we talked about ___ last week you said ____, but you just told me ____. Can you help me understand this better?"

Another thing you can do is anchor the questions to a particular time frame. Remember that young children have a difficult time understanding various time frames. If they need the help, it will be useful to use significant and memorable events to help them remember things. Examples of these events can include birthdays, holidays, day or night, winter or summer (hot or cold outside), and even the timing of TV shows to anchor children's memories to certain events.

Finally, going back to the rules of the interviewing process, if there are concerns about the risk of suggestibility for a particular child, it is important to be certain that children are told not to guess at their answer and are forewarned that you may ask questions more than once. Some suggest that all interviews with children should be audio- or videotaped. While I do not necessarily agree with this in all child custody evaluation interviews with children, I do agree that in cases in which there are allegations of abuse, especially sexual abuse, it is important at least to audio-tape the interviews to be certain at a later date exactly what the child said and whether or not questions were appropriately asked, reducing the risk of suggestibility.

Overall, regardless of whether you agree with those researchers who are very concerned about suggestibility or generally agree with those researchers who do not believe that suggestibility is as significant a concern in child custody matters, it is best to ask children questions in nonleading and open ways, often starting with "who," "what," "how," and "where" words. It is also important to avoid suggestive questions, avoid giving the child help, avoid repetitive questions, avoid positive reinforcement for certain answers, and maintain a neutral demeanor in which you gain rapport and neither support or intimidate the child (Bourg et al., 1999; Lamb, Hershkowitz, Orbach, & Esplin, 2008).

> "Who," "what," "how," "tell me," and "where" questions all reduce the risk of influencing children during interviews.

# Children and Their Language

Interviewers who have only limited experience in interviewing children may not recognize that one of the major differences in interviewing children relates to the language that children understand (Walker, 1999). As we seek to elicit information from children and to understand their relationships with their parents, it is critical that our questions and statements be at an age-appropriate level. In reviewing the chapter on developmental issues, we note that language skills significantly improve between ages 3 and 6, with much further language growth occurring from the ages of 6 to 12. During the preschool and early grade school years, children's ability to understand abstract reasoning and time is more limited, and our discussions with these children need to be at a more concrete and very specific level. Similarly, children in that age range have a greater difficulty verbalizing feelings or talking about things that they like and do not like about each of their parents. Obviously, a child custody evaluator will not talk about custody with children in general, because it is a legal concept they generally do not understand. However, children do understand that they spend some of their time with their mom and some of their time with their dad, and they can begin to think about how they enjoy their time with each of their parents.

I find that one way to begin talking with children and understanding their language skills is to ask them what divorce means. Once the evaluator has established some rapport with the child and the child is at ease in the interview situation, has explained the limits of confidentiality, and has told the child that the evaluation is designed to help his mom and dad or a judge reach a decision about his life, questioning his understanding of divorce helps the evaluator understand both the language skills of the child and the extent of the child's awareness of the evaluation process itself.

Some children, as if primed by their parents, come in and start talking about the divorce and custody in words that are clearly not child-oriented. I have had 5-year-old children come into my office and say, "I want to have custody with my mommy," and it was clear that they had no idea what they were talking about. In such situations, it is quite likely that someone has suggested that the child tell the evaluator that. When a child uses adult words, especially when not prompted by the evaluator, and it is totally out of context at the given point in the evaluation, it is quite likely that the child's statements were rehearsed by one of her parents. On the other hand, if I am talking about divorce with the child, and the child spontaneously states that she feels scared at daddy's house because her father does not let her sleep with a nightlight, I can assume that the emotion is more accurate as to what the child is truly experiencing.

Talking in the child's language is even more critical when we attempt to understand issues of possible physical abuse, drug and alcohol abuse, mental illness, sexual abuse, and the like from the child's perspective. For example, in issues of possible sexual abuse, we need to hear child words, not adult words, from the child, as we try to explore the child's experiences. As noted earlier, children are potentially suggestible, so it is important to use nonleading questions to elicit information. As with the adult, if the evaluator acts somewhat perplexed and conveys he does not understand, a child is often willing to provide additional information that helps the adult evaluator understand what the child is trying to explain. Evaluators who are sensitive to children's language, anxiety, and emotions during the discussion can do a more thorough job of truly understanding the child and gathering the information that is needed.

# Gathering Information About the Child's Experiences

It is important to try to elicit information about the child's likes and dislikes about each parent. It is important to assess whether or not the child can talk about both good and bad traits for each parent. Children who are afraid to talk about their parents' traits, or who can talk only about good traits for one parent and bad traits about the other, may have a sense of anxiety associated either with the evaluation process, the divorce, or the quality of the relationship with one of the parents. If, in particular, a child can focus on only the good traits of one parent and the bad traits of the other parent, it is quite likely that a certain degree of psychological splitting is in operation, and the evaluator will need to understand this further. By having two or more sessions with a child and seeing siblings in various combinations (individually and conjointly), the evaluator can compare and contrast their words and get a truer understanding of the child's "real" feelings. This level of splitting may relate to some level of estrangement or alienation in children that needs to be fully understood. This will be discussed in more detail in Chapter 13.

Another issue that is important to understand through the eyes of the child is the limits and discipline within each household and with each parent. Over the course of several interviews, I might see how the child talks about her mother's anger and frustrations, and things that make the mother upset with the child. We can talk about punishments the child receives and whether or not her parents spank her, send her to her room, yell at or berate her, and so forth. With somewhat older children, we can talk about not only what makes the child angry, but also what her parents do when she gets angry. With multiple siblings, we can understand what each parent does when the siblings argue with one another and see whether there is a difference in the amount of fighting between siblings in each household. Ideally, we will learn that the parents try to talk with the child, negotiate, and work out problems between them, rather than use corporal punishment or verbal abuse.

Another issue to understand is the structure and routine in each household. Some parents are fairly rigid in their routine and structure, with a set schedule of activities. Mealtimes and bedtimes are generally consistent, and a child tends to gain a sense of security and confidence because family life is relatively structured. In contrast, some children have a different routine nearly every day, and it appears that there is almost no routine in their lives. I look for differences in the routines of each parent and try to understand the extent to which they are similar to one another and the extent to which they are a potential problem for the child.

When a young child spends a portion of her time in each household, and the routines are quite disparate between the households, she may have more difficulty. This may lead us to recommend that the parents develop similar routines and structures. As a child gets older, this may be less problematic, as long as she is able to do her school work, get to her school and activities on time, and maintain her friendships while staying at both houses. In general, as children get older, participate in a variety of activities, and have homework and jobs, their daily routine may become a bit less structured and more fragmented. It is important, however, to understand whether or not each parent is structuring regular mealtimes, bedtime, and schoolwork time, probably the three most important routines for school-age and adolescent children.

> Try to gather as much information as possible about the child's life; that is, her friends, her schooling, her interests, the routines in her two homes, and her relationships with each parent.

By trying to understand all of these issues, we can hope to get a complete picture of the relationship between the child and each of her parents. The more we understand the child's behavior in each home, the child's likes and dislikes about each parent, the nature of each parent's limits and discipline, as well as the structure in each home, we get a better idea about the child's experiences and the extent to which he feels secure and insecure with each of his parents. If the parents are already separated and each parent is living in a separate home, this understanding will also provide a good opportunity for recognizing the ability of each parent to adequately meet the child's needs independent of the other. It is my hope that through the interviews with each child, I can develop a broader perspective of the child's relationship with each parent and use this to complement the understanding derived from the interviews and testing with each parent.

In addition to these few critical areas, there are several other areas in which evaluators want to understand the child's experiences. It is important to understand how all children express their feelings to their parents. Again, this is somewhat easier when assessing older children who express themselves verbally. With younger children, it is difficult to get this sense, and the evaluator will probably need to rely on the descriptions of the parents for this information. With older children, however, we can often determine through direct and indirect observations and questions how they express themselves to their parents. Many children are afraid to tell their parents how they feel about things. This may be especially true for adolescents. Other children, however, find a time and place to talk about almost everything with each of their parents. In all families, but even more so with families going through a divorce,

I often find that individual children express their feelings differently to each of their parents. By understanding these issues of emotional closeness and security, I can relate them to my recommendations for custody and parenting.

Another important issue to understand is the extent to which the child feels caught in the middle of a loyalty conflict between her parents. With younger children, it can be difficult to understand without some evidence from parents or by observing parents and children together. With older children, I will ask direct questions about loyalty issues as we start talking about their experiences. It is easy to ask children how they feel when one parent talks badly about the other, and sometimes we can directly ask whether or not children are worried that pleasing one parent will upset the other. Children who experience tremendous loyalty conflicts often feel anxious when talking about their efforts to please one of their parents, and it is usually because of the insecurity they feel about displeasing the other parent. It is often difficult to ascribe a sense of blame to this because the conflicted child does not wish to hurt or say anything bad about either parent. Instead, the best we might understand is the existence of the conflicts within the child, based on his inability to express any dislikes about either parent during the interviews.

The final area to understand about the child and her life is her various support systems. This is discussed in more detail in Chapter 14, on relocation evaluations in the context of social capital. In all cases, however, it is important to understand the extent to which the child's support systems help her deal with her anxiety and conflicts, and allow her to have a "normal" everyday life. A child's support systems include her friends, teachers, extended relatives, family friends, activities, and often a therapist. Some children feel very isolated, afraid to talk with anyone about their experiences and their fears. At the other extreme, some children seem to talk to everyone, and they are very needy, struggling with the emotions they experience. For both types of children, it is likely that their support systems are failing them and that the anxiety they are experiencing through their parents is overwhelming to them. Hopefully, children can have the opportunity to maintain the same support systems following separation and divorce that they experienced before the separation, as this allows them to ease into a more simplified postdivorce adjustment. Such a transition is made more difficult when there is a tremendous amount of disruption for the child in terms of activities, peers, and so on. Evaluating this issue is critical for understanding not only the extent of the distress that the child experiences but also how she deals with the distress and the extent to which the parents understand this as a problem for the child and work to solve it.

Some parents are so locked in their own issues, especially in the midst of the custody battle, that they forget about the child's support systems and how beneficial they can be. This is critical to understand, both as a result of the child's experiences and needs, and as it relates to the parents' ability to meet those needs. For example, I recently completed an evaluation in which a mother who was feeling very lonely because her child spent the majority of his time with the father was seeking full custody, even though it would mean a significant change in the support systems for the child. This mother even had a difficult time encouraging the child's participation in Scouts because the mother felt lonely whenever the child was away from her. In evaluating the child, it became clear that his support systems, in particular peers and Scouts, were very important to him. While the child wished to have more time with his mother, it was not that critical for him in comparison to some of these support systems. In formulating the appropriate parenting plan for this child, it was important to understand and find a way to maintain the child's support systems while increasing the amount of time spent with his mother. Ignoring the support systems, it would have been too easy to miss an important element in this child's life.

## Directly Assessing the Parent–Child Bond

A fundamental purpose for observing children is to understand the attachment and bond between a child and her parents. In young children, we must see children and parents together, observing the way they relate with one another. Do they play together, smile and laugh with one another, exchange affection with one another, or stay relatively distant and isolated from one another? Does the child seem attentive to the parent when the parent enters the room, or does the child seem disinterested? When the parent is in the room, it is important to listen to the words of the parent. Parents may want to talk about things that are very inappropriate to talk about in front of the child because they have a felt need to provide more information to the examiner. This helps us to understand the parent's ability to utilize adequate boundaries and keep the child free from anxiety. If the parent does say inappropriate things during the interview, for example, something negative about the other parent or something about the litigation, I try to understand how the child feels about it, responds to it, and interacts with the parent about it. I have seen children get into arguments with their parents about things that parents say, and this provides valuable information about the interaction between parent and child. During a recent evaluation, a father was telling me that his son's mother always says bad things about him in front of his son. The boy got into an argument with his father about this, defending his mother. In this way, I could directly see the psychological splitting of his parents into "good" and "bad." In another assessment, a girl who has been "afraid" to see her father and was critical, controlling, and omnipotent in the interview with her father simultaneously drew a picture with rainbows and gave it to her father, with the signature "love" attached. Thus, I could directly see the ambivalence the girl felt toward him, suggesting that her fear of giving up control might provoke anxiety for her. Obviously, such direct observation is useful for understanding both the individual functioning of the parent and child and their interaction with each other.

We can provide structured and unstructured tasks for parent and child together. Encouraging a father and his daughter to draw a picture together, for example, will help us see how they can work together to complete a task. Are they cooperative, are they playful, do they use each other's assistance, or do they become quite competitive with one another? As we observe these behaviors, we can develop some hypotheses about the child's relationship with the parent, which will need to be checked out in other ways (e.g., with collateral sources or interviews). Unstructured play, in which the child initiates an activity of her choosing, is also quite useful because it gives an opportunity to see how responsive the parent is to the child in *her* space. Many parents can interact quite well with a child when the parent chooses the activity, but they may feel awkward and insecure when the child chooses the activity. Through this observation, we can see how well the parent can go to the level of the child and, at the very least, attempt to interact in a neutral or positive way with the child and her activity. While we observe all of this, we are also observing whether the parent or child is having fun, whether they both are relaxed, or whether the time is as tension-filled as the relationship between the parents.

With older children, it is still important to observe parents and children together. With such children, I try to talk with them about their relationship and their perception of how things work in the family. Through such discussions, we hear of the child's wishes, feelings, and fears. Children usually feel most free to express themselves verbally without the parents present. Interviewing them together allows the evaluator to see if the child still feels safe in expressing herself in front of the parents. I find that most children are pleased to have an opportunity to talk individually with the evaluator about their life, their relationships, their desires, and their feelings, separate from their parents, and also enjoy the opportunity to talk with their parents about family life. Some children are relaxed, spontaneous, and open when seen with their parents, while others may appear resistant and more rebellious, perhaps struggling with issues of autonomy and independence. By directly observing the interaction between the child and parent we can better understand all of the feelings, including potential hostility, empathy, willingness to compromise, or resistance of both parent and adolescent, and thus understand their relationship more completely. Sometimes, especially in evaluations in which there are allegations of abuse or alienation, an adolescent wants less time with one parent than that parent wants with him. In order to understand the nature of their relationship and the reasons why the child wants less time with a particular parent, I need to see them together and watch the interaction and the ways in which the adolescent and each of the parents function as we discuss these issues.

Sometimes, during the course of an evaluation, a child will reveal some information that is markedly different from the story the parent told. Seeing the two of them together may assist the evaluator in better understanding the "truth" of the experience. Anytime I see an older child and her parents together, however, it is important to minimize the anxiety the child feels as I try to see how the parent can understand the child from the child's perspective. Just as a conjoint interview between parents helps me better understand their conflict and the nature of it, when there is conflict and tension between a child and a parent, the conjoint interview with them will help me in evaluating and understanding the source of that conflict and tension.

## Siblings Together, or Not?

When I do training for new child custody evaluators, I am often asked whether I see siblings together or separately. Some parents have a preference about how this should be done, as do some evaluators. Through the years, I have found there are no rules for determining what makes the most sense, except to keep an open mind about the process. By and large, however, I always spend some time with siblings together and some time with them individually. The advantages of seeing siblings together can include a reduction of anxiety for the children, an opportunity to learn more about the family and the family dynamics, and an opportunity to observe the nature of the relationship between the siblings. With younger children, observing their play together can be quite beneficial, and if there are two children, especially opposite-sex children, I sometimes see a mirroring of the parent conflict. Observing siblings' affect when together, watching their level of cooperation during play, and hearing their words provides a tremendous amount of information about the family's dynamics.

In contrast, however, if I see siblings only together and individual children are not seen by themselves, there may be problems. One child may speak for the sibling group, and I have a difficult time knowing whether or not that child's opinion is shared by others or is being imposed upon the other siblings. In a family, it is typical that one child will be stronger than another, and if there are some family secrets or significant problems that this child does not wish to have divulged, it is often difficult for another child to speak in front of the more powerful sibling. Children run the risk of having no confidentiality when seen with a sibling, because the child may fear, accurately or inaccurately, that her brother will tell the parents what was said. Thus, there could be a tendency for greater silence, with a strong reluctance to talk about her parents and the structures within the home. Some children demand to be seen individually, and other children refuse to be seen unless with a sibling. Because it is our goal to understand the family dynamics and interactions as much as possible, it is generally recommended that children be seen both individually and conjointly, especially in the more complicated evaluations.

## Use of Play and Other Techniques in Understanding Children

In addition to talking with children, evaluators sometimes use a child's symbolic play as a means of trying to understand issues related to her parents and her parents' divorce. When I wrote my original book in 1994 on child custody evaluations, I encouraged evaluators to consider using symbolic play as a way to better understand children, especially young children. However, since that time, my views on this have changed. While I still believe it is possible to use play as a means of gaining rapport and helping reduce the child's anxiety, I have come to believe that there is tremendous risk in relying on children's play as a means of gathering accurate family data.

Over the years, I have come to recognize that there is no scientific basis on which to use play and other techniques to gather family data (see, e.g., Murrie, Martindale, & Epstein, 2009). Drawings cannot tell me if a child was abused. Sand tray play does not confirm the nature of children's relationships with parents. Play with dollhouses may or may not replicate children's experiences in their family. There is no research that supports an evaluator reaching conclusions about children and their experiences on the basis of these techniques.

At the same time, evaluators will use these techniques to gain rapport and relate to young children. They may even use these techniques in the same manner that psychological testing is used (see Chapter 8), that is, to develop hypotheses about what is going on in children's lives and relationships that need to be tested elsewhere. Therapists do not determine truth via these techniques. Instead, child therapists use these techniques to help children become more relaxed and to play out their inner feelings. Therapists realize that they are only generating hypotheses about the lives of children. Therapists then have several sessions, and perhaps several months, to test these hypotheses. In a similar way, child custody evaluators may use these techniques to gain rapport and help children feel relaxed enough to share their feelings. However, a child custody evaluator should never rely on the play techniques or drawings as evidence of the child's feelings and experiences.

## Home Visits

Some evaluators find that doing home visits can be very beneficial. Home visits may be logistically difficult. However, I find them of great benefit when seeing children under age 7, and while they may be a lesser benefit as children get older, I still enjoy seeing children and parents in their natural environment. Home visits may significantly reduce the anxiety that the child might experience as a result of the evaluation itself. In the child's own home, I can observe firsthand the place a parent has provided for the child and get a qualitative feel for the differences (or similarities) between the parents in this regard. During an interview with a child, I might ask questions about the child's bedroom and the family sleeping arrangements, which is quite important in understanding the child's sense of space and privacy within the home. Nevertheless, asking about it and seeing it firsthand are two different things.

Home visits allow me to view the child interacting with his own toys, in his own room, and often in a more natural environment with his own siblings. Because home visits are always scheduled ahead of time, it is extremely rare to find any real level of disorganization or serious problems when conducting a home visit, though on occasion a home visit will provide information that shows a serious problem in the ability of one parent to make space for the child at his or her home. I once conducted a home visit with a parent whose home was so chaotic—laundry was strewn all over the place, the kitchen was a mess—and the children indicated that this was fairly normal, something the mother confirmed. The chaos was significant. In a different evaluation, however, there was laundry in the bedrooms and laundry room, but the mother reported that she and the children had returned the night before from a week-long vacation and she was doing their laundry before the children went to their father's home. Not only was there no other evidence of chaos, but her explanation of the "mess" in the house made sense.

Evaluators who routinely use home visits indicate that they provide a natural understanding of the children in their home environment and may ease the anxiety for the child during the evaluation process. Evaluators who use home visits on a more limited basis tend to look for specific reasons why a home visit will be beneficial in a given evaluation and then try to gather as much information as possible related to that specific question. It is important for evaluators to know that a home visit can be a technique for discovering additional information that can be useful in formulating the appropriate parenting plan for children.

In doing the home visits, it is useful to spend time with the child touring the house, often with other family members, and also spend time alone in the child's room. The time in the child's room provides a good opportunity to talk with the child about his relationships with his parents. I use the time to talk about the routines in the home and learn more about the child's friends and activities in that home. It is also useful to talk about the "other" parent so that the child feels safe; he does not have to worry about this parent listening to what he has to say.

## The Preference of the Child

Many evaluators dispute whether or not children should be included in the decision-making process for where they should live. As indicated, I typically do not ask children with whom they would like to live, because it raises their anxiety and continues to put them in the middle of the parental dispute. Nonetheless, even relatively young children (e.g., 7, 8, and 9 years old) spontaneously mention a preference about where they want to live and how they would like to spend their time with their parents. Adolescents, in particular, have a very strong preference on this issue.

Regarding this issue, my task is twofold. First, I need to understand the child's rationale for this request. Sometimes the request is being made at the suggestion of one parent or the other. In this case, it may not relate to the child's preference at all, but to the child feeling overwhelmed because of having to express her mother's or father's wishes. Thus, I need to understand whether it is truly the *child's* preference, or the child's words mirroring the preference of one of the parents. Clues to this can be discerned by listening to the timing of the child's request, or the exact words from the child, and the way in which those words match the parents' words regarding this. Obviously, the closer the words, and/or the quicker the child states his preference without any prompting from me, the more suspicious I become.

The second task, however, is even more complicated. If I discover the child is truly expressing her own preference, I need to understand all the issues that are associated with the child making such a preferential statement. I need to understand the nature of the conflict between the child and the parent with whom she does not wish to live (if there is one), and the way the child's preference may fit into developmental issues noted in Chapter 5. When an adolescent expresses a strong wish to be primarily in one parent's home and to desire a relationship with the other parent that is on her terms in relation to school, job, and peer activities, I am likely to give a tremendous amount of weight to this child's preference. This would be expected developmentally, given all of the issues that adolescents must deal with. On the other hand, an 8-year-old child who expresses a desire to move into her father's home and away from her mother and siblings may be reflecting a desire for preferential treatment from her father, conflicts with siblings, a need for privacy, and so on, which needs to be understood more completely. Regardless of the age of the child, it is important to understand fully the child's desires and the ways in which those desires relate to her conflicts, the parents' conflicts, and/or her normal developmental issues. More weight must be given to the wishes of an older child, but all children need to have their feelings and wishes heard and understood.

It is my belief that while it is best for an evaluator not to ask the child his or her preference, when a child has stated her preference and it does not appear to be a mimic of a parent, that must be given weight when I define parenting plans. Not doing so risks alienating the child and leaving her to feel as if adults do not listen to her. While I may have very valid reasons for not recommending the parenting plan requested by the child I must give the child an opportunity to feel heard and understood. It may be necessary to explain directly to some children why I am recommending something different from what they requested. In most jurisdictions, the child's wishes are a factor to be considered, along with the capacity and maturity of the child to make sound and reasonable wishes. In these situations, the adolescent's wishes are often granted, unless there is a significantly overriding factor that might interfere. On the other hand, young children who express their preferences are all too often ignored, and I believe that could be a mistake.

Finally, there is one other place in which a child's preference is a very important issue, even for younger children. This is in the relocation of parents, and the possible move to another community. A move can have such a profound impact on children that we need to ask children to think about this impact upon them, especially if they are of at least school age. In relocation evaluations, the preference of the child might be given added weight because of the child's specific wishes and the rationale behind these wishes. I have found that when confronted with this issue, many 8-, 9-, and 10-year-olds can provide a tremendous amount of thinking about what they expect this to feel like, and most of these children have very strong preferences about whether or not they wish to move with one of their parents and change the relationship with the other parent to become more of a visiting one. While this issue will be discussed in greater detail in Chapter 14, it is important to point out that children's preferences in relocation evaluations are a very important piece of knowledge for the evaluator. Thus, while most evaluators do not like to ask children where they want to live, we must listen carefully to those who express a preference.

Finally, I believe that the child custody evaluator can explore the child's wishes a bit more thoroughly in a careful way. Many children wish to have a voice in the outcome of the evaluation. While most custody evaluators are trained not to ask children who they want to live with, it is important to provide an opportunity for a child to express his wishes about the custody outcome, *if the child has such wishes.* I find that this dilemma can be most easily solved by asking the child about his relationships with each parent, and then saying to the child something like,

> You know, one of the things about a custody evaluation is that it is about your life, not your parents' and not mine. You've told me about some of your feelings about your mother and your father, and I wonder if you've thought about how you would like to spend time with each of them. While the ultimate decision will be made by either your parents or the judge, if you have any thoughts about how you like to spend your time with each of your parents, and if you want to share those thoughts with me, I can use that information in making my recommendations. But just so you know, I don't make my recommendations simply based on what you tell me you'd like, but based on all of the issues that I think are important in your life. As we talk, if you have any questions about that, please let me know.

Thus, children can be encouraged to share their feelings and wishes without being put on the spot to make a decision or choose between their parents. What I generally find is that some children are quite articulate in explaining how and why they would like to spend time with each parent, having given it much thought. They may be comfortable with their parents knowing how they feel and are not concerned about confidentiality. Other children are avoidant of their feelings, reluctant to take a stand and be in the middle of the conflict. They not only tell me that they have no preference between their parents, but they even try not to think about how these issues affect them.

# Cautions in Interviewing Children

I have discussed the need to shield children from too much interrogation during the evaluation process. In spite of this, I do advocate a certain confrontation of children, especially when trying to understand the complex issues connected to the child's feelings, fears, wishes, and needs. I try to keep such confrontation relatively minimal, but I always ask for clarification from children, rarely taking at face value what they initially tell me. Children generally feel a certain degree of stress when they come into the evaluation, and I suggest that we balance the amount we push them with the amount we hold back. If we push too hard, we run the risk of adding to the child's alienation and anxiety related to the divorce. If we do not push hard enough, we run the risk of not getting enough information about the child's real feelings and of not having enough information for a good understanding of the complex issues seen through the child's eyes. Again, because the task of the evaluation is to understand the child's needs vis-à-vis the issues of the parents' divorce, we should push hard enough to complete the task, while simultaneously minimizing the risk of increasing the child's emotional distress. This is a tough balance, one that gets easier as we gain experience and learn from our mistakes.

By the time we have completed the interviews with the children and parents, reviewed the written materials supplied by the parents and/or their attorneys, and spoken with the collateral sources, it is time to write the report. The next chapter will address psychological testing and parenting questionnaires, Chapter 9 will address collateral information, and Chapter 10 will discuss the process by which evaluators take all of the information, synthesize it, and integrate it into a comprehensive report that will educate the parents and help the attorneys and the courts reach a mutually acceptable solution to the conflict.

## THE BOTTOM LINE

Interviews and observations of children are critical in a custody evaluation. Remember, it is the child's life that is the focus of the evaluation, in spite of the time spent with parents and focused on parents' personalities, the parental conflicts, and each parent's strengths and weaknesses. Key ingredients in interviewing children include the following:

- Gaining rapport
- Providing structure and rules for the process
- Clarifying the limits of confidentiality
- Understanding the risks of suggestibility
- Recognizing the limitations of children and their language skills
- Ensuring that children have an opportunity to fully express their joy, fears, wishes, feelings, and concerns about each parent and about the parenting plan

# 8 Use of Psychological Testing in Custody Evaluations

Among professionals, controversy exists regarding the use of psychological testing in child custody evaluations. The view from some is that there is no psychological test that specifically identifies parenting capacity, and that psychological tests cannot differentiate parenting abilities. The view from others supports that psychologists can use psychological tests and parenting inventories to develop a set of hypotheses about each parent's respective parenting ability and that the tests may help to differentiate abilities between the parents. This chapter addresses issues related to the use of psychological testing in child custody evaluations, including a description of the commonly used tests, applicability of validity/reliability issues in custody evaluations, benefits and risks of using psychological tests and instruments in child custody evaluations, and a suggested way to integrate the relevant test data into reports.

The decision of whether or not to use psychological tests and parenting instruments should rest solely with the child custody evaluator and should be based on the scope of the evaluation, the issues involved, and the other data available to the evaluator. It is expected that the evaluator will use multiple sources for gathering data (Association of Family Conciliation Courts [AFCC], 2006; American Psychological Association, 2009), and the decision to include data from psychological tests and instruments should rest with the evaluator. Forensic evaluations include a measure of malingering and deception, and response bias can be assessed by the use of some psychological tests.

I believe it is best to include some psychological tests and parenting inventories in nearly all custody evaluations but to maintain caution in interpreting and potentially overinterpreting the test data. In my opinion, it is not the use of testing per se that is the issue, but rather the way in which psychological test data are interpreted and reported and the weight given to psychological test data by the child custody evaluator that concern me.

# Review of the Literature

In 1993, Brodzinsky wrote about the risks and benefits of using psychological testing in child custody evaluations. Over the following years there has been considerable literature focused on this issue—much of it was done in books, along with a few articles (see e.g., Gould, 1998; Otto, Edens, & Barcus, 2000; P. Stahl, 1999). Most recently, Flens (2005) focused on using psychological tests in a responsible way in child custody evaluations. This chapter will address these issues in a rather limited fashion, and the reader is encouraged to go to those other sources for more in-depth consideration of the use of psychological tests in child custody evaluations.

The recently revised version of the American Psychological Association's (2009) *Guidelines for Child Custody Evaluations in Family Law Proceedings* provides limited guidance for psychologist child custody evaluators about psychological testing. These *Guidelines* state,

> Psychologists strive to employ optimally diverse and accurate methods for addressing the questions raised in a specific child custody evaluation. Direct methods of data gathering typically include such components as psychological testing, clinical interview, and behavioral observation. (Guideline 10)
>
> Psychologists are encouraged to consider and also to document the ways in which involvement in a child custody dispute may impact the behavior of persons from whom data are collected. For example, psychologists may choose to acknowledge, when reporting personality test results, how research on validity scale interpretation demonstrates that child custody litigations often display increased elevations. (Guideline 11)

Similarly, the AFCC (2006), in its revised *Model Standards of Practice for Child Custody Evaluations,* states,

> Child custody evaluators not trained and experienced in the selection and administration of formal assessment instruments and not reasonably skilled in data interpretation shall not conduct testing. (Standard 6.2)
>
> When formal assessment instruments are employed, child custody evaluators shall be prepared to articulate the bases for selecting the specific instruments used. (Standard 6.3)
>
> Evaluators shall be mindful of issues pertaining to the applicability of psychometric test data to the matters before the court and shall be familiar with published normative data applicable to custody litigants. Evaluators shall carefully examine the available written documentation on the reliability and validity of assessment instruments, data gathering techniques, and tests under consideration for use in an evaluation. (Standard 6.3)

Formal assessment instruments shall be used for the purpose for which they have been validated and the testing shall be conducted according to the instructions. (Standard 6.4)

The Judicial Council for the state of California has "Uniform Standards of Practice for Court-Ordered Child Custody Evaluations" (Rule of Court 5.220). These Standards state,

All evaluations must include . . . A written explanation of the process that clearly describes the . . . Procedures used and the time required to gather and assess information *and, if psychological tests will be used, the role of the results in confirming or questioning other information or previous conclusions.* (emphasis added) (Rule (e) 1 (A) and (B))

All of these guidelines suggest the need for evaluators to use caution and competence in the administration and interpretation of psychological tests when conducting a child custody evaluation.

At the same time, research on custody evaluation practices in the United States found that more than 90% of psychologists who perform child custody evaluations use at least some psychological tests as an integral part of their custody evaluation practices (e.g., Ackerman & Ackerman, 1997). In particular, this research revealed that 91% of psychologists used some version of the Minnesota Multiphasic Personality Inventory (MMPI-2) and nearly 50% used the Rorschach Inkblot Test and/or intelligence testing in routine child custody evaluations. A growing number of psychologists, about 33%, were using the Millon Clinical Multiaxial Inventory (MCMI-III), as well. A smaller percentage of psychologists were using other clinical instruments or parenting-related questionnaires, including instruments developed by Barry Bricklin (e.g., Bricklin Perceptual Skills, 1984; Parent Awareness Skills Survey, 1994; and Perception of Relationship Test, 1992; see Bricklin, 1995). Given these data, it appears that practitioners find psychological tests and parenting inventories to be a valuable aid in child custody evaluations.

There has been a growing body of psychological literature associated with using psychological tests in custody evaluations. Otto and Collins (1995) describe the use of the MMPI-2 or MMPI-A (Minnesota Multiphasic Personality Inventory–Adolescent) in child custody evaluations. They state:

Given the rationale and basis for the Minnesota instruments, a strong case can be made for including them in some child custody evaluations. The Minnesota instruments can be used to assess the emotional functioning and adjustment of the parents, . . . and (adolescent) children. . . . To the degree that minimization or denial of problems and shortcomings is a potential concern in child custody evaluations, the Minnesota tests' validity scales may also prove of some value.

Dyer (1997) reports concerns about using psychological tests in custody evaluations (see later discussion). Writing about the Millon instruments, he states,

> Many attorneys object to the use of the MCMI-II in child custody evaluations because of the statement in the manual that the instrument should not be used with normals. . . . The rationale (that the test can be used in these types of evaluations) is that if child custody litigation progresses to the point where a judge orders the litigants to submit to an evaluation, then this constitutes a significantly serious degree of interpersonal difficulty to label the evaluation as a clinical case.

When I wrote my original books on custody evaluations, there was little published research on the use of the Rorschach in child custody evaluation practices, but in the past several years there has been growing debate on the use of the Rorschach in child custody evaluations. Lee (1996) was one of the first to speak about the use of the Rorschach in child custody evaluations and presented some of her findings at various conferences. She reported that school-age children in high-conflict divorces are more vulnerable than they appear on the surface.

More recently, however, there has been considerable debate about the use of the Rorschach in any court-connected forensic evaluations. Critics contend that the normative data for Rorschach scores are seriously in error and make normal individuals appear maladjusted. They contend that validity and reliability are insufficient to allow Rorschach data to be admitted into court (see, e.g., Garb, Wood, Lillenfeld, & Nezworski, 2002; Grove, Barden, Garb, & Lillenfeld, 2002). In contrast, proponents disagree and state that there has been sufficient research on the validity and reliability of Rorschach data to use the test to identify personality traits in forensic testimony (see, e.g., Calloway, 2005; Medoff, 2003; Ritzler, Erard, & Pettigrew, 2002).

While I no longer use the Rorschach, I still believe that those who utilize the Rorschach in child custody evaluations can do so, as long as they do not rely too heavily on Rorschach data in reaching their conclusions.

# Traditional Psychological Tests

## Objective Personality Tests

The two most commonly used "objective" personality tests in child custody evaluations are the MMPI-2 and the MCMI-III. Both have been extensively researched for use as personality tests, and both are being used to a significant degree in child custody evaluations. Their "objective" status is defined by the way in which they are scored and normed, though the interpretation of test scores is still potentially impacted by the subjective interpretation of the psychologist. While the following information will be redundant to psychologists who are familiar with psychological tests, I will provide a brief description of each test, how it is scored, and the personality features that are measured by each test.

The MMPI-2 is a 567-item true/false test. The individual reads and answers each item as it applies to him or her. Each item is loaded onto a particular scale, 10 main clinical and 3 main validity scales on the MMPI-2. The clinical scales measure various personality traits. The validity scales are designed to measure test-taking attitudes such as truthfulness, defensiveness, fake-good, or fake-bad.

Along with the main validity and clinical scales, there are a number of supplementary scales on the MMPI-2 that also aid in our understanding of clinical and personality traits. The research on and understanding of these supplementary scales is growing, as is their interpretation in forensic work. Some of the supplementary scales are validity measures (e.g., the TRIN and VRIN scales) and others measure additional personality traits. They are considered supplementary because they are an outgrowth of research that has been ongoing since the introduction of the original MMPI.

In general, the MMPI-2 is an instrument that provides hypotheses about personality traits that might fluctuate according to stress, one's current life situation, or one's therapy. The MMPI-2 also measures characterological traits that might be consistent with chronic personality disorders. While child custody evaluators do not make psychiatric diagnoses, the personality traits identified on the MMPI-2 are typically consistent with Axis I and Axis II personality traits found in the fourth edition of the *Diagnostic and Statistical Manual of Mental Disorders* (*DSM-IV*; American Psychiatric Association, 1994).

The MCMI-III measures chronic personality traits that are often seen in Axis II of the *DSM-IV*. The MCMI-III is a 175-item instrument that is taken in the same manner as the MMPI-2 and reflects the respondent's true/false scoring of each item. The MCMI-III also has validity and clinical scales, and the clinical scales measure characterological disturbances. Unlike the MMPI and MMPI-2, the MCMI-III is not based on norm referencing. Instead, the MCMI-III uses base rate scores as the standard score into which raw scores are translated.

As stated in the *MCMI-III Manual* (Millon, 2006),

Base Rate (BR) scores define a continuum of the pervasiveness and severity of a psychological attribute against which any individual can be evaluated. Using a continuum is an acknowledgment that the difference between a clinical disorder and normal functioning, especially with personality scales, is one of degree rather than kind.

BR scores of 60 correspond to the median raw score. For all of the clinical scales, a person who scores in the range of 75–84 on a given scale may display some behaviors consistent with that scale. A person who scores 85 or above appears to display a more prominent degree of features. This differentiation is significant because it helps the evaluator make hypotheses and differentiate between each parent's respective abilities.

For both the MMPI-2 and MCMI-III, there is a small but growing body of research specific to child custody evaluations (see, e.g., Bathurst, Gottfried, & Gottfried, 1997; Halon, 2001; McCann et al., 2001). In general, this research identifies that child custody litigants are more defensive and tend to present themselves in a favorable light to a degree much greater than noncustody litigants. They also tend to be more self-centered and histrionic than noncustody litigants. On the MCMI-III in particular, female custody litigants also score higher than men on the Histrionic scale. Given these data, it is important that custody evaluators use normative data from research on custody litigants rather than research on the general population when developing hypotheses about the parents being evaluated.

The child custody evaluator is encouraged to use the data from psychological tests only to form hypotheses about personality traits and behaviors, which can be further explored through collateral interviews, direct interviews, or observations. I encourage all custody evaluators to keep abreast of ongoing research on these instruments as it applies to child custody evaluations.

A third objective instrument that is increasingly being used in forensic evaluations is the Personality Assessment Inventory (PAI). The PAI is a 344-item test that yields data in 22 scales, including four validity scales, 11 clinical scales, five treatment scales, and two interpersonal scales. There is growing research on the use of the PAI in forensic matters (Edens, Cruise, & Buffington-Vollum, 2001; Hawes & Boccaccini, 2009), though none that I am aware of specific to child custody evaluations. Additionally, there are no survey data that identify the extent of the use of the PAI in child custody matters. Nonetheless, there is growing anecdotal evidence that the PAI is being used by some child custody evaluators. All of this suggests that there will be an increased use of this psychological test in such cases.

The PAI is sold by Psychological Assessment Resources (PAR). According to the PAR website description of the PAI (http://www3.parinc.com/products/product.aspx?Productid=PAI, last searched on July 27, 2009), the PAI clinical scales are "essentially grouped into 3 broad classes of disorders: those within the neurotic spectrum, those within the psychotic spectrum, and those associated with behavior disorder or impulse control problems." The PAI treatment scales "include two indicators of potential for harm to self or others, two measures of the respondent's environmental circumstances, and one indicator of the respondent's motivation for treatment." The interpersonal scales were "developed to provide an assessment of the respondent's interpersonal style along two dimensions: a warmly affiliative versus a cold rejecting style, and a dominating/controlling versus a meekly submissive style." Given that this test has well-researched validity scales, several clinical scales and an interpersonal dimension with the interpersonal scales, and given that this test is shorter and easier to administer than the MMPI-2 or MCMI-III, it will not be surprising if the PAI becomes an increasingly popular psychological test in child custody evaluations.

## Projective Personality Tests

By definition, a projective test is one that is scored differently from objective tests such as the MMPI-2, the MCMI-III, and the PAI. The presumption that people project their personality dynamics in their stories or drawings, or when identifying the inkblot figures in the Rorschach, identifies these tests as "projective." The Rorschach, the Thematic Apperception Test (TAT), and drawings are examples of projective tests. They are projective because they are presumed to reveal aspects of a person's psychological functioning by the way in which the individual approaches the task.

The Rorschach is an ink-blot test in which an individual views a series of 10 cards with ink-blot drawings and tells what he or she sees. It is presumed that the content of what is seen is a projection of the individual's personality dynamics, almost a "psychological fingerprint." On the TAT and other apperception tests (e.g., Children's Apperception Test or Family Apperception Test), an individual looks at a picture depicting activities and tells a story about what is happening in the picture. It is presumed that the stories are a projection of the individual's psychological dynamics.

Because the Rorschach is the projective test most commonly used and it is the only one on which there is some research about its use in child custody evaluations, it is the one on which I will focus the most. Additionally, the Rorschach has a systematic scoring system (Exner, 1995), which makes this "projective" test more "objective." Use of the Exner system allows the psychologist to have a variety of scores from which interpretations can be made. The interpretation of scores and the integration of this interpretation into the child custody evaluation is still under the subjective control of the evaluator. The Rorschach purportedly measures things such as reality testing, disordered thinking, internal resources and coping skills, modulation of affect, level of depression, levels of narcissism, and other personality dynamics. The Rorschach tends to provide information across the range of Axis I and Axis II personality dynamics. Unlike the MMPI-2 and MCMI-III, the administration and scoring of the Rorschach requires a high level of training and sophistication and is dependent on the training of the psychologist. The MMPI and MCMI are not subject to this same variability because they are objectively (and frequently computer) scored and more easily interpreted.

# Tests Designed Specifically
# for Custody Evaluations

In the 1990s, two new types of instruments were designed specifically for use in custody evaluations. The ASPECT (Ackerman Schoendorf Scales for Parent Evaluation of Custody; 1992) was designed to be an objective clinical tool to aid in the task of making child custody recommendations. The ASPECT incorporates assessment tools that many clinicians use and yields a quantitative score for each parent. The instrument includes a Parent

Questionnaire, has specific questions for parents and children, and integrates the scores of psychological tests including the MMPI-2, Rorschach, intelligence tests for parents, drawings by the parents, and an IQ measure for children.

The ASPECT yields three scaled scores, Observational (based on the parent's appearance and presentation), Social (based on the parent's interactions with others, including the child) and Cognitive-Emotional (based on the test scores). For each parent, the ASPECT produces an overall score called the Parental Custody Index that is designed to be a guide in custody decisions.

The other group of tests is a variety of instruments developed by Barry Bricklin that includes the Bricklin Perceptual Scales (BPS), the Parent Awareness Skills Survey (PASS), and the Perceptions of Relationships Test (PORT). These instruments are administered to adults (PASS) or children (BPS and PORT) and are designed to help identify issues related to custody and access. The PASS yields scores indicating a parent's awareness of various social issues, the ability of the parent to explore adequate solutions to problems, communication issues with children, and the value of acknowledging the child's feelings. The BPS is designed to measure the child's perception of the parent's competence, consistency, supportiveness, and possession of admirable traits, and the PORT is designed to assess the child's closeness with each parent. In his 1995 book, Bricklin provides a rationale for the use of these instruments in custody evaluations. Many evaluators have found them to be a useful adjunct for understanding parental competence.

However, unlike the personality tests described earlier, there is little research on the Bricklin scales, the ASPECT, and the PORT. Citing the *Ethical Principles of Psychologists* (American Psychological Association, 2002), the *Standards for Educational and Psychological Testing* (American Psychological Association, 1999), and general *Forensic Practice Guidelines* (Committee on Ethical Guidelines, 1991). Otto et al. (2000) identified that these instruments are neither valid nor reliable and have significant limitations in almost every area of their potential use. Those authors recommend against using these instruments in child custody evaluations. I would concur.

Although the concept of specialized instruments for child custody evaluations is exciting, I believe these instruments should be used as adjunct information rather than definitive instruments in custody evaluations. While the PORT may be consistent with judicial decisions 95% of the time, this does not help the evaluator discern relative strengths and weaknesses of each parent or understand the complex issues of high-conflict divorce.

# Parenting Inventories

Currently, there are several parenting instruments that are being used in child custody evaluations. The Parenting Stress Index (PSI; Abidin, 1990), originally designed as a tool for assessing parental stress related to child abuse, is used to assess stress in parents of children who are 12 years of age and under. The test measures sources of stress within six areas of the child's domain (Adaptability, Acceptability of Child to Parent, Mood, Demandingness, Distractibility, and Reinforcing the Parent). High scores in the child's domain are associated with parents who feel that their children display qualities that make it difficult to fulfill one's parenting role. Elevated scores suggest that characteristics of the child are major factors in the parent's overall stress. The test also measures sources of stress in seven areas of the parent's domain (Depression, Guilt or Unhappiness, Attachment, Restrictions Imposed by the Parental Role, Sense of Competence, Social Isolation, Relationship With Spouse, and Health). Elevated scores in these areas suggest that stress and potential dysfunction are likely to be related to dimensions of the parent's functioning.

On the PSI, parents answer a series of statements along a 5-point Likert-type scale ranging from "Strongly Agree" to "Strongly Disagree." The normal range of scores for all domains is between the 15th and the 80th percentile. Interpretation of scores within this range is done cautiously. A significant score of 85 or above on any of the subscales may indicate that the parent is experiencing significant stress in that area of the parent–child relationship. The evaluator should ask interview questions that corroborate or negate this and then integrate the test data with the other evaluation data when interpreting the scores.

A second parenting instrument, the Parent–Child Relationship Inventory (PCRI; Gerard, 1994) is a self-report inventory designed to measure how parents of 3- to 15-year-old children view the task of parenting and how they feel about their children. Using a 4-point Likert-type scale similar to the PSI (also ranging from "Strongly Agree" to "Strongly Disagree"), the PCRI measures scales of Parental Support, Satisfaction With Parenting, Involvement, Communication, Limit Setting, Autonomy, and Role Orientation. With a mean score of 50 and an average range of 40 to 60, the PCRI is especially useful when parents achieve a low score on any of the scales, reflecting problem areas in that scale.

In the context of child custody evaluations, my opinion is that the PCRI is useful for measuring parenting attitudes. I often find parents who score fairly high on one or more scales (e.g., over 60). Unfortunately, the test designers did not develop a measure of defensiveness on this instrument so it is difficult to differentiate between parents who legitimately feel strong satisfaction with parenting (for example) and those who want to appear as if they feel satisfaction. Integrating these data with other interview test data is crucial in interpreting PCRI scores.

A lesser known instrument, the Parent Behavior Checklist (PBC; Fox, 1994), was designed to help identify parenting strengths and needs for parents of 1- to 5-year-old children. Also using a 4-point Likert-type scale (ranging from "Almost Always/Always" to "Almost Never/Never"), this instrument measures parent expectations and behaviors, not attitudes. The three scales of the PBC are Discipline, Nurturing, and Expectations. I find the PBC to be particularly useful in child custody evaluations when parents seem to have unusually high expectations, low nurturing, or potentially harsh disciplinary practices. Comparing the pattern of scores across scales can provide the evaluator with important hypotheses about the parent–child relationship, such as when the parent scores low in Nurturing and high in Expectations and Discipline. Again, though scores may suggest problems in the parent–child relationship, they need to be confirmed from other sources.

The Achenbach Child Behavior Checklist (CBCL; Achenbach, 1991), while not a true parenting inventory, is a practical instrument for parents of children between 2 and 18 years of age. It provides data on parent observation of their children's behaviors. Scores are derived in areas such as Aggressive Behavior, Anxious/Depressed, Attention Problems, Delinquent Behavior, Social Problems, Somatic Complaints, Thought Problems, and Withdrawal. A particularly useful way to use the CBCL is to administer it to parents and any teachers to determine whether they are consistent in their perceptions of the child. When there is a significant difference of scores between parents and the evaluator determines that one of the parents is more accurate than the other (based on teacher CBCL ratings, observational data, or collateral reports), the evaluator might look for other evidence that one parent is more intuitive or observant in assessing how the child is functioning.

All of these inventories are useful in that they provide some quantifiable way of understanding the parent–child relationship. Depending on the particular scores, the evaluator can make hypotheses from which to interpret and understand potential strengths and weaknesses in the parenting relationships. While it would be inappropriate to use parenting inventories as a primary determinant of one's recommendations, they provide very useful information about the parent–child dynamics evaluated in child custody evaluations.

# Tests for Children

The research by Ackerman and Ackerman (1997) suggests that children are less likely to be given psychological tests in child custody evaluations, yet when they are, evaluators may use projective tests such as drawings, the Rorschach, or one of the apperception tests (e.g., Thematic Apperception Test, Children's Apperception Test, or Family Apperception Test). Evaluators also use a variety of indirect tools with children, such as dollhouse or sand tray play, or other tools used by play therapists. All of these techniques use symbolic tasks to hypothesize about or gain some understanding of the psychological dynamics of the child.

Perhaps the most widely researched of these instruments is the Rorschach, and there is growing research on the use of the Rorschach to assess vulnerability in children of divorce. In particular, Johnston and Roseby (1997) focused on the vulnerability found in children's Rorschach results in their studies of children exposed to high-conflict divorce. Researchers who worked with Johnston and Roseby were able to use the Rorschach to assess feelings of vulnerability and inadequacy, levels of depression and disorganization, and other concerns within children of high-conflict divorce. Their data on under-lying psychological dynamics is quite useful, because so many school-age children appear to be functioning well. As described earlier, and even more so with children, the use of the Rorschach requires specialized training and expe-rience. When used appropriately, though, the Rorschach may provide infor-mation about the psychological functioning and possible psychological disturbances of children and may also allow the evaluator to be more specific in treatment recommendations.

# Benefits of Using Tests

High-conflict custody litigants, who are more likely to require a child custody evaluation, have a potential for distortion, deception, and significant person-ality dysfunction (Johnston & Roseby, 1997). Psychological tests have scales that might help in understanding a parent's deception and distortion. They have scales that might help in identifying parenting deficits, such as a propen-sity to be violent, abuse substances, and/or have poor impulse control. The Rorschach has the potential to identify perceptual accuracy, good or bad real-ity testing, and disordered thinking in parents. Psychological tests can assist the evaluator to understand a parent's relationship capacity and the potential for matching the parent's abilities with the particular needs of the child.

Children rely on their parents to help them learn about the world. When two parents have a different level of perceptual accuracy and different styles in relating to the world, they may put children in a bind as the children try to figure out what to believe. When the evaluator has data to identify such per-sonality characteristics as a capacity for empathy, positive coping skills, denial and projection, perceptual accuracy, disordered thinking, emotional availability, hostility, distrust and suspiciousness, defensiveness and guarded-ness, and a tendency to be self-focused, she can assess the ability of each parent to meet the child's needs. These data may also help the evaluator understand the goodness of fit between the parenting traits displayed by each parent and the needs of the child and the child's ability to benefit from them.

In summary, a high-conflict divorce creates its own set of requirements for coping, and the Rorschach and other test instruments may help the evaluator understand a parent's coping ability and levels of narcissism and rage. As will be described in Chapter 11, many of the parents who engage in high-conflict divorce have significant, chronic personality disturbances. While custody evaluators do not diagnose parents, understanding the nature of these distur-bances assists evaluators in understanding the extent to which the areas of disturbance interfere with parenting or co-parenting issues. The benefit of using tests is that they place more information at the evaluator's disposal and provide empirical data from which to make hypotheses and to understand the complex issues described earlier in this book.

# Risks in Using Tests

Unfortunately, these benefits do not come without some potentially significant risks. Brodzinsky (1993), and later Otto et al. (2000), raised concerns about the misuse of testing in child custody evaluations. Brodzinsky found that lawyers and judges often expect too much from psychological tests and may push psychologists to go beyond their limits in using psychological tests to help answer the ultimate question of custody; he also found that lawyers may demand "objectively needless testing" for strategic reasons. Brodzinsky feared that data from psychological tests would be misused against parents in litigation. He cited a case in which a psychologist identified the presence of a disorder simply on the basis of a computerized interpretation of the MMPI and then made unsubstantiated assumptions in his report about the effects of that disorder on parenting, now and in the future. Brodzinsky felt that psychologists who engage in such practices are working beyond the bounds of their knowledge.

In his research, Brodzinsky found that many psychologists do not understand forensic issues, and he raised a concern that psychologists tend to overtest due to a financial incentive. In light of the Ackerman and Ackerman research (1997), there is some potential validity to this concern, since evaluators who use testing generally charge more for the evaluation than evaluators who do not use psychological tests.

In describing the pitfalls that psychologists face when using psychometric instruments in child custody evaluations, Dyer (1997) also reports that psychologists need to understand each test's characteristics and have their own independent ability to interpret the scores rather than rely on computer-generated reports. He notes that custody evaluations are designed to assist the court in making determinations of the relative strengths and weaknesses of each parent, and he fears the temptation to make decisions and recommendations based on which of the parties scores better on the tests. He deems such a practice to be "inappropriate."

Roseby (1995) reports that mental health professionals experience considerable pressure to answer questions within the win/lose framework of litigation. She states, "In this way a custody evaluation can take on the appearance of a pathology hunt which often holds the litigating divorced family to a high standard of mental health than intact and nonlitigating divorcing families." She suggests that a likely outcome of this process is to "unnecessarily heighten feelings of shame" within the parents and that this leads to an escalation of the conflict, which leaves the child vulnerable long after the litigation is over.

Talia (1997), an attorney, describes concerns about the intrusive effects of testing for parents and wonders if the benefits that may be derived from testing are sufficient to outweigh that risk. She is concerned about the overgeneralization some evaluators make on the basis of test results that are more apt to focus on pathology rather than parenting strengths. She has raised concern that psychological tests do not predict who will make a good parent nor do they provide much concrete information about parent–child relationships.

A final concern that has been raised is over evaluators who give too much weight to any piece of data from a single test or instrument.

As indicated earlier in this book, custody evaluations are designed to assess psychological factors affecting the best interest of the child, parenting capacity of the respective parents, the needs of the child, and the functional ability of each parent to meet those needs. The issues facing a child custody evaluator are complex and require a broad-based understanding of all family dynamics before adequate recommendations can be made.

In my view, *overreliance* on psychological testing is a significant risk because evaluators, attorneys, and the courts could look for simplistic answers to these difficult questions. But I also believe that tests *do* provide invaluable data regarding psychological dynamics that relate to parenting strengths and weaknesses. The data provided by the multitude of tests can be a valuable tool for understanding these complex issues, as long as they are used with care.

## Computerized Test Results

In recent years, there has been a significant growth in the use of computerized test scoring for each of these instruments. There are computer programs to aid in the scoring and interpretation of the MMPI-2, the MCMI-III, the PAI, the Rorschach, the PCRI, the PSI, and many other psychometric tests. They have taken a lot of the work out of using psychological tests and reduced the risk of manual scoring errors. Some psychologists simply use the computerized scoring services to generate scaled scores for the relevant instrument. Others may use the scoring services to generate an interpretive report. How the psychologist uses the data derived from the use of computer scoring services is potentially critical.

If the psychologist uses the scoring services to generate scaled scores, but then interprets the test data herself, the psychologist knows the basis of the interpretation. However, if the psychologist gets a computer-generated interpretive report, the psychologist has no knowledge of the paradigms by which the company developed the interpretive report. The psychologist does not know whether the interpretive report is accurate. Worse yet, I have seen many times where a psychologist pulls certain statements from the interpretive reports, in essence picking and choosing which statements to include in the custody evaluation report. To the extent that the psychologist relies on the test data as fact about who the person is and how the person functions, rather than using the test data to formulate hypotheses about who the person is and how the person functions, and to the extent that the interpretive report is less than accurate, and to the extent that the psychologist picks certain statements from interpretive reports and ignores others, the test data are at risk of being quite nonobjective.

## THE BOTTOM LINE

Given the preceding analysis, it is my view that if evaluators are going to use psychological tests and parenting inventories in their evaluation, the following are important:

- Be certain that the use of testing is indicated for any particular evaluation.
- Instruments given to one parent are also given to the other parent. If there are stepparents, the instruments should be given to both stepparents.
- Instruments should be used appropriately and within the bounds of validity, reliability, standardization, and administration. Tests must be administered according to the procedures outlined in test manuals. Tests should never be given to parents to take home.
- Be cautious of anything that attempts to take the complexity and conceptual thinking out of custody evaluations. Computer-generated interpretive reports and instruments designed to choose a "primary caretaking parent" should not be used for that purpose. As mentioned earlier, these instruments should be used only to develop hypotheses that the evaluator integrates with other evaluation data.
- Do not over generalize from any one test or make definitive statements about a particular test that are beyond the data of the test. Avoid descriptions of "profiles" for which there is no validity (e.g., a profile of a sex offender on the MMPI-2).
- It is unethical to use psychological tests alone as the foundation for custody recommendations. Instead, tests and inventories *can* be used as a foundation for making hypotheses about personality dynamics as long as the evaluator integrates those dynamics with the other data gathered in the course of the evaluation for the custody recommendations.
- Evaluators should remember that we are asked by the court to offer recommendations and opinions about many different aspects of custodial determination and parenting issues, such as therapy, use of alternative dispute resolution techniques, and more. Testing can be quite useful in guiding recommendations in those areas, as well.

# 9

# Gathering
# Collateral Data

In my original book on child custody evaluations (P. Stahl, 1994), I provided some limited guidelines for the use of collateral information in the child custody evaluation process. In that section, I focused primarily on the professional collateral witnesses who can provide balanced and neutral information about family members and the relationships between them. However, that information was quite limited. Since then, there has been additional literature focusing on this topic. For purposes of this chapter, I will focus on what collateral data are, the benefits of gathering and integrating collateral data into the overall custody evaluation data, and the process by which child custody evaluators gather collateral data.

A survey of Association of Family and Conciliation Court (AFCC) member custody evaluators, more than half of whom were quite experienced, showed that 100% of those surveyed indicated that they always included "collateral interviews as an integral part of their custody evaluations" (Kirkland, McMillan, & Kirkland, 2004). At the same time, however, only 77% required participants to sign releases authorizing the third-party contact, 49% followed a formal outline for collateral interviews, and while 81% reported using both telephone and in-person interviews, 16% used only telephone contact. This survey suggests that it is part of the standard of care to include collateral data in a child custody evaluation.

The AFCC's *Model Standards of Practice for Child Custody Evaluation* (2006) addresses the issue of collaterals in great detail. Among other things, the *Model Standards* state,

> Valid collateral source information is critical to a thorough evaluation. . . . Evaluators shall be mindful of the importance of gathering information from multiple sources in order to thoroughly explore alternative hypotheses concerning issues pertinent to the evaluation. Evaluators shall recognize the importance of securing information from collateral sources who, in the judgment of the evaluators, are likely to have access to salient and critical data. . . . Child custody evaluators shall

disclose situations where uncorroborated information was utilized in the formulation of an opinion expressed by the evaluator. . . . When assessing the reports of participants in the evaluation, evaluators shall seek from other sources information that may serve either to confirm or disconfirm participant reports on any salient issue, unless doing so is not feasible. . . . In utilizing collateral sources, evaluators shall seek information that will facilitate the confirmation or disconfirmation of hypotheses under consideration. . . . All collateral sources contacted shall be disclosed by the child custody evaluator. . . . The subjects of the evaluation shall provide explicit authorization for the child custody evaluator to contact collateral sources unless the authority is provided in the order appointing the evaluator or is statutorily provided. The child custody evaluator shall inform collateral sources that there is no confidentiality in the information that is being discussed between the collateral sources and the evaluator. (Standards 11.1–11.6)

The AFCC *Model Standards* will be more thoroughly discussed in this chapter.

# What Are Collateral Data?

Collateral data can be defined as all of the data that is gathered that is not directly from interviews, observations, and psychological test data. Collateral data can include the material sent from attorneys and other material provided by one or both of the parents. Oftentimes, this information will include court pleadings and declarations, medical and therapeutic records, school records, and other such information that provides important material related to the child custody evaluation. Sometimes the evaluator is given a small amount of information, but I have also seen cases in which there are numerous boxes of material to go through. Experience tells me that the volume of material is directly related to the level of conflict. At the same time, if attorneys or parents want the evaluator to read certain material, it is incumbent on the evaluator to read everything provided unless the court order specifies differently.

Collateral data can also include information gathered from parents' friends as well as from relatives, teachers, pediatricians, therapists, and other professionals. All collateral data are useful in understanding family relationships. Frequently, some of this information is in writing. For example, it is my usual practice to have friends and family members send such information in letter format. I reserve the right to call the people who write to me, yet I find that I rarely need to do that. In general, I find that friends and relatives often write letters that are supportive of the parents they are close to. On occasion, however, some friends and family members are more neutral, speaking positively about both parents, and at other times, friends and family members may write negatively about the parent one would expect them to support.

# Benefits of Using Collateral Data

Gould (1999) observed, "Information from a family member may provide a rich source of direct observational data, yet it may be confounded by the observer's self-interest derived from his or her relationship with the parent." As noted previously, I am somewhat skeptical of data collected from friends and family members. At the same time, I believe it is crucial for the child custody evaluator to gather some form of collateral data in nearly all evaluations.

Over time, I have come to learn the value of gathering collateral information in most child custody evaluations. These potential benefits include the following:

- Evaluators need to have a mind-set of disconfirmation rather than confirmation. Reviewing collateral information and talking with collateral sources allows for that.
- Parents in the midst of a custody dispute tend to present themselves in the most favorable light and the other parent more negatively. Collateral data can help balance this defensiveness and positive impression management by the parents.
- It is common for evaluators to get contradictory information from each of the parents and/or the children, and collateral data can help resolve the contradictions.
- Evaluators need a complete data set regarding the child's and parent's behavior, and collateral data help to complete the information about family members and their relationships.
- Collateral data include potential information about parents and/or children that cannot be obtained through clinical interview, testing, and observation.
- Collateral data can help to verify or refute claims made about the parents by one another or by others.
- Collateral data may help the evaluator judge the credibility of informants who have given information by way of declaration.
- Ultimately, from a process standpoint, gathering collateral data helps to satisfy the need for a thorough inquiry.

Elaborating on these items, as stated in Chapter 1, child custody evaluators need to keep an open mind throughout the course of the evaluation, developing multiple hypotheses about what is occurring in the family and about what conclusions will be in the children's best interests. After interviewing the parents, observing them with their children, and gathering psychological test data, there are still questions about these issues. When the evaluator remains skeptical about the potential conclusions, the gathering of collateral information can help put everything into perspective. Teachers can inform the evaluator which parent (or both) is actively involved in the child's education, therapists can inform the evaluator how each of the parents (and perhaps the children) are dealing with the family conflicts and

> Collateral data are critical and help the evaluator confirm or question information gathered in interviews with parents and children.

dynamics, prior therapists may help clear up the allegations of domestic violence by informing the evaluator of how domestic violence issues surfaced years earlier, and coaches can inform the evaluator how each parent supports the child's extracurricular life. Information from collateral sources can help inform the evaluator about the everyday life of the family beyond what can be gathered during the interviews and testing.

## Record Review

As noted already, collateral data include the review of records. Sometimes parents find it difficult to tell the evaluator all of their concerns. Reviewing the parents' court declarations helps to round out all of the information. Additionally, there are many times when a parent will say one thing in the evaluation interviews, but the collateral record will have different information. The evaluator can then use appropriate and confrontational questions to sort out those differences. This can be especially helpful when a parent reports doing a great job of meeting the child's educational needs, but the records suggest that the parent has frequently gotten the child to school late or the child has not completed homework on the parent's watch. In those ways, record review is very helpful.

A record review may be even more critical, however, when there are significant allegations, such as allegations of domestic violence. A review of the records will reveal why a prior judge granted a restraining order. Hospital records may show the impact of bruises caused by incidents of violence. Therapist records may reveal that issues of violence were discussed in therapy sessions several years before the evaluation. On the other hand, collateral data may reveal that there is no prior evidence of any violence between the parties. While the absence of collateral data may not mean that violence did not occur, the collateral data gathered may help in understanding the history of the alleged violence.

## Gathering Lists of Collateral Sources

Essentially, the gathering of collateral sources is a simple process. When gathering my informed consent from parents, I tell them that I will be seeking information from collateral witnesses. I inform them that I will invite them to have friends and family members send information and that I will be wanting to review relevant records and talk to relevant professionals. I then inform parents that their job is to create a list of those persons they want me to talk to. I ask for contact information and compare the lists provided by each parent. I encourage parents to talk with their attorney about possible relevant collateral witnesses I should contact. This list is usually included on the intake form that parents fill out about their family.

Once I get the list from each parent, I talk with parents in the first interview about those persons. I explore whether or not there are other contacts that I have not heard about. By the end of the first session, I try to confirm that I have a complete listing of everyone that the parent believes may be sources of relevant collateral information.

My next task is to draft authorizations to talk with all of these relevant collateral witnesses and ask each parent to sign the authorizations. I always ask parents to authorize a two-way conversation, such that the collateral witness can talk to me about the family members and I can talk with them as well. I clarify on the authorization form that there is no confidentiality expected in the conversations that we will have. This guarantees that parents understand the limits of such confidentiality and also ensures that when I forward the signed authorization to the collateral witness, the witness has written confirmation that there is no confidentiality. This is consistent with the requirement in the AFCC *Model Standards* (2006).

## _____ Who to Talk To: A Concentric-Circle Approach

Austin (2002) was the first to recommend that child custody evaluators use a concentric circle approach for gathering collateral data. Austin suggested developing several concentric circles and placing persons into the circle that matches their knowledge of and closeness to the family. For example, Austin identified that there are people who are close to the family, that is, in the innermost of the concentric circles, who will have the richest and most complete information about family members. At the same time, these persons are likely to be the most biased and to take sides in the dispute.

In the second, broader circle are the professionals who may have considerable family data, but only within the narrow areas of knowledge that they experience family members. For example, teachers know a lot about what occurs educationally, but do not know much about what occurs medically or in the child's extracurricular world. Similarly, a Little League coach may know a great deal about each parent's participation in their child's baseball games, but is unlikely to know anything about the routines in each parent's home and the way in which each parent nurtures and supports the child emotionally, except for what is observed at baseball games. Third, while a pediatrician may know a lot about each parent's participation in medical decisions, she may know very little about each parent's support of the child's education. The child's therapist may know a great deal about each parent's support of the child's emotional well-being and the child's inner feelings, but he may know nothing about each parent's participation in the child's social life.

In the outermost circle are those few people who may know very little about the family, but may have very specific information about an event or some particular parent–child information. This may include the school parent who overhears an argument between a parent and the child's teacher, a woman in the community who witnesses an exchange between parents and children, or even a semiprofessional who has very limited contact with family members, such as a Scout leader. These persons may have very critical information about a specific event that was witnessed but know absolutely nothing else about any of the family members.

According to Austin, the best approach in contacting collateral witnesses is to make sure that you have sample witnesses from each collateral circle. He also recommends choosing collateral witnesses who are more likely to be credible because they have had the opportunities to observe parents and children together. Austin and Kirkpatrick (2002) identified that it may be useful to consider the relationship between the collateral informants and the parent who suggests the collateral informant. There are times when a collateral witness has something to gain by providing testimony that supports a parent. Austin believes that a witness who is closer to a parent is potentially less credible and that a collateral witness who is more distant emotionally from the parent is potentially more credible. He also suggests contacting potentially biased and unreliable collateral informants as a way to demonstrate to the parents that the evaluator did a thorough job and thereby gain greater acceptance by the parents.

> Gather collateral information from three types of people: those very close to the family, such as extended family and friends; those professionally involved with the family, such as teachers and therapists; and those more distantly involved with the family who may have very narrow but useful information to share.

As I think about the process of conducting child custody evaluations, I agree with Austin. I gather information from the inner concentric circle by asking for this information in writing. I gather information from the middle concentric circle by talking with relevant professionals, such as teachers, therapists, day-care personnel, pediatricians, coaches, tutors, police officers, and social service workers. In each given case, one or more persons will fit into this category. In many cases, there are no persons in the outer concentric circle, but occasionally persons are identified who have very specific information about a particular event in the family's life. Finally, I try to determine whether there is evidence that a particular collateral witness is less than credible. At times, parents' therapists are less credible when they appear to be unwavering in their support of their client, especially if they cannot acknowledge their client's weaknesses. If a child therapist has not met with one of the parents, the child therapist may be less credible if recommending a particular outcome. Finally, it is important to recognize that even teachers and pediatricians may be less than credible if they are too close to one of the parents and have little or no contact with the other parent, and yet are making suggestions for custodial outcomes. In my opinion, it is the evaluator's job to consider the credibility of all collateral witnesses.

Finally, there is rarely a need to call all of the persons identified by the parents. It is helpful to call persons in a balanced way; that is, contacting roughly the same number of collateral witnesses from each parent's list.

However, as the AFCC *Model Standards* state, it is important for the evaluator to contact the witnesses that the evaluator believes to be relevant and not necessarily all of them.

## Interviewing Collateral Sources

Once you decide who to talk to, there are a few steps to take before making the relevant calls. First, fax or e-mail the authorization to the proposed collateral witness. Again, make sure that the authorization states the limits of confidentiality and informs the collateral witness of how the information will be used. Then, when making the phone call, begin the call by clarifying your role, stating that you are a neutrally appointed evaluator focused on the best interests of the child, and reminding the potential witness that the information will likely be used in the report.

The next step is to determine what questions to ask of the collateral witness. In general, I like to ask questions that help identify the relationship between the witness and each parent and/or children, the nature and frequency of the contacts, observations regarding strengths and weaknesses of each parent, observations regarding parental interactions and communication and discipline styles, and what the children state about their relationship with each parent. Ideally, this will yield considerable information. For professionals in the second concentric circle and individuals in the outer concentric circle, it is useful to clarify the basis for the information that the witness is trying to provide.

Finally, it is important to end the phone call by providing the witness with a chance to ask questions and asking if the witness wants to add any further information. Some witnesses want to know what has been written down about the phone call, and I offer read my notes back to those witnesses to confirm my understanding of what I have been told. Finally, I offer to give the witness my phone number in case the witness wants me to know anything else after the phone call is over.

### THE BOTTOM LINE

As noted in this chapter, I believe quite strongly that collateral information is critical in nearly all child custody evaluations. In fact, if resources and time are limited, I would rather gather collateral data than psychological test data in most cases. I want to make sure that collateral witnesses know that they do not have to talk with me. I want them to know that their information will be included in my report. I want to use the collateral data to help confirm or disconfirm hypotheses that I have formulated during the course of the evaluation. Finally, I want to integrate all of the collateral data with the rest of the data gathered during the evaluation process to better understand the family relationships and make recommendations consistent with the best interests of the child.

# 10

# Sharing the Results of the Evaluation

## *The Evaluation Report*

After gathering all of the data, it is time to write the report. The evaluation report is the culmination of all of our psychological and forensic work. It is through the report that we evaluators inform the parties, the attorneys, and the judge of our findings, our analysis of those findings as it relates to the psychological best interests of the children, and our conclusions and recommendations. This chapter will address the relevant material that must be included in each report and provide a format for incorporating this material into your report.

I believe that it is most helpful when the evaluator plans ahead in gathering data, thinking from the start about the report that must be written at the end of the process. Knowing how I plan to organize my report helps me organize the entire evaluation process. Formulating a plan for the report before seeing our clients will help guarantee that the evaluation report accurately flows from the evaluation process itself. While there are many different ways to write the evaluation report, there are certain principles that must be adhered to in the writing of a report, and certain information must be included so that it is useful for the family, the attorneys, and the court. The report is used by the attorneys and court to understand the family dynamics and to help determine the ultimate custody and access plan for the family. The report is the vehicle through which we educate the judge and attorneys about the family. It becomes a document of the court. Consequently, certain information must be included in order for the report to be useful to the attorneys and the court.

In my experience, both from the history of reports that I have written and from my conversations with many judges, judges require a variety things from the report. They want the report to focus on the issues and problems of the family. The report must be credible, well-reasoned, clear, and thoughtful; it must be fair, balanced, and neutral, avoiding advocacy for one parent and accentuating positives when possible. Evaluators should avoid jargon and diagnosis, yet remain behaviorally focused, and should offer recommendations that are child-focused and flow from the data gathered in the evaluation. As noted previously, this chapter will describe the necessary information to include and will discuss many of the issues surrounding the writing of recommendations and their specificity.

## AFCC *Model Standards*

The Association of Family Conciliation Courts (AFCC; 2006) *Model Standards* address report writing. In the section titled "Presentation of Data," the *Model Standards* guide evaluators to offer opinions only in those areas in which they are competent, identify that the opinions expressed by evaluators shall be based on information and data obtained through application of reliable methods, and clarify that evaluators need to differentiate among information gathered, observations made, data collected, inferences made, and opinions formulated. Additionally, it is important for evaluators to provide information about personality characteristics of only those persons they have personally evaluated. Finally, when it is appropriate, evaluators need to articulate limits to the evaluation conclusions. In my opinion, the goals set out by these *Model Standards* are an important objective for the evaluator to follow.

> Formulate conclusions only about persons whom you have personally evaluated. Articulate the limits to your conclusions where relevant.

## Basic Characteristics of a Quality Report

Regardless of one's report writing style, there are a number of features that are important in all child custody reports. Because the report is the evaluator's written testimony, the report must be objective. The report's objectivity is evidenced by balance in focusing on the relevant issues in the case, the relevant strengths and weaknesses of each parent, and each parent's style of parenting, and by providing an analysis of the data that addresses all of the relevant multiple hypotheses and the evaluator's conclusions regarding them.

Another way to ensure objectivity is to outline the evaluator's multiple methods of data gathering. When the report identifies the methodology used and the evaluator shows evidence of a balanced approach in the gathering of data from multiple sources, the objectivity is identified. Additionally, if the report conforms to professional standards, as exemplified by the American Psychological Association *Guidelines*, the AFCC *Model Standards*, or the *California Rules of Court*, it is more likely to be objective.

> Evaluation reports need to be objective, based on multiple methods of data collection. Findings must distinguish among clinical judgments, philosophical positions, and research-based judgments.

The third critical principle associated with a quality report is the evaluator's analysis of the data. The evaluator's analysis within the report should distinguish between clinical judgments, philosophical positions, and researched-based judgments (American Bar Association, 2001). Finally, the report should avoid technical language, while at the same time provide useful psychological information.

# Information That Must Be in Every Report

## Identifying Information and Statements of Informed Consent

The first section of my report outlines the identifying information, including the names of the parties, dates of the evaluation, and the court case number. I also include a statement about informed consent and information about the limits of confidentiality. An example of this follows:

Complete written and verbal informed consent was obtained from Mr. and Ms. Smith before undertaking this court-appointed child custody evaluation. A thorough discussion of the procedures was discussed with each of the parents. Limits of confidentiality, specifically that there was no confidentiality within the process, was discussed with both parents, with all of the children, and with all collateral informants.

## Procedures

Listing the procedures helps the reader know what the evaluator did and helps ensure that the process is balanced. Many judges have told me that they want to see, right at the beginning, what procedures the evaluator followed in completing the evaluation. In this section we describe all interviews, whether conjoint or individual, in office or in the home, giving the dates when people were seen. According to the AFCC *Model Standards* and the *California Rules of Court*, it is important to include the amount of time spent on these procedures, largely because it helps the reader know that the process was fair and balanced. If there is a reason why significantly more time was spent with one parent than the other or when there is some other imbalance in the process, it is important to explain the reason(s) for this. If clients bring in (or their attorneys send) written material, audiotapes, or videotapes for the evaluator to review, that should be noted as well. It is very important to detail the collateral contacts who were called, explaining their role with the family (e.g., teacher or babysitter). If psychological testing is used, it is important to name the tests that were administered. Sometimes evaluator teams work together, and if different people share in the process of the evaluation, it is important to describe who did what part of the evaluation. This is especially true if a nonpsychologist evaluator has a psychologist provide psychological testing to assist in the evaluation process. Similarly, if one evaluator sees the adults and another evaluator interviews the children, this information should be described as well. It must be clear from the written report what the evaluation procedures were and who participated in the evaluation.

Such a complete description of the evaluation procedure is necessary for the attorneys and the judge to know that a complete, credible evaluation was done. Also, listing all of the collateral sources the evaluator spoke with clarifies the collateral record and follows the requirements of the *Model Standards*.

## Background Information

In the report, I like to describe the reasons for the referral and provide relevant background information that helps the reader understand the family's difficulties and the evaluation questions. Obviously, if the questions and problems of the family are more complicated, this initial section of the evaluation will need to be more comprehensive. Rather than simply indicating that the evaluation is to assess custody and access planning, I provide a description of the problems between the parents, their history of conflict and their difficulties resolving differences, and some statement of how each parent believes that the custody and access issue needs to be settled. It is important to outline each parent's view of the problems and the solutions each parent desires. Once that is outlined, the specific reasons for the evaluation are clearer and can then be delineated.

For example, in a recent evaluation, the father felt that the mother was attempting to alienate the children against him and was both covertly and overtly attempting to disrupt his access with the children. This was the primary motivation for the father to seek custody of the children. In contrast, the mother felt the father was extremely hostile and degrading to both her and the children and was not at all sensitive to the younger child's insecurity over the transfer to his care. In addition, each described the other as distorting the truth and lying, and each felt that the other was doing a poor job of taking care of the children when in the other's care. They could not speak to one another without arguing and becoming totally enraged, and they rarely could allow a transfer to take place without some type of outside assistance. This was the backdrop for the evaluation, which had several questions around parental competency, potential distortions of reality, domestic violence, high conflict, possible parental alienation, and more. By being specific about the reasons for an evaluation at the beginning, it is possible to write a comprehensive report that answers those questions in detail, leading to the overall recommendations of the evaluator. At times, I list all of the multiple hypotheses that were formulated in order to clarify for the reader the direction that I am taking in the evaluation report.

## The Parents

Once I have completed the background information and outlined the evaluation procedures, I describe the interviews with the family members. It is important for evaluators to devote a section of the report to the mother, another section of the report to the father, and another section of the report to the children. Describe each parent individually, usually in a narrative style that gives a complete sense of each parent's "story" of the problems. I find that it is best to break each of these sections into five parts as detailed below.

Initially, provide some idea of the parent's affect, how he related, how defensive or open he was, how much he blamed the other parent, and how focused or rambling his style was. In this way, we are reporting some beginning sense of the way in which we perceived the parent.

Next, elaborate on the parent's concerns regarding the other parent and the issues for the evaluation. This is usually an elaboration of the issues outlined more briefly in the background section already completed. In this section, I provide more of the details of the concerns and describe the parent's "evidence" for those concerns. It is important in this section to be clear that I am only describing the parent's perceptions and not yet reporting on my own findings. Sometimes, in this section, I will also address how the parent responded to some of my questioning, especially when the allegations do not seem clear. This section of the report should provide a clear picture of who the parent is, and how he portrays his concerns, complete with his evidence (or lack thereof).

Third, it is important to give a sense of the parent's own childhood. While I do not believe there is a need to give a complete history of the parent's childhood, I definitely provide information when I believe that a parent's behavior during divorce mirrors concerns about his own childhood. For example, a man whose own father abandoned his family when he was 10 years old might be seeking custody of his three latency-age children in order to prove that he is not irresponsible like his own father had been. He does not want his children to hurt like he did, and, as such, he is driven by the need to "make right" the wrong that was done in his own childhood. It is important in this section of the report to provide such information and to tie it to the referral questions and parental concerns.

Fourth, it is important to give each parent a chance to respond to the critical concerns raised by the other parent. For example, when there are allegations of domestic violence, it is critical in this part to identify each parent's view of the problems and each parent's responses to the allegations made by the other parent. Within that context, it is important to identify each parent's ability to see his or her own role in the family problems.

Finally, I always describe the parent's perceptions of his child's functioning and needs. Focus on the parenting qualities identified in the evaluation and the parent's ability to understand the child developmentally and to respond to the child's emotional needs. Describe the parent's ability to provide routines for the child and to understand issues of limit setting and discipline. For parents who have a good understanding of their child and his needs, the report is generally positive. However, for parents who are focused largely on issues that do not pertain directly to their children, it is important to point out how each time I asked questions about the child, the parent kept avoiding the issues related to the children and maintained criticism of the other parent. I highlight those parenting traits that identify each parent's style of parenting, such as whether the parent showed evidence of being authoritative, authoritarian, or overly permissive. I identify parents who have difficulty separating their own anger and needs from the needs of the children. In more complex situations, such as with alienation, relocation, high conflict, or domestic violence, this part of the report is critical because too many parents forget about the kids when they continue their barrage against each other. I am always surprised when parents who want custody of their children cannot focus for even a few minutes on their children and their needs, and instead either rigidly criticize the other parent or ramble on to other issues that have nothing to do with their child. This part of the report is the best place to put this critical information.

> The report should include sufficient information to allow the reader to understand each parent, the concerns and wishes of each parent, and each parent's observations of the child and her needs.

After completing the interview sections on each parent, I write a section focused on my clinical understanding of each parent. In this section, I am relying on all of the clinical material gathered, whether from psychological testing, the clinical interviews, our observations of the parent and child together, or other components of the evaluation. While doing this, I provide a more complete sense of the parent's psychological functioning, defenses, and ability to meet the child's needs. I do this without jargon or diagnosis, focusing instead on the behaviors and attitudes that are critical to the evaluation findings. When the pathology is more extreme, it is best to describe the behaviors that create concerns rather than provide a diagnosis of the parent. For example, judges need to know if a parent is volatile, externalizes blame, denies any wrongdoing, gets delusional and paranoid at times, has made threats to hurt the other parent and the children, and so on, rather than just be told that the parent shows strong evidence of a borderline personality disorder. Such descriptive writing makes it easier to understand why an evaluator recommends supervised and limited access with the children.

In this clinical section, I also address the significant strengths (e.g., coaches the sports team, understands emotional needs, etc.) and weaknesses (e.g., drug abuse, temper outbursts, etc.) that relate to the initial evaluation questions, and any other findings that I might have in this area. For the dad who is psychologically healthy, has actively participated in the child's schooling, and is responsible about encouraging a healthy relationship with the mother, I will note that here. Then, when I recommend either primary physical custody to the father or shared physical custody with the mother, it is clear that I had no concerns about the father's functioning as a parent. In a different type of evaluation, even if I am not certain that a parent is alienating the children against the other parent, I can describe the parent's style of exploding rage and difficulty separating his own hurts and fears from his perception of his children's hurts and fears. Then, when I make a recommendation for therapy for the dad, it will make sense because it relates to the needs of the children. Ultimately, by the end of this section, I attempt to connect clinical findings to the issues of parenting and to the parent's ability to meet the needs of his children. If the evaluator remembers to keep the referral questions and the needs of the children as the primary focus in her report, the judge and attorneys will better understand the reasons for all of the evaluator's recommendations. At the end of the section on one parent, we now go back and do the same for the other.

When possible, I try to have the report flow naturally from one parent to the other, tying in the issues between them. No matter how it is done, it is important to report on both parents in these sections of the report and to do so in a narrative way that describes the issues presented by both parents and the responses to the allegations of the other parent, and then to focus on how those relevant issues relate to the psychological best interests of the children.

## The Children

The next major section of the report is about the children. In this section, I write about my observations and impressions of the children, especially their perceptions of their parents and the divorce. It is best if this section is written from a developmental perspective so that the reader has a clear understanding of the child's needs. Essentially, during this section, there are five primary issues that must be included in each report.

As with the adults, I write about how the children related in the evaluation, whether they were scared, open, defensive, prompted by parents, inhibited, and so on, focusing on their general demeanor during the entire evaluation process. I will note if there is a difference in how they interacted with either parent, or if I did a home visit, I will note any differences in how they responded in the office compared with the home. If the child is seen with siblings, I note something about the sibling interaction, as well, and whether there was a difference for the child when seen individually or conjointly with his siblings. The first part of this section is focused on the overall behavior during the sessions.

Next, it is important to report on the child's feelings and concerns. As indicated in Chapter 5, verbal children usually have a lot to say about their parents, likes and dislikes about them, and feelings that they may have about their parents' divorce. As mentioned earlier, I never ensure confidentiality to the child, but in this section I may make general statements about what the child reports. At the same time, if the child is comfortable sharing everything about what he has said, and the issues are clear, I may use quotes as a way of adding emphasis to my understanding of the child's statements. Whenever possible, it is useful to relate these concerns to statements made by either parent, again as a way of having the report flow smoothly.

For example, if I have been reporting on mom's attempts at alienating the children against dad and on dad's temper outbursts, I can connect that here when reporting on the child's concerns about both his mom and dad saying terribly mean things about each other to him, and how this makes him feel sad and scared. Similarly, I can report that the child "hates it" when his mom does not "let" him see his dad just because she is "angry" at the dad (child's quotes). Thus, from understanding the child's concerns and feelings, I can understand the behaviors described in the reports about the parents and provide that information in my report to the court. As such, my purpose in this section is to make clear to the reader any significant feelings and concerns raised by the child during the evaluation process and to report them in a way that makes sense in the context of the rest of the evaluation report.

Third, the report needs to include information on the child's perception of her relationship with parents, siblings, friends, community, school, and other aspects of her life. Obviously, in the context of a custody evaluation, there are many complex issues that need to be understood, and by providing this general view of the child's perception of her functioning, I have a better idea of what to recommend for the child. For example, if there is a question of relocation and the child tells me that she does not want to move away from her dad, friends, and activities because of what they all mean to her, I will report that in this part. This will make sense when I later make my recommendations. Similarly, if a child tells me that she has no friends at her dad's house and is usually quite lonely there, even though she loves him, I report this. This information will be consistent with my later recommendation against a fairly equal time-share between the parents. In essence, this section of the report allows me to tie together the child's perceptions of himself in the family with the sense of himself in the larger world.

Because it is expected that evaluators observe the children and their parents together, this also must be reported upon. In this portion, I encourage being quite specific about your observations, again tying them in with the referral questions and concerns. For example, if mom says that dad is mean and the kids do not like him, it is important to observe and note whether or not the kids were afraid of him, loving toward him, or ambivalent. Similarly, you will want to note how well dad was able to interact with the children and how he responded when the kids pushed his limits. I often see children who have too much power and parents who are overwhelmed by their child's acting out behavior. This is important to note, especially when we later recommend parenting classes for the dad and therapy for the child.

Finally, if you have not yet done so, summarize your findings about the child or children in a general way. In this portion of the report, integrate your observations of the child's interactions in the interviews, the child's perceptions of his parents and his relationships to the larger world, the child's feelings and concerns, and your observations of the child's direct interactions with his parents. With more than one child, you might do this in a general way for all of the children (if warranted) or you may do this specifically for each child (when there are differences). In essence, close this section with your understanding of the children. Summarize your perception of who

> Judges rarely know much about the children, so this section must inform the judge about the children's emotional, academic, and social functioning, along with their feelings and wishes and how they relate to each parent. Describe each child broadly, not just in relation to his or her parents' divorce.

each child is, how each child feels about the issues related to the evaluation, and how you perceive the children to be functioning in their world.

## Collateral Information

At times, I list everything that I have read for my child custody evaluation. I have found, in reviewing other evaluator's reports, that only about one third of evaluators do this. As long as I am fairly certain that both sides have seen all of the material that was sent to me, I do not list everything I have read. However, I state that I have read everything that has been given or sent to me. I also include in the report the most relevant of the information that is useful for consideration of my findings, being careful to include important information that might not be consistent with my findings (as required by California Rule of Court 5.220).

After reporting about the written collateral information I gathered, I then include in my report the information from collateral witnesses. Because collateral sources have been told that everything they tell me is not confidential, I include most, if not all, of what each collateral witness shares with me. I do this for every collateral witness, even therapists. At times, child therapists may want limited confidentiality, and while I cannot promise confidentiality, I can limit how much of their information I put in my report. In addition to including what collateral witnesses tell me, I also include a statement related to each witness I attempted to speak with but who either did not respond or refused to speak with me.

## Analysis and Summary

After gathering all the data and reporting on the family data, it is time to integrate the report into a comprehensive understanding of the family dynamics and the needs related to the children. Thus, the next critical section in the evaluation report is the summary and analysis. Attorneys and judges rely on this section to integrate all of the information and provide a complete understanding of all of the family's issues. With this in mind, the summary needs to reiterate the main referral questions, but to do so now with the evaluator's understanding of the answers to those questions. Whereas the earlier parts of the report focused on the individual dynamics of the adults as well as the individual and relationship dynamics with the children, a strong summary takes those data and provides a clear picture of the intertwined relationships within the family. Whereas the earlier section about the adults relayed each parent's concerns about the other parent, the summary gives us a chance to address how we evaluate those concerns, while explaining why we do or do not see things the same as the parents. In essence, whereas the child's or the parents' issues reflect a narrow view of the family, my summary will paint a broad picture of all issues that are relevant to the custody evaluation and the needs of the children.

For example, consider an evaluation that is focused on issues related to alienation, reality testing, and truth telling by the parents; children's fears; the nature and extent of parental hostility; and the father's alleged rage. In the summary, the evaluator will describe the data that lead to the conclusions and that pull together all the information in the report. Just as the narrative becomes a bridge between the referral questions and the summary, the summary becomes a bridge between the narrative and the recommendations. By the time the reader has completed the review of the summary, the recommendations that follow should be clear and obvious. A report that is written concisely, yet thoroughly, leaves nothing to the imagination and is essentially foolproof in cross-examination by an attorney. If the narrative and summary are vague, neither the attorneys nor the judge will have any idea why the recommendations are being made, and the report will be subject to a higher degree of cross-examination, almost forcing the case to trial. In addition, if the evaluator has not presented the material thoroughly and concisely, the parents will not understand why the recommendations are being made. Thus, a summary that is clearly focused on the children and their needs, the parents' strengths and weaknesses and their respective ability to meet those needs, and all of the broad issues in the case is less likely to be questioned by each parent when the recommendations are being made.

With that in mind, it is important to point out that over the last 10 years, since publication of *Complex Issues in Child Custody Evaluations,* I have had the opportunity to critique numerous child custody evaluation reports. More on the process of critiquing will be discussed in Chapter 17. What has become clear, however, is that the lack of a quality Analysis section is a significant weakness in most of the reports I have read. This critical section needs to include not only the summary of relevant information but also the evaluator's analysis of the relevant data. This allows the evaluator to explain the connection between the relevant data and the conclusions.

As noted in Chapter 1, the state of California has Rules of Court that define certain aspects of the evaluation process. There are two critical elements that are relevant to this section. First, it is expected that evaluators will "describe any limitations that result from unobtainable information, failure of a party to cooperate, or the circumstances of particular interviews" (California Rules of Court 5.220). I agree with this; it is very important for evaluators to inform the court about the missing pieces. This should not have to be discovered by cross-examination, because the requirement for neutrality means that the evaluator will notify the court on his or her own of those limitations. The requirement to report on limitations also exists in the AFCC *Model Standards.*

The second and in my mind the most critical requirement is that evaluators will "present all relevant information, including information that does not support the conclusions reached" (California Rules of Court, Rule 5.220). All too often, as I read other people's custody evaluation reports, it seems as if all data are like a train going in one direction. This is not consistent with most families and their emotional functioning. Typically, the data lead in many different directions, some supporting one conclusion and some supporting other conclusions.

It is in the Analysis section that evaluators describe their conclusions and outline the data that support, and do not support, those conclusions. This is where a thorough risk/benefit analysis of the various custodial options provides the most helpful information to the court. Remember that few cases are cut and dried, especially when considering complex issues such as domestic violence, relocation, alienation, and the multiple issues existing in high-conflict families. Outline your findings of the parenting strengths and weaknesses of each parent. Outline the risks and benefits of primary mother-custody, primary father-custody, and some type of shared custody. Differentiate between the horizontal co-parent relationship and the vertical parenting relationship when clarifying the alternatives that must be decided and the various parenting time-share arrangements. Be certain to follow the AFCC (2006) *Model Standards,* which call for you to "differentiate among information gathered, observations made, data collected, inferences made, and opinions formulated." Make sure you explain the reasons for the conclusions and describe the data that are used to formulate those conclusions. In colloquial terms, this means that you must "connect the dots" so that the conclusions match the relevant family data.

> While presentation of data is useful, the most important section of the report is the evaluator's analysis of the data. Explain what data led to your conclusions and always include the consideration of data that do not support your conclusions as well as data that do support your conclusions.

Finally, this is also where you will need to integrate the law into your report. For example, if I am doing a relocation evaluation in California, I list the various factors set out in *In re Marriage of LaMusga* (2004; see also Chapter 14) and provide the data relevant to each of those factors. If I am doing a high-conflict evaluation in Arizona, I list the statutory factors in Arizona Statute 25-403 relevant to the best interests of the child and provide the data relevant to each of those factors. Ultimately, in my opinion, if you do all of this, then your report will be most helpful to the court for its own analysis of the critical issues of the case. Only after this is done can you make specific recommendations. The next section will focus on the nature of those recommendations.

In later chapters, and in Appendix F ("Sample Alienation Analysis and Recommendations") and Appendix G ("Sample Relocation Analysis and Recommendations"), there will be examples of the way in which this analysis can potentially be written.

## Recommendations

In my original book on child custody evaluations (P. Stahl, 1994), I wrote,

Among various evaluators and attorneys, there is some controversy about whether evaluators should make specific recommendations about custody. There are some attorneys and evaluators who believe that our knowledge base is too limited to provide the necessary predictability related to the issues involved in custody disputes. Some attorneys take the position that it is a breach of judicial authority for evaluators to make recommendations about the ultimate issue of custody, since that is meant to be within the purview of the law. They argue that judges often give up their judicial authority to evaluators by accepting recommendations without change, and they believe that the law does not allow anyone other than judges to make judicial decisions. Some evaluators take the position that making recommendations around custody and visitation is unethical because there is no scientific proof that our recommendations are valid and predictable for the family. Those attorneys and evaluators would suggest that evaluators should provide all of our information without making specific recommendations, and allow the attorneys and judge to infer recommendations from our report. They would rather let the judge use his/her judicial authority to make orders based on the information and summary which is in our report. (p. 97)

When I wrote that book, I suggested that there was value in evaluators making such recommendations. Since that time, however, the controversy has been renewed. Tippins and Wittman (2005) suggested that evaluators should stop after the Summary and Analysis sections and not make specific recommendations. Essentially, they took the position that there is not sufficient research from which to extrapolate from the evaluation data to the recommendations and that the task of formulating the conclusions is solely in the judge's role. They also suggested that there was too much opportunity for evaluators' personal values to enter into the decision-making and that by not making recommendations, any value judgments that would be made would be by the judge. Finally, they suggested that judges might rely too heavily on the evaluation report and make decisions that could affect a parent's basic rights (i.e., the right to the care and custody of a child) when the evaluator might be wrong. For these and other reasons, they recommended against custody evaluators making recommendations.

In the same issue of *Family Court Review* that contained the Tippins and Wittman article, several other authors contributed to the debate (see nearly the entire April 2005 issue of *Family Court Review*). Many authors agreed with Tippins and Wittman and others disagreed. My conclusion (P. Stahl, 2005) was that evaluators should provide a thorough analysis, as mentioned earlier, in a way that allowed judges to consider other data and different possible outcomes if the case went to trial. Additionally, in relocation evaluations, I suggested that evaluators consider *not* making a specific recommendation about the move, because the decision often rests on the weighting needing to be done (see Chapter 14), and it is my opinion that, by and large, judges are the ones who should weigh the different options. As such, I believe that evaluators should be allowed to make recommendations when judges want them, as long as they make clear both the data that support those recommendations and the data that do not support those recommendations. The rest of this chapter will focus on the nature and type of recommendations to be made in most evaluations.

For many judges and attorneys, the *main* purpose for using mental health experts is to do a custody evaluation that provides a clear understanding of family dynamics and specific recommendations for resolving the conflicts and providing an opportunity for the family that might end the litigious process. With that in mind, it is important that any recommendations made by the evaluator make sense. As noted previously, the recommendations must flow naturally from the data of the family and the evaluator's analysis of the data, integrated with the law, child development and divorce research, and the best knowledge that exists related to the issues of custody and shared parenting.

Keep in mind that, frequently, when a family comes to a custody evaluation, each parent is afraid that one of them will win and the other will lose. It is quite common for parents to view things in this all-or-none manner, and the litigious process is typically filled with people who view themselves as winners and people who view themselves as losers. It is very common for children to come to the evaluation wondering which parent is going to win, and the entire process tends to reinforce everyone's splitting and competition. Recommendations that are focused on the issues and that provide clarity about the best interests of the child and provide the opportunity for both parents to understand why the evaluator believes that the conclusions are best for their children are the most useful. Recommendations must be practical, child-focused, and a logical consequence of the material found in the report. If the evaluator recommends the child to be in therapy or the use of a Parent Coordinator or co-parenting counseling for the parents, such recommendations must be goal-specific and it must be clear how such recommendations will benefit the child. With such recommendations, both parents can feel as if they have been heard, and ultimately they can feel that their children have benefited from the evaluator's recommendations.

I believe that after the completion of a thorough evaluation, the evaluator will know more about the complete family dynamics than anyone outside of the family unit. The attorneys, as advocates for their clients, know what their clients tell them and have only limited contact with the rest of the family members. The judge has had little opportunity to see the parents and has very little understanding of the children and their functioning. With this in mind, it is my belief that the evaluation recommendations are necessary and should be as specific as necessary to help the family resolve all conflicts. Sometimes recommendations may be arbitrary and designed to help the parents reach some level of resolution. We know that it is in the children's best interest for settlement to occur, and therefore we work for the possibility of resolution in our recommendations.

For example, when we specify that the exchange of the child should occur at the end of school on a Thursday with the return to the other parent's care at the beginning of school on a Monday each week, the specifics of the relatively equal shared parenting plan may be related to logistics and the need for parents to be away from each other during the exchanges more than anything else. Clearly, there is nothing in psychological research that says what time children should transfer between homes, but if the evaluator is trying to be specific about the time that the children are with each parent and provide an opportunity for the exchange to be free of conflict, this recommendation will make sense. In addition, it is important to recognize that some couples, if left to themselves, will fight over the minutest of details. Thus, if the evaluator were to make a broad recommendation for equal time with each parent and not specify when and how the exchanges were to take place, some parents would argue over not only the definition of equal time but also the actual time that each parent's custodial responsibilities were to begin and end. These same parents would argue about what to do if one parent is late for the exchange, or if school is out, or if there is a Monday holiday, and so on. I encourage you to think ahead to the potential sources of conflict and make recommendations that can prevent such conflict. This will be discussed more in the next chapter.

## THE BOTTOM LINE

When the evaluation is complete, the thorough evaluator will have a tremendous amount of information with which to write a report. Attorneys and judges do not wish to read reports of 50 or more pages, as they often find them too wordy. It is hoped the evaluator has pared down the information into a comprehensive and concise report that provides the necessary information to answer the referral questions without overloading the reader with additional, but less than useful, information. I try to write a concise report based on the following outline:

- A beginning that outlines the reasons for the evaluation
- A complete description of the procedures used in the evaluation
- A thorough assessment of the parents and children
- A summary that synthesizes and integrates all of the important information
- An analysis that clarifies the reasons for the evaluator's conclusions, while also describing the data that do not support the conclusions
- Recommendations that make sense and that meet the best interests of the children

# PART III

## Complex Issues to Be Evaluated

# 11 Nonviolent High-Conflict Families

Research on high-conflict families (Johnston, 1994; Johnston & Campbell, 1988; Johnston & Roseby, 1997; Johnston, Roseby, & Kuehnle, 2009) reveals a continuum of problems between divorcing parents and a variety of factors that contribute to the problems. Some families are mildly entrenched in conflict and can benefit from guidance and structured recommendations. The more difficult of these families may seem to make little progress, even with rather extensive intervention (e.g., therapy and case management). Some parents have personality traits that exacerbate conflicts, perhaps by exaggerating or being quite rigid. In the next section, I will focus on the way in which the parents' respective personality traits contribute to the degree and nature of the conflict. One of the most challenging tasks for many child custody evaluators is to identify the nature of and sources of conflict within the family. In nearly all instances (except perhaps for some families where relocation is an issue) conflict drives the questions that lead to a child custody evaluation. In this chapter, I will talk about conflict, its sources, and the various means to identify who contributes to the conflicts, and how to differentiate between each person's contributions to the conflicts within the family.

At the same time, I need to be clear that in this chapter I am focusing on high conflict *without* domestic violence. Domestic violence and its many forms are a very different topic, one that will be discussed in Chapter 12.

Low-conflict families are those in which parents, either by themselves or with the aid of their attorneys or a mediator, resolve issues. They learn how to resolve financial, property, and child custody and access issues. These parents are not derogatory of each other in front of the children, they rarely go to court, and they draft their own agreement, which is signed by the judge. While there is no clear research to identify the percentage of families low in conflict, I estimate that this is probably 20% to 30% of the divorced and never-married population. These families are identified in greater detail by Ahrons (2004) as "Parenting Pals." Essentially, these parents get along with one another, often see each other at holidays and birthdays, and seamlessly integrate the children's lives, however they are shared between the two homes. It is rare for a child custody evaluator to see a low-conflict family.

The medium-conflict families, which I estimate to be approximately 50% to 60% of the families, struggle at times. They may be actively in conflict or disengaged. Estimates suggest that about 40% of all divorced families become disengaged over time (Maccoby & Mnookin, 1992). At the beginning of their divorce, they often struggle to reach a marital settlement agreement, often letting financial, property, and access issues get in the way of each other. Many of these parents have difficulty with each other in public, and they typically provoke mild loyalty conflicts in their children. Typically, when these parents are together, the tension is high and observable by other parents, teachers, and the children. They have significant difficulty resolving their differences. It is quite common for these parents to be critical of each other in court documents, and they will often return to court at times of conflict. When seeing a mediator, they may require several mediation sessions, and in those jurisdictions that include judges in settlement negotiations, they may need several settlement sessions with the judge. There is ample research to suggest that medium-conflict families benefit tremendously by quality parent education programs (Arbuthnot, Kramer, & Gordon, 1997). Many of these families also need a focused evaluation, but usually not the more comprehensive evaluations discussed in this book. When couples are in medium conflict and one parent needs, or wants, to move with the children, it is rare for them to resolve the relocation request without court intervention and evaluation. Finally, when these families cannot resolve their differences and a judge makes orders, the medium-conflict couple usually follows judicial orders. Ahrons (2004) refers to these parents as "Cooperative Colleagues," especially when they learn to manage their conflicts and follow court orders over time.

In contrast, the high-conflict couples often look at judicial orders as merely suggestions (Bruniers, 2000). These parents are referred to by Ahrons (2004) as "Angry Associates" or "Fiery Foes," depending on the extent of their conflict. These parents have extreme difficulty following orders, settling their parenting plan, and resolving financial issues. They often let one set of problems interfere with the other set of problems. Many of these parents seem to hate each other more than they love their children. These parents make allegations of parental alienation (see Chapter 13), substance abuse, domestic violence (see Chapter 12), and other serious problems. Many of these parents have restraining orders against them or orders that limit their ability to be together in the same place at the same time, even at their children's events. Such parents have extremely derogatory attitudes toward one another. Some of these parents merge their own feelings with those of their children and have very poor boundaries with their children. In many of these families, there is additional conflict instigated by extended family members and friends. Sometimes, even therapists and attorneys get drawn into the conflicts. Many judges refer to these families as "frequent fliers," the 10% to 15% of the families that take up 85% to 90% of the court's time. These are the cases that are often seen in evaluations like the ones described in this book.

> High-conflict parents are the "frequent fliers" of the family court system.

The dynamics that contribute to this level of conflict will be discussed more fully in this chapter, with a focus on personality features of the parents, as well as the way that the system contributes to the conflicts between the parents.

In many ways, it appears that the life of the child stops while the arguments between the parents continue. For many of these families, every issue becomes a potential source of conflict. Sometimes this is related to the history of the relationship and the power dynamics between the parents. Sometimes one parent will not let go of the conflict because it keeps them "together" in their relationship (albeit a destructive one). Ultimately, both parents and the children are significantly affected in a negative way as a result of this unresolved conflict.

## Contribution of Personality Features

Over the past 30 years, a growing body of literature has developed on personality styles, in particular narcissistic and borderline styles. Millon (1996) focused not only on the disorders themselves but also on those personality traits and features that impact upon relationships rather than the individual. He has grouped personality disorders into types, one of which he refers to as Cluster B disorders: disorders that are conflict-inducing. Many custody evaluators observe that in most high-conflict families, one or both parents exhibit either narcissistic, obsessive-compulsive, histrionic, paranoid, or borderline traits or features. Millon stated that personality disorders are caused not only by the internal structures but also by the social system in which these people interact. The court system, with its litigation and conflict, is certainly an external system that may cause people who have such personality traits to act as if they have personality disorders. This is consistent with the commonly expressed phrase that "those in criminal court are bad people on their best behavior but those in family court are good people on their worst behavior."

Such parents may become rigid in their perception of each other and tend to deal with things in their extremes. Many parents are polarized, viewing themselves as all good and the other as all bad. These parents focus on the traits in the other parent that reinforce this perception, and they approach each new conflict as verification of just how difficult the other parent is. These parents experience chronic externalization of blame, possessing little insight into their own role in the conflicts. They usually have little empathy for the impact of this conflict on their children. They routinely feel self-justified, believing that their actions are best for their children. No matter how much helping professionals try to keep the focus on the child, these parents remain focused on the conflict.

Generally, those with personality disorders have characteristics that include the following traits:

- They have an enduring pattern of thinking and behaviors that may be pervasive in many aspects of their life.

- They create problems for others and are generally disruptive; they do not adapt well.
- They externalize issues, blame others, and have poor or limited insight into their own contribution to the problems.
- They may also show signs of depression, self-destructive behavior, aggressiveness, or brief psychotic episodes (or behaviors that appear psychotic).
- These parents tend to use emotional persuasion when in conflict, escalating their emotions, often becoming louder, blaming, and increasing the seriousness of their allegations.
- Many confuse emotional facts with actual facts. Those parents generate facts to support how they feel, and their emotions are often triggered by cognitive distortions. They believe "facts" that are not true, even though they feel as if they are true. This often leads to cognitive distortions, exaggerations, and overt fears. They tend toward dyscontrol or overcontrol.
- Parents with severe narcissistic personality disorders, or who act as if they have such disorders, lack empathy for both the children and their ex-spouse and have a strong sense of entitlement in court proceedings.

> Personality issues, such as narcissism, anger, anxiety, fear, a tendency to overreact, paranoia, and so on, are a major source of conflict for parents engaged in high-conflict divorce.

While these parents tend to be motivated by a diverse set of emotions, I believe that most of them take this rather rigid position out of fear, often the overwhelming fear that if they let their defenses down, they will be taken advantage of. Many parents say, "If I give in just this one time, she will always take advantage of me," or, "If I give him an inch, he'll take a mile." Sometimes this is accurate and sometimes this is based on fear. Many parents fear being controlled by the other parent. For the more disturbed of these parents, giving in may represent a fear of loss of self. This rigidity ensures conflict. Because these families routinely go back to court, they are also afraid that any relaxing of their position might give the other parent an advantage in court. What is lost in the conflict are the needs of the children.

Another source of the fear is that winning or losing is so integrally tied to self-esteem. Narcissistic parents fear losing custody and control lest they feel abandoned and depressed. Borderline parents must win in order to contain their internal chaos and rage. While losing might mean different things to each parent (e.g., shame, loss, abandonment, rage, etc.), the key ingredient is how *unbearable* such a loss will feel to the parent.

Judges and attorneys express their extreme frustration over these families. As noted already, judges often refer to these families as "frequent fliers." Many come back to court several times a year, and just as it appears that a settlement has been reached, a new issue will arise. Lacking a reasonable dispute-resolution mechanism, these parents feel justified in taking each other to

court and letting "the judge settle it." Each issue is perceived as a new opportunity for victory and is feared as a potential loss. These characterological personality dynamics, along with each parent's righteous self-justification and fear,
create the high degree of conflict and the perpetuation of the court battle.

At the same time, away from the conflict, many of these parents seem concerned for their children's needs and feelings and are capable of good parenting skills. They may be nurturing and set reasonable limits with their children.
They are frequently involved in their child's day-to-day activities, participate
in schoolwork, and provide encouragement and support to their children.
Many of these parents can be loving, spontaneous, and supportive of their
children, even when they are cold, rigid, angry, and fearful toward the other
parent. In the abstract, they understand the value of the child's relationship
with the other parent, and they may even recognize that the conflict is problematic for their children. Despite this acknowledgment, it is difficult for them
to relax their rigid positions and attitudes toward the other parent and extri-
cate their child (and themselves) from the conflict.

For many high-conflict families, it seems that the parents' characterological
personality dynamics get manifested in a relationship disorder with the other
parent. They may be able to manage some of their chronic traits, including
their narcissism, overreaction, rigidity, and anger, in some of their other relationships. They may be pleasant to coworkers, showing few pathological traits
in their work environment. With their children, they may not personalize experiences or show signs of narcissistic injury. When seeing such parents in a child
custody evaluation, it is important to understand how (and whether) the vulnerabilities that exist in the parent–parent relationship are manifested in the
parent–child relationship.

In contrast, the history of the conflict, the emotions of the divorce, the lack of
trust, and the fear of letting go bring out the worst in these parents in any interactions with each other. It appears that the couple's relationship has been unable to
withstand the previous love, the loss of that love, and the rejection and hurt that
followed. In the newly formed divorce relationship, dysfunctional personality traits
flourish, while in other relationships, including with the children, healthier personality traits may abound. For those parents who are less disturbed, the pathological
personality traits may surface only in the context of the conflicted relationship
between the parents. Each parent's negative individual traits clash and the conflicts
continue. Left unchecked, these families return to court year after year to solve
what might appear to the neutral observer to be the most minor of issues.

These families require strategies and interventions that assist them in taking care of their children and reducing their conflict. The evaluator should
determine whether or not therapy or parent education is an appropriate recommendation for either or both of the parents, because such interventions
may be quite useful for high-conflict parents. However, these interventions
are not totally sufficient for these families. Evaluators will want to consider
whether some form of dispute-resolution intervention, such as the use of a
Parent Coordinator, will work for the high-conflict family.

# Contributions From Other Sources

In addition to the personality features of the parents, there are a number of other potential sources that contribute to the high-conflict nature of some parents. One potential source is the nature of litigation itself. The court system is typically focused on polarization and blame, which reinforces the polarization and blame that many parents feel in these situations. Unless judges are sensitive to these issues, they may reinforce some of the problems by criticizing both parents when only one is exacerbating most of the problems. Within that context, there is often limited encouragement of problem-solving skills, though more recently some jurisdictions are encouraging parents to participate in specialized high-conflict programs designed to teach problem-solving skills, as well as focus these parents on the needs of the child.

At other times, some lawyers seem to hate each other as much as or more than the parents do. They may personalize their client's feelings and needs. They ratchet up the conflict, sometimes for a variety of reasons. While I do not want to criticize the work done by good attorneys, even the good attorneys know when they are faced with a lawyer who instigates and stirs up the trouble between parents. I have known many attorneys who will not take cases that involve one of those more difficult attorneys from their community. It is almost as if the attorney has a personality disorder, or acts like he or she has one.

Therapists may contribute in a way that exacerbates problems (L. Greenberg, Gould, Gould-Saltmann, & Stahl, 2003). Sometimes, a child's therapist, who has never met one of the parents, will send a letter to the judge regarding the alleged abuse that children have suffered and make recommendations for custody. In many jurisdictions, that might be an ethical violation because the therapist is making such a recommendation without seeing one of the parents. Along the same lines, adult therapists often provide "supportive" therapy, without any knowledge about how the supportive therapy allows their client to avoid taking personal responsibility for the client's contributions to the problem. In that vein, when the client talks to the therapist, all the therapist does is accept and agree with everything the client says, without questioning the client about his or her behaviors and attitudes that may be exacerbating the problems. While I do not mean to say that therapy should not be supportive, I have found that supportive therapy alone, without some level of focus on the client's behavior, can be counterproductive. These problems can sometimes become evident when talking to therapists who are collateral sources of information in particular cases.

The final source of conflict comes from friends and extended family who support and encourage the "tribal warfare" (Johnston & Campbell, 1988). Again, while it is appropriate to support a loved family member or friend, it is not helpful to do so in a way that exacerbates the family conflict. In some families, the conflict is quite entrenched and extends beyond just the divorcing parents. Like the proverbial "Hatfields and McCoys," these parents get armies of support for their battle against the other parent. In such families, relationships become increasingly fragmented, as children are not able to see some family members because of their role in the conflict.

For example, I once evaluated a family with two school-age girls who were refusing to see their mother. Their mother had two parents and two siblings, each of whom took sides. The maternal grandparents and one sibling took mother's side in the dispute and the other sibling took father's side. The children never saw their maternal grandparents or the aunt who supported the mother, but frequently saw the aunt who supported the father. This was detrimental to the children. As this type of conflict in such families increases, positions harden, resolution is all but impossible, and the children suffer in the process.

> In addition to personality features, litigation, attorneys, therapists, and the "tribal warfare" of families and friends can exacerbate the conflict between divorcing parents.

As such, in addition to the way in which personality traits and disorders often contribute to high conflict, the court system, attorneys, therapists, and family members and friends may all contribute to the level of conflict that may occur.

## Recommendations for High-Conflict Families

### Therapy

It is common for evaluators to make recommendations for therapy at the conclusion of an evaluation. With high-conflict families, I strongly encourage specific recommendations that relate to the psychological and personality issues identified in the evaluation. For the parents, this might include the following:

- Therapy or counseling that encourages parents to develop empathy and understanding of their children's feelings and needs
- Teaching parents to differentiate between their own thoughts, feelings, and needs and those of their children
- Teaching parents to take personal responsibility
- Teaching parents to consider alternative solutions and improving problem-solving skills

With this in mind, it is obvious that supportive therapy will not work with this population. It may be critical to confront these parents therapeutically to focus them on the issues that are contributing to the conflicts with their ex-spouse.

Therapy or counseling is also likely needed to help children learn to cope. Children cope best when they learn active skills for coping, such as understanding their feelings, learning to express their feelings in a healthy way, and learning to separate their feelings from the loy-

> When recommending therapy for high-conflict adults, clarify and specify the goals that you believe will benefit both the children and their parents in helping the children and the parent.

alty conflicts and the conflicts of their parents (Fields & Prinz, 1997; Shelton & Harold, 2007). To the extent that children feel caught in the middle or are used as spies or messengers of communication, such therapy can help them learn to get out of the middle and cope more successfully with the tension of their parents' divorce.

## Structured Recommendations

Another important intervention for these families is providing structured recommendations. During the custody evaluation, evaluators learn the routines in each household, the strengths and weaknesses of each parent, and the quality of the relationships between the child and each parent. For high-conflict families, a lack of specificity promotes parental conflict, and conflict breeds insecurity for the children. I suggest that evaluators recommend specific and concrete plans to assist parents in fulfilling the tasks of parallel parenting (see discussion that follows) and reducing the likelihood that they remain engaged in conflict. The more specific we make our recommendations, the more we can help parents know the rules and help the neutral decision-maker enforce the rules.

Some families have a rather vague schedule outlined in their divorce order stating something like "the children are to be with father every Wednesday overnight and every other weekend. Each parent has the opportunity for a summer vacation in each calendar year." Some are even vaguer and state that "father has reasonable rights of access." While such phrases may be acceptable for many low-conflict and medium-conflict families that are flexible and manage their conflicts, they will not work for high-conflict parents. High-conflict parents argue about the beginning and ending times of the overnight, how to define the times of the weekend, the length and times of vacations, and even how to resolve the likely occurrence that each parent desires the same vacation dates. For these families, the evaluator might recommend something like the following:

> The children are to be with father from his pick-up of the children at school at the end of their school day each Wednesday until he returns them to school the following Thursday morning. He will have the children every other weekend (with the start date noted so that an observer can easily determine whose weekend is whose) beginning at his pick-up at school on Friday afternoon until his return of the children to school on Monday morning. In the event of a three-day holiday weekend, in which the children are off school either Friday or Monday, his time with the children will extend to include that additional day; for example, he will return the children to school on Tuesday morning following a Monday holiday. In the event there is no school on an exchange day, the father will drop the children off at mother's home at 8:30 a.m.
>
> Additionally, it is recommended that each parent can have the children for up to 14 consecutive days for a vacation in each calendar year. Such vacations can occur only during the summer school break, except as outlined in the holiday schedule below. Requests for vacation

must be made by February 28 of each calendar year for the following summer, and in the event there is a dispute over requested dates, father has first choice in even-numbered years and mother has first choice in odd-numbered years.

Another way to maintain a structured schedule is to develop a holiday plan that is clear. Certainly, it will depend on the age of the children and the family expectations. Schools in different parts of the country are on different schedules, as well. An example of a structured holiday and vacation schedule follows:

For holidays, birthdays, and school vacation, I recommend the following:

Thanksgiving break to be with Father all odd-numbered years and Mother in all even-numbered years.

I recommend an equal split of the Christmas break from school, switching at 1:00 p.m. Christmas Day. In all odd-numbered years I recommend that Mother have the first half of the Christmas vacation. In all even-numbered years, I recommend that Mother have the second half of the Christmas vacation. The intent of this recommendation is that each parent will have one half of the break. In the event that the vacation does not split evenly, I recommend that it be adjusted as necessary by the Parent Coordinator.

I would recommend that Spring Break be treated as a whole, including the weekend days, with Father having the children in all odd-numbered years, and Mother having them in all even-numbered years.

The children should be with Father on his birthday from 4:00 p.m.–8:00 p.m. (if Father's birthday naturally falls on his time, no special date will be made) and for the entire Father's Day weekend and with Mother on her birthday from 4:00 p.m.–8:00 p.m. (if Mother's birthday naturally falls on her time, no special date will be made) and the entire Mother's Day weekend. Additionally, I would recommend alternating the children's birthdays in the same fashion.

As can be seen by this lengthy and detailed recommendation, less room exists for each parent to manipulate or feel manipulated by the other. The rules are quite clear. In the event of a dispute, it will be relatively easy for the Parent Coordinator (or police if they are called into the case) to resolve. The recommendation should also include a provision that the neutral decision-maker can make adjustments or modifications in the event of certain situations, such as a family emergency, a special longer vacation, the children's summer schedule, or the needs of one or more family members. Typically, such adjustments will be put in writing so that there is no dispute about how or why the adjustment was made.

> Because high-conflict parents have trouble agreeing on the meaning of almost anything, be as specific as you can in your recommendations. This reduces the likelihood that they will continue to argue about what you meant.

Flexibility does not work for these high-conflict families unless there is a dispute resolution mechanism such as a neutral decision-maker, because flexibility is a breeding ground for new conflict. Parents can feel more comfortable with a structured recommendation if it can be adjusted in the event a specific need arises. The preceding is only one example of the areas in which concrete and specific recommendations can be made, and it is the task of the evaluator to identify the level and sources of conflict within the family so that appropriate recommendations in all risk areas can be made.

## Neutral Decision-Maker (Parent Coordinator)

In a variety of jurisdictions, courts have begun to use attorneys and mental health practitioners as neutral decision-makers to assist families in such day-to-day disputes. These families frequently return to court, and the court system is incapable of handling the types or frequency of problems that these families bring. Instead, courts require the assistance of a decision-maker who acts on behalf of the children. This person is empowered by the family and the court to act on behalf of the children to resolve conflicts in an expeditious manner. If neither parent has control, both can relax their fear of being taken advantage of by the other. While each parent may periodically become frustrated with the decisions of the neutral decision-maker, each parent usually trusts that person more than the other parent.

An example of recommendation for neutral decision-making might be the following:

A Parent Coordinator should be appointed to assist the parties in resolving their disputes. I would recommend that this Parent Coordinator have decision-making authority in all day-to-day areas except for significant changes in the time-share. At a minimum, the Parent Coordinator needs to have authority to settle disputes in the areas of child care, after-school activities, times and locations of exchanges, disputes about vacations, therapy for the child, and each parent's participation in the child's events. Both parents are discouraged from engaging in conflict within their child's hearing and are directed to use the Parent Coordinator for such disputes. Both parents should refrain from calling the police except in an emergency, without first discussing their concern with the Parent Coordinator. The Parent Coordinator needs to have the authority to alter the basic time-share if he or she deems that one parent is causing significant problems for the child. Finally, at a minimum, the parents should meet with the Parent Coordinator once per month to discuss their child and the child's needs and to work toward preventing future problems from occurring.

In fact, it is this evaluator's opinion that the use of a Parent Coordinator is the single most important thing that these parents can do to help their child. Each parent needs to focus more on his or her own parenting and learn to be less critical of the other. If they can learn to resolve their disputes away from their child and work toward being the best parent each can be during the times they have their child, almost any time-share in which both parents are actively involved in their child's life will be workable and successful for their child.

As noted in the recommendation, not only is the neutral third-party role included, but so is the task of taking responsibility for healthy parenting. When the evaluator makes a recommendation for someone to take on this role, it will be helpful to explain the benefits for the parents. By the time a family is seen for a child custody evaluation, many parents are tired of fighting and of the delays and costs of the court process. The evaluator can help parents recognize the benefits of using a neutral decision-maker such as a Parent Coordinator by talking to parents about the lowered cost and the quicker decisions and assuring parents that neither parent will have undue power over the other. This may help many parents accept this as an alternative mechanism for their dispute resolution.

> The Parent Coordinator makes decisions for the high-conflict parents so that the child's life can proceed seamlessly and with less intrusion by that conflict.

It appears that there are three primary benefits from this role: helping families more quickly resolve their differences, unclogging the courts of some of their most difficult families, and helping families with very young children manage the nuances of integrating changing developmental needs of the child into their parenting plan.

When I first suggested this process in my earlier book (P. Stahl, 1999), there was little published about the Parent Coordinator role. At that time, I had previously described the process as one in which a professional is appointed by the court to act in a quasi-judicial manner to make day-to-day decisions for divorced families in conflict. The major task of the Parent Coordinator is to make decisions that help a family stay out of court and keep their children out of the middle of the conflict. Parent Coordinators need to be decisive. Just as young children often have difficulty sharing, high-conflict divorced parents often have difficulty sharing their children. While the Parent Coordinator needs to understand the parents' position and feelings, it is more important for the Parent Coordinator to make decisions that are in the child's best interests, without taking a lot of time (P. Stahl, 1995). Since that time, several articles have focused on the role of the Parent Coordinator (see, e.g., Boyan & Termini, 2005; Sullivan, 2004). Additionally, the Association of Family and Conciliation Courts (AFCC) has recently published *Guidelines for Parenting Coordination* (AFCC Task Force on Parenting Coordination, 2005). All of this literature has helped our understanding of the role, which is clearly focused on encouraging parents to reduce their conflict to improve things for children of high-conflict divorce.

A Parent Coordinator is faced with making major decisions on a regular and consistent basis. For most mental health practitioners, quick decision-making is the most difficult task of being a Parent Coordinator. Someone who accepts this task must recognize that the child relies on the Parent Coordinator to make decisions on his behalf. When the Parent Coordinator keeps the focus on meeting the needs of the child, it becomes easier to make quick decisions that support and promote the child's healthy adjustment.

The role of the Parent Coordinator is a multifaceted one in which the Parent Coordinator is part detective (as parents describe their different stories, the Parent Coordinator tries to understand the "whole truth"), part educator (the Parent Coordinator helps parents learn to share their children, understand each child's developmental needs, resolve problems, and move on with their lives following the divorce), part mental health professional (the Parent Coordinator understands the parents' and child's feelings and attitudes), part judge (the Parent Coordinator makes timely decisions), and part advocate for the children (children's needs are the Parent Coordinator's first priority). Just like evaluators, Parent Coordinators may talk with other professionals and may need to meet with the children to carry out their work. The task is complex because of the ongoing conflict between the parents.

It is necessary for the Parent Coordinator's scope to be defined by court order. In most jurisdictions, Parent Coordinators cannot be ordered by the court (see, e.g., *Ruisi v. Theriot*, 1997, in California). Instead, this court-appointed role is stipulated to by the parents and grants the Parent Coordinator very specific and usually limited authorities. This is because courts cannot delegate judicial tasks to nonjudicial officers. With that in mind, Parent Coordinators generally are granted the authority to make decisions about schedules, overnight access, choice of schools, extracurricular activities, troubles at transfers, holiday scheduling, parenting differences, health issues, children's therapy, and/or problematic behaviors on the part of one or both parents. The Parent Coordinator needs to understand the impact on the children before making decisions in any of these areas.

In my view, Parent Coordinator work is perhaps the toughest in the family court arena. Parents who require Parent Coordinators are engaged in the most destructive conflict, tend to have limited psychological resources and coping skills, and tend to thrive on chaos in their lives. The Parent Coordinator must have time-management skills, which may be difficult to manage for some mental health professionals. I have heard fewer concerns with time management when an attorney is the Parent Coordinator. However, being a Parent Coordinator requires training in child development and conflict resolution, and attorneys sometimes may have more problems with those aspects of the job.

Because many of these parents are highly litigious and vehemently express their displeasure over decisions, the job requires the mental toughness of a judge and the empathy of a psychologist to withstand the pressures that some parents apply. While this might be difficult for some, I know many Parent Coordinators who find gratification in being able to support children in these families, while helping parents reduce the intensity of their conflict.

## Parallel Parenting

A fourth intervention involves parallel parenting. Psychologists describe young children who play next to each other but interact very little with each other to be in "parallel play." In the same way, parents who parent their children at different times, but who have little or no direct interaction, are engaged in parallel parenting. This occurs when they engage in the same tasks, as long as they have little or no contact with one another.

Although much of the divorce literature focuses on the goal of cooperative co-parenting, in which parents communicate and work with one another to raise their children in a cooperative fashion, high-conflict families fail miserably at this task. Each parent usually thinks his or her style is the only way to parent and is often quite critical of the other. Interactions stimulate the conflict, reducing benefits to the children.

The goal of parallel parenting is to reduce the level of conflict and make sure that the tasks of parenting are accomplished by one or both parents. It is important for parents, in conjunction with the courts and/or neutral decision-maker, to specify which parent is responsible for various parenting tasks. Parents develop a plan that identifies how each parent will participate in the child's extracurricular activities, help with schoolwork, take care of medical needs, and so on. Plans are developed to ensure that parents communicate with each other with less conflict. Faxes and/or e-mails may be used when the conflict is high. Each parent is encouraged to develop his or her separate routine and structure. With such a plan, for example, the child will not be exposed to both parents attending the same field trip and making things miserable with their conflict.

> Not all parents can co-parent effectively. Encourage high-conflict parents to parallel parent. There is a much higher chance of success, and the children can be taken out of the middle more easily.

I find that the integration of these recommendations leads to the ideal intervention for many families. While the literature suggests that high-conflict parents cannot share parenting, Johnston (1994) states that parallel parenting may work. I agree and find that this is the goal to encourage. Parents with a high level of conflict must first learn to disengage before they can parent together. Parallel parenting allows them the freedom to parent separately. Working with the neutral decision-maker allows them to develop the skills to co-parent and use them later in raising their children, after the conflicts have diminished.

To help these parents disengage and then learn to work together, it can be helpful for the neutral decision-maker to meet with the parents periodically to develop a schedule of the child's activities and each parent's participation in those activities. The Parent Coordinator can focus on the process of parallel parenting and help parents to disengage from conflict. Together, they can develop routines for the child and help coordinate a similar routine in each household, schedule times for phone calls between children and the other parent, and assist each parent in doing those tasks that each parent does best. With this process, there are no winners or losers, and the child benefits from separate and parallel interaction with both parents and the reduced amount of conflict to which she is exposed. Once a neutral decision-maker is in place and the process of parallel parenting is ensured, parents can detach from each other and reduce the intensity of their conflict.

In thinking further about parallel parenting, it is clear that certain skills are required by the parents in these families (P. Stahl, 2008b). The first step of parallel parenting is "disengagement." These parents need to avoid communication about minor things in the child's life. They need to avoid telling each other how to parent or criticizing each other. Instead, only limited and basic information is provided, and all of it is done via e-mail, letter, or fax. They communicate orally or leave voice messages only in emergencies when no other method of communication will work to deal with the emergency. In their written communication, parents need to be encouraged to be factual and concise and business-like, avoid sarcasm and impulsive emotions, and not share the communications with the children. Parents who parallel parent must support different styles of parenting and accept more than one "right way" to parent in order to avoid conflict. When engaged in parallel parenting, each parent needs to be less rigid and more accepting of the child's other parent. It is important to note that many children of divorce adjust well to two very different homes. Ultimately, parents who parallel parent can learn to parent differently and continue to raise their children in a healthy way.

### Using a Parent Communication Notebook

Parents who are engaged in parallel parenting do not communicate very well with one another, but they still need to communicate about the day-to-day issues regarding their children, especially when children are quite young. The Notebook should include highlights of the very young child's emotions and behaviors during the time that the child is with each parent. The Notebook is transitioned between parents during the exchange of the child. When children are very young, the Notebook should have information about the child's health, feeding, and sleeping patterns. It should include information about the child's emerging language and the child's mood, including what soothes or upsets the child. Ultimately, the Notebook should include all relevant information about the child's day-to-day functioning and needs.

In order to ensure that such communication goes well, it may need to be monitored by the Parent Coordinator.

# A Case for Sole Legal Custody
# or Decision-Making to One Parent _____

Finally, one of the key areas that may need a recommendation is the question of sole versus joint legal custody or other ways to encourage parents in their decision-making. It is important to point out right away a few limitations associated with this topic. First, there is no specific research that can be applied to understanding when a family should have both parents sharing legal custody and decision-making versus one parent having sole legal custody and the decision-making responsibilities. In addition, because the concept of best interests of the child is so vague, it is not surprising that judges are not always sure how to apply the best-interests concept in the real world. With that in mind, it seems likely that most judges order joint legal custody without question in order to ensure that neither parent loses any rights, and I suspect that most evaluators recommend joint legal custody in most cases in order to ensure fairness to both parents. Unfortunately, by the time a family has gotten to the point of needing an evaluation, the likelihood of those parents successfully sharing custody and decision-making is poor. With that in mind and based on a workshop I participated in with two judges and another psychologist in Arizona, I have sorted out the tasks that are necessary for parents to share custody as opposed to those situations where one parent should be the sole decision-maker. The following suggestions are based on this workshop.

Joint legal custody requires parents who are able to make periodic agreements about the daily activities of the child and make periodic adjustments to the access schedule when things come up. These parents must be able to agree on where children go to school and what medical and dental issues should be undertaken. Joint legal custody is very workable for those parents earlier identified as "Parenting Pals" or "Cooperative Colleagues." Without considerable help, joint legal custody is likely to be a dismal failure for "Angry Associates" or "Fiery Foes." This help may come in the form of co-parent counseling, but it also may come in the form of using a Parent Coordinator. Parents who want to co-parent cooperatively need to have resolved their anger, have accepted the status of their divorce, no longer feel abandoned, and be adaptable (Glassman, 2007). With parallel parenting and co-parent counseling or the use of Parent Coordination, parents with a greater degree of hostility and distrust may be able to share legal custody.

In contrast, joint legal custody is unlikely to be successful when there is domestic violence, especially of the Coercive–Controlling type (see Chapter 12); when parents have used a Parent Coordinator and failed; when there are frequent violations of court orders; and especially when there is one parent who is primarily stirring the trouble between them. Unfortunately, judges and evaluators all too often have what I have referred to as "truth lies somewhere in the middle" bias (P. Stahl, 2006). While it is true that it is common for both parents to contribute equally to the conflict, in many of these high-conflict cases one parent is the prime initiator of the conflict and the other parent is largely the reactor. In those cases, there may be a case to make for granting the reacting parent sole legal custody or at least primary decision-making if the two parents cannot agree on things.

Thus, evaluators need to recognize that in high-conflict situations, there are many options. These can include:

- Joint legal custody
- Sole legal custody to one parent
- The use of a Parent Coordinator or other interventionist to see if the family will benefit from this service
- The use of a Parent Coordinator or child's attorney to balance the power when giving either parent sole legal custody or that parent has the risk of abusing that power
- With both parents sharing joint legal custody, allowing one parent to make the decisions in even-numbered years and the other parent to make the decisions in odd-numbered years

## THE BOTTOM LINE

The critical task for the evaluator is to sort out and identify the relevant issues regarding the high-conflict nature of the relationship. By the time a family goes to a complex and comprehensive child custody evaluation, the likelihood is that we are dealing with a high-conflict couple who are more likely "Fiery Foes" or "Angry Associates" than a low- or medium-conflict couple who are "Parenting Pals" or "Cooperative Colleagues." With high-conflict parents, it is important to sort out not only each parent's personality features that are contributing to the conflict but also any other factors, such as the litigation or contributions from others. Then it will be possible to determine whether one parent or both are the main cause of the conflict. Once that is done, it is hoped that the correct recommendations can be made for the family.

One thing to keep in mind is that for some families the level of conflict is not resolved for years. With such families, neither parent trusts the Parent Coordinator; in fact, the use of a Parent Coordinator only provides one more opportunity for engaging in conflict and battling over power and control. Those families will require a very structured court order that leaves little room for dispute and potential sanctions from the court in the event that either parent violates the order. Those families will have no room for flexibility, unless mutually agreed upon.

In contrast, many high-conflict parents do trust the Parent Coordinator, benefit from a clear and precise order, and are encouraged by parallel parenting. They neutralize their balance of power and reduce the likelihood that conflict will erupt in front of the children. Because the Parent Coordinator can make decisions in a timely way (e.g., whether or not the child will participate in Little League and how each parent can participate with the child), the child's life is less likely to be halted or disrupted by the conflict.

At the beginning of this chapter, I differentiated between domestic violence families and high-conflict families. While the goals for domestic violence families are to end the violence, ensure safety for victims and children, support therapeutic interventions for batterers and victims, and normalize the relationship that the child has with each parent, the goals for nonviolent but high-conflict families are to reduce the level of conflict to which the child is exposed and ensure that each parent has the opportunity to do the best possible job of parenting during the time that each parent has the child. This also helps to ensure that the child's life, including schooling, extracurricular activities, and peer relationships, can be predictable and develop in a healthy way.

# 12    Domestic Violence

In the past few decades, there has been an increased focus on understanding domestic violence and its various dynamics and how it affects the family, particularly the children. While the debate about what conditions precipitate domestic violence has grown, so has the social awareness.

In the year 2009 alone, I learned about several cases in which fathers murdered their ex-spouse, or committed murder–suicide, and where children or other relatives were murdered as well. Judges hear evidence of violence, put restraining orders in place, and yet women and their children are killed. These cases receive considerable publicity, judges are blamed when they do not allow a parent to move when the request for the move is for safety reasons, and communities act to prevent these tragedies from happening. While it is clearly tragic when someone is killed due to domestic violence, it is also tragic when a broad brush is used to deal with allegations of violence, and relationships between children and a parent are affected because of unnecessary limitations in those relationships. While it is important to ensure the protection of children and victims, it is also important to ensure that in the absence of significant risk, children and parents can maintain healthy and secure relationships. This chapter will focus on addressing the relevant research on domestic violence that will help guide these cases in the right direction.

When I wrote about domestic violence in my 1999 book (P. Stahl, 1999), I identified research by Newmark, Harrell, and Salem (1995) on domestic violence and mediation, and Hanks (1992) and Johnston (1994) on different typologies of domestic violence in the context of marriage and divorce, along with other research at that time. In 1996, the National Council of Juvenile and Family Court Judges (NCJFCJ) encouraged states to adopt rebuttable presumption legislation that perpetrators of domestic violence should not have custody, either joint or sole, of their children. Since that time, about 25 states have adopted such laws, and the rest all include domestic violence as a factor in determining child custody matters.

Domestic violence advocates, who have continued to try to protect victims and children and to end the cycles of violence in families, have continued to endorse research focusing on the power and control dynamics that are consistent with domestic violence. They cite research that suggests that the majority of domestic violence is perpetrated by men against women and that there is significant risk to women and children around the time of separation. At the same time, others have endorsed community research that suggests that domestic violence is perpetrated equally by men and women, and that while the dangerous violence that gains the publicity is real, it is much less frequent than the typical violence that occurs in families. The tension between these two groups has increased, as they cite different research and reach different conclusions about violence in families and the ways in which violence affects women and children.

This tension led the Association of Family and Conciliation Courts and the NCJFCJ (Salem & Dunford-Jackson, 2008) to bring researchers from various disciplines together to discuss the various findings to see if they could open a productive dialog about domestic violence and hopefully reach some consensus on the disparate data from the research on domestic violence. This resulted in the Wingspread Conference that was held in February 2007 (Ver Steegh & Dalton, 2008). Participants at the conference included members of the domestic violence advocacy community, family court judges and administrators, lawyers, mental health professionals, others working in the family court system, and academic professionals in the fields of law and social science. The result of that conference was a special issue of *Family Court Review*, published in the summer of 2008. In this chapter, I will focus on the emerging research and publications associated with the Wingspread Conference and integrate that knowledge with guidance on performing child custody evaluations when there are allegations of domestic violence.

> The Wingspread Conference on Domestic Violence was convened to develop a more broad-based understanding of domestic violence and its many forms in families, especially families of divorce.

## The Concept of Differentiation

One of the key results of Wingspread was an agreement that the concept that one size fits all is not appropriate in domestic violence cases. While the cases that gain publicity are terrible and tragic and are likely the result of a long-standing pattern of power and control, not all families with domestic violent behaviors fit this pattern. As the research has shown for years, while all violence is harmful and for some it is potentially lethal, the majority of violence in families is different. For years, Hanks (1992), Johnston (1994), and others (see, e.g., Ver Steegh, 2005; Zibbell, 2005) have identified that family violence is sometimes referred to as common couples violence, situational couples violence, or separation-related violence, in addition to the violence that is attributed to power and control. The participants at Wingspread agreed that there are different forms that domestic violence takes in families and that not all violence is of the power-and-control type.

Participants recognized that there was some tension in dealing with these issues. On the one hand, family relationships can be compromised if all domestic violence is seen as the power-and-control type that needs strict interventions and should result in limited or supervised access between the violent parent and a child. On the other hand, safety can be compromised if we allow open and unrestricted access in those cases where there is legitimate risk. The only way to manage these tensions is to ensure that judges and those who report to judges—mediators and evaluators—consider lethality, the risk of future violence, and the presence of other forms of intimidation when looking at these families. As Dunford-Jackson and Jordan (2003) wrote, the risk of getting it wrong is very high. While they meant that the risk of missing the signs of domestic violence could lead to serious consequences, such as future violence and the risk of homicide, others might also think that there is risk of children losing a relationship with a parent if there is no risk of violence. Thus, the key task for those working with families of violence is to understand the various risks involved with all families.

Another key task highlighted by the Wingspread participants was to identify a language that all could agree upon. They recognized that the research identified many different types of violence and that there was considerable overlap in the terms being used. They reached agreement on the reality that domestic violence must be differentiated along various dimensions. Participants were concerned that there might be some over-adherence to typologies and that there might not be good enough screening instruments to reliably identify which families might fit into which category of violence. Again, this could lead to some families being at risk, either the risk of future violence or the risk of family relationships being compromised. By identifying the value of differentiation and developing an agreed-upon language for different types of violence, it was hoped that better clarity and improved decisions could be made.

Third, it was determined that one of the reasons for the discrepancy between the research identified by the advocates and the research identified by those who work in family courts was that they were largely working with different samples. The domestic violence advocates focused primarily on data gathered from domestic violence shelters, police, and hospital records. Death review panels, in which citizens reviewed the history of family violence that resulted in the death of a victim, has also contributed to our knowledge about such family violence. In contrast, the research identified by others was focused on data gathered in community samples and that reflected large numbers of family relationships. This resulted in confusion, dissent, and disagreements among researchers, and disparities in gender-related research findings. As I discuss the findings of both groups, I will identify the gender differences in the differentiated groups, as well as prevalence and frequency issues. Finally, there are very different findings associated with severity and consequences of the violence based on

> It is important to recognize the need to differentiate among families experiencing domestic violence, because one size does not fit all.

the different types. I will provide information about each of the various types as I focus on these issues.

In the rest of this chapter, I will discuss the different types of violence identified by the Wingspread participants and described in the literature. Differentiation allows for the development of appropriate parenting plans for families with different types of violence and moves away from the one-size-fits-all paradigm that claims all intimate partner violence is power-and-control battering or is simply common couples violence. I will identify the ways that evaluators need to integrate the literature so as to ensure safety where safety is the primary issue, while simultaneously encouraging family relationships when safety is not a risk. I will start by focusing on the different types of domestic violence identified in the literature, using the language agreed upon by the participants at the Wingspread Conference. I will identify each group in order, based upon the apparent frequency in families.

## Situational Couples Violence (SCV)

While other names have been used for Situational Couples Violence, including Common Couples Violence, families who engage in this type of violence have intermittent violence, initiated by both genders, over time, *without* any evidence of power and control being a central dynamic of the relationship. In these couples, it is common for the partners to be angry with one another. Over time, and in some circumstances, the anger flares up into some type of violence. Another key ingredient for this type of violence is that neither partner is in fear of the other. For the most part, injuries are very rare when a couple engages in SCV, and serious injuries occur less than 4% of the time (see e.g., J. Kelly & Johnson, 2008). In this population, minor forms of violence, such as pushing, shoving, and grabbing, are the most common. Different families appear to have different frequencies of such violence, and generally, this type of violence decreases over time. Unlike those families who engage in Coercive–Controlling Violence (see next section), partners who engage in SCV are quick to acknowledge their actions and recognize that it was unhealthy for the couple, and the violence generally stops after separation.

> Situational Couples Violence has also been referred to as Common Couples Violence.

It is common in many families for this type of violence to be instigated rather equally by both men and women. However, there are other families in which one partner initiates SCV most of the time. When this occurs, women initiate SCV more frequently than men. Common forms of emotional violence in this group include cursing, yelling, and name-calling; jealousy may also be a part of this type of violence, but not isolation and stalking or other controlling types of behavior. Two other important pieces of data regarding SCV are that the risks for violence are higher with aggressive, delinquent, and antisocial teenagers and young adults, and that the rates of violence are higher in dating couples than in older, married couples.

## Coercive–Controlling Violence (CCV)

The hallmark of this type of violence, which has often been referred to as Battering or Intimate Partner Violence, is that intimidation, power, coercion, control, and emotional abuse *are central dynamics* of this type of violence. This type is primarily male initiated, with only a small number of heterosexual females initiating this type of violence (see, e.g., J. Kelly & Johnson, 2008). In spite of the publicity that these types of families receive, the incidence of CCV in the general population is *lower* than the incidence of SCV. Another difference is that injuries to the victim are much more common in CCV than in SCV, and these injuries are often much more severe. Additionally, perpetrators, and often the victims, of CCV are much more likely to engage in denial, blame, and minimizing than the perpetrators of SCV. Unlike SCV couples, the victims in CCV families do live in fear and often walk on eggshells when interacting with their partners. Finally, at the time of separation, there is an *increased rather than decreased* risk of violence. This is why we are so likely to see serious incidents, including homicide, after separation with CCV than with any other type of domestic violence.

> Coercive–Controlling Violence has also been referred to as Battering, Intimate Partner Violence, and Male Controlling Violence

A hypothesis about the preceding data lies in the reasons for the violence. In SCV, the violence is largely the result of anger and impulsiveness that has escalated in one or both partners, and it appears that the violence in CCV is largely the result of a need to control the victim. Different reasons have been hypothesized for this need to control, including male privilege, strong jealousy, and strong feelings of dependency (e.g., Bornstein, 2006; Holtzworth-Monroe & Stuart, 1994). Regardless of cause, all perpetrators of CCV control their partner and use a combination of emotional, psychological, verbal, physical, economic, and sexual violence to maintain the control. Typical emotional abuse includes cursing, humiliating, screaming, isolation from family and friends, checking up on the whereabouts of the victim partner, monitoring phone calls and mail, threatening to harm children and pets, and controlling all the money. It is also hypothesized that many perpetrators of CCV have personality disorders.

Again, as noted previously, this type of violence is the most severe and is most likely to result in serious injuries, with a higher level of risk after separation. When confronted with this type of violence, it is critical for the evaluator to do a risk assessment that includes determining the risk of ongoing violence. Factors that increase this risk include the following:

- Past violence and abuse
- Emotional dependency

- Relationship problems
- A history of control
- Mental health problems
- Substance abuse problems
- Threats and fantasies of serious harm
- Availability of weapons
- Obsessive attitudes and behaviors
- Disregard or contempt for authority
- The existence of a recent stressor

It is critical for evaluators, when faced with dynamics of domestic violence, especially the dynamics of CCV, to assess for lethality and continued risk. Gathering data about these risk factors may help in determining which families are more likely than others to erupt into more serious and harmful violence. While the absence of these risk factors does not mean that there is no risk, the presence of one or more of these factors significantly increases the risk of ongoing violence within a family.

## Separation Instigated Violence (SIV)

The third major type of violence is referred to as Separation Instigated Violence. As its name suggests, this type of violence occurs when a couple has problems at the time of separation *but has no prior history of any type of violence.* In these families, not only has there been no prior violence, but neither partner describes coercive, controlling, or intimidating behaviors (e.g., J. Kelly & Johnson, 2008). Like the SCV couples, the SIV couples seem to have problems with short-term impulse control and anger, as the stress of separating seems to lead to the violent behaviors. Yet, unlike either of the two previous groups, the violence represents an *atypical* loss of self-control. Additionally, while the SCV couple will typically acknowledge the past violence, for the SIV couple, the perpetrators of this violence (both male and female) not only acknowledge the violence, but they are often embarrassed, bewildered, and ashamed of their uncharacteristic actions. Like the SCV couple, but unlike the CCV couple, the SIV couple will typically comply with court orders and neither partner is fearful of the other.

Finally, while the SCV parents tend to have significant parenting problems, largely due to a long history of impulse control and anger management problems, and the CCV parents have significant parenting problems due to the problems with power and control (to be elaborated upon later), the SIV parents tend to have fewer parenting problems. In fact, not only are the parents ashamed of their actions, their children are often bewildered by the actions of their parents, and may exhibit signs of posttraumatic stress disorder (PTSD) due to exposure to the shock of their parents' uncharacteristically violent behavior.

# Approaching the Family's Domestic Violence Issues

At this point, I hope it is obvious that violence within the family can take many forms. For CCV families, the physical abuse can include behaviors such as hitting, kicking, biting, slapping, spitting, pushing, shoving, pulling hair, throwing or breaking things, and other forms of physical abuse. More harmful violence can include stabbing, shooting, actions that lead to internal injuries, use of weapons, and strangling. Additionally, as described earlier, there is often emotional, psychological, verbal, economic, and potentially sexual violence in CCV families. Violence is most devastating to the victim when several of these patterns are combined. The victim and children in such families live in a chronic state of intimidation and fear that can be debilitating. Even when the physical violence has diminished, continued threats of such violence, with occasional acting out, is perhaps the most traumatic for children and families. When there is a blend of psychological, physical, economic, and other violence that is perpetrated in an intermittent fashion over time, often with little or no apparent cause or warning, the abuse is perhaps the most devastating and overwhelming.

With CCV, it is rare to find violence that is mutual. Mutual violence occurs only in SCV and SIV families. Again, as noted already, the victim in CCV tends to live in more fear, and is usually threatened and intimidated by the actions of the perpetrator of the coercive, controlling behaviors.

# Parenting Problems of CCV Domestic Violence Parents

## Perpetrators

According to many sources, perpetrators of CCV violence have a number of significant problems in their parenting (e.g., Bancroft & Silverman, 2002). While not absolute, the risk of the following parenting problems is much greater for the primary perpetrators of CCV violence:

- Uses coercive discipline tactics, including physical abuse of child
- Is alternately overly permissive and rigidly authoritarian
- Reverses roles with child erratically
- Violates child's emotional boundaries and may perpetrate sexual abuse
- Emotionally abuses the child with mind games, put-downs, and social isolation
- May encourage immoral and criminal behaviors in the child
- May abduct or threaten to abduct child

- Shows lack of empathy for the impact on child of exposure to the violence
- Is intolerant of developmentally appropriate behavior or "special needs"
- Demands that child demonstrate affection and loyalty
- Uses access to coerce or harass other parent
- Rewards child for rejecting/punishing the other parent
- Is unable to focus on child's needs
- Has limited awareness of child's personality, preferred activities, achievements, and the like
- Has angry outbursts, breakdowns into rage, especially when discussing child's situation
- Denies child's expression of ideas, feelings, in favor of own
- Is convinced that all child's feelings/needs are either identical to own or manipulated by other parent
- Has impulsive responses, with occasionally odd or bizarre remarks about child

The child custody evaluator will be looking for evidence of these types of parenting problems, along with the potential strengths of the parent, when there are allegations of domestic violence.

## Victims

Similarly, victims of CCV violence are at risk of experiencing potential parenting problems (e.g., Jaffe, Johnston, Crooks, & Bala, 2008). These potential parenting problems include the following:

- Anxiety, depression, PTSD symptoms
- May use drugs/alcohol to numb pain
- Preoccupied with demands of the abuser
- Physically and emotionally exhausted and unavailable
- Less warm, more permissive, or coercive and power assertive
- Role-reversal with child
- Unable to protect child from abusive partner
- Brainwashed by abuser to accept that child is abused
- Lacks confidence in parenting/poor self-esteem
- Difficulty managing children (especially boys)
- Acts irrationally or with seemingly poor judgment

Parenting problems and poor parenting practices are common in both parents when domestic violence occurs, especially in the CCV type of violence.

Again, just as with the perpetrators of violence, when evaluating the victims of CCV it is important not only to look for evidence of these risks, but also for the strengths that the parent brings to the role of parenting.

# Gathering the Data

## History of the Family's Domestic Violence

The first step in differentiating between these types of families is taking a good history. It is important to get a separate history from each parent about all aspects of the marital relationship. Because so many parents (both victims and perpetrators) are good at hiding family violence, I believe that the history of conflict and the potential for violence needs to be explored in all evaluations, not only when it has been alleged by one of the parents. It is important to ask questions that will elicit information about the nature and extent of any violence, whether physical, emotional, economic, sexual, or any other type.

Even when there are no corroborating documents (e.g., police reports, medical reports, etc.), allegations of abuse should be taken seriously and thoroughly investigated. In custody evaluations, it is common to hear disparate stories from each parent, and it may be difficult to sort out the truth until a rather complete picture is generated. Women tend to overreport their violent behavior and men tend to underreport their violence (Hanks, 1992). At times, there will be police and medical reports, statements from therapists and others, pictures of injuries, taped threats, or other clear evidence that may help the evaluator in determining "the truth of the family." In other instances, however, there may be none of the above, and sorting out these truths may be more difficult. Lack of collateral evidence does not mean that violence has not occurred, but collateral documents should always be reviewed before forming an opinion on the veracity of the allegations. Psychological testing may also be useful. While such testing cannot confirm or refute an allegation of abuse, it can shed some light on the personality dynamics of the parents that may also be used in forming an opinion on truth.

In the individual interviews with each parent, you will need to ask questions that help gather information about the pattern of abuse, any trigger events, and the first, most recent, and worst of such incidents. When emotional abuse is alleged, ask questions to elicit information about violence, physical aggressions, or assaults on a person or object. In some families, intimidation is ongoing and severe, and there does not need to be ongoing physical violence to exacerbate the intimidation within the family. It is important to remember that victims of violence may exhibit symptoms associated with PTSD, giving less coherent and more emotionally charged histories. Some violent acts may not be perceived by either party as violent. Other symptoms of the victim may include incapacitating depression, being angry at the children, and being traumatized by the children when they act violently.

Look for patterns and history that help differentiate between families and whether there is a risk of ongoing assault. The most robust predictor of violence is past behavior, which is much more useful than personality traits. You want to know the age of the perpetrator at the first offense and whether or not the person is currently on, or has a history of, probation or parole. A history of probation failures is a positive indicator of future risk, as is the involvement of other agencies (e.g., Child Protective Services). Check criminal histories, if allowed in your jurisdiction, and look for charges of abuse, assaults, and the like. Get copies of any restraining orders and the documentation that supported the issuance of the restraining order, because they are likely to provide specific data regarding the abuse. With CCV families, there is greater risk of future violence when violence has been long term, there has been no treatment or interventions, the perpetrator externalizes blame and/or denies problems, and the perpetrator focuses on the victim.

On the other hand, there is a lower risk of renewed violence in CCV families when there is acknowledgment of the violence, guilt and remorse that focus on the impact on the victim and/or children, responsibility for violent behavior, empathy for the effect of the violence on the children, awareness of children's needs, an understanding that the abuse has served to maintain control in the relationship, and a motivation to change.

If there has been violence, it is important to differentiate among the types outlined previously. Finally, as mentioned earlier, it is important to assess for risks of lethality. If the evaluator sees a risk for ongoing violence and assesses for lethality, the evaluator can provide the family and the court with direction to reduce the violence and meet the needs of the children.

## Specific Questions to Ask Parents

There are a number of questions that evaluators might ask to elicit a better understanding of the violence issues. Some questions are obvious and directly connected to the issue of family violence. Others are designed to get an understanding of the parents' empathy and attitudes about themselves. Some are related to specific incidents. Possible questions include the following:

- Describe the first, the most recent, and the worst incidents of violence between you and the other parent.
- How did your parents deal with conflict? What did you see?
- How do you think your child feels when you and your spouse are angry (or violent) with each other?
- What do you like most about your child?
- Describe a tender moment with your child.
- When was the last tender moment with your child?
- When was the last time your child got angry at you? How was it handled?
- When was the last time you got angry at your child? How was it handled?
- Give five adjectives to describe your childhood. Why did you pick them?
- Define discipline and what it means to you.
- Has your child ever tried to intervene in your fights? Has your child ever tried to call the police? What happened?

- Has your child ever been directly threatened or injured? How?
- Have you or your spouse ever blamed the fight on your child?
- Has your child ever been threatened with loss of toys or pets or told to keep secrets?
- Has your child ever been forced to watch abuse?
- Has your child ever been abducted to gain compliance by the other parent?
- Is your child having school problems, especially being frequently tired in school?

For specific incidents about domestic violence, ask:

- What did the child see? Hear? Do?
- How close was the child to the violence?
- Did your child hide, flee, or try to intervene?

## The Children in These Families

A critical issue with domestic violence is the exposure of children to the violence. Such exposure can include but is not limited to seeing the violence, hearing the violence, seeing the effects of the violence (e.g., broken dishes, hole in the wall, bruises, etc.), or even just noticing the tension following the violent outbursts. Even when children are not direct witnesses of violence, they may experience symptoms of posttraumatic stress, regression, vulnerability, and other forms of psychological injury. If abused themselves, they are likely to exhibit many of the signs commonly seen in abused children. However, many children who witness domestic violence between their parents but who are not themselves victims of abuse exhibit psychological symptoms as well. Many of these children are in love/hate relationships with both parents.

In families with more than one child, it is common for each child to have a different reaction to the violence and the specific responsive role taken by each child, which may alter the child's role within the family. One sibling may take care of the others, another sibling might take care of the mother, and another sibling might start acting like the perpetrator of the violence. Siblings may become abusive with one another, or may soothe each other. Violence is always overwhelming for children, and parents may or may not have the capacity to soothe the child. The severity of the violence is not directly connected to the child's experience of trauma. If the child does not see the violence and does not intervene, the trauma is more likely due to the child's vulnerability and perceptions than to the actual event itself.

These children need a differential assessment that helps in understanding their vulnerabilities and future needs. They typically exhibit a range of emotions, including hopelessness and guilt, rage, depression, vulnerability, hypervigilance, fear, and so on. Because the family violence may be a secret, it is important to speak to collateral sources who can provide information on the child's relationships with peers, parents, authority figures, and others. Talk to the teachers and find out if the child sleeps in school. Many of these children are hypervigilant at night and sleep during the day.

The two parents will often provide very different views of their children, and the evaluator will need to form her own opinion of the level of fear, insecurity, or pathology in these children. Because this population of children is at a high level of risk, a thorough, independent assessment of each child is critical. The assessment of the children in these families may also help in understanding the family's pattern of violence. Interviews with the children may provide the evaluator with necessary data to understand the family pattern of conflict.

Finally, look at the extent to which the children themselves are at risk. This might be a risk of child abuse, but it might also be a risk of abduction or threat by an angry and vindictive parent. Understand both the level of direct threat that the child is exposed to and the threat perceived by the child. In families with a history of domestic violence, it is not uncommon for children to express fear of being around a violent parent, and assessing the difference between the real risk and the child's perceived risk (if there is a difference) is important before formulating a custody and/or treatment plan for the family. The evaluator must assess and understand ways in which the child can feel more secure and less vulnerable, a task that will be important for protecting these children. By understanding the direct and indirect impact of family violence upon the children, by understanding the level of the child's psychological vulnerabilities, and by understanding the risk that these children are exposed to (either real or perceived), you can formulate a careful plan for access and custody, and treatment for the family.

# The Alphabet Soup of Data
# Used to Formulate Conclusions

In their article, Jaffe et al. (2008) identified a decision-tree process designed to help evaluators and judges formulate sound decisions for these families. They suggested consideration of a number of factors in determining whether or not there should be a primary parent or shared physical custody, whether or not there should be joint legal custody, and in more serious situations, whether there should be supervised or unsupervised access between children and parents who have been violent. They identified the "5 P's" and the "3 R's" that are critical for reaching these determinations. They are as follows:

## Pattern

The first "P" factor to consider is the pattern. As described earlier, CCV families have significantly greater risk after separation than do SIV and SCV families. Gathering the data to determine which type of violence is the first step in differentiating a parenting plan that has the least risks for future violence and is more likely to be in children's best interests.

## Potency

Potency refers to lethality. By gathering data to understand the risks of lethality (as outlined previously), the evaluator can help the court understand the potential short-term risks associated with having parents together at exchanges and the potential risks to children when spending unsupervised access with the perpetrator of the violence. Potency is a very important consideration.

## Primary Perpetrator

One of the key ingredients to understand when there are allegations of violence is whether or not there is one primary perpetrator or two perpetrators. While it is true that there may be more than one perpetrator of violence in SCV and SIV families, some of those families may have only one primary perpetrator. Additionally, as mentioned, it is critical to understand that in CCV families there likely is only one primary perpetrator. When there is only one primary perpetrator of violence, it is important to manage the ongoing access, taking into account the risks that are greater when there is one primary perpetrator as opposed to two.

## Parenting Problems

The fourth "P" factor is the quality of parenting by each of the parents. As is the case in all evaluations, it is critical to understand the quality of parenting. The list of parenting risks in both perpetrators and victims in CCV families previously identified in this chapter is a starting point for evaluating the potential risk factors for parents who engage in violent behaviors. Evaluators need to assess the quality of each parent's parenting in domestic violence families and factor this into the overall parenting plan.

## Perspective of the Child

The fifth "P" factor is the perspective of the child. It is important to understand what the child has experienced related to the family violence. It is important to know if the child is afraid, is refusing access, is estranged from a parent due to the history of exposure to the violence, or is in need of protection. Some children are immature and inconsistent in their stories and other children are reasonably mature and able to focus on their observations and feelings. Some children want to spend time with both parents and other children express concern about spending time with one of their parents. Understanding the child's feeling and fears is critical to creating an appropriate parenting plan for the children.

Within the Perspective of the Child are three more factors. These "R" factors are as follows:

### Reflective Functioning

This is related to empathy. How much can the adults reflect on the experiences of the child and understand what the child has been exposed to and experienced? Higher reflective functioning is consistent with lower risk of harm, if access is granted.

### Responsibility

Does a parent take responsibility for what has happened or blame the victim and children for the family violence? Parents who take responsibility are less likely to put children in harm's way. On the other hand, when parents do not take responsibility for their behavior, they cannot apologize to children and are likely to continue engaging in behaviors that are harmful to children.

### Repair

Children need to heal. The repair function is consistent with helping children heal. Parents who can express empathy and take responsibility for their behavior are likely to help the child repair the insecurities and vulnerabilities that were caused by the family violence.

# Using the PPPPP Analysis With the RRR Concepts to Reach a Decision About the Parenting Plan _____

> High potency violence, with a primary perpetrator and a pattern of CCV, especially with a child who is afraid, will result in significant restrictions in the parenting time.

Jaffe et al. (2008) suggest using these eight factors in reaching a decision about the parenting plan. The various options are along a continuum, ranging from limited or no access to open and complete access. At one end of the continuum, they suggest that a pattern of CCV, continued high potency, with one primary perpetrator, significant parenting problems, and a child who is afraid to be alone with that parent would lead to supervised or limited contact with that parent. There might be no contact if the child is extremely afraid and the parent takes no responsibility, cannot help the child heal, and lacks empathy for the impact of this violence and his behaviors on the child.

In the middle of the continuum, families engaged in SCV, where there is low potency, both parents equally involved in initiating the violence, fewer parenting problems by one parent and some problems by the other parent, and children who want contact with both parents, might have a plan in which the children spend quality time with each parent, but more time with the parent with fewer parenting problems. Additionally, in order to continue reducing any risk of anger problems surfacing in front of the children, it may be necessary to have the exchanges take place with some monitoring or in a public place, thus reducing the risk that conflict or violence will erupt at the exchange of the children. Additionally, those CCV parents who have gone through quality intervention programs and are prepared to help with the repair and healing for the children, where there is now a low risk of potency, might also be somewhere in the middle of the continuum.

> Low potency violence, without a primary perpetrator and no pattern of violence other than one incident of SIV, especially with two good parents and a child who wants to be with both parents, will result in no restrictions on parenting time.

At the other end of the continuum, parents who were both very involved parents with a history of healthy parenting, who had one incident of SIV, and where there is no concern about risk of future violence, with children who want quality time with both parents, might have a parenting plan with relatively equal, 50–50 custody.

## Therapeutic and Structural Interventions

In addition to the parenting plan, the evaluator will likely make some form of therapeutic recommendation. With primary perpetrators who engage in CCV, a 52-week batterers' program is currently seen as the best available strategy. While the research suggests that this model is effective for only about a third of participants (Gondolf, 2004), such a cognitive-behavioral intervention is designed to help perpetrators raise their awareness of precursors to their battering behaviors, recognize that violence is a choice they do not have to make, learn new ways of dealing with their impulses, and raise empathy for their victims and the children in these families.

For both parents who engage in SCV, especially when the violence is caused by anger problems and impulsive behaviors, a shorter anger management program may be the intervention of choice. Such a program will focus mostly on stress reduction techniques and teaching skills to help impulsive parents learn more appropriate outlets for their anger.

When impulse control problems and violence are secondary to a psychiatric problem or substance abuse, medication and/or treatment for the substance abuse or psychiatric problem would be indicated. Because many parents who become violent experience strong feelings of inadequacy, dependency, and vulnerability, psychotherapy may also be a useful adjunct. However, it is important to point out that therapy alone is usually not sufficient with primary perpetrators of CCV. These parents are likely to require a lengthy batterers' treatment program that is strongly focused on the issues of domestic violence.

For the adult victims of domestic violence, treatment is often needed to build ego functioning, help raise awareness around issues of domestic violence, reduce dependency, and improve self-esteem. Many of these victims do not know how to recognize when they are in danger. Therapy that focuses on the risks of violence is important to preclude or prevent involvement in future violent relationships. In SCV families in which there is mutual aggression and for families in which the violence appears to be separation-instigated and related to the postdivorce trauma, it is often helpful for both parents to participate in some form of anger management work. The goals of this work are to reduce the likelihood of provocation, increase the likelihood of empathy for one's children, and reduce the extent to which each parent contributes to the cycle of domestic violence. Just as the perpetrators of domestic violence might benefit from individual psychotherapy in conjunction with batterers' interventions, victims may need insight into how their own personal issues contribute to their victimization. Parenting classes may be necessary for many parents when violence has been a pattern in the family.

It is quite likely that the children in these families will benefit from individual or group psychotherapy. There is certainly evidence to support that they can benefit from group interaction to help normalize issues of divorce and help them focus on and understand issues of violence within the family. An example of such a program is Kid's Turn, a nonprofit program in the San Francisco Bay Area (Bolen, 1993). In this group program, children participate with each other in age-appropriate groups to understand their feelings associated with the dynamics of divorce and violence when they have experienced it, and how these issues affect friendships, relationships, and the like. At the same time, parents must meet in separate groups to learn about the impact of the conflicts on their children. Because many of these children are anxious and experience feelings of vulnerability and inadequacy, individual psychotherapy may be indicated.

For many of these children, reunification with the violent parent may be healthiest and safest if it occurs in therapeutic sessions in which the child can express his or her fears and feel reassured by the violent parent. Once the child recognizes that he or she is safe and the parent has taken responsibility for controlling the assaultive behavior, it will then be possible to begin unsupervised and increasingly frequent contact. In the most severe cases, therapeutic work is a necessity before any meaningful access can take place (Deutsch, 2008).

Finally, as indicated earlier, there is a strong need for a structural intervention in the form of a clear and direct court order. Just as with the alienated families described in the next chapter, many of these families benefit from some form of Special Master, Parent Coordinator, or case manager.

## THE BOTTOM LINE

As mentioned at the beginning of the chapter, these cases run the risk of getting out of control with significant harm coming to families. At the time that this chapter was written, a woman in Arizona was murdered by her husband, who then killed himself. Apparently, a few days before, the mother had gone to court to try to get permission to move out of state. While she had previously gotten a restraining order against the father, she apparently did not express to the judge the extent to which she feared for her life based on alleged threats by her husband. The judge was worried that, if he allowed her to move out of state, the children would no longer have any relationship with their father. He denied the request to move, and a few days later, two parents were dead.

A few years earlier, in Reno, Nevada, a woman was killed in her home and the family court judge was shot a short time later from a parking lot four blocks away from the court house (the judge has since recovered). This judge had angered the father with his ruling a few days earlier. Judges, evaluators, advocates, and parents all worry about such scenarios, and the judge who made the Arizona decision was being sharply criticized in the press, while the court system in Reno, which thought it had good security, was extremely concerned.

After working with these families for approximately 30 years, it is clear to me that humans will make mistakes. We do not have the ability to predict *which* parent will actually lose control and murder someone or *which* parent, even with significant risk factors present, will not. However, as evaluators, it is critical that we are thorough and try to gather the necessary information to differentiate the type of violence, to understand the risk factors associated with ongoing violence, gather data about the five "P" factors and the three "R" factors, and ultimately make the best set of recommendations we can based on our analysis of those data.

Finally, I hope that those who started the dialog at the Wingspread Conference are able to continue doing the necessary research to develop better screening tools that allow for more nuanced differentiation and will work to get the necessary resources to continue to improve safety for families with a history of violence. It is my understanding that a future issue of *Family Court Review* will focus on domestic violence and the research that has followed the Wingspread Conference. Much continues to be learned about these families and how to ensure safety for children and victims in CCV families and reasonable and structured access between parents and children in other families with a history of violence.

# 13 The Alienated Child[1]

Since 1980, when Wallerstein and Kelly first wrote about children who refused visitation with a parent, there has been considerable controversy about this topic. Much of the controversy exploded after Gardner coined the phrase "Parental Alienation Syndrome" (PAS) in 1987. Since that time, scholars have debated whether or not there is a syndrome related to parental alienation. Some have argued that there is no syndrome and that this is mostly a creation of Gardner's with no validity (Bruch, 2001; Isman, 1996; Wood, 1994). Others have argued that PAS does exist and that it is damaging to children (Lund, 1995; Rand, 1997a, 1997b; Warshak, 2001). Some have argued that the primary cause of children refusing to visit the other parent is found in the behavior of the aligned parent, the one the child enjoys spending time with (Gardner, 1995; Lampel, 1996), while others have argued that there are multiple causes that lead to children refusing contact with one parent (J. Kelly & Johnston, 2001; P. Stahl, 1999). There is also significant controversy over how to deal with alienation, with some arguing for a change in custody when alienation dynamics exist and others arguing for more caution. This chapter will address the multiple issues that child custody evaluators need to know to understand alienated children, focus on the assessment questions involved in these cases, and discuss potential remedies in these situations.

Gardner's early definition hypothesized that the primary cause of the child becoming alienated is the behavior of the aligned parent. His medical model suggested that if we have a child who is refusing visitation and a parent who is supporting that refusal, then we have parental alienation operating. This linear model, in which there is a single cause and an obvious effect, was a key component in his understanding of alienation. In contrast, a more comprehensive clinical model recognizes that multiple causes might contribute to an effect. In order to take the focus off of the parents and their behaviors and because it is hypothesized that multiple forces contribute to a child's alienation, J. Kelly and Johnston (2001) suggested the term "the alienated child" as a way of stating that children can become alienated not solely through the behaviors of the parent. By bringing the focus back to the child, as was done when Wallerstein and Kelly (1980) first discussed this phenomenon, their model suggests that the child's behavior and the multiple contributions to this behavior are more important than the single cause, which is the behavior and emotions of the aligned parent.

In a personal communication, J. Kelly (May 16, 2009) defined an alienated child as:

> One who persistently expresses strong, negative feelings (such as anger, hatred, contempt, and fear) and beliefs about his or her parent that do not accurately reflect the child's prior experience with that parent. This definition of "alienated child" does not include children who have experienced child abuse or family violence. Children who have been abused or exposed to family violence may become traumatized and/or emotionally estranged from the abusive parent, and may resist contact with that parent. These children would NOT be described as "alienated children."
>
> In rejecting a parent, an alienated child demonstrates contemptuous and aggressive views and behaviors that are developmentally inappropriate and significantly disproportionate to the child's actual experience with the rejected parent. The beliefs and behaviors are typically irrational, distorted, or exaggerated, and these children develop significant and long-lasting difficulties in their emotional development and interpersonal relationships. The expression of strong dislike or anger from a child toward a parent should never be used, in the absence of other evidence, to determine whether a child has been abused. Both mothers and fathers may be rejected by children, and both boys and girls may become alienated children, most typically between the ages of 8 and 16.

For purposes of this chapter, I will incorporate J. Kelly's definition of the alienated child.

## Contributions to the Child's Alienated Response

J. Kelly and Johnston (2001) hypothesized that the child's response of alienation occurs as a result of many factors, each of which contributes a portion of the force that results in the child's response. These can include the following:

- The personality of the aligned parent and that parent's negative beliefs and behaviors that reinforce the child's aligned response. This is consistent with Gardner's (1995) hypothesis that children are likely to respond in an alienated way when there is a hostile parent who is very critical toward the other parent.

- The personality and responses of the rejected parent, both historically in the relationship as well as in response to the child's initial alienation.

- Because alienation occurs within the context of the divorce, a more conflicted divorce and intense litigation can also contribute to the child's response, especially when the child is exposed to the litigation and the conflict by one or both parents.

- The marital history, especially when there has been intense marital conflict, or when there are intense emotions around the separation (such as shame or humiliation).

- The myriad of aligned professionals and/or extended family and friends who contribute their own pressures on the parents and/or the child to resist contact with one parent.

- Siblings can also be a factor, especially when an older sibling refuses contact with a parent, as this can contribute to a younger sibling becoming afraid or resistant.

- Finally, a critical component to whether or not the child will become alienated is found in the child's age, cognitive capacity, temperament, and vulnerability. It is hypothesized that children under age 7 are less likely to become alienated because they are less able to "hold onto" the resistance when they are with the otherwise-rejected parent, but that older children can more easily become alienated and will often take a strong position, primarily because of the forces noted above.

In addition to this multiple causation, J. Kelly and Johnston (2001) hypothesized that there is a continuum in the relationship between children and each parent that may typically range from an equal attachment with each parent, through an affinity or an alignment between a child and one parent to an estrangement or alienation from one parent. A child who previously had significant problems in a relationship with one parent (e.g., as a result of child abuse or family dynamics that included domestic violence) and who refuses contact would be considered estranged but not alienated. Such estrangement is usually seen as a healthy response to an untenable situation.

> Almost like physics, there are many forces that have the potential to contribute to a child becoming alienated from a parent and resisting contact with that parent.

In contrast, it is considered pathological alienation when a child who previously had a healthy attachment with each parent is now rejecting one parent as a result of some combination of these forces. Thus, any consideration or evaluation of family dynamics to understand a child's rejection of a parent must consider the family history and the history of the child's relationship with each parent. Finally, regardless of one's conceptualization of this phenomenon, most scholars view this type of alienation as being pathological.

# Parent Contributions to the Development of Alienation

Divorce research suggests that it is common, especially in the early stages of divorce, for both parents to engage in inappropriate behavior, especially behavior in which the parents are hostile toward and critical of each other before, during, and after separation. In high-conflict families (see Chapter 11), this increases the likelihood that children will hear both subtle and overt derogatory messages from one or both parents about the other parent. It appears that the parents who overtly or unwittingly alienate their child against the other parent are most likely to be angry, emotionally fragile, and potentially dependent on their children for self-esteem (Friedlander & Walters, 2010). Many of these parents have poor impulse control and rather rigid black-or-white-type beliefs. While Gardner (1995) hypothesized that some of these parents are psychotic, it is my opinion that the parent who has poor boundaries with his or her child and who tends to be rather inflexible in relationships and exhibit either rigid thinking or emotional fragileness is the most likely contributor to the child's alienation. Especially in the first year of divorce, but lasting much longer for some parents, it can be very difficult for one parent to forgive the other. This is more likely when one parent is rejected in favor of a new partner or spouse. Along with that, some parents love their children conditionally, so those children get the message that if they love the other parent, this parent will not love them. This sets up, within the child, the untenable position of having to choose between parents.

As mentioned previously, it is not only the personality and behaviors of the aligned parent that contribute to the child's rejection, but also the behaviors and personality of the rejected parent (Drozd & Olesen, 2004; Johnston, Walters, & Olesen, 2005). In my experience, it is not uncommon for rejected parents to have limited parenting skills and a tenuous relationship with their child prior to separation and to claim alienation when the child's reaction is more consistent with the alignment noted earlier. These rejected parents also have limited awareness of the ways in which their behavior has contributed to the child's rejection. I have seen numerous examples in which a relatively passive parent, in combination with a somewhat hostile and rejecting parent, will allow the angry parent to make the rules and create an environment in which children will resist contact with the rejected parent. When this process continues for some time, it increases the risk that the child will become more severely alienated. Thus, the rejected parent's passivity becomes a contributor to this dynamic.

> Both parents potentially contribute to the child's unwarranted rejection of one parent, and both parents must be included in any interventions designed to solve it.

The understanding of alienation and its components has grown a great deal recently, especially the extent to which both parents engage in behaviors and attitudes that foster the likelihood that a child will reject contact with a parent. *Family Court Review* devoted a special issue to the topic in January 2010. This issue identified some promising new approaches to consider when intervening with very severe rejection of a parent. More research is needed to understand the extent to which both parents contribute to the child's alienation and what to do about it. However, the child custody evaluator needs to focus on the attitudes and behaviors of both parents in order to understand each parent's contributions to the child's alienation. I will provide more information on the evaluation of alienation in the following discussion.

# Child Contributions to the Development of Alienation

Much has been written about children's reactions to conflict in divorce (Johnston & Roseby, 1997; Johnston, Roseby, & Kuehnle, 2009; P. Stahl, 1999). It is clear that some children can be overwhelmed by exposure to conflict and are at risk of experiencing significant regression. One form of this regression is referred to as splitting. Vertical splitting is normative developmentally, as very young children experience the sense of a good or bad parent and good or bad self. This typically occurs between the ages of 2 and 4, during the early stages of separation and individuation, until children develop some internal feelings of ambivalence. However, for children aged 7 and above, who are most susceptible to becoming alienated (J. Kelly & Johnston, 2001), this regression in splitting takes on a horizontal dimension, in which children tend to view one parent as all good and the other parent as all bad. For some children, taking sides in the war reduces their anxiety, even if it sets up unhealthy relationships with one of their parents.

Another contribution from the child can be the anxious attachment or hostile–dependent relationship between the child and one parent. Like the school-phobic child who refuses to attend school due to communication of the mother's anxiety to the child (Eisenberg, 1958), these children refuse to visit with one parent because of the communication of one parent's anxiety about that other parent to the child. For many of these children, there is an enmeshed quality to the relationship between the child and the aligned parent, and the child cannot have his or her own independent thoughts and feelings, especially toward the other parent.

Another potential source of the child's contribution lies in the need some children have to take emotional care of a parent. These children fear how the aligned parent might react if they visit the other parent, and they cling to the aligned parent to protect him or her.

> Children have many reasons for rejecting a parent, some based on legitimate reasons and some based on the forces that contribute to alienation.

The child's temperament is hypothesized to be a contributing source, as well, because some children are simply more anxious and have difficulty adjusting to change.

Some children reject a parent due to the realistic estrangement associated with the abuse or very poor parenting of the rejected parent (Drozd & Olesen, 2004). Except when the rejection is understandable, the rejection of a parent is always harmful to children. More research is needed to understand the extent to which children's emotions contribute to their alienation, but the research to date clearly suggests harm is the result (Baker, 2005a, 2005b, 2007a).

# Typical Alienated Behaviors in Children

While attitudes are important in understanding a child's alienation, understanding the child's behaviors is critical. We can expect to see some or all of the following behaviors in children who are alienated:

- A near or complete rejection of one parent in favor of the other. While there may be some ambivalence in this, as the alienation becomes more extreme, the child becomes more absolute in his or her refusal to see the other parent.
- A fusion of thinking in which the child and the aligned parent think alike. The child even use the terms *us* or *we* to define attitudes and beliefs, rather than *I*. This is especially likely in those situations in which the alienation is related to an enmeshed relationship with the aligned parent.
- Superficial and trumped-up or exaggerated complaints about the rejected parent that have little or no substance
- Inconsistent and contradictory statements and behaviors. For example, at times, when in the presence of the aligned parent, the child may be vehement in rejection of the other parent. At other times, when in the presence of the rejected parent, the child may be ambivalent and act in friendly and positive ways.
- A strong tendency to become over-involved in the adult issues of the divorce. This is often parent driven, such as when parents tell their child about issues like child support, who has caused the divorce, and so forth. Some children are enlisted as spies to report information about the rejected parent back to the aligned parent. At other times, this is child driven, as some children go out of their way to look at court papers, listen in on phone conversations between adults, and the like.
- A tendency, when confronted about why they are rejecting a parent, to be vague in their reasons and possibly just say that the parent is "mean." They tend to refuse to answer specific questions about the history of the relationship and to stay focused on the exaggerated complaints.
- In interviews, using the same phrases or expressions as the aligned parent. This is consistent with the merged thinking often found between such parents and children.

- Acting as spies for the aligned parent. I know of children who were told to search a parent's computer for information on bank accounts. In the same vein, alienated children are often asked to keep secrets from the rejected parent. This contributes to the child's anxiety and need to choose between the parents.
- Often, similar to the views of the aligned parent, seeing the world in rigid and all-or-nothing ways. Thus, one parent becomes all good and the other becomes all bad.

While there are other examples in the literature, these are the most common ways that an alienated child will behave.

## Emotional Impact of Alienation on Children

A great deal has been written about the impact of alienation on children (Baker, 2005a; Johnston & Roseby, 1997; Johnston, Walters, & Friedlander, 2001; J. Kelly & Johnston, 2001). It is beyond the scope of this chapter to go into depth about this, but it is important to briefly summarize these negative effects. When children are caught up in the midst of this conflict and become alienated, the emotional response can be devastating to the child's development. The degree of damage to the child's psyche will vary depending on the intensity of the alienation and the age and vulnerability of the child. However, the impact is never benign because of the fact of the child's distortions and confusions. It is my view that the distortion of history and the distortion of the relationship with one parent is potentially the most damaging effect on children.

In addition to this, alienated children are at risk of developing disturbances in many of their relationships. They often become manipulative and feel overly powerful. They may be resistant to authority and act out at school. Some of these children may use this manipulation to extort the aligned parent because of this manipulation. As they get older, there is a strong likelihood that they will develop a disturbance in their identity. None of this can be healthy for the child who is caught up in the conflict between his or her parents and who becomes alienated from one parent.

One of the most intriguing questions evaluators, judges, and attorneys need to consider is why some children are resistant to the pressures of such alienation and keep positive contact with both parents, and why some children are more vulnerable to these pressures and reject one parent. In my experience, the children who are most resistant to becoming alienated:

- Accept the reality of the otherwise rejected parent
- Have enough contact with the other parent
- May have an older sibling or someone else that the child respects who is not so alienated

- Are not too vulnerable emotionally; they likely have a healthy temperament
- Have a healthy self-esteem that makes them less susceptible to alienation
- Have someone, such as the judge or Parent Coordinator, who has taken a strong role in countering the alienated position and undermining the process of alienation
- Have an otherwise-rejected parent who is reasonably self-protective and who can openly discuss relevant issues with the child in a way that is sensitive to the child and the other parent's feelings. Such a parent does not counterattack. Oftentimes, these rejected parents need help and coaching on how to act in a self-protective manner without fueling the child's conflicts.

In contrast, the children who are most susceptible to the forces that result in alienation:

- May be passive and dependent, have a difficult temperament, or have low self-esteem
- May experience a great deal of secondary gain from their alienated symptoms
- Are likely to have a tenuous, anxious, or hostile–dependent and fragile relationship with the aligned parent
- Are likely to have been conditionally loved
- May have other symptoms exacerbating their emotions, including but not limited to sleep or eating disorders, drug abuse, depression, psychosomatic problems, confusion, and school problems
- May be self-centered, have exceptionally strong feelings of entitlement, and are used to getting their way

> Regardless of cause, a child who is truly alienated and rejecting a parent is at risk for serious psychological problems.

Again, as with the other issues, more research is needed to understand the role that children's temperament and these other features affect the likelihood that a particular child will become alienated.

## Dynamics of the Larger System

As noted in Chapter 11 on high conflict, other forces outside the family often contribute to children becoming alienated. In addition to the parent and child dynamics that contribute to the development of alienation, relatives and friends of the family often join in the conflict in what Janet Johnston has called "tribal warfare" (Johnston & Campbell, 1988). They may help to stir up the conflict and contribute to the extent that a child is embroiled in the middle of it. While therapists are often helpful in reducing alienation symptoms, there are times when therapists take a unitary view of the problems and reinforce the notion that one parent is good and the other is bad (L. Greenberg, Gould, Gould-Saltmann, & Stahl, 2003). A third possible contributor outside of the family is the excessive litigation by attorneys and the extent to which the legal professionals add to the polarizing in the case. Family law matters are usually polarizing to some extent, and the polarizing in alienation cases tends to mirror the polarizing in the family.

Many observers recognize that the court system takes too long to resolve issues, especially for high-conflict families. When high-conflict families experience significant delays in judicial decision-making or when court-ordered evaluations take too long, families tend to become polarized and alienation dynamics flourish. Finally, at times it appears that the entire family law system is focused on pathology and blame rather than problem solving and conflict resolution (American Bar Association, 2000). Such dynamics can create a fertile environment for alienation to develop in a family that might otherwise resolve their differences.

## Evaluation of Alienation

In any evaluation of allegations of alienation, the process is a complex one (Lee & Olesen, 2001; P. Stahl, 1999). Evaluators believe that alienation of children is certainly possible and should be taken seriously (Baker, 2007b). At a minimum, it is important to focus on the following potential components:

- The attitude, beliefs, and behaviors of the aligned parent
- The attitude, beliefs, and behaviors of the rejected parent
- The overall functioning of the child, including temperament and psychological, emotional, and academic functioning. Consideration of the child's peer relationships, extracurricular interests and activities, and support systems is also important.
- The history of the family relationships. This needs to include an assessment of marital conflict, domestic violence, and abuse. Also to be evaluated is the history of the child's attachment to and relationship with each parent and the extent to which each parent has legitimately supported the relationship with the other parent.
- The level of parental cooperation or conflict and the extent to which the child is exposed to and brought into the middle of the conflict

In 1999, I described a number of issues to focus on when evaluating these cases. As mentioned at that time, a comprehensive evaluation focuses on all aspects of the family relationships. When a referral is made alleging parental alienation or if the evaluator suspects that such a process exists within the family, it is important for the evaluator to focus on several key elements. Not surprisingly, there are special dynamics to evaluate in the aligned parent, in the alienated parent, and most particularly in the child who is the object of the alienation. Observation of the child with each parent will be a critical element of the evaluation process.

## The Aligned Parent

Though severely alienating behavior is fairly rare, I have found that it is quite easy to observe and recognize. Such signs of alienation include direct interference with visits, giving the alienated parent false information about school and the child's activities, and making inflammatory or critical statements against the alienated parent. Such parents may tell the evaluator:

- "I tell the kids that they don't have to go with their father if they don't want to; they always have a terrible time over there."
- "Everything she says is crazy; the kids simply can't trust her."
- "The kids know that we can't do anything because he never pays his child support."
- "We hate it when she has her boyfriend over."

In each of these examples, the evaluator notices that the aligned parent makes absolute statements ("always" or "never") or merges his or her feelings with those of the children ("we hate"). These are two of the features that are most pronounced in parents who foster the rejection of the other parent, that is, the extremes of splitting (as observed in the absolute statements) and the problems with boundaries (as observed in the merged feelings statements).

When the evaluator hears such things, it is important to ask for specific examples from both of the parents and the children. If absolute statements are made, the evaluator needs to determine whether the aligned parent can be more positive or can differentiate between the child's feelings and his or her own. These examples will either provide legitimate reasons for the feelings (e.g., dad is truly not paying child support, or there are specific visitation problems for the children when mother's boyfriend is present), or they will reflect the polarized feelings of the aligned parent. It is best if the evaluator's questions are subtle and less obvious, but if the parent is unrelenting, more direct questions will need to be asked.

The evaluator will also want to understand whether or not the parent can recall more positive aspects of the relationship between the child and the rejected parent. In situations where alienation is alleged but not occurring, it may very well be that the rejected parent has never really had a good relationship with the child, and the aligned parent can provide a detailed description of the problems in the relationship. On the other hand, if alienation is occurring, the evaluator can usually pinpoint a time frame or period in which a change occurred in the relationship between the child and the rejected parent. This change is usually associated with an intense emotional reaction on the part of the aligned parent (e.g., the discovery of a new girlfriend) among many other precipitating factors, including emotional need states within the aligned parent.

More difficult to assess, however, are the subtle behaviors and statements often made by aligned parents. It is unlikely that the evaluator will be able to determine whether alienation exists without exploring the concerns of the alleged aligned parent. For example, a father might report that the mother always refers to him as "Mr. Smith" (his last name) to the children. The evaluator will look for clues that this is occurring and will likely ask questions that include the phrase "their dad" to see how mother responds. The evaluator might even ask the mother, "How do you think it affects the children when you refer to their father as 'Mr. Smith'?" Usually, an aligned parent will have no awareness of how those behaviors affect the children and is likely to respond with a statement reflecting the merged feelings, such as, "Well, we know he's never been a very good dad, so they don't mind."

Because the subtle signs can be numerous, it is important to follow up on all concerns raised by the rejected parent. Most alienating behavior will fall into one or more of the following categories:

- Unbalanced accounts of behaviors—talking in extremes and absolutes
- Merging of feelings between aligned parent and children, for example, "We don't like the Tuesday night dinner visit"
- Denial of the relationship between the child and the alienated parent, as if she or he has no right to it any more
- Behaviors that directly and/or indirectly thwart the relationship between the child and the other parent
- Intrusive behaviors such as frequent phone calls (e.g., two to three times per day or more) to the other parent's home during visits
- Encouraging the children to act as spies during visits
- Informing children about adult issues, such as child support, reasons for the divorce, and so forth
- Forcing the children to be messengers of communications
- Derogatory and blaming statements about the other parent
- Tribal warfare in which other family members or family friends get brought into the battle between the parents

Because alienating behaviors fall along a continuum, the evaluator must look for and explore any indicators that are found of the alienation. The evaluator will notice that the aligned parent is often very angry, vindictive, vengeful, and extremely labile or extreme in views, and struggles with emotional boundaries. In evaluating the aligned parent, it is critical to understand the rationale for those behaviors and what causes them. It could be that the alienating behaviors are the direct result of either *actual* or *perceived* shortcomings in the rejected parent. If real problems in the rejected parent are found, the evaluator will make recommendations to correct them. However, if the aligned parent is acting on the basis of perceived problems, it will be important to recommend interventions that encourage the aligned parent to alter his or her perceptions and to recognize the many ways that the alienation is negatively affecting the children.

## The Rejected Parent

For the rejected parent, there is a potentially different set of dynamics to explore. Rejected parents tend to fall into two groups. There is a group of parents who had a healthy relationship with the child prior to the separation, but who are now being shut out of the child's life. These parents are truly being rejected by the child by the behavior or attitudes of the aligned parent, along with the other forces previously identified. The second group of rejected parents are those who claim that alienation is the significant source of the problems with their children, but who tend to be fairly defensive, are avoidant in relationships, externalize blame, and have a very difficult time seeing their own role in problems with the children. Such parents are often very controlling and powerful and are used to having things their own way in their relationships. After separation, they expect their relationship with the children to be *as they want it to be.* These parents are often less child centered and have less empathy than others. When the relationship does not work out the way they want, they are quick to blame the other parent for alienating the children and for creating problems with their children. I will discuss these two groups separately.

### Rejected Parents Who Previously Had a Healthy Relationship With Their Child

Parents in this category seem to be truly rejected and have children who are alienated as defined by J. Kelly (2009) earlier. These parents are often insightful, able to reflect on a wide variety of possibilities for their children's behavior, and are willing to look inward to find a source of some problems. Typically, these parents have had a history in which they were close to their children and actively participated in their children's lives and activities. These parents can have a nurturing quality, though there may be a tendency toward some passivity and difficulty dealing with overwhelming emotions. Such parents may accept some blame for the divorce, especially if the parent is the one who initiated the divorce. These dynamics provide a fertile atmosphere for the alienation to flourish.

In these families, the aligned parent is likely to experience extreme and overreactive emotions, and the rejected parent is usually more passive, nurturing, and sensitive. The rejected parent is often overwhelmed and does not know what to do when faced with the aligned parent's attitudes and behaviors. Rather than confront the aligned parent or the child, these rejected parents have a tendency to detach. This detachment reinforces the aligned parent's vengeful attitudes and behaviors, and the detachment is often bewildering to the child, reinforcing the child's distorted thinking and rejection. In my experience, these rejected parents may exhibit sensitivity to the children, nurturing behavior, passivity, insight, and a tendency to be overwhelmed with intense emotions.

### Rejected Parents Who Previously
### Had a Poor Relationship With Their Child

On the other hand, many of these parents have had very little to do with their children prior to the separation and divorce. They may have been workaholics who came home late at night. They may have been fairly self-centered individuals who were more involved in their own activities than the activities of their children. Many of these parents may quickly become involved in a new relationship and are insensitive to the feelings of their children about this new relationship. Rather than recognize that their children may have their own, independent feelings about the parent's behavior or the parent's new partner, they are quick to blame the other parent for the children's feelings. Blame is common for these parents.

When exploring the history of the relationship between these parents and their children, we often find that there is a general absence of a quality relationship in the formative years of development. There is a superficial nature to the relationship caused by years of neglect or a history in which the other parent was truly the "primary parent" in the marital relationship. These parents may show up for the "Kodak moments," but do so in a more self-centered way, often for their own enjoyment and interest rather than to participate with their children. These parents may report active involvement in activities such as coaching the children's sports, yet upon further exploration, we find the child often felt pushed into these activities and felt distant from the parent-coach. Often these parents are not even that interested in the child after the divorce. They claim alienation primarily as a way of continuing the control and blame that they exhibited during the marriage. In parents who claim alienation but are more likely to be the cause of the rift with their children, we look for indicators like defensiveness, control, externalization of blame, self-centeredness, and superficiality.

Thus, both parents have a central role in the potential development of the alienation. Their respective contributions need to be understood before the evaluator can objectively understand the nature of the alienation and related allegations.

## The Children

Perhaps the most critical part of an evaluation in which there are allegations of alienation is understanding the children and their functioning. J. Kelly and Johnston (2001) observed that most children who become a party to the alienation process are in the age range of 7 to 15 years. It appears that many child variables contribute to whether or not they become entangled in the alienation behaviors of their parents. These variables may include the child's temperament, ego functioning, prior relationships with each parent, the child's immediate reaction to the separation of the parents, and the child's general level of anxiety and distress. Evaluators need to look at all of these factors. In evaluating the nature of the child's current relationship with each parent, I would suggest evaluating whether:

- The child's alignment with one parent is due to shared interests
- There is a history of problems in the child's relationship with either parent
- The child loves both parents and has little or no preference between the parents
- The child is being alienated from one parent largely because of the actions of the alienating parent
- The child is alienated from one parent because of that parent's own actions and inability to understand or improve the relationship with the child

As with the adults, these children fall along a continuum. Questions directed toward the children are designed to help the evaluator understand the nature and severity of the child's negative feelings toward the rejected parent. One clue that suggests the child is alienated rather than estranged, is when the child uses words that are identical to those of the aligned parent. Another indicator of alienation is when the child expresses moral indignation and outrage that seems more appropriate for a parent's feelings. Similarly, if the child uses absolute statements, such as "always" or "never," when criticizing the other parent, this is a clue that alienation is occurring. Statements such as the following would suggest that alienation is occurring:

- "Things have been terrible since he left us."
- "He's always mean to us."
- "I can't believe she left us for that jerk."
- "He used to be nice, but now he's always with *her* [the new girlfriend]."

On the other hand, some children tell very moving stories of how they have not liked or have been fearful of the rejected parent for a long time. They can give specific details of abuse, angry behavior, and more, prior to separation. These children often feel relieved when their parents get divorced because they are now free of those problems. The differential understanding will come from the child's clear account of inappropriate behavior, detachment in the relationship, and a convincing sense of real problems (as opposed to the moral indignation of the alienated child).

When we listen to these children in those cases where the child is detached from the rejected parent, there is little evidence that these children are put in the middle by the aligned parent. Rather, there may be a sadness in these children, who wish (or may have wished in the past) for a different quality to the relationship with the rejected parent. Many of these children have observed significant spousal abuse during the marriage or have observed one parent being controlling and hostile to the other parent. It is the sadness and ambivalence about the lack of a relationship that is one of the key differential indicators that these children, while certainly aligned with one parent and rejecting of the other, are not being alienated.

For both of these types of children—those who are alienated because of the multiple causes described already as well as those who are primarily aligned because of significant problems in the past relationship with the rejected parent—there is usually a desire to have little or no contact with the rejected parent. Alienated children usually have no initial or ongoing legitimate reason for this, and their stated reasons appear on the surface to be flimsy, although they believe adamantly in their justifications. Those children who have a legitimate reason for being aligned against a parent are usually able to articulate this.

Another differential in these children often emerges during the joint interviews and observations with each parent. The alienated child is usually enmeshed in the relationship with the aligned parent, often experiencing an anxious, insecure, or hostile–dependent relationship with that parent. These children may feel a need to emotionally care for the aligned parent, and the refusal of visits is a manifestation of that need. The enmeshed and/or hostile-dependent nature of the relationship, or the "parentification" of the child, is usually apparent during the observations with the aligned parent. In conjoint interviews with the rejected parent, these children will often be cold and indifferent to that parent, showing little ambivalence or remorse for their absolute unwillingness to maintain a relationship. In less severe alienation, if the joint interview is long enough, the evaluator might see a shift, or softening, of the child's alienated stance toward those parents with whom they previously had a positive relationship. It is almost as if they finally allow themselves to have fun when they think no one is noticing.

In contrast, a child who is aligned but not alienated usually has a fun and playful relationship with the aligned parent, the boundaries are clear, and the relationship does not appear enmeshed. When seen with the rejected parent, the sadness and ambivalence are more obvious. These children want the rejected parent to take responsibility for the problems in the relationship. They might want to rekindle the relationship, but only if the rejected parent shows some insight and understanding of the child's feelings.

## Other Reasons for Alignment With One Parent: What to Look for in the Children

There are two other dynamics that are important to look for in these children. First, many children seem to be aligned with one parent primarily because of shared interests or a "goodness of fit" in the personality dynamics with one parent. There is a natural affinity between an active, sports-oriented child and her active, sports-oriented parent. Other children may have a stronger affinity with the parent who has effectively been the primary parent and may have a strong desire to be with that parent. These dynamics have nothing to do with alienation but are related to the quality of the child's relationships with each parent. Such alignment occurs in all families, not just families of divorce. Unlike alienated children, however, these children also want to spend time with the other parent, though on a more limited basis. The evaluator will notice that the child's reasoning is related to these interests or the quality of the relationship rather than imagined problems in the relationship with the rejected parent.

Second, conflict takes an emotional toll on children. As the level of conflict between parents increases and as children are caught in the middle of these conflicts, the child's level of anxiety and vulnerability increases. For many of these children, aligning with a parent helps take them out of the middle and reduces their anxiety and vulnerability. When pressed, these children will prefer a relationship with both parents and show no real history of any significant problems with either parent. By making a choice to be primarily with one parent, these children are making a statement that they need to be free of the conflict. For some, it may not even matter which parent they live with, as long as they are removed from the conflict.

In fact, when the child's anxiety is driving the split, the intensity and severity of the child's feelings may be greater than the other forces, including the intensity of the alienating parent's behaviors. Unlike children who are alienated primarily because of the aligned parent or children who are aligned because of a rift in the relationship with the rejected parent, these anxious and vulnerable children are experiencing alignment or alienation as a direct result of the conflict and the behaviors of both parents.

> Any evaluation of alienation dynamics must include looking at the contributions of each parent, the children, and other potential sources of conflict.

# Concluding the Evaluation

As we near the completion of our evaluation, we need to understand each participant thoroughly. For the alleged aligned parent, the feelings and negative behaviors toward the other parent will be on a continuum from mild to severe. As we evaluate the rejected parent's behavior, we will be looking at the degree to which that parent has contributed to the rift in the relationship with the child, the need states of that parent, and whether that parent can see his or her own role in the problems. Finally, as we look at the child, we are looking for clues along a continuum of alignment to alienation and to the degree of conflict the child has been exposed to. Our recommendations and the interventions will vary according to the dynamics observed. By carefully observing each participant's role in the alienation dynamics, we can help to pinpoint family recommendations that will hopefully work toward alleviating these problems for the child.

## When Alienation Is Present

Given the wide range of situations in which alienation can manifest itself, the range of recommendations will also vary according to the dynamics of the family. However, there is one constant for all of these families that appears to be most beneficial. In cases where some form of true alienation is functioning, it is important for all family members to participate in some form of parent education related to issues of divorce. Recent research on parent education (Arbuthnot, Kramer, & Gordon, 1997) suggests that for all families, but especially those with the milder forms of alienation, improvement can be made by helping the parents gain a better understanding of how their postdivorce behavior affects the children.

As alienation dynamics become more severe, it is equally clear that some form of direction from the court is critical in helping to ensure ongoing contact between the rejected parent and the children (Sullivan & Kelly, 2001). When children are willing to go with the rejected parent, visits of longer blocks of time are often helpful, especially if there is little or no intrusion from the aligned parent. Long weekends several times per month and maybe 1- or 2-week blocks of time in the summer may help offset some of the aligned behaviors. When the court tells the parents and the child that there must be contact with the rejected parent, this also takes the child off the hook for having to decide. This may be quite helpful for those children who are feeling anxious but who are less determined to avoid the alienated parent. As discussed in Chapter 5, consideration of the child's temperament, age, and emotional functioning should be made whenever we recommend forced blocks of time for the child to be with the alienated parent.

## Recommended Interventions and Custodial Options

Depending on the intensity of the alienation and the other dynamics operating in the family, these families should have the entire range of options available to them. In cases where the alienation is mild to moderate, parent education that focuses on the impact of these issues on children and court orders that ensure that the child spends sufficient time with both parents are likely to be sufficient. Specialized education programs for children may also be quite useful in reducing the child's likelihood of becoming alienated. Therapy for the parents may be needed as well. The aligned parent may need help in separating his thoughts and feelings from the child and in learning to keep the child out of the middle of the conflict. Helping the aligned parent understand the value to the child of maintaining her relationship with the rejected parent is also critical. The otherwise-rejected parent may need help in setting reasonable limits and developing empathy for the child and the aligned parent. Therapy for the child is usually focused on reducing the rigid black-or-white thinking and helping the child to separate her feelings from those of the parents.

Therapists who work with high-conflict families may need specialized training to understand the dynamics involved. Therapeutic models suggest the need for both therapy and an educational component to be successful (Friedlander & Walters, 2010; Garber, 2004; Johnston et al., 2001). It is suggested that any therapeutic intervention be supported by court orders and that when families have more than one therapist involved, the therapists coordinate treatment to make sure that the goals are consistent and focused on reducing the alienation (Sullivan & Kelly, 2001).

Many of these families will need the services of a Parent Coordinator. As identified in Chapter 11, a Parent Coordinator is usually a licensed mental health professional or attorney who is in a quasi-judicial role to monitor the family and make recommendations to the court on an ongoing and regular basis (AFCC Task Force on Parenting Coordination, 2005). Parent Coordinators need sufficient training to develop a comprehensive understanding of the family dynamics, the time and availability for intensive case management, and the authority to monitor and enforce compliance with the intervention plan. The Parent Coordinator may help ensure that contact with the otherwise-rejected parent occurs as ordered and may also make ongoing recommendations designed to reduce the likelihood that the alienation will continue.

One of the most controversial aspects of alienation comes from Gardner's recommendation of an immediate change of custody in severe cases of alienation. In general, he took the position that whenever there was severe alienation the courts should order a change of custody to the rejected parent, and he has reported that this was successful in nearly 100% of the cases in which the courts ordered such a change (Gardner, 1987). I have always felt that this solution is theoretical and has not been sufficiently tested by adequate research. Johnston and Roseby (1997) expressed concern that more vulnerable children might regress, and some could even be suicidal if the court ordered such a change in custody. I have always felt that certain cases might clearly be appropriate for a change in custody while others would likely be inappropriate for such a rigid position.

While my thoughts are also theoretical and we clearly need more research in this area, I have felt that for many children, especially adolescents who are doing reasonably well in all other aspects of their life, an abrupt change of custody to fix the alleged alienation would be risky. We might be creating new problems that are more severe for the child than the ones we are trying to fix. My thoughts have been more consistent with the recommendations of J. Kelly and Johnston (2001) in which therapeutic and child-centered recommendations are indicated. In such cases, it may be more appropriate to resolve the alienation via a combination of increased time with the rejected parent, use of court-ordered therapy, and the appointment of a Parent Coordinator. I have often felt that court-ordered joint physical custody may be more appropriate, as well. We need to be especially careful with adolescents, though forcing time with the rejected parent is more likely to be successful with school-age children. The key is to arrange for a neutral child custody evaluation, by someone trained in the dynamics of alienation, before making any decision. Thus, rather than arbitrarily changing custody from one parent to the other, I believe that a range of potential options exists. This range of options includes:

- A change of custody to the other parent
- Joint physical custody with the child spending approximately equal time with each parent in a court-ordered arrangement

- Continued primary custody with the aligned parent while using therapy and parent coordination to assist in supporting and improving the child's relationship with the rejected parent
- Continued primary custody with the alienated parent while encouraging the rejected parent to withdraw from the child's life until the child is older and more stable and ready to deal with the conflicts that may occur in trying to maintain both relationships

It is my experience that as a very general rule, younger children can be more easily forced by the courts to spend time with a rejected parent, but as children move toward adolescence, it may be more difficult to force that contact between the child and parent. In addition, while some children might struggle if they have an abrupt change of custody, they might do fine if there is a transitional change to joint physical custody. Then, if the forces that contributed to the alienation continue, the change of custody to the previously rejected parent may be easier for the child.

> Custody evaluators can be most helpful by presenting various options and interventions to the court with the suggested risks and benefits of each.

## Parentectomies: Do They Help?

As indicated earlier, perhaps the most controversial element of all the alienation literature has been stimulated by Dr. Gardner's recommendation for a swift change of custody in those families identified as exhibiting severe parental alienation. There may also be a severe limitation on the child's contact with the aligned parent, at least for the first few months after the change of custody. While there are certainly times when an evaluator might recommend a change of custody from one parent to the other, doing so solely on the basis of a finding of severe alienation may not be in the child's best interests. When a child has a strong attachment, even if it is an unhealthy one, to the aligned parent, it can be emotionally damaging to the child if the relationship is abruptly terminated.

It is important to remember that children in these families are often in an enmeshed relationship with the aligned parent and often feel a strong need to protect that parent. They may be in a hostile–dependent relationship with the aligned parent. An abrupt change in custody may cause significant problems for the child. We must be careful that the proposed solution to alienation does not cause more problems for the child than did the alienation. I have never seen a change of custody by itself lead to a reduction in conflict and improvement in the situation for the child. While it may temporarily help the relationship between the child and the rejected parent, it often comes at an exorbitant price for the child.

Even with a Parent Coordinator and therapeutic support, many of these children continue to long for a relationship with the aligned parent. Sometimes these dynamics will resurface several years later. Rather than a complete change of custody, I believe that a more balanced time-share in which the child has time to be with each parent for a relatively equal period of time in larger chunks (such as 2-week blocks or most of the summer) may be more beneficial to the child. Even when this is difficult to achieve, I would always consider the impact to the child of the change of custody and whether this solution will be worse than the alienation that is occurring.

For some families, it will be impossible to help the rejected parent ever have a viable relationship with the child, in spite of the best therapeutic and structural efforts. Some courts are taking to punishing children, placing them in juvenile halls and psychiatric hospitals because they will not see a parent. I do not agree with this approach. I believe that these children should be in therapy, with part of the therapeutic work centered on the rejected parent withdrawing from the child's life. It is important to do this carefully so that the child does not feel abandoned by the alienated parent. The rejected parent needs to be taught to say the following to the child (in his or her own words, but with the overall intent completely clear):

> I know how hard it is for you when you feel pain. I know that you and I don't see things the same way, and maybe we never will. I am sorry for whatever I have done to cause you to feel pain, and I know that our divorce has been terrible for you. I love you and don't want you to be in the middle of the war between your (mom/dad) and me. I know it's terrible for you, and rather than have you continue to experience that pain, I am going to withdraw for a while.
>
> I want you to remember three things. First, I do love you and want what is best for you. Second, I will always be there for you if you need anything. Third, if you ever change your mind, and want to rebuild our relationship, nothing would make me happier. I'm only withdrawing for now to help you feel less pain and take you out of the middle of our war. I'll keep in contact with you every few months or so. I'll keep sending you birthday and Christmas cards. I hope you get them, and I hope you'll write back. I'll always make sure you know where I am and how to reach me if I move. More than anything, I want you to have peace in your life, and some day, I hope I can be a part of it. I love you and I always will.

While this is a painful thing for a rejected parent to do, sometimes it is the only viable solution for an intractable situation. I would certainly encourage such a child to remain in therapy, at least periodically, to explore how the situation is working out. I would also encourage the parent to continue sending the cards, inviting a reunification with the child. At the present time, there is no research on these children and families to know if this actually helps, but anecdotal evidence for some children suggests that it might.

## Some Promising Alternatives

In recent years, three psychologists have started a program to help high-conflict, alienated families learn to deal with their issues (Sullivan, Ward, & Deutsch, 2010). According to the Overcoming Barriers website, http://overcoming barriers.org/, the program is a summer camp lasting for several days that is

> designed to help children and families where one or more children is in danger of losing a relationship (or has lost this relationship) with one of her parents. The psycho-educational part of this family camp will help both parents see the value of the other in the child's life as well as help children become more free to feel and show connection with both parents. Families will learn how to repair ruptured relationships in a safe and healthy environment in beautiful Starksboro, Vermont. This camp will offer fun camp activities as well as the unique opportunity to create new beginnings and new memories with the assistance of a skilled, supportive staff who understand the complexities of these relationships.

In their evaluation of the program, participants felt that the program was quite successful, and many of the children resolved and improved their relationships with a previously rejected parent. Their article provides quite detailed information about the program and the curriculum.

Another program with similar results offers a different hope for some of these families. "Family Bridges" (Warshak, 2010) provides a court-ordered 4-day educational program that reunites children and rejected parents, often at a site far removed from the aligned parent. While there are some promising results with this program, it requires significant resources and the availability of trained personnel. It has had less success than Overcoming Barriers in improving behaviors and attitudes of the aligned parents. In her critique of the program, J. Kelly (2010) suggests that more research is needed before understanding which families might benefit from such a program and which ones will not. Warshak's (2010) article provides quite detailed information about those programs and the curriculum.

I encourage readers to pay attention to these growing trends in therapeutic and educational programs and to consider each of them when evaluating severe cases of alienation.

## THE BOTTOM LINE

In my opinion, families in which children are rejecting a parent without good cause are among the most difficult of cases to resolve. All family members are struggling with intense emotions. Sorting out the history of the family takes considerable time and effort. Figuring out what to do when severe alienation is identified can be very difficult, especially when there are few good options. As described in

Chapter 10, I encourage evaluators to describe the risks and benefits of multiple outcomes before settling on one particular conclusion. In these alienation cases, I encourage evaluators to inform the court of the risks and benefits of primary physical custody with the aligned parent, some form of shared physical custody, or a change of custody to primary with the rejected parent. I would explain to the court the value of therapy and psycho-educational efforts and specify the goals for each family member. I would also explain the value of using a Parent Coordinator to monitor compliance and encourage coordination of the therapeutic work. Only after providing a comprehensive analysis of the options can a final determination be made of what is best for any particular family.

Ultimately, until there is more research to understand all the forces that contribute to a child's potential alienation, until we have more research on understanding and differentiating between a child's alienation realistic estrangement, and until there is more research on the effects of different custody and access options and additional research on various interventions, I would discourage any arbitrary and rigid response to dealing with these families.

Relevant research was published in the January 2010 *Family Court Review* that summarized what was known about alienation at that time, but more needs to be learned before we can proceed with any particular strategy in all cases. The summary by Fidler and Bala (2010) and the therapeutic-related article by Friedlander and Walters (2010) are excellent resources for those who want to learn more about these issues.

Finally, at the time of this writing, the American Psychiatric Association was developing their new *Diagnostic and Statistical Manual*, to be known as *DSM-V.* While I do not believe in using diagnoses in forensic work (S. Greenberg, Shuman, & Meyer, 2004), there is a proposal under review for inclusion of "Parental Alienation Disorder." There was no definition on the website (American Psychiatric Association, 2010) of this proposed disorder. At the same time, there are political efforts in some states to abolish the use of terms such as *alienation* in the family court because alienation is an untested theory. To my knowledge, there is only one study of the use of the term *alienation* in the courts (Bala, Hunt, & McCarney, 2010), and that was in the Canadian courts. The authors found a growing use of the term in the courts from 1989 to 2008 and revealed a multifaceted set of cases and different judicial responses, depending on the perceptions of the judge and the resources and conflicts of the parents. If Parental Alienation is included in the *DSM-V,* it would certainly be considered suitable for inclusion in the courts. At the same time, with my own informal discussions with colleagues, there is certainly some controversy over whether or not this proposed diagnosis should be included. I encourage all evaluators and interested observers to monitor these actions as they evolve.

# Note

1. This chapter is adapted in part from an article (P. Stahl, 2004) copyrighted by the author and published in the *Wisconsin Journal of Family Law,* 24(1), 2004, and from P. Stahl (1999), and incorporates the newest research in the field.

# 14 Relocation Evaluations

Relocation evaluations, in my opinion, are unique. Like all evaluations, they require the evaluator to have multiple interviews with each parent, interviews with most children, observations of the child with each parent, collateral contacts with relevant people in the family's life, and a complete report focusing on the data that have been collected. Relocation evaluations are unique because they are so connected to the legal rules in your state and the fact that you are addressing the questions surrounding the move as well as the best interests of the child. As I will explain later in the chapter, the move-related issues that are being evaluated are one significant component of the evaluation, but so is the custodial arrangement and parenting plan in the event that the move does, or does not, take place. This chapter will outline all of the critical move-related issues and focus on the way in which judges often consider and decide relocation cases.

In my work teaching judges, attorneys, mediators, and child custody evaluators, I often ask my audiences what types of situations are the most difficult and challenging. Without a doubt, the most common response is relocation cases. Mediators do not like them because even low-conflict families often have difficulty reaching agreement on a parenting plan when one parent wants (or has) to move. Attorneys do not like relocation cases because there is no room for negotiation, and they often feel as if the law is stacked against their client, especially if the attorney is representing the parent who wants to move. Judges do not like relocation cases because it is often hard to choose between two good parents when the motive of one or the other is in good faith. Finally, child custody evaluators do not like relocation cases because they are so complex and there is no middle ground from which to make a choice. Evaluators often struggle with the legal aspects of relocation cases because many evaluators have difficulty keeping up with case law in their state. Finally, many child custody evaluators believe that it is in the child's best interests for both parents to be regularly involved in the child's life. This causes evaluators trouble when they need to make a recommendation that does not allow for this. For these and other reasons, many people struggle with these cases.

On the other hand, I believe that when you understand the legal issues in your state and understand the risk factors and protective factors that the literature describes related to relocation, you can focus on providing sound assessment information for the judge, even in the absence of an actual recommendation about whether or not the children should move with the moving parent.

In a mobile society, a parent often has to choose between a career, a new relationship, moving to be near the comfort of family and friends, and the parenting of his or her child. When one parent needs (or wants) to move with the children and the other parent wants the children and the other parent to stay, children become victims in a battle over parenting time, custody, and access. In increasing numbers, judges are seeking the assistance of child custody evaluators in order to determine "the best interests of the child" in these relocation cases. For the child custody evaluator, move-away cases are often emotionally sensitive, usually because there is no middle ground that can minimize potential risks to the child. The stakes are even higher in long-distance and international moves, as things become even more complicated and knowledge of the legal issues becomes even more critical.

> In a mobile society, there can be many reasons why one parent wants to move. Understanding the motive is critical.

What often makes these cases so difficult is that typically there are few alternatives available, the impact on the child is potentially severe, and parents tend to be rather rigid in their positions. The parent who wants to move sees no other alternative, and the nonmoving parent worries about the impact on the children and is likely to experience sadness and distress at the loss of his child. For many families, one parent feels she must move and the other feels that she should not take the children away. There is little room for negotiation, and after the judge reaches a decision, one parent seems to have won and the other to have lost. The sad reality in most relocation cases is that one parent does gain, one parent does lose, and the children are likely to suffer some losses no matter the outcome.

# Legal Considerations in Relocation Evaluations: Relevant Case Law

Like many areas of family law and child custody evaluation, there is a scarcity of research, but a growing amount of literature, in this area. Much of the literature can be found in the case laws across the country (and the world) that have contributed to the thinking in relocation law. This literature has changed over time, and in many U.S. states, the legal issues and decisions have changed in as little as 5 to 10 years. Consistent with the Association of Family Conciliation Courts (2006) *Model Standards,* I believe that evaluators need to understand case law in the jurisdictions in which they practice. I also believe strongly that case law decisions can help guide the way in which evaluators consider relevant issues in front of them.

In this chapter, I will discuss the statutory and case law to help focus on the critical issues that child custody evaluators need for approaching relocation evaluations. I will then discuss the relevant psychological literature on relocation. It is important to note that both the law and the literature discuss critical and relevant factors that need to be considered. I will focus on the critical factors that must be considered by child custody evaluators in their reports, depending on the particular facts of a case. Finally, I will conclude this chapter with a call to avoid bias in this work. There are two possible biases in relocation work. Some practitioners believe that moves are most always harmful and that the burden should be on the moving parent to show how a move will substantially enhance the life of the child. Other practitioners think that custodial parents should automatically have the right to move their children with them, citing the thinking that what is good for the custodial parent is automatically good for the child. I believe that all relocation cases need an approach that acknowledges that the move of the children may be in the child's best interests and a change of custody may be in the child's best interests, and that the facts of each case will lead to the correct decision by the court. As evaluators, we provide helpful information to the court for making this decision.

I will use case law in the state of California as an example of how case law in a variety of states has evolved since 1990. This extensive section will guide the reader in understanding the complexity of relocation law and the importance to evaluators in understanding this complexity. Since 1990, the statutory law in California has not changed, in that Family Code § 7501 has always stated, in essence, that the custodial parent has a presumptive right to move the child, absent a showing of harm to the child. That statute would suggest that moves would generally be allowed. However, the prevailing case law in the early 1990s was *In re Marriage of McGinnis* (1992), which, in spite of Family Code § 7501, essentially stated that the moving parent had to show that the child's life would substantially benefit from the proposed move. This put the burden on the moving parent to show that the move would be in the child's interests. At that time, few parents who requested to move were able to do so with their children.

Then, in 1996, the California Supreme Court made a substantive change when they held in *In re Marriage of Burgess* (1996, 25, 28–29) that

> a parent seeking to relocate after dissolution of marriage is not required to establish that the move is "necessary" in order to be awarded physical custody of a minor child. Similarly, a parent who has been awarded physical custody of a child under an existing custody order also is not required to show that a proposed move is "necessary" and instead "has the right to change the residence of the child, subject to the power of the court to restrain a removal that would prejudice the rights or welfare of the child." (from Family Code § 7501)

Another key provision of *Burgess* was Footnote 12, which states, "A different analysis may be required when parents share joint physical custody of the minor children under an existing order and in fact, and one parent seeks to relocate with the minor children." In such cases, the custody order

> may be modified or terminated upon the petition of one or both parents or on the court's own motion if it is shown that the best interest of the child requires modification or termination of the order. The trial court must determine de novo what arrangement for primary custody is in the best interest of the minor children.

In spite of the fact that the first cited case after *Burgess* denied the relocation of the moving parent (*Cassady v. Signorelli*,[1] 1996), by and large, most case law decisions for the next 9 years continued the trend of generally allowing moves by custodial parents. Along the way, there were many other case law decisions by the California appellate courts that generally allowed the move by a custodial parent, either by upholding a trial judge's decision to allow the move or by overturning the trial judge's decision to deny the move. Some of those decisions focused on the percentage of time required to be considered the "custodial parent"—which ranged from 60% to 65%. Given Footnote 12 in *Burgess,* this was critical in helping to determine whether or not there was a sole-custodial parent or whether there was a joint physical custody order in place. Another case, *In re Marriage Edlund v. Hales* (1998), decided that neither judges nor custody evaluators could ask the moving parent what she (or he) would do if the court denied the request to move with the child. The rationale for that was that it would put the parent who wants to move in the difficult position of choosing between her or his goals for the future (e.g., job, pending marriage, return to family, etc.) and the child. To my knowledge, evaluators and judges in other states can ask that question, and it may be a relevant consideration in any relocation request.

> Custody evaluators need to understand the statutory and case law in order to provide helpful information to the court about the family.

The California courts also affirmed an international move from California to Australia in *Condon* (*In re Marriage of Condon*, 1998, 533). This case not only added to the discussion about sole versus joint custody but also authorized courts to impose restrictions associated with international moves, including the ordering of bonds to help ensure that funds are available in the event that the orders for access are not followed. This case provides guidance for evaluators in California who are involved in international relocations.

Two other Appellate Court cases are worth noting. In another international case, *Abargil* (*In re Marriage of Abargil*, 2003), the court was faced with two Israeli citizens who came to the United States on tourist visas and overstayed. They had a son who lived primarily with the mother and visited the father. Mother went to Israel to visit her dying mother, taking the son with her. While she was in Israel, Father filed for divorce. When Mother attempted to return to the United States to deal with the divorce case, she was barred from entering the country because of having overstayed her tourist visa. This sanction was stayed, however, to allow her to return for the trial. In this case, Father asserted that he could not return to Israel to visit the child because he was applying for permanent residency and could not leave the country for an extended time. After the 5-day trial, the court authorized Mother to have custody of the child in Israel, noting that she had been the child's primary caregiver and finding that she was more likely to facilitate access with the father than if the parental roles were reversed.

In the other interesting California case, *Campos* (*In re Marriage of Campos, supra,* 108 Cal.App.4th 839), Father had sought modification of custody when Mother requested to move from Santa Barbara to Moorpark, California, which is about 50 miles away. The superior court denied Father's motion, indicating that Mother did not have bad faith in her move. The appellate court reversed and remanded the matter for an evidentiary hearing to determine whether the proposed move would be detrimental to the welfare of the children. The court of appeal recognized that even when the custodial parent has a good faith reason for the proposed move, "a change of custody may be ordered in a 'move away' case where, as a result of the move, the children will suffer detriment rendering a change of custody essential or expedient for their welfare" (*In re Marriage of Campos, supra,* 108 Cal.App.4th, 843).

Along with these cases, there were many other published relocation appeals between 1994 and 2003, all but two of which affirmed trial court decisions, most of which allowed moves by custodial parents, citing *Burgess.*

In 2001, the case of *LaMusga*[2] (*In re Marriage of LaMusga,* 2004) began, as Ms. Navarro, the mother in this case, requested a move from California to Ohio. At trial, there was testimony that the move might increase harm to the children's relationship with their father. Citing the decision by the California Supreme Court, the trial court decision stated,

> The issue is not whether either of these parents is competent and qualified to be custodial parents, I think the evidence indicates that they are. That is not the question. The question is whether there is sufficient evidence at this point to determine, one, that the best interests of the children is served by relocating with Mother to Ohio, or whether the best interests are served by a change of physical custody if [the mother] is to relocate.

Mother appealed that decision, and the appellate court reversed the judgment, citing *Burgess* and concluding, "although the [superior] court referred several times during the hearing to 'best interest' as the applicable standard, its order was not truly based on that criterion as it applies in the context of this custodial parent's relocation." The court of appeal concluded that the superior court

> neither proceeded from the presumption that Mother had a right to change the residence of the children, nor took into account this paramount need for stability and continuity in the existing custodial arrangement. Instead, it placed undue emphasis on the detriment that would be caused to the children's relationship with Father if they moved.

Subsequent to that decision, Father appealed to the California Supreme Court, and the court held hearings and received seven amicus briefs in 2002 and 2003. Ultimately, the California Supreme Court overturned the appellate court's decision.

In overturning the appellate court's decision, the state Supreme Court stated a number of critical things. The court noted that

> [t]he Court of Appeal in the present case held that the superior court abused its discretion in ordering that primary physical custody of the children would be transferred to the father if the mother moved to Ohio. The Court of Appeal concluded that the superior court "neither proceeded from the presumption that Mother had a right to change the residence of the children, nor took into account this paramount need for stability and continuity in the existing custodial arrangement. Instead, it placed undue emphasis on the detriment that would be caused to the children's relationship with Father if they moved. We disagree."

The court reaffirmed *Burgess* that

> the paramount need for continuity and stability in custody arrangements— and the harm that may result from disruption of established patterns of care and emotional bonds with the primary caretaker—weigh heavily in favor of maintaining ongoing custody arrangements. (*Burgess, supra,* 1996, 32–33).

However, the California Supreme Court stated that

> the superior court did not place "undue emphasis" on the detriment to the children's relationship with their father that would be caused by the proposed move. The weight to be accorded to such factors must be left to the court's sound discretion. The Court of Appeal erred in substituting its judgment for that of the superior court.

In their decision, the court pointed out that both the court and the appellate court were correct in considering detriment in *Edlund v. Hales.* The California Supreme Court reiterated in *LaMusga* that the "noncustodial parent has the burden of showing that the planned move will cause detriment to the child in order for the court to reevaluate an existing custody order." Thus, the state Supreme Court reaffirmed that, according to California law, the noncustodial parent has the initial burden of showing that there is detriment in the proposed move. This is one of the more salient findings in the *LaMusga* decision.

Another focus of the decision that I believe is salient is their discussion on good-faith versus bad-faith motives. The court reminded that, in the *Burgess* decision, the court had previously stated that a finding that the proposed move constitutes bad faith "may be relevant" in determining custody arrangements (*Burgess, supra,* 1996, 36, fn. 6.). Essentially, the court in *LaMusga* described that these are not discrete issues, adding,

> Absolute concepts of good faith versus bad faith often are difficult to apply because human beings may act for a complex variety of some-times conflicting motives. As the superior court in the present case observed after finding that the mother was not acting in bad faith because she had legitimate reasons for the move and was not acting for the specific purpose of limiting the father's contact with his children said, "I think it's far more subtle than that."

The court concluded that

> [e]ven if the custodial parent has legitimate reasons for the proposed change in the child's residence and is not acting simply to frustrate the noncustodial parent's contact with the child, the court still may consider whether one reason for the move is to lessen the child's contact with the noncustodial parent and whether that indicates, when considered in light of all the relevant factors, that a change in custody would be in the child's best interests.

Ultimately, the court refined *Burgess* by stating,

> [W]e conclude that just as a custodial parent does not have to establish that a planned move is "necessary," neither does the noncustodial parent have to establish that a change of custody is "essential" to prevent detriment to the children from the planned move. Rather, the noncustodial parent bears the initial burden of showing that the proposed relocation of the children's residence would cause detriment to the children, requiring a reevaluation of the children's custody. The likely impact of the proposed move on the noncustodial parent's relationship with the children is a relevant factor in determining whether the move would cause detriment to the children and, when considered in light of all of the relevant factors, may be sufficient to justify a change in custody. If the noncustodial parent makes such an initial showing of detriment, the court must perform the delicate and difficult task of determining whether a change in custody is in the best interests of the children.

This substantial change in California statutory law created a two-part test: First that the noncustodial parent must first show detriment associated with the move of the child. Then, once that showing is reached, the court needs to determine whether a change of custody is in the best interests of the child. In my opinion, this two-part test has been a key in court decisions after *LaMusga*.

The other key finding in *LaMusga*, in my opinion, is that relocation law is not amenable to inflexible rules[3] and that the trial court needs to consider a variety of factors before deciding whether to modify a custody order in light of the custodial parent's proposal to change the residence of the child. According to the court,

> Among the factors that the court ordinarily should consider when deciding whether to modify a custody order in light of the custodial parent's proposal to change the residence of the child are the following: the children's interest in stability and continuity in the custodial arrangement; the distance of the move; the age of the children; the children's relationship with both parents; the relationship between the parents including, but not limited to, their ability to communicate and cooperate effectively and their willingness to put the interests of the children above their individual interests; the wishes of the children if they are mature enough for such an inquiry to be appropriate; the reasons for the proposed move; and the extent to which the parents currently are sharing custody.

# Legal Considerations in Relocation Evaluations: Relevant Statutory Law

In addition to case law, many states have statutory laws that define relocation issues (e.g., Elrod, 2006). I will use Arizona's statutory law to help define how relocation cases are addressed. Child custody law is defined in Chapter 25 of the Arizona statutes. AZ 25-403 identifies critical issues related to the best interests of the child, and AZ 25-408 identifies critical issues in relocation cases. Both identify critical factors determined by the legislature to be important for the court to consider. The most relevant best-interest factors in AZ 25-403 for the child custody evaluator include the following:

- The wishes of the child's parent or parents as to custody
- The wishes of the children as to the custodian
- The interaction and interrelationship of the children with the parent or parents, the child's siblings and any other person who may significantly affect the child's best interest
- The child's adjustment to home, school and community
- The mental and physical health of all individuals involved

- Which parent is more likely to allow the child frequent and meaningful continuing contact with the other parent
- Whether one parent, both parents or neither parent has provided primary care of the child
- The nature and extent of coercion or duress used by a parent in obtaining an agreement regarding custody

The critical 25-408 relocation factors include:

- The factors prescribed under section 25-403
- Whether the relocation is being made or opposed in good faith and not to interfere with or to frustrate the relationship between the child and the other parent or the other parent's right of access to the child
- The prospective advantage of the move for improving the general quality of life for the custodial parent or for the child
- The likelihood that the parent with whom the child will reside after the relocation will comply with parenting time orders
- Whether the relocation will allow a realistic opportunity for parenting time with each parent
- The extent to which moving or not moving will affect the emotional, physical or developmental needs of the child
- The motives of the parents and the validity of the reasons given for moving or opposing the move including the extent to which either parent may intend to gain a financial advantage regarding continuing child support obligations
- The potential effect of relocation on the child's stability

Other states have various factors identified in the law, and custody evaluators are urged to know the law in their respective jurisdiction(s) when doing this work (for more information on the legal issues in relocation, see Austin & Gould, 2006). Later in the chapter I will be addressing all relevant factors that evaluators might be likely to face in doing a relocation evaluation. In my view, these factors are critical for the child custody evaluator to understand so that the evaluator can write a report that is helpful to the court.

> Custody evaluators can provide relevant information to the court about the data associated with the factors in statutory or case law.

Ultimately, these cases and statutory laws provide the landscape in which the court and evaluators need to approach relocation evaluations in California or Arizona. While evaluators in other states will not need to follow these principles, they are being cited in this chapter for instructional purposes. Remember that evaluators in California may not ask the parent requesting to move what she or he will do if the court denies the move (though in many other states it is considered to be both relevant and allowable). To be helpful to the court, evaluators need to provide information about potential detriment to the child in the event that the move will take place and provide responses to the relevant factors identified in the law and in the psychological literature, which will be discussed later in the chapter. In international cases, the evaluator will want to address the Hague Convention issues and the special risks involved in a move of such great distance. Finally, I believe strongly that whereas it is often appropriate for child custody evaluators to make recommendations in non-relocation evaluations, it is often inappropriate for evaluators to make a specific recommendation about the move itself. This was made clear in the *LaMusga* decision where the court stated, "The weight to be accorded to such factors must be left to the court's sound discretion." With that in mind, the evaluator's best option, in my opinion, will be to describe the factors and the data associated with each of the factors and leave the weighting up to the court, unless everything aligns in one direction. That conclusion and a suggested way to write the relocation report will be addressed more fully at the end of this chapter.

## The Psychological Literature Related to Relocation

While there was been some literature in this area prior to 1995, it grew substantially with the amicus brief filed by Wallerstein and Tanke (1996) in *Burgess*. Wallerstein drew on her research on the effects of divorce on children and applied it to her analysis of moves. Their brief was the primary source of information used by the California Supreme Court in its decision in the *Burgess* (1996) case. In my opinion, this article provided the key focus in favor of supporting Mother's right to move in that case. Miller (1995) and Shear (1996) addressed many of the issues facing the court in move-away cases associated with the law in New York and California, respectively. Subsequent to *Burgess,* Warshak (2000b) wrote an article in response to Wallerstein, addressing his key concerns and pointing out that he believed that Wallerstein presented only some of the research on divorce in making her case. He provided other research to support the belief that bright-line rules are not appropriate in relocation cases. Prior to the court reaching a decision in *LaMusga,* there were seven amicus briefs focusing on both theoretical and case-specific issues, five that I believe were primarily pro-Mother (and pro-move) and two that were primarily pro-Father (and anti-move). Interestingly, while the *Burgess* decision cited Wallerstein and Tanke's brief and used its rationales consistently in its decision, the court in *LaMusga* acknowledged receipt of the seven briefs but stayed focused on the legal issues and case-specific issues in rendering its decision. All of these briefs in the legal arena provide excellent information that should help inform evaluators about the critical issues in relocation cases.[4]

At the same time, there have been a number of articles guiding child custody evaluators in conducting relocation evaluations (Austin, 2000; Austin &

Gould, 2006; Kelly & Lamb, 2003; P. Stahl, 2006) since publication of *Complex Issues in Child Custody Evaluations* (P. Stahl, 1999). In this section, I will highlight the critical information from these articles to provide the necessary framework for evaluators to consider in relocation cases and as a way of guiding evaluators in their work.

Berkow (1996) pointed out that the benefit of a custody evaluation in relocation cases is for the court to hear "the child's voice" as advocated by Wallerstein in the *Burgess* amicus brief. Berkow believes that a custody evaluation "is very helpful to the court in determining several factual issues critical to the best interest analysis." While pointing out that it is not the job of the custody evaluator to make a legal assessment of whether the proposed move is or is not in the best interests in the child, she states that an evaluation focused on certain issues is critical to the court making an intelligent decision in a move-away case.

These issues include whether there is a working shared custody arrangement; the reasons for the move, both stated and unstated; the history of the moving parent either facilitating or interfering with the noncustodial parent's access to the child; the child's developmental and individual needs at this point in time and how they can be expected to change in the future; the child's significant relationships with siblings, step-siblings, teachers, playmates, and others, and what impact the proposed relocation may have on these relationships; the child's special needs, if any, and how they might be affected in the new location; what a child wishes in the context of the child's age and ability to formulate an intelligent preference; whether there are any less disruptive alternatives to propose instead of the relocation; and if there are alternative parenting plans under the proposed relocation, considering the financial and logistical circumstances. Berkow believes that child custody evaluations that focus on such relevant issues are a major contribution to the judicial decision for these families.

Justice Miller (1995) notes that, as early as 1981, the New York Court of Appeals apparently recognized the legitimacy of considering a parent's right to a "fresh start," among other factors bearing on the child's best interest. According to Miller, the most significant message contained in various New York cases is the court's clear, unequivocal concern for the child's welfare above all else. New York courts have typically held a two-part test of whether relocation would deprive the noncustodial parent of "regular and meaningful access to the child." If there is deprivation, exceptional circumstances must be shown to allow the move. If there is no deprivation, the custodial parent need not show exceptional circumstances. However, if the court finds that the relocation will deprive the noncustodial parent of meaningful access, a presumption arises that relocation is not in the best interest of the child. Miller states that once it has been determined that the custodial parent has demonstrated the requisite exceptional circumstances to justify the relocation, the focus then turns to whether the relocation is in the child's best interests. According to Miller, whether a given relocation is in the best interests of a child is based on the given facts in each case. Central to this inquiry is an analysis of the quality and quantity of access enjoyed by the noncustodial parent and child prior to the proposed move, and whether the relationship can adequately be preserved at a greater distance with less frequent, but more intensive prolonged access. Considering the writing of Berkow, this analysis can be provided by the child custody evaluator.

Justice Miller (1995) suggests that the court must look at the following five factors in determining what is in the best interests of the child:

1. Whether the move is likely to enhance the quality of life for both the custodial parent and the child
2. The motives of the custodial parent who wishes to move, in order to determine whether the motive behind the move is to defeat or "frustrate" visitation
3. The noncustodial parent's motives for opposing removal
4. The noncustodial parent's visitation rights since it is in the best interests of the child to have a "healthy and close relationship with both parents, as well as other family members"
5. Whether a "realistic and reasonable visitation schedule can be reached if the move is allowed"

Justice Miller believes that there shall be no presumptions for or against a proposed move. She proposed that the custodial parent desiring to relocate shall bear the initial burden of coming forward with evidence that the motivation underlying the move is one of good faith and is not sparked by a desire to interfere maliciously with the relationship or access schedule of the child and noncustodial parent; that a rational basis exists for believing that the relocation will provide a better life for the family unit, the parent, or the child; that the child will enjoy a healthy, decent lifestyle in the new community (i.e., adequate schooling, housing, financial support); and that the proposed access program will provide the noncustodial parent with sufficient access to permit and encourage the development of a meaningful relationship between the noncustodial parent and child.[5] Justice Miller's most important point is that

> [t]he flexibility implicit in the recommended approach to relocation cases permits the courts to weigh the relative importance to the child of such close relationships with the noncustodial parent against all other factors in determining whether to permit the move, alter visitation, or even change custody. The basic change proposed is not a matter of preference between fathers and mothers, but rather one of focus on the child considering all factors impacting upon that child's best interest unimpeded by rigid preconditions.

According to Wallerstein and Tanke (1996), children of divorce often experience feelings of anxiety and self-blame for the marital failure, and though the legal system "pays lip service to their needs with the best interest standard," all too often those needs are obscured by the advocacy of warring parents. The court needs to assess the impact of possible disruptions on the child. The court needs to extend its understanding of best interests to include the potential impact on the child if a move does take place and also if the move does *not* take place. The best interests of the child cannot be identified without a consideration of the child's feelings, as understood by sensitive and caring adults who are independent of the battling parents.

Wallerstein and Tanke (1996) wrote that the psychological adjustment of the custodial parent has consistently been found to be related to the child adjustment, but the psychological adjustment of the noncustodial parent has not. While not wishing to diminish the important role of the father in the child's growing up years, they believe that there is no significant connection between frequency of visits and time spent in the father's home and the development of the nurturing father–child relationship on the positive outcome in the child or adolescent. When a court prohibits a move by the custodial parent, it may force that parent to choose between custody of the child and possible opportunities (e.g., a new marriage, an important job opportunity, or a return to the help provided by extended family) that may benefit the entire family unit, including the child, adding that children are not Ping-Pong balls and travel plans need to be tailored to the age, temperament, and wishes of the child.

Ultimately, Wallerstein and Tanke (1996) concluded that the best interests of the child are best served within the nurturing and protection provided by high-quality parent–child relationships and that the needs of children should have greater protection than the rights of the adversarial parents or process. They stated, "[E]specially at the time of the contemplated move, the court should be responsive to the child's voice, amplifying it above the din of competing parents." Again, presumably, child custody evaluators can provide a venue for the child's voice.

In response to the amicus brief filed by Wallerstein and Tanke in *Burgess,* Warshak (2000b) took issue with the presumption that is implied in their writing. He suggested that they discussed only some of the divorce research in their brief, and he provided considerable other research data to highlight the importance of the child's relationship with the noncustodial parent. Among other things, Warshak described that much of the research Wallerstein relied upon in her analysis has come from mother-custody studies. He added that this was inconsistent with findings in her initial research with Kelly (Wallerstein & Kelly, 1980), where they pointed out that their

> findings regarding the centrality of both parents to the psychological health of children and adolescents alike leads us to hold that, where possible, divorcing parents should be encouraged and helped to shape post divorce arrangements which permit and foster continuity in the children's relations with both parent.

Warshak (2010) cited Hetherington (Hetherington & Kelly, 2002) by stating,

> [W]hen the father is not available, both the constructive and destructive behavior of the divorced mother are funneled more directly to the child. A good relationship with a non-custodial father cannot buffer the adverse effects of a destructive relationship between the mother and child in the same way that occurs with a residential father who is regularly available.

Warshak continued by pointing out that just because the noncustodial father's adjustment does not correlate with the child's adjustment, does not mean that the child is unaffected by the father's absence. He felt that problems in the child's psychological adjustment following divorce are least likely to occur if both parents assume a role in helping children cope successfully. He also points out that Hetherington found that children benefit from low conflict, an absence of denigration between parents, high parental agreement, and availability of the noncustodial father, if the father is not extremely deviant or destructive, are associated with positive adjustment in children.

Warshak (2000a) also focused on the findings of Lamb, Sternberg, and Thompson (1997), who found that nonresidential parents who maintain parental roles (providing guidance, discipline, supervision, and educational assistance) may affect their children more profoundly and in a more positive way than those who are limited to functioning as occasional visiting companions. Along with this, Warshak (2000a) pointed out that Wallerstein and Tanke (1996) failed to include research that showed that a majority of children consistently complain about the loss of contact with the noncustodial parent as the major drawback of divorce and studies in which predictable and frequent contact with a reasonably well-adjusted and mature noncustodial father was linked with better adjustment. Ultimately, Warshak (2000b) reported that many studies conclude that "[a]ccess to both parents seemed to be the most protective factor, in that it was associated with better academic adjustment." He added that the Lamb et al. (1997) research concluded,

> To maintain high quality relationships with their children, parents need to have sufficiently extensive and regular interaction with them, but the amount of time involved is usually less important than the quality of the interaction it fosters. Time distribution arrangements that ensure the involvement of both parents in important aspects of their children's everyday lives and routines—including bedtime and waking rituals, transitions to and from school, extracurricular and recreational activities—are likely to keep nonresidential parents playing psychologically important and central roles in the lives of their children.

Ultimately, Warshak (2000a) concluded that there is no perfect relocation disposition. He said that within each family, every possible arrangement has its advantages and disadvantages. He pointed out that the relocation disposition that is optimal for one family may not be best for another. He felt that bright-line rules cannot alleviate the difficult task before the court without doing damage to some families. Warshak added that relocation decisions must be tailored to fit the circumstances and needs of each individual family rather than force every family into the same mold. Statutes, case law, research, and experts can provide valuable input into the decision, but, he added, "The best path for ensuring the best interests of children is to remain open to all of the evidence and encourage all parties to do the same."

In 1999, I described much of the relocation literature that was in existence at that time, concluding that the custody evaluator needs to focus on relevant family and move-related factors that are important in any child custody evaluation. This list of factors highlighted the importance of focusing on what Warshak (2000b) described as "all of the evidence" so that the court would have the most useful information in reaching its judgment. Because I have already focused on so many factors, there is no need to repeat the relevant factors described at that time.

In 2000, Austin provided important information for his relocation risk assessment model. He suggested that evaluators and judges are using inferential decision-making to make predictions about what the child's life will be like in the future under different sets of living conditions. He pointed out that at that time, there was little research on the effects of relocation for all children, including children of divorce in particular. He described that attachment research supports that children are capable of forming strong attachments to multiple caretakers and that the divorce research suggests that children show the best adjustment to divorce when they have quality access to both parents in an atmosphere of relatively low conflict, and that child competency research suggests that positive parenting, community support, and self-regulation skills help children cope with stressors. He added that relocation is a potential stressor for children in general and children of divorce in particular.

Like many others before him, Austin (2000) provided a listing of factors that he believed to be important in sorting through the critical issues of relocation for children of divorce. For Austin, these factors included:

- History of involvement by noncustodial parent, including post-separation involvement
- Geographical distance
- Cognitive and emotional status of the child
- Psychological health of both parents
- History of child or spouse maltreatment
- Age of child
- Degree of conflict between the parents
- The custodial parent's psychological resources

Austin (2000) then described that practical considerations associated with economics, transportation schedules, and the wishes of the child would also be important considerations. At that time, he worried about child custody evaluators overpredicting harm because they are so focused on the need for both parents to be involved that they do not address all of the relevant issues. In this way, Austin raised a concern similar to one of mine (P. Stahl, 2006), that some evaluators might be biased against moves. He described that the most constructive role for evaluators would be to utilize data from the family and integrate those data with research and thinking about relocation cases, and then to identify critical variables, assess risks, and make clear the limitations of their predictions and their opinions.

In 2003, two important articles were published (Braver, Ellman, & Fabricius, 2003; Kelly & Lamb, 2003). Braver et al. published research associated with their sample of psychology undergraduate students at Arizona State University. They surveyed students to discover whether they had experienced either of their parents moving more than an hour away from the other parent. They reported that these students reported a preponderance of negative effects associated with parental moves by mother or father, with or without the child, as compared with divorced families in which neither parent moved away. These negative effects included, among other things:

- Receiving less financial support
- Worrying more about that support
- Feeling more hostility in their interpersonal relationships
- Suffering more distress from parents' divorce
- Perceiving parents less favorably as sources of emotional support and as role models
- Believing the quality of their parents' relationships with each other to be worse
- Rating themselves less favorably on general physical health, life satisfaction, and personal and emotional adjustment

While Braver et al. (2003) recognized that their data could not establish with certainty that moves cause children harm, they concluded that there is no empirical basis on which to justify a legal presumption that a move by a custodial parent to benefit the parent's life will necessarily confer equivalent benefits on the child. In spite of acknowledging some disadvantages, they recommended that courts be allowed to consider the strategic use of conditional change-of-custody orders when a parent wishes to relocate, though they added that no court should issue a conditional change-of-custody order if it believes that any custodial change would yield important disadvantages for the child. At the very least, they suggested that courts and legislatures should discourage moves by custodial parents, at least in cases in which the child enjoys a good relationship with the other parent and the move is not prompted by the need to otherwise remove the child from a detrimental environment.

At the same time, Kelly and Lamb (2003) published an article focused on critical issues in relocation. They focused on attachment, legal trends that were encouraging custodial parents the rebuttable presumptive right to move, and, like others before them, encouraged courts to consider a number of factors before deciding on any request to move. Their factors were similar to Austin's and included the following:

- Psychological adjustment and parenting capacities of relocating parents
- Psychological adjustment and parenting skills of non-moving parents
- Extent and focus of conflict
- Economic realities following relocation
- The distance between the two homes

In addition, Kelly and Lamb focused on the importance of maintaining the child's relationship with both parents and encouraged parents to use mediation, maintain communication between both parents and children, and modify access schedules to accommodate a child's developmental needs.

> Custody evaluators also want to provide relevant data associated with factors identified in the psychological and legal literature in order to assist the court.

Also around that time amicus briefs filed in the *LaMusga* case highlighted the rich research in the field. Much of it reiterated the Wallerstein and Tanke (1996) brief in *Burgess* and the Warshak (2000b) response to it. In addition to that which was previously stated, the brief filed by Wallerstein (2003) supporting Mother's position pointed out that the research showing that children benefit from participation of both parents in their lives deals, without exception, with mothers and fathers who voluntarily make and agree to cooperative arrangements. The authors of this brief believed that parents opposing the move are in a subset of families that are high-conflict families, which means much of the research Warshak relied upon does not apply in those cases.

Shear (2003), in a brief supportive of Father's position, reiterated much of Warshak's research. Additionally, she pointed out that many relocation cases involved moves with children under the age of 6 and that relocation is a particular risk for very young children. Both Shear and Warshak think that in many of the cases, the parent seeking to restrain the move is the parent most attuned to the child's developmental needs. Shear believes that as a society, we need to assist parents in meeting those needs, not castigate them for voicing concern. The notion that children have only one psychological parent has been thoroughly discredited by a large body of evidence that has demonstrated that infants normally develop close attachments to both of their parents, that this occurs at about the same time (approximately 6 months of age), and that they do best when they have the opportunity to establish and maintain such attachments. They note that attachment is actually about the reciprocal connectedness between children and both parents. They concluded that relocation cases should always be about the best interests of the child rather than holding a presumption favoring a move, when deciding whether a relocation is appropriate.

In 2006, I invited a series of articles about relocation and presumptions for a special issue of the *Journal of Child Custody*. In that issue, Austin and Gould (2006) continued to refine Austin's position regarding relocation issues in child custody matters. Elrod (2006) surveyed state laws to understand which states had presumptions for or against moves and which states had no presumptions in either direction. L. Greenberg, Gould-Saltmann, and Schneider (2006) focused on the problems with presumptions in all child custody matters. Fabricius and Braver (2006) provided more research data to support their earlier research (Braver et al., 2003). Lott (2006) described many of the legal issues in relocation cases and identified what judges may want from a child custody evaluation. Finally, I (P. Stahl, 2006) described the concerns about bias in relocation cases and suggested using factors to help avoid those biases. Each of these articles added important information related to relocation, and it is beyond the scope of this chapter to summarize them. They nevertheless are all important and useful references for the child custody evaluator in relocation matters.

Most recently, Austin (2008a, 2008b) has continued to refine his relocation risk assessment model. With this model, he suggests that relocation is always a risk factor for children, except in domestic violence cases. He then highlighted those factors that, depending on the findings associated with those factors, either increase that risk or provide protection against the risk of relocation. He summarized those factors as:

- The age of child
- The distance of the move
- The child's strengths and vulnerabilities
- The degree of nonresidential parental involvement
- The strengths, resources, and vulnerabilities of the moving parent
- Parenting effectiveness of both parents
- The history and degree of parental conflict
- The history of any domestic violence
- The ability of the residential parent to support the other parent emotionally following a move
- The residential parent's ability to be a responsible gatekeeper
- The recency of the separation and divorce

Austin (2008a, 2008b) concluded that "distance makes it more difficult to craft a parenting time plan that keeps the nonmoving parent involved and requires the evaluator and court to have a harm-mitigation mind set when there is going to be a long-distance parenting plan put into place." He concluded, "The evaluator can be most helpful to the court by communicating both an estimate of the risk (i.e., probability) and likely short- and long-term consequences of the alternative residential arrangements in the relocation context."

# Societal Issues That Often
# Lead to Requests to Move

What are the societal issues that the custody evaluator needs to understand in addressing these cases? Most parents who want to move cite employment, remarriage, and economic hardship as their reasons for wanting to move. The nonmoving parent often claims that the move is designed to interfere with the relationship between himself and the child.

Employers and the military are not necessarily family friendly. Most people change jobs several times during their adult life—corporations downsize, companies move various operations, military bases close and the military moves people to where they are needed, all regardless of the impact on children in child custody matters. When this occurs, people are faced with choosing between the other parent's access to the child or their own career options/enhancement. The courts have long recognized the necessity and rights of parents to move for employment reasons and, as noted earlier, are likely to grant a move for such reasons to a primary custodial parent.

Parents may wish to move for a remarriage. Many parents get involved in a relationship that requires a move. The future stepparent may reside out of state, or a current stepparent may be transferred to another location. Some stepparents may be unemployed and need to find a job in another state. For these families, it is the blend of remarriage and employment economics that forces the move. Given the relative lack of value placed upon stepparents in the courts, these cases may require a somewhat different analysis. The courts and the evaluator are usually concerned about the direct impact on the relationship between the biological parent and the child.

Economic hardship may cause a move. In high-cost-of-living locales, a single parent may need to move in with relatives or to a location with a lower cost of living, even if there are no relatives nearby. With the recession in 2008–2010, people needed to move in order to find employment or because their house had been foreclosed. In such cases, the court will often assess the reality of the hardship before allowing the move.

In contrast, there is usually only one primary reason that parents oppose moves. This is so the noncustodial parent can maintain frequent and continuing contact with the child. Prior to the 1990s, when it was more common for mothers to raise children and fathers to work, it was not unusual for the noncustodial father to move away from his children sometime after the divorce. While many of those fathers continued their relationship with their children, they were less concerned with the frequency of such contact, as long as they could maintain some relationship with their child. As modern-day fathers have become more directly involved in child raising and participating more fully in their child's day-to-day life, it is not surprising that they find themselves in opposition to proposed moves.

Some fathers allege that the mother wants to move to control or interfere with the child's relationship with him. They maintain that there is no legitimate reason for the move; instead they believe it is born out of revenge or spite. They oppose the move because they can see no positive impact that a move could have on their child. As noted previously, it is critical to understand the motive(s) for moving, and most state laws (both case law and statutory law) consider the motive for the move as a critical factor before deciding on the move.

Often ignored in this debate is the parent who "chooses" to move away from the child, regardless of the reason. While noncustodial parents are often upset by the desire of the custodial parent to move, no one seems to object when the noncustodial parent moves. Yet such moves may be very difficult for the child. The child can experience feelings of abandonment, anger, disappointment, and resentment, and may wish for the return of the relocating parent. This may worsen the child's adjustment to the divorce. For the potential custody evaluator, while it is still rare, there could be an increasing number of evaluations to address appropriate access issues for these families.

# Factors for the Evaluator to Consider

Given the issues noted earlier in the literature and the laws, it is clear that evaluators must focus on the relevant factors noted in the literature and the law when evaluating families for relocation. Judge Dennis Duggan (Albany, New York) has presented numerous workshops for evaluators and judges related to relocation over the years. He has surveyed all 50 states and many countries around the world. From that, Duggan has identified 34 factors that show up in at least one state or country in its relocation statutes or case law (see also Duggan, 2007). In this section, I will describe those factors identified by P. Stahl, Austin, Kelly and Lamb, and Duggan that are relevant to the work of child custody evaluators. When helpful, I will also provide a brief description of each to help evaluators use them while assisting the court in making a ruling that is in the best interests of the child.

## The Actual Time-Sharing Arrangement by the Parents and the History of That Arrangement

One of the most important issues for the evaluator to understand is the *actual* relationship between the child and each parent during the marriage, the early stages of the divorce, and presently. This helps to establish a baseline from which to assess the potential risk to the child's relationship with the other parent if the child were to move. The evaluator will be trying to understand the qualitative and quantitative aspects of the relationships and how much the child relies on each parent for day-to-day needs. This will help the evaluator determine whether the parents have been practicing joint physical custody, or whether one parent has been the primary custodial parent. In many jurisdictions, this analysis is critical for understanding the potential impact of a move on the child and will be a significant factor in the best interest analysis.

Once evaluators understand the history, they can then assess the qualitative nature of the relationships. They will want to know who participates in day-to-day activities, such as helping with homework, reading at bedtime, driving to activities and doctor's appointments, and other daily tasks. Evaluators will want to know to whom the child goes when afraid, excited, angry, or hurt. They will assess the relative attachments and the extent to which the child feels a preference for either mother or father, or if the child is equally close to both. By understanding these facts, evaluators can better understand the current nature of the relationships between the child and each parent.

The evaluator also needs to assess the relationship between the parents. If they share joint legal and joint physical custody, how is their co-parenting arrangement working? When one parent has primary physical custody, the evaluator will want to know how that parent encourages the relationship between the child and the other parent and whether the custody was established voluntarily or as a result of a previous court decision. Because the court is likely to allow a primary custodial parent with a reasonable motive to move, or to allow a move when joint custodial parents share an unworkable plan, this information is critical.

## The Age, Maturity, Interests, Activities, and Special Needs (When Relevant) of the Child

Once the evaluator has assessed the custodial relationship, it is important to understand the developmental issues of the child. As was described in Chapter 5, children of different ages have varying developmental needs. For example, with young children, it will be important to understand how they can be expected to maintain and grow the attachment with the noncustodial parent if distance becomes an issue. Certainly, before age 3 and possibly up to age 4 or 5, a young child requires relatively frequent contact with each parent in order to establish and maintain a relationship. The evaluator must understand how each parent perceives relationships being affected by a move. The evaluator will want to understand the child's capacity to maintain a relationship when significant time might pass between visits.

For school-age children, the evaluator must assess the potential impact on the relationship between the child and the noncustodial parent if the child can visit only for blocks of time, such as vacations, holidays, and summers. The evaluator will want to understand the child's capacity to use the telephone, fax, e-mail, video cameras, and other technologies that might be useful in maintaining an established relationship. The evaluator will also want to know how the noncustodial parent can foster and maintain the relationship with the child at a long distance.

Adolescence may bring a whole range of new issues, such as the adolescent's lack of desire to relocate away from her friends. Teenagers are able to hold and maintain relationships over long distance, but the impact of those relationships is reduced when much of their time is spent with friends. As we encourage and guide adolescents toward adulthood, it is important for the evaluator to understand how each parent will be able to contribute to this task, especially from a distance. Adolescents may state a preference to stay in their community because of strong attachments to friends. This can pose a problem for the evaluator when there are siblings, and the evaluator attempts to meet the needs of all children. Another dilemma is found with the teenager who wants to be with the parent who allows the most freedom but does not necessarily provide the best structure to meet the teen's needs.

Evaluators also want to consider that there may be other relationships that are likely to be affected by the move. Many children have close friends or may be involved in cherished activities (such as Little League, dance, music, etc.). I have had many children express an unwillingness to move because of their preferred activities. Other potential losses for the child would be step-siblings, stepparents, and other close family members. The evaluator needs to understand and report to the court about these potential losses, and evaluate the extent to which the child will be hurt by these losses.

For all children, it is important to understand any special needs, such as medical, educational, or psychological needs, that may contribute to understanding the relevant psychological issues associated with the relocation. One location may have better educational opportunities for a special needs child. One location may have better medical facilities if there is such a need. To the extent special needs are relevant for the particular family, the evaluator should understand those needs within the context of the relocation. Whatever the developmental issues, it is important for the evaluator to understand and integrate them for the particular family.

## Social Capital in Each Location

Children benefit from relationships with a wide array of people, including relatives and extended family. It is important for the evaluator to consider the child's relationships with others in each location. There may be significant relatives on both sides of the family in the location of the proposed move, or there may be few such relationships in both locations. This is an important factor that evaluators can gather data about and share with the court.

## Gender, Temperament, and Fit Between Each Parent and Child

Another issue to understand is the extent to which gender, temperament, or psychological fit is an issue for this family. While there is no specific research that differentiates between the relative value of mothers or fathers for boys and girls, the move might stimulate a problem that is gender related. For example, it might be more detrimental for a teenage son to be moved from his noncustodial father because the father's ability to be a role model will be limited by the move. While a similar scenario might be problematic for a latency-age daughter, the impact could be different and the evaluator needs to understand the gender issue.

Similarly, while many children adjust to a variety of circumstances, some have a temperament that makes adjustment more difficult. The evaluator must understand the child's temperament and whether it might affect the child's adjustment to the proposed move. For some children, especially those who have had difficulty adjusting to significant changes in their life, a move from one's home and community could be detrimental. At the same time, a change of primary custody may be problematic for a child with a temperament that makes adjustment more difficult. A child who had trouble adjusting to the divorce itself may have difficulty adjusting to a family change related to the move. The evaluator must bring an understanding of these issues to the court's attention.

The third criterion, "goodness of fit," reflects the extent to which a parent and child blend or clash in their personalities. For example, a child who is very athletic and interested in sports might miss the parent who is also athletic and a part-time coach differently than a child who is artistic would miss an athletic parent. Similarly, a child who is temperamentally fidgety may do better with a parent who is temperamentally calming. Because many families are being evaluated for the first time and a judicial custody determination has never been made, the evaluator can offer insight to the court on the quality of the relationships and in the psychological connections between each parent and the child. While this is important for all custody evaluations, it is especially crucial in move-away cases.

## Potential Loss to the Child: What Is the Child Likely to Experience if the Proposed Move Does or Does Not Take Place?

When a move is proposed, one of the significant issues is the expected loss to the child. The evaluator in these cases is being asked to assess the nature of the expected loss. This is related to the previous issues, such as the extent and quality of the attachments, the involvement of the noncustodial parent in the child's day-to-day life, goodness of fit, and child development. It is common for the parent who is left behind to express a fear that the child will lose a significant relationship and that such a loss will be detrimental to the child. In contrast, the parent who wants to move typically states that the loss will be minimal to the child. The task for evaluators is to understand their own assessment of this loss and what the child is actually likely to experience, rather than what either parent is alleging will occur.

At the same time, it is important for the evaluator to assess the impact on the child if the move is not allowed to take place or if there is a change of custody and the previously custodial parent moves. In their amicus brief, Wallerstein and Tanke (1995) cites the example of a mother, the primary custodial parent, who wanted to return to school to become a doctor. The move was denied by the court. Wallerstein suggested that the child, a school-age girl, might feel guilty that she prevented her mother from going to medical school. Wallerstein suggests that if the mother becomes depressed because her goal was thwarted, this will also negatively impact the child. This example illustrates the importance of evaluating any potential negative impact on the child if the move does not take place, not merely the impact on the child if the move does occur.

## The Child's Adjustment to Home, School, and Community and the Length of Time That the Child Has Been in a Stable Environment

Just as the evaluator is making predictions about the future life of the child in either the current or future location, it is important to understand how the child has adjusted in his present environment. Some children make adjustments easily and others have a more difficult temperament and struggle with adjustments. All of this needs to be considered by the evaluator in helping the court understand the child's best interests in a relocation case.

### The Preference of a Mature Child

As stated by Wallerstein (1995, 2003), it is important to understand the child's feelings. As children get older, their ideas and wishes sometimes become the overriding determinant, especially in a relocation case. Some children express clear wishes concerning the proposed move, even if it means a change of custody to the other parent. When evaluating the child's statements, it is important to evaluate the reasons that are articulated by the child. Some children have very clear and obvious reasons for their wishes, and others appear to be lobbying on behalf of one of their parents. Differentiating this is an important and potentially difficult task for the evaluator. Other children are reluctant to state their feelings and may be more concerned about protecting one of their parents than stating their own feelings. Especially for children over the age of 10, it is important to understand the child's stated wishes and feelings and incorporate them into the recommendations being made.

## The Reasons for the Move, and Whether or Not the Proposed Move Is in Good Faith or Designed to Thwart the Legitimate Relationship Between the Child and the Other Parent

The court needs to understand the reasons for the move. Parents might state their reasons to the court in their formal declarations, but the task for the evaluator is to understand whether or not there are hidden factors not being discussed by the parent. For example, a parent might state that he wants to move to be closer to out-of-state relatives. However, the evaluator might actually learn that there is more extended family close by, and it might appear that the primary reason for the move is to interfere with access by the other parent. Often, there is no hidden agenda in wanting to move, but if there is one, it usually relates to interfering with the other parent's relationship with the child. Some parents may hope to get an increase in child support if they move. By taking the time to explore these issues with the parents, the evaluator can be secure in stating whether or not there appears to be a hidden agenda.

## The Reasons for Opposing the Move and Whether or Not the Opposition Is in Good Faith or Designed to Thwart the Legitimate Need of the Custodial Parent to Move

The court similarly needs to understand the reasons for opposing the move. While a move is typically opposed by parents who are worried that their relationship with the children will be negatively affected, some parents may oppose the move largely to make life difficult for the moving parent. This occurs when the opposing parent is angry and has a history of making life difficult for the parent who wishes to move. It may occur within the context of domestic violence allegations. This is easier to spot when the parent opposing the move has not exercised court-ordered access or when that parent has previously moved but does not want the relocating parent to move on with her life.

## The Advantages of Moving for Both the Parent and the Child

Some states require that there be a clear advantage available to both parent and child before allowing the move. If you work in one of those jurisdictions, it is important to assess the proposed improvements in the quality of life for parent and child. It should not be assumed that just because a parent's life improves, the child's life will also improve. The evaluator needs to assess the potential change and whether or not the child's life is likely to improve in the new location.

## The Distance of the Move, Including the Travel Time and Cost of Travel Between Homes

Another variable to be evaluated is the logistical realities for the parents. Some moves make it more difficult for the child to see the other parent. Evaluators need to understand how frequently the child can travel, whether travel will need to be by plane and how easy it is to arrange flights, and whether the parents can afford to pay for frequent visits. For very young children who cannot travel by themselves, it will be important to understand how the moving parent envisions access with the other parent taking place. Some parents are quite rigid when it comes to access plans, and others are quite flexible. Flexibility is an important trait when trying to facilitate long-distance access.

## Is the Move Representative of Stability or a Pattern of Instability on the Part of the Moving Parent?

Divorce is a time of potential instability for many children. Whether or not this move is representative of more instability is a critical variable to understand. Changes brought about by divorce are usually stressful to children. Changes brought about by moves are potentially stressful as well. If the requested move is part of an ongoing pattern of instability, the evaluator must note that to the court. For example, I have seen children who have moved four or more times in 3 years following the initial separation, reflective of instability. An out-of-state move might represent more instability or may be the necessary step to reaching relative stability. The evaluator must assess this. This would be especially true if the reason for the move is weak and the evaluator could anticipate another move of even greater distance in the future. Because children require stability following their parents' divorce, the relative stability of each parent will need to be assessed by the evaluator before making a recommendation.

## The Feasibility of a Move by the Noncustodial Parent

In California, as previously discussed, evaluators cannot ask the moving parent what she or he will do if the move of the child is not allowed. In those states where such a question is allowed, it is always helpful to ask the parent opposing the move if he or she is willing to consider moving closer to the children in the event the move is allowed by the court. At the very least, this might help in understanding the potential for settlement after the move.

## Whether or Not the Moving Parent Is Likely to Comply With an Access Order

This is consistent with the good faith motive issue. The evaluator will want to look for evidence that the parent requesting the move has a history of compliance, or of noncompliance, with court orders. Obviously, a history of noncompliance would suggest increased risk associated with moving and getting away from the close watch and jurisdiction of the court.

## The Permanence (or Lack Thereof) of the Proposed Situation

In some circumstances, the proposed move is temporary or less stable. The evaluator will want to consider this issue. For example, a work-related move might be temporary and for only a year, or a new relationship might be so new that it may not yet be stable and secure. In those circumstances, the lack of permanence may be a significant risk factor for the move.

## The Mental and Physical Health of All Persons Involved

A significant factor to evaluate is the mental health of the moving parent, especially if there have been problems with that parent facilitating a relationship with the other parent. Relatively healthy parents who have encouraged and supported the relationship with the other parent are likely to continue that pattern after the move. On the other hand, parents who have a pattern of interfering with the other parent's access may use the relocation to further the interference. The evaluator will want to consider whether the primary reason for the move is really to interfere with the other parent's relationship with the child. For some families, this may be the determining factor in whether the court allows the move.

With regard to mental health issues, the evaluator needs to understand the level of pathology in the adults, the level of conflict between the adults, the extent to which the move is designed primarily to get away from the other parent, any pathology in the children due to their parents' high conflict or emotional disturbance, and the extent to which the children will be affected by the reduction in conflict as opposed to the change in relationships.

## Whether or Not There Are Any False Allegations of Abuse

This is self-explanatory. If there is a history of false allegations, it is likely that the court will be concerned that if the parent who has made those false allegations gets to move with the children, the risk of future allegations might be high.

## Gatekeeping

In recent years, the issue of gatekeeping has gotten increased attention in divorce (Allen & Hawkins, 1999; Pruett, Williams, Insabella, & Little, 2003). Essentially, gatekeeping has been referred to in gender terms as the extent to which a mother restricts or is open to the father's involvement with the child. Studied first in married families, the concept has now been applied to divorced families as well. Gatekeeping occurs along a continuum. At one end of the continuum, a mother encourages the father's frequent and open access to the children. At the other extreme end of the continuum, a mother is extremely restrictive in the extent to which she supports the father's involvement with the children. Such restrictive gatekeeping is usually seen as harmful to children. In addition to this continuum, the evaluator must consider the possibility that restrictive gatekeeping serves a protective function. Such protective gatekeeping might serve to protect children from the influences of harmful or abusive parenting, or parenting that might be neglectful of children's needs. Evaluators should keep in mind that it is common for a parent who alleges restrictive gatekeeping to be the kind of parent against whom protective gatekeeping is warranted.

## Special Issues in International Cases

One of the more interesting areas of relocation is international relocation. In the many years that I have been doing child custody evaluation work, I have been appointed only three times to do an international relocation evaluation, though I have served as a consultant in approximately 5 to 10 such cases. An informal survey of colleagues shows that few have done any international relocation cases and that it is rare for evaluators to have been appointed to more than a handful over the course of their career. An informal survey of judges showed that few have presided over international moves, and while there is some case law in that area, it is rather limited. Earlier in this chapter, I wrote about *Condon* and *Abargil,* two California international relocation cases. I know of only a few attorneys who specialize in international relocation issues. Nonetheless, this is an interesting and important area for child custody evaluators to understand.

> International relocation cases have their own critical factors.

In addition to the usual factors for relocation evaluations, the main factor that the child custody evaluator will want to investigate is whether the country to which the moving parent wants to take the child is a partner with the United States on the international Hague Convention on Private International Law (U.S. Department of State, 2009). There is a clear divide, in that most North, Central, and South American countries; most of Europe; and South Africa, Australia, and New Zealand are all partners, while most of Africa, the Middle East, and Asia are not partners to the Hague Convention. The Hague Convention is designed to help host countries get the return of children who have been removed to another Hague Convention country, but non-signing countries will not typically participate in that. In addition, if a child is moved legally to a Hague Convention country, it is anticipated that the country to which the child has moved will support court orders and enforce access promised in those orders from the original home country. Unfortunately, not

all Hague Convention countries are alike, and several are seen as very compliant while others are seen as generally noncompliant—for example, Brazil,
Germany, Greece, and Mexico, to name a few (Morley, 2009; U.S.
Department of State, 2009). A specific concern is found in Japan, a country
that is not a party to the Hague Convention and where Japanese civil law
stresses that in cases where custody cannot be reached by agreement between
the parents, the Japanese court will not resolve issues based on the best interests of the child. According to the U.S. State Department website, compliance
with family court rulings is voluntary in Japan, which renders any ruling unen-
forceable by the family court. According to this website, foreign parents are
greatly disadvantaged in Japanese courts, even in getting enforceable access.
According to the website, the Department of State is not aware of any case in
which children removed from the United States to Japan have been ordered
returned to the United States by the Japanese courts, even when the left-behind
parent has a U.S. custody decree. Such specialized knowledge can generally be
gained by consulting with an international relocation expert[6] and going to the
State Department website.

In addition, the evaluator will want to understand the history of the family
and the motives for wanting to move. Morley (2009) suggests that these cases
often involve conflict between the parent who wants to return to her home
country and the parent who does not want to lose access to his children. He
describes three types of cases. First, he refers to the "trailing spouse" who
moves to the United States with her husband, but has a completely different
experience after the move. She often feels lonely, misses her family, and feels
very isolated in her new community while her husband goes off to work.
When the marriage dissolves, she wants to return to her native country and
family, which is easy to do if there are no children but causes an international
dispute if there are. In the second example, a U.S. citizen falls in love while
traveling overseas, brings his wife back to the United States, where they have
a child, and when the marriage starts to deteriorate, she just wants to go
home. The third type of case involves a foreigner who comes to the United
States for work or school, gets married, has children, and when the marriage
disintegrates, the foreigner wants to return to her home country. When doing
these evaluations, it is important to understand the history of each parent, the
reasons they got together, relevant cultural issues, and the reasons that the
marriage fell apart and the foreigner wants to return to her native country.
All of this will be important because it relates to motive, both in wanting to
move and in opposing the move.

## Avoiding Bias

As described in Chapter 1, evaluators need to be mindful of potential biases
in their work. I believe that this is especially tricky in relocation cases because
of the tendency to seek the optimal outcome for children, which would, in

most circumstances, include the active and regular involvement of both parents in the child's life. However, a relocation case, by its very nature, cannot allow for that. Courts have long recognized that adults have the absolute right to live wherever they want, just as they have recognized that parents have the absolute right to care for their children. These rights collide in a relocation case. With the growing trend toward shared custody and more equal involvement of both parents, relocation cases challenge the potentially optimal solution of having both parents regularly involved in the child's life.

With that in mind, it is easy for an evaluator who believes that both parents are necessary to recommend against a move in the hope that both parents will continue to reside in the same general vicinity. However, I believe that this is the wrong approach in relocation cases, as long as the law does not require both parents to live in the same general vicinity following a divorce. Instead, it is important for the evaluator to do the required task of understanding all of the relevant factors in his jurisdiction and provide data on those relevant factors in the custody evaluation report. It is important to approach each relocation evaluation with the expectation that the parent who seeks to move will move and the parent who opposes the move will not move. With that in mind, a relocation evaluation is like an initial best interests test where relatively equal shared physical custody is not an option. The choice for the evaluator will be to recommend either primary custody to the moving parent in the new location or primary custody to the nonmoving parent in the current location. Using the data from those factors will help guide and inform the evaluator in making that recommendation.

In my opinion, many relocation cases are a close call. When that is the case, it is always important for the evaluator to be clear in the analysis that the data led to a close call and to state that before making any recommendation. Additionally, as described in Chapter 1, there are times when I believe an evaluator should not make a specific recommendation, either because there is not sufficient data on which to base a recommendation or because it involves the weighting of factors, which is the judge's job rather than the evaluator's job.

> It is important to use factors to help the evaluator avoid a pro-move or against-move bias.

In some relocation evaluations, the data generally line up one way or the other, such that it is clear that the child should be primarily with the moving parent in the new location or that it is clear that the child should remain with the nonmoving parent in the current location. In those circumstances, I will routinely recommend what I believe to be in the child's best interests. However, when it is a close call, I identify for the court those factors that support the move with the parent to the new location and those factors that support remaining with the nonmoving parent in the current location. I then suggest that the court provide the weighting of those factors in order to make a decision about the child's best interests.

For example, in one recent case, in which two parents shared equal custody and one parent needed to move as a result of a military transfer, I recommended to the court that if the court believed that the school-age child's interest in stability and continuity in her community, school, and friends was greater than the child's interest in regularly being with her younger half-sibling, she should remain with the nonmoving parent, but if the court weighted it oppositely, she should move with the moving parent to the new location. In another such case, I recommended to the court that if the court believed that the 12-year-old child's well-reasoned preference to move was of greater weight than the child's interest in stability and continuity in his community, school, and friends that the child should move with the moving parent to the new location, but if the court weighted it oppositely, he should remain with the nonmoving parent in the current location. In those examples, I believed the court needed to weight the relevant factors. At times, there may be a cluster of factors that lends itself one way or the other. Rather than risk any bias creeping into such a case, I believe it is critical to provide the relevant data to the court and let the court make the decision.

Thus, as can be seen from this discussion, I strongly believe that evaluators in relocation cases can best serve the family and the court by providing relevant data associated with each of the relevant factors in that jurisdiction, providing guidance to the court about the psychological risks and protective factors (Austin's relocation assessment model), and then carefully applying that data before making their recommendation. This is the best way to ensure that evaluator biases are avoided.

## THE BOTTOM LINE

Because relocation law is complex and not directly related to the psychological best interests of the child, it may be best to decline making a recommendation on the ultimate issue of whether the child should be in the custody of the moving parent in the new location or in the custody of the nonmoving parent in the old location. After consideration of all of the relevant factors assessed, including relevant risk factors and protective factors identified, with a special focus on the critical legal factors identified in statutory or case law, I will often make two sets of recommendations: one if the court allows the child to move and the other if the court denies the move of the child and yet the parent moves anyway. I may provide a third set of recommendations in the event that both parents live relatively near one another in either the current location or the new one.

To be most helpful to the court and the family, evaluators need to provide clear data from which the court can make its decision. Experience tells me that when the court believes that the evidence is largely equal, but the child could do just as well in the current location with the nonmoving parent or in the new location with the moving parent, motive will be a critical factor, along with a history of caregiving and the child's wishes. In those circumstances, courts will often deny the move and leave custody with the nonmoving parent, granting frequent and appropriate access to the moving parent based on the distance and logistical issues of the family (e.g., financial resources).

It is always important to remember that relocation cases are to be decided on the unique facts of each case. If the court believes that the motive for the move is largely sound, the court will then look to the preponderance of evidence, the standard usually applied in family law matters. If the preponderance of evidence in critical areas (e.g., the history of attachment; the loss to the children of one parent vs. other; social capital in each location; the support of the other parent's relationship with the children; the willingness of each parent to use technology to support the relationship with the other parent; the risks of restrictive gatekeeping; the history of the actual parenting plan; the quality of the moving parent's life and the benefit to the child from the proposed move; any history domestic violence; the nature of an intensity of conflict between the parents; each parent's ability to put his or her respective needs secondary to those of the child; and any other relevant factors) generally leans in one direction, the court will rightfully decide based on the evidence in that direction. However, if the court believes that the preponderance of evidence in critical areas is mixed, judges who are avoiding their own potential bias for or against relocation will determine the appropriate weight to be applied to that evidence and reach the decision it believes is in the child's best interests. To me, that is the essence of good judging and the appropriate use of judicial discretion.

# Notes

1. In this case, the trial judge believed that the mother had no sound reason to move, ruled that she had always interfered with the child's relationship with the father, and determined that there was no benefit to moving. The appellate court upheld the judge's decision to deny the move.

2. Although I was the evaluator in the *LaMusga* case, the only information in the book is from the public record contained in the state Supreme Court decision.

3. There had been a feeling in California that *Burgess* was being interpreted as a bright-line rule (see, e.g., Warshak, 2000b), in which any parent who was considered by the court to be the primary parent had the absolute right to move, absent a showing that the motive was suspect and designed to interfere with the other parent's access.

4. For information on the amicus briefs, see the Liz Library webpage on Child Development and Well-Being: http://www.thelizlibrary.org/site-index/site-index-frame.html#soulhttp://www.thelizlibrary.org/site-index/site-index-body.html#Relocation

5. Note that this two-part test is a different two-part test than that defined in the *LaMusga* decision of the California Supreme Court.

6. Two such experts known to the author are William Hilton, San Jose, California, and Jeremy Morley, New York, New York.

# PART IV

## Other Critical Issues

# 15

# Tackling the Terror of Testifying[1]

O ne of the more difficult tasks for the evaluator occurs when a case goes to trial and she or he has to prepare for testifying in court. For many evaluators, this is a daunting task, stimulating fear, feelings of inadequacy, and insecurity. This is especially true for the relatively novice evaluator who has limited court experience and has done little testifying in the past. Contemplating the experience can be terrifying, but developing confidence can help.

Because the basic tools used by an evaluator are interviewing, psychological testing, observation, report writing, and other such clinical skills, few evaluators are adequately trained in the art and technique of testifying. Excellent resources for forensic psychologists (Brodsky, 1991, 1999, 2004) provide direction for mental health professionals in the courts. However, those books are designed for forensic experts who do court-connected work in many areas, not just custody evaluations. There has been little written to teach evaluators about testifying within the context of custody evaluations. The purpose of this chapter is to focus on the experience of preparing for and giving testimony in court. It includes discussions of legal procedures and issues related to testifying. This knowledge will reduce the evaluator's anxiety about testifying and help maintain his professionalism.

Once a report has been completed and sent to the attorneys, it is not uncommon for parties to reach their own settlement. However, all too often and for reasons having little or nothing to do with the quality of the evaluation, one parent or the other will challenge the evaluator's recommendations and ask to have a judicial hearing on the matter. If one of the parents objects to implementing the evaluator's recommendations, a trial will be necessary. In such instances, the evaluator will usually be the key and may be the only neutral and objective witness to present data, opinions, and recommendations to the court.

# The Deposition

When a case is set for a trial or hearing, either or both attorneys may want to take the evaluator's deposition. Taking a deposition is a formal legal procedure in which a witness gives testimony, under oath, before a court reporter. The attorney who gives notice of the deposition will question the witness first. The other attorney usually will be given the chance to follow. The purpose of the deposition is discovery. In essence, the attorney taking your deposition is trying to understand more thoroughly what you did, why you did it, if this is typical for your practice, and what you believe your findings mean. The attorney will be seeking clarification on things that she does not understand in your report and may also be asking you about things that are not in your report. The attorney will want to know what you would say if the case does go to trial.

During the deposition, just as at a trial, the other attorney has the right to make objections for the record. These are usually technical and may relate to the form of the question or about the area of inquiry. However, with no judge present, the objection will not be ruled upon at the moment; instead it will be preserved, and if your deposition testimony is actually used at trial, the judge will rule on the objection at that time. Be prepared to answer the question even if there has been an objection. Of course, if you have your own attorney with you and your attorney makes an objection and tells you not to answer the question, you would likely choose to follow your attorney's advice and not answer the question.

After the deposition, the court reporter will prepare a transcript and you will be given the opportunity to review the transcript. The purpose of the review is to check that the testimony was correctly transcribed; it is not to change your testimony or try to make your testimony sound better by editing it. Any substantive changes made can, and probably will, be brought up by the attorney in court. At the same time, court reporters sometimes make mistakes, and it is critical to make sure that the testimony has been transcribed accurately.

> A deposition is testimony taken by an attorney and is focused on understanding what you did, why you made the recommendations that you made, and what you are likely to say at trial. While a judge is not present, it is just as formal as courtroom testimony.

The deposition usually takes place in the attorney's office, but occasionally the attorney may request that it occur in the evaluator's office. This gives the attorney the opportunity to see such things as what books you have in your office and takes away the convenient opportunity ("That's in my office, I'll have to get it for you later") for you to avoid disclosing items that you may not want the attorney to know about immediately. If asked if the deposition can take place in your office, a simple, "It really won't accommodate the process" should suffice.

The major purpose of the deposition is to assist the attorney in preparing for trial by testing the evaluator's opinion and recommendations and the basis for the recommendations. In addition, the attorney may want to see how the evaluator performs as a witness and to pin down the evaluator's testimony. The deposition transcript may be used at trial. If the evaluator answers a question differently at trial than at deposition, the attorney may use the deposition transcript to impeach or question the evaluator about the change in testimony.

Typically at trial, the first person taking your testimony will be doing what is known as direct examination, and the second attorney will be doing cross-examination. In a deposition, however, the roles are reversed, in that the deposing attorney is usually the one who is challenging your results and conclusions, and the follow-up attorney is the one who is more likely to support your process and conclusions. In both trial and deposition, each attorney takes turns asking their questions. The sequence at trial is direct examination, cross-examination, "re-direct" in which follow-up questions can be asked, followed by "re-cross-examination." This process continues until questions are concluded.

The purpose of an evaluator testifying at a trial is to assist the judge, the trier of fact, in making a decision. The job of the evaluator in testifying is the same, regardless of whether it is at a deposition or a trial, and regardless of who is asking the direct or cross-examining questions.

## The Process at Trial

Whether or not the evaluator likes it, the evaluator must remember that a trial is an adversarial process in which each side is attempting to provide relevant facts that primarily support its position to assist the court in making a determination of custody and access issues. The process is formal one, regulated by rules of civil procedure, rules of evidence, and state and local court rules. The petitioner of the case presents her side to the court first, followed by the respondent. For each witness, the attorney who calls the witness asks the first questions. This process is referred to as direct examination.

Before asking questions about the evaluation, the attorney will establish the witness's qualifications to testify as an expert by asking questions about his education, professional experience, and experience testifying. This process is called "voir dire." During voir dire, the opposing attorney may attempt to challenge the witness's ability to testify as an expert or narrow the scope of the testimony. This is an uphill battle because the court has already accepted you as an expert when you were

> Voir dire is the process to establish your credentials and to outline the scope of your expertise.

appointed to do the evaluation. In my experience, this voir dire is likely to happen when the attorney who is not happy with your report and recommendations was not the attorney who agreed in the first place to having you appointed to do the evaluation. Do not take this process personally, as the attorney is simply doing his job by trying to keep your report out of evidence.

Keep in mind, however, that the judge will usually accept you as an expert if you were originally appointed by the court in that role.

After voir dire, the first attorney asks questions that are referred to as the "direct examination." The purposes of the direct examination at trial are to lay the foundation for putting the report in evidence, to have the evaluator answer questions about the evaluation process, and to support the evaluator's conclusions. During direct examination, the attorney will be asking open-ended questions, trying to get you to explain who you evaluated, what you did in the evaluation, when you did it, why you did what you did, what you found, what you believe, why you believe what you believe, what you are recommending, and why you are making those recommendations. You are likely to be asked what data support your recommendations and what data do not support your recommendations. You are likely to be asked if you considered other options and recommendations and what those were. Ultimately, you will be given wide latitude to explain what you did, why you did it, and how your findings were consistent with your conclusions.

> Direct examination goes first and incorporates open-ended questions starting with "why," "what," "who," "where," and "how." Avoid narratives but give thorough answers to these open-ended questions.

Following the direct examination is the "cross-examination," in which the other side poses questions designed to cast doubt in the judge's mind about either your process or your conclusions. During cross-examination, you will be asked about the things you did not do and why you did not do them. You will be asked about the data that support the parent you recommended against. You will be asked about missing data, data you did not collect, and data you were not able to collect. You will be asked about your choice of collateral witnesses and why you did not call everyone that her client wanted you to call. You can expect to be challenged on your process and on your conclusions. Do not take this personally, as the attorney is doing her job, supporting the goals of her client.

> The best answers to cross-examination questions are frequently short, perhaps nothing more than "yes" or "no."

During this question-and-answer process, the attorneys are to conduct themselves according to rules of evidence and local court rules. As noted earlier, during a deposition, there is no one there to control the proceedings, so objections can be made for the record. At a deposition, you must still answer the questions asked, but before any part of a deposition is used or admitted into evidence, the judge needs to rule on all objections related to the portion offered.

During the trial, it is the judge's job to control the proceedings. When an objection is raised, judges will either sustain or overrule the objection. If it is sustained, you will not answer the question. If it is overruled, you will. The judge may also ask questions to try to help clarify what you have testified to and to get answers for questions the judge has about your report and your conclusions. At the conclusion of your testimony, the hearing/trial will continue until both sides are finished calling witnesses and providing argument to the court. When this process is concluded, the judge considers all the evidence and makes a decision.

For the inexperienced evaluator, testifying in court can be a terrifying process. The rest of this chapter is designed to assist the evaluator in preparing for testimony, approaching the testimony, and remaining professional. The suggestions made in this chapter are based upon my experience and training, as well as discussions with attorneys and judges. I encourage all evaluators to pay attention to local court rules and their state's rules of evidence. Contact your local court to get the local court rules. Search the Internet (or call the state bar association) to get rules of evidence. Perhaps the best way to learn is to spend a day at the local courthouse observing other evaluators in their testimony. The suggestions in this chapter are basic tools to reduce anxiety and to help the evaluator stay in control of the testifying process.

# Preparing for the Testimony

Perhaps the single most important thing the evaluator can do to prepare for testimony is to write a clear, well-organized, and thorough report. It should provide sufficient information to the attorneys and the court about the evaluator's process, data, and reasons for the conclusions and recommendations. As noted earlier, if you write a thorough report and provide a concise, well-organized analysis, this will help the direct examination as the attorney can ask specific questions focused on the appropriate details of the report, and the opposing attorney will have a harder time attacking it. As you write your report, think about whether your analysis can support your conclusions if the case goes to a trial.

In contrast, when the report is either too brief or too long or when it does not flow in a coherent and integrated manner, it may be difficult for either attorney to understand the rationale behind the recommendations. This is likely to invite either a conference call from the attorneys, a deposition, or a trial. The strongest settlement tool an attorney can have is a well-reasoned and well-written report.

However, not even a well-done evaluation and a well-written report can prevent a trial in some cases. As noted in Chapter 14, relocation cases are often very difficult to settle. In other types of cases, if the two sides cannot agree on custody and access based on your report, one side or the other is going to request your testimony, either in support of their case or to challenge your conclusions. Whether for deposition or trial, you must prepare for your testimony before it begins.

Preparation for testimony at deposition or trial begins with being thoroughly familiar with your work and your report. Review your report, notes, and any materials provided to you. In most jurisdictions, you will not be able to speak with the attorneys substantively unless in a joint conference call. In other jurisdictions, you might be able to talk with each of the attorneys about your report and your conclusions. J. Gould (personal communication, 2005) has suggested that the evaluator prepare written questions for both attorneys to help in the examination of the report. I have known attorneys to send a letter to the evaluator with a copy to the other attorney prior to testimony with questions for the evaluator. Ultimately, state and local court rules will determine what types of communication attorneys and the evaluator can have prior to testifying.

Where an expert represents one side, the attorney hiring you will prepare you for testimony and you may assist the attorney in developing questions for trial.

> Being prepared means being thoroughly familiar with your file and your data, and in control of your emotions. Stay calm, relaxed, and emotionally balanced before, during, and after your testimony.

Remember that you may be asked in deposition or trial whether you talked with the other attorney or whether you reviewed anything in preparation for testifying. It is a legitimate question, and it is perfectly proper to review your file and to speak with the attorney prior to testimony. You just have to know that you can be asked what was discussed. Thus, when you have discussions with the attorney who has hired you, be prepared to answer questions about those conversations.

Your appearance at deposition or court may be demanded by subpoena or may be arranged by an informal agreement between the attorneys. If it is by subpoena, the document will tell you what to bring, for example, "your complete file" or "all notes, correspondence, and any documents you reviewed along with your report." In most states, expert witnesses are entitled to their customary expert fees for a deposition. You are also entitled to be paid at the beginning of the deposition. Prior to the deposition, you should make sure that you have advised the attorney what your deposition fee is and be clear on who will pay it and when it will be paid.

An important part of preparation is to have your file completely organized. This allows you to find things easily. Arrive a few minutes early. It makes a bad impression when you keep attorneys or the judge waiting. Bring enough copies of your curriculum vitae for each attorney and the judge, even if you think they already have it. Planning ahead, arriving on time, and having things organized will give you time to relax and prepare yourself emotionally for your testimony. This will allow you to maintain your own control during what may be an anxious or tense experience. If you arrive late, your file is disorganized, or you feel rushed, it will be more difficult to stay focused and calm during your testimony.

A final thing to pay attention to is your appearance. Do not dress so that your appearance invites notice. Do not wear clanking, flashy jewelry or a loud tie. Be professional and subdued in your appearance. Always remember that your appearance will provide the first impression to the court, regardless of your skill and qualifications.

# Testifying Procedures

There are certain important testifying procedures. For example, it is important to speak calmly, slowly, and clearly. This ensures that the judge and attorneys hear you accurately and allows the court reporter to record your testimony accurately. Spell words that may not be familiar to the court reporter. Avoid an argumentative tone that might alienate an attorney or the judge. Do not use sarcasm or joke on the stand. By staying calm, speaking clearly and slowly, and maintaining an even tone of voice, you will improve the credibility of your testimony.

Always allow the attorney to finish the question before beginning your answer. Not only is this courteous, but it allows you time to think through your answer before giving it. Attorneys and judges have told me that one of their biggest frustrations about testimony is when expert witnesses presume they know the question before it is complete, giving their answer too early. Additionally, the court reporter cannot record the proceedings when two people are speaking at once.

In direct testimony, it is best to provide as much information as possible in answer to the questions, without giving any long narratives. If the attorney asking the question needs more information, she will usually ask for elaboration. If you begin to speak too long, the other attorney may object that your answer is a narrative. If you expect that you will need to give a long answer to a particular question, you might announce that your answer will be lengthy and ask the court for permission for giving a longer than usual answer to the question. With experience, you will recognize what answers are generally considered of reasonable length and what answers are of the narrative variety. Once you learn to understand this basic difference between a reasonably long answer and a narrative, you can always ask the court's permission in advance. When I have asked permission from a judge to give an answer that is expected to be a narrative, I have never had a judge refuse.

In contrast, it is generally best to give short, brief answers to the questions you are asked during cross-examination. Stay focused on the data in your report and answer questions honestly. Do not volunteer information that you have not been asked or any information that is irrelevant to the case just to impress anyone. If you say, "I'm the county's expert in relocation," you are only inviting questions about your history with these cases. Not only will you appear arrogant, but now you have to answer questions about yourself rather than the case. Do not get defensive or sarcastic if the attorney asks questions you are unsure how to answer. Simply impress everyone with your knowledge of the facts of the particular case.

Many judges consider it wise for the evaluator to take a few seconds after a question is asked before responding. This allows you to reflect on the answer and be more certain that you are saying what you want to say. This is true both for questions you are not sure how you want to answer and for complex questions. By pausing and reflecting on the question before you answer, you are more assured that your testimony is what you want it to be. If you need to refer to your file, by all means do so, but do not look at your notes or through your file without asking the court's permission. Also remember, if you look for something in your notes, the attorney may want to see what you are looking at and can ask to see your notes and then ask questions about what is in them.

Another reason for pausing is related to the court process itself. One attorney may object to the form or nature of the question being asked. Pausing gives the other attorney the opportunity to object prior to the start of your answer. When an objection is made at deposition, it is important to wait for the attorneys to complete their arguments before answering the question. At a deposition, after an objection is made, you still answer the question. As previously stated, if that testimony is used in court, the judge will hear the objection prior to reading the answer from a deposition. In the courtroom, it is always important to allow both attorneys to complete their arguments regarding the objection and to wait for the judge to make a ruling. You should not interrupt the judge, and you should not give an answer when the judge has sustained an objection. If a question has been asked that you want to answer, it is important to wait until you have the right opportunity. You may be able to provide the necessary information embedded in your answer to another question. However, you may never get the opportunity to say what you want to say about a particular piece of data. If there is something that you think of that you want to add to a prior answer, you can always pause after answering a question and ask the judge, "I'd like to amend a prior answer. Can I say a little more?" Then, tell the judge what question you are amending, and after the judge gives permission to amend the prior question, go ahead and do so.

It is important that your testimony remain independent and objective at all times. Remember, prior to testifying, you swore to "tell the truth, the whole truth, and nothing but the truth" in your oath. To me, this means providing not only the information that you want to give and that supports your conclusions but also information that might not be as flattering to your work. While your recommendations are likely to favor one parent over the other in some areas, it is important not to become an advocate for that parent. Even when you are hired as an expert for one side, you are still a neutral professional working to educate the court and to help the court understand the data that support the best interests of the child. If you are the court-appointed expert, remember that you are an advocate for the data and for the child's best interests. If you become an advocate for one parent during your testimony, the other side might question whether you have lost your objectivity or become biased in your answers. Even worse, the judge might think you are not objective and reject your testimony and work.

Being a neutral evaluator and being balanced means you are independent of either party and do not come from a biased point of view. This is in contrast to the way you might present yourself if you were hired as a consultant for one party. As a consultant you are not independent; you work for that party. As an independent evaluator, however, you have performed the evaluation process in a neutral and balanced manner, and you do not try to prove one side's case. You treat the parties equally in your investigation. If there were circumstances where you did something different with respect to one party than the other, you will explain your reasons, preferably in your report and definitely in your testimony. As long as differences in treatment of the parties were legitimately justified, you will still be viewed as neutral, objective, and independent. As long as you remember that your task is not to determine what is best for either parent but to make a recommendation for what is in the best interests of the child, you can maintain your neutrality.

At the same time, you should be able to take a stand on issues. The only person who will be pleased with your testimony if you cannot take a stand is the person who is challenging your report. Evaluators who are too wishy-washy and unable to take a stand, perhaps out of fear of offending someone, will frustrate the attorneys and the court. The court needs evidence on which to base a decision in the best interests of the child. You are the vehicle for providing that evidence. Neutrality does not mean that you do not reveal one parent's strengths and the other parent's problems if they are relevant to the ability to parent and the best interests of the child. It is not a pleasant task to talk about a person's problems and weaknesses as a parent, but that is part of your job. If it is relevant to the best interests of the child, you must be prepared to say it.

> Stay focused on the data, be clear and concise in your testimony, and avoid weak, wishy-washy responses.

Another thing you will want to do periodically is look at the judge. The attorney who is questioning you is the one with whom you are having a dialogue, but an occasional turn to the judge, particularly if you are making an important point, is helpful. Do not feel intimidated if the judge appears to be scrutinizing you. The judge is trying to determine how much weight to put on your testimony and needs to get a feel for your expertise. If the judge asks you a question, answer it. Do not look at the attorney first. Remember, it is the judge who needs to know your testimony because it is the judge who makes the decisions.

## Stick to the Data

Those who argue that child custody evaluators should not make recommendations claim that child custody evaluators reach conclusions that go beyond the data. Melton, Petrila, Poythress, and Slobogin (2007) state, "Indeed, there is probably no forensic question on which overreaching by mental health professionals has been so common and so egregious" (p. 540).

One of the clearest ways to ensure your independence as an expert witness is to provide answers that can be supported by your data. As evaluators, we are sometimes tempted to elaborate beyond what the data can support. In some of the tough evaluations described earlier (e.g., child alienation, domestic violence, or relocation), we might not have enough data even at the end of a thorough evaluation to be sure whether or not someone is interfering with the child's relationship with the other parent, whether or not abuse has taken place, or whether a parent should or should not move. If we have given psychological testing, there might be conflicting evidence from the tests, the interviews, and the observations that also interfere with our level of certainty. Collateral sources might also provide conflicting data. If you have described those inconsistent data in your report, it will be easier to explain it in your testimony. As evaluators, we are sometimes cautious regarding our recommendations because of mixed data. If, as described in Chapter 1, you provided data in your report that supported your conclusions and also the data that did not support your conclusions, it is easier to avoid speculation beyond that which the data can support.

At the same time, evaluators do make recommendations about specific items for which there may be little direct data. In those instances, we use indirect data and our understanding of developmental and divorce research to support our recommendations. For example, if we have given a recommendation for an exchange of a child at a particular time on the weekend, there is unlikely to be data that support a specific time other than specific family logistics. However, we know from the research on high-conflict families that structure and consistency reduce conflict. Additionally, we know that young children need consistency and simplicity of schedules. Thus, we can testify with relative confidence about such a recommendation even if the evaluation data might not lead directly to the specificity of such a recommendation. We might not know whether someone has been abusive to the other parent or child even after reviewing all of the data. As stated in the section on report writing, it may be best to be clear that you do not know all of the answers to the referral questions when that is the case, even after gathering all evaluation data.

Another area of possible concern is when the evaluator has not seen one parent and is asked in testimony to provide data about that parent. This would be in those instances where one parent has not agreed to participate with a court-ordered evaluation or if the court order directs only one parent to participate in a psychological evaluation. If you have seen only one parent, you cannot make statements about the other parent. For example, if you have seen only the father, you cannot say, "Mother is depressed and unable to care for the children." Instead you would say, "Father expresses concern that mother is depressed and is unable to care for the children, but I have not been able to evaluate this matter."

A third way of sticking to the data is to admit when you do not know something, when you have been unable to find an answer to a particular question, or when you have made a mistake. Frequently in complex custody evaluations, there will be some things that the evaluator cannot answer. Along with this, psychological research is still evolving, so it may be difficult to make precise recommendations when there is limited information. While evaluators typically make specific recommendations, they need to be cautious in report writing and during their testimony to express clearly what they do and do not know.

Finally, there may be times when the evaluator does not have enough data because something was missed. For example, if you did not talk to the pediatrician, you may need to explain why you did not. It is rare that one piece of data will sway an opinion gathered from multiple sources, but if you are asked questions about the pediatrician's testimony and realize that talking with her might have helped, admit it. If asked by the court to do something that you did not do, offer to do so if later asked. Judges are critical of evaluators who are reluctant to admit mistakes for fear of looking bad. When evaluators make mistakes, it is important to clarify and acknowledge them. Sometimes inexperienced evaluators can become defensive and arrogant. A simple statement that you could have done something you did not do would be better. For example, in a recent case where the evaluator had not done a thorough alcohol assessment, the evaluator strengthened his testimony by admitting that a more thorough alcohol assessment most likely could have been helpful.

## Avoid Ipse Dixit Assertions

When answering questions, it is always important to explain the data that lead to your reasoning and conclusions. At times, however, I have heard experienced witnesses say something without having the data to make the assertion. Such statements are referred to as "ipse dixit" statements, meaning statements that should be believed simply because the witness said them. Attorneys will try to expose analytical gaps in your reasoning if you do not have the data to support your statements. As an expert witness, while you may rely on your experience to help in formulating your opinions, you are still expected to explain how your experience leads to your conclusions and how your experience is reliably applied to the data and how your experience is a sufficient basis for your opinions (Zervopoulos, 2010).

These principles are identified in the Federal Rules of Evidence. Rule 702 states,

> If scientific, technical or other specialized knowledge will assist the trier of fact to understand the evidence or to determine a fact in issue, a witness qualified as an expert by knowledge, skill, experience, training or education, may testify thereto in the form of an opinion or otherwise, if (1) the testimony is based upon sufficient facts or data, (2) the testimony is the product of reliable principles and methods, and (3) the witness has applied the principles and methods reliably to the facts of the case.

The principles related to this Rule require a child custody evaluator to be able to explain the basis for his conclusions.

According to Zervopoulos (2010), four steps are required to apply these principles. They are:

1. Determine whether the witness is qualified as an expert by knowledge, skill, experience, training, or education.

2. Determine whether the expert's methods follow applicable professional standards of the relevant professional specialty.

3. Evaluate the empirical and logical connections between the data arising from the expert's methods and the expert's conclusions.

4. Gauge the connection between the expert's conclusions and the proffered expert opinion. (p. 28)

Assuming that you have the requisite knowledge, skill, experience, training, and education and that you have applied reliable principles in completing the evaluation, your report and testimony must explain how you know what you say you know. Your conclusions must always be based on the data gathered in your evaluation so that you avoid ipse dixit reasoning.

# Dealing With Hypothetical Questions

Attorneys often ask hypothetical questions during cross-examination, adjusting some of the facts to see whether your recommendation might change. This tactic is used to question the evaluator's recommendations and to support the consideration of a different recommendation. Hypothetical questions involve situations that the cross-examining attorney will attempt to show as factual. By asking you about your recommendations under hypothetical situations, the attorney is attempting to lay the foundation that if the court accepts the facts in the hypothetical, a different conclusion might result. This also happens when you are hired by one side and you have only reviewed the report and other case data and have not seen any family members. In that circumstance, you can answer only hypothetical questions about the family.

In that circumstance, it is important to answer the hypothetical questions objectively. It is easy for an evaluator to look like an advocate rather than an impartial expert if he is not careful. If the hypothetical facts would lead to a different recommendation, it is important to state so. This is probably the best time to pause, think through your answer, and describe out loud why your recommendation would or would not change as a result of these hypothetical facts. One effective way of dealing with hypothetical questions is to state clearly that the facts as presented in the hypothetical are not consistent with the facts of the case as you understood them when you evaluated the family.

However, if the data were as the hypothetical question implied, be sure to tell the complete truth in response to the hypothetical question.

Similarly, if you get asked a difficult, negative question about the parent whose requests you are supporting or the parent whose attorney hired you if you are hired by one side, answer it honestly. If you can, relate the question and your answer to the ability to parent. Again, avoid becoming an advocate and be direct and clear in acknowledging weaknesses in the parent whose position you are otherwise supporting. If the data show that the parent is not perfect, answer the question honestly. Stick to the data you have gathered and report accurately on the strengths and weaknesses of each parent. Answering questions directly and honestly assists the judge in reaching a sound conclusion. If you avoid the tough questions, minimize strengths in the parent you are recommending against and weaknesses in the parent you are supporting, it will be more difficult for the court to view you as unbiased, making it more difficult for the court to use the information in your evaluation in a helpful way.

## Remain Professional

Being professional means being prepared. You need to be prepared for both direct and cross-examination prior to any testimony. As stated, you need to know everything in your file, the strengths and weaknesses of each parent, and the rationale used in reaching your conclusions. Experience may help you anticipate questions. A novice evaluator might wish to consult with a more experienced evaluator to aid in testimony preparation. Role-playing with colleagues or going to court to observe a colleague helps prepare you for your testimony in any case. Even if you feel experienced, you must prepare for testimony in every case. Ultimately, you will want to anticipate the kinds of questions the judge might ask and the important, factual data you want to discuss so you can teach the judge what she needs to know.

At times, you will have a direct examining attorney who does not ask you the correct questions, and you have data you want to give the judge. Elaborating on your answers to the direct examination may give you the chance to provide that information to the court. In some jurisdictions, it is considered appropriate to meet with the attorney who is calling you to go over your testimony ahead of time, though in most it is not. Make certain that this does not violate local court rules prohibiting ex parte communication at all levels of the process.

Finally, as a professional, never debate the cross-examining attorney. Judges and attorneys get frustrated with evaluators who end up arguing with an attorney. Rather than argue, simply answer the attorney's questions. Do not ask questions of the attorneys. After answering a hypothetical

> Always remain neutral and balanced in your testimony, ensuring your unbiased professionalism.

question with the statement, "Those are not the facts that I am aware of in this case," answer the question as if the hypothetical facts were true. If you are annoyed by the cross-examining attorney and her style of questioning, it is even more important to keep your answers short and succinct, focused directly on the question. Answer "yes" or "no" questions with either a "yes" or "no" answer without elaboration.

## Trick Questions

Never take questions from the cross-examining attorney personally. Remember, it is her job to raise a question in the judge's mind about your qualifications, process, or recommendations. Sometimes cross-examining attorneys will ask provocative questions to try to trip you up. Sometimes it may appear as if they are trying to blame you for your recommendations. I know of an attorney who once asked an evaluator, "Is it really your intent to deprive this child of a relationship with her mother?" Such a question can leave an evaluator feeling defensive. Sometimes a cross-examining attorney might ask about you about your experience or the number of times you have recommended for joint, sole-to-mother, or sole-to-father custody. Such questions are designed so the attorney can claim you are biased. Answer those questions briefly, honestly, and without emotion. At other times, the attorney might ask you whether you have children or about your own marital status. You probably do not need to answer these questions. Anytime you believe the question is personal and not relevant to your professional role in the case, you can answer, "I don't believe that question is relevant to my professional role." An attorney who still wants you to answer the question will ask the judge to direct you to answer. Then, do as the judge directs.

Never let your frustration interfere with professional testimony. Attorneys are trained to try to upset you. Do not give the attorney that advantage with your testimony. The attorney may ask trick questions, designed to throw you off base. For example, an attorney on cross-examination might ask a question in an incredulous tone, like, "Are you actually saying that Mrs. Smith is the best choice for primary parent?" The tone of the question suggests that there might be no reason to make that recommendation. The best way to handle this type of question is simply and nondefensively to say, "Yes, that is my recommendation based on the information I collected during the evaluation."

Another trick is to ask a complex question that accurately reflects part of what you said, while distorting another part of your testimony. An attorney once asked me to read a passage from my earlier book about the developmental needs of preschool children. She only wanted me to read two paragraphs. This left out important contrary information that was in the following two paragraphs. I read the section as asked, hoping for an opportunity to state the rest but did not argue it. In re-direct, the other attorney asked me to finish the section so that my entire opinion as stated in the book could be given to the court. If I had attempted to read more than asked, it would have been objected to and might have made me look biased.

Similarly, if you are asked, "So, is it your opinion that the domestic violence allegations made by my client may not have happened as she alleged, and therefore are unfounded?" you might say that the allegations did not seem to happen exactly as she claimed, "but nowhere in my report did I say that the allegations were unfounded." Listen carefully for the entire question. Acknowledge what is true, and clarify what is falsely implied by the question.

Sometimes, attorneys question me about something *they say I said* in my report, *but I know I did not say it*. Such a question might be, "Isn't it true that you saw no evidence of problems in the parent–child relationship when you observed my client with his child?"

> Pay attention to the questions so you can avoid being tricked by the attorney challenging your conclusions.

even when I never said this. You will not fall for this trick if you know your report exceedingly well prior to giving testimony. If such a question comes up, my response always is, "Could you please show me where I said that and then I would be happy to respond."

Ultimately, you will maintain you professionalism by staying neutral, calm, and self-assured. By sticking to the facts of the case, by avoiding an appearance of becoming an advocate for one side, by refusing to debate a cross-examining attorney who tries to provoke you, by refusing to take personally attacks on your professional or personal beliefs, and by answering questions directly and within the bounds of the data, you keep your professionalism intact and ensure the court that you are truly a professional expert and that there is a sound basis for your recommendations.

## Do's and Don'ts for Testifying in Court

- Look confident and secure—be overprepared.
- Write a balanced, thorough report.
- Know your report and everything in the file.
- Speak calmly, slowly, and clearly—avoid an argumentative tone.
- Avoid the splitting and polarization in the courtroom by becoming too much of an advocate for one side.
- If you are sure about something, say it unequivocally.
- Avoid jargon, both in your reports and your testimony.
- Avoid overexplaining or becoming too technical.
- Allow the attorney to finish the question before answering.
- Avoid talking when attorneys and the judge are discussing an issue; wait when an objection is made.
- Stop and think before answering tough questions; stop talking when you have finished answering the question.
- Refrain from speculation beyond what the data support.

- Give no opinions about anyone not seen as part of the evaluation.
- If you do not know something, or if you have made an omission or mistake, admit it.
- If asked a hypothetical question, answer it honestly.
- Do not allow yourself to get emotional; do not allow your feelings to be hurt or get angry.
- Remember that the judge's job is to support a fair trial and control the proceedings.
- Stay cool, honest, direct, nondefensive, balanced, neutral, and decisive.
- Avoid being unprepared, defensive, sarcastic, rigid, or one-sided, and try to take control of the trial.

## THE BOTTOM LINE

Testimony is like teaching. When you testify, you are teaching the judge, the attorneys, and the parents about the relevant issues involved in the particular case you are testifying about. If you did a court-appointed evaluation, you are teaching them about the data you collected, the strengths and weaknesses of each parent, the attachment of the child with each parent, the relevant child development and divorce research, and the relevant psychological issues of that family that pertain to the best interests of the child. If you are hired as an expert by one side, you may be teaching the judge about the strengths and weaknesses of the work of the court-appointed child custody evaluator, or the research about a particular topic, such as conflict, domestic violence, relocation, attachment, or overnights with each parent. Regardless of your particular role, it is always important to take the oath to heart and always remember to tell the truth, the whole truth, and nothing but the truth. Never take sides on the outcome of the case, yet always feel free to advocate forcefully in your testimony for the data you are presenting, as long as you are certain to testify to the rest of the data as well.

# Note

1. This chapter is an adaptation of Chapter 10 in Stahl, P., *Complex Issues in Child Custody Evaluations* (Sage, 1999).

# 16

# Critiquing Evaluations

As mentioned in a previous chapter, over the past several years I have spent considerable time critiquing evaluations and have developed a protocol for these critiques. There has been only a limited amount of literature in this area (Gould, Kirkpatrick, Austin, & Martindale, 2004; P. Stahl, 1996) over the past 15 years. Additionally, the National Council of Juvenile and Family Court Judges (NCJFCJ) developed a protocol for critiquing evaluations in domestic violence cases (Dalton, Drozd, & Wong, 2005). The purpose of this chapter is to provide you with an outline of these protocols for critiquing your own evaluation before sending it to the courts and the attorneys. I believe that if evaluators pay attention to how psychologists, attorneys, and judges critique other people's work, it may help improve the overall quality of the custody evaluations performed.

Essentially, the protocols start with a focus on the experience and qualifications of the evaluator. Especially for cases with domestic violence allegations, the NCJFCJ suggests that judges ensure that the evaluator has been trained to understand the dynamics of domestic violence and has focused on safety issues as well as the overall parenting plan. When I am asked to critique an evaluation, I always want to know about the qualifications and experience of the child custody evaluator. This is the first step in ensuring that the evaluation is being competently performed. However, because it is common for attorneys and the court to appoint evaluators with sufficient training and experience, it is rare that I find that an evaluator is not qualified.

> Do you have the necessary training and experience to conduct the evaluation that has been referred to you?

With this concept in mind, however, I would encourage you to ensure that you are qualified to perform evaluations and that you have sufficient training and experience to perform evaluations in the specific area of your case.

Even before the interviews take place, I look to find out if the evaluator gave each of the parents a thorough written and verbal informed consent. Did the evaluator explain that she would be making specific recommendations to the court and that one or both parents might not be happy with the recommendations that would follow? Did the evaluator inform the parents

Did you provide the parents with appropriate informed consent, especially about the limits of confidentiality?

of the limits of confidentiality and inform the parents of the state's reporting laws? I would urge that before performing an evaluation, the evaluator should think about his procedures, informed consent, and the need to let parents know what his role is, what the parents' responsibilities are, and what he will do in the evaluation. I always let parents know that I will be asking many questions and they should not assume that I believe one parent more than the other. I inform parents that I do not ever know what to believe until I get a chance to check things out. When I critique someone else's evaluation, I look for evidence that the evaluator did those things.

The next step is to ensure that the procedures are thorough and balanced. As noted in Chapter 1, various *Model Standards* (Associated Family and Conciliation Courts [AFCC], 2006), *Guidelines* (American Psychological Association, 2009), and Rules of Court (e.g., California Rule of Court 5.220) require evaluators to use balanced procedures. At times, such balance is not possible, and in those situations, the evaluator is expected to explain what led to the unbalanced procedures. Using both the NCJFCJ document and my own experience, I look at the procedures to ensure that there has been sufficient time spent with all adults, with the children, and with observations of parents and children together. I look to see what collateral witnesses were contacted and if there was any evidence that significant collateral witnesses were ignored. In some cases, those significant witnesses might be therapists, day-care workers, teachers, pediatricians, or other first-line neutral collateral people who would likely have critical family information. These procedures should be sufficient to ensure that enough time was spent in gathering data for a thorough assessment of the family dynamics and to answer the evaluation questions. When you are nearing the end of your evaluation, I would urge you to stop to consider whether you spent sufficient time with the family, reviewed all the written collateral data, and contacted relevant and necessary collateral witnesses. If not, then I would urge you to do whatever other procedures necessary until you are satisfied.

The third step is to look at the data that have been collected. Have all of the relevant questions been explored? When mother told the evaluator important information, did the evaluator ask father for his side of the story? Was domestic violence explored, even if it was not identified as a possible issue? Was there evidence that the evaluator used a standard protocol in interviewing children and adults, or was there little or no pattern to the questions that were asked? In the children's interviews, did the evaluator inform the children about the limits of confidentiality? Did the evaluator demonstrate awareness that children's statements might be encouraged by one or both parents? Did the evaluator seem to understand the potential for suggestibility and ask mostly open-ended questions, asking other questions only as follow-up when appropriate?

The next thing I look at are the observations of parents with their children. I am shocked at the number of the evaluations I critique where the evaluator has not seen children in the family because they are either too old or, more commonly, too young. In my view, this is unacceptable. Has the evaluator taken notes of the observation and were those notes written (or dictated) in a timely manner? Were home visits performed? While this is not necessary in any evaluation, I believe that home visits provide richer, more "natural" data than observations that are done in the office. At the same time, it is important to understand that the observations are simply one part of the process. When critiquing the evaluation, I look to see if there are inconsistencies between what the evaluator sees in the home visit and the data gathered from the interviews. If so, I look to see if the evaluator has an explanation for this. With that in mind, I urge evaluators to have a purpose to their observations, to explain the nature of inconsistencies that might exist between observational data and interview data, and to make certain that they see all children with the parents.

> Were your procedures, including interviews and observations, thorough and balanced?

If psychological testing or parenting questionnaires were administered, I look to see whether they were used appropriately. Was there some rationale for the use of specific tests? Were the same tests given to each parent? If not, was there a legitimate reason for this? Were the tests administered according to the instructions in the test manual? I have seen instances where evaluators let parents take the test protocols home and fill out the test at home, faxing it back to the office. There is no excuse for not administering the test appropriately and monitoring the administration in some fashion. Were the tests scored accurately? Were test data used to formulate the basis of conclusions, as opposed to using test data to formulate hypotheses about the individuals involved? For example, I have seen many evaluation reports in which it appears that the Rorschach data were used as the basis for the evaluator's conclusions. Is there evidence that the evaluator understood and utilized custody litigant norms, if they exist (e.g., Bathurst, Gottfried, & Gottfried, 1997)? If there is some controversy about a particular test, and the evaluator seemed to rely heavily on that test, did the evaluator acknowledge that in the limitations section of the report? For example, there is controversy about the use of the MCMI–III (Millon Clinical Multiaxial Inventory) and the Rorschach in custody evaluations, and there is literature suggesting that evaluators would not want to use drawings or apperception tests in custody evaluations. Ultimately, did the evaluator explain how different test data yielded contradictory results and did the evaluator discuss inconsistencies between test data and other observational, interview, or clinical data? I would urge all evaluators to think about these questions in the context of testing that you might use.

> If psychological testing is used, is it used appropriately and only to formulate hypotheses?

Regarding the collateral data, I look for evidence that the evaluator talked with relevant collateral witnesses and reviewed all the written collateral data that was given to the evaluator. Did the evaluator list all of the people she talked with? For example, I have reviewed a number of evaluations where the evaluator did not list all of the people spoken to, yet utilized some of that data in reaching conclusions. How did the evaluator reconcile the differences between collateral data that support the positions taken by one parent versus the data supporting the positions taken by the other parent? Did the evaluator show evidence of integrating the collateral data, especially the written data, with the interview and with the observational and/or psychological test data? Did the evaluator use the statements of one witness to override all the other data that was received? I am always concerned about the use of a "sample of 1," and in several evaluations I have reviewed, the data from one witness led to the evaluator's conclusions, as if the rest of the evaluation data did not even exist. Ultimately, I recommend that evaluators critique their own use of collateral data and encourage you to be certain that you have followed the *Model Standards* (AFCC, 2006) and listed all of the collateral information you have considered. When you speak to witnesses, it is important to identify who said what. For example, I have seen a number of evaluations in which it was impossible to know which of the different witnesses said something. This leaves the reader unable to

> Were all potential collateral sources identified and were all statements attributed to the correct sources?

determine the source of relevant evaluation data. If you think about how the attorney who will not like your recommendations will interpret your report, you will want to ensure that you are balanced in your use of collateral information and that you have indicated how the collateral information led to your conclusions.

The next thing I look at is the Analysis section of the report. In all the years that I have been reviewing evaluations, this is the section that has been most troublesome. Too many evaluators present a very weak analysis of their evaluation data. As described in Chapter 10, it is my belief that this is the most important section of the report because it allows evaluators to explain how they considered *all* of the data in reaching their conclusions. When critiquing this section of an evaluation, I look to see whether the evaluator included the data that did not support the conclusions in the analysis or used only data that did support the conclusion (California Rule of Court 5.220). Did the evaluator explain his analysis

> Is your Analysis section thorough and complete? Does your analysis provide sufficient understanding of the risks and benefits of various custodial options and connect the data to the factors that may be in your state's laws?

of the risks/benefits of different custodial options (e.g., primary mother-custody, primary father-custody, or shared physical custody)? Did the evaluator consider the relevant law in the analysis? For example, in states with specific statutory or case law factors associated with best interests or relocation, did the evaluator address the factors? As noted in Chapter 10, it is important to list the factors and provide the evaluation data that relate to the factors. If the evaluator does not do this, the evaluation is less helpful to the judge, who must apply the factors in the law to his decision. As such, I would urge you always to review your analysis in an evaluation before sending it in. Make certain that you have written a thorough analysis of all data, explained the risks and benefits of various custodial options, and provided the court with the necessary data related to factors that the court must consider when making its ruling in the case.

The next area of my critique focuses directly on the recommendations. Ultimately, my main question is, "Do the recommendations make sense given the data gathered?" I have often read reports in which I am thinking that a certain set of recommendations will follow, yet they do not. Attorneys often call me when they have observed the same thing, and they do not understand what the recommendations are based upon. Consistent with the lack of a quality Analysis section, the evaluator in such a situation has not explained the reasons for the ultimate conclusions and recommendations. With that in mind, I would urge you to not only make sure that your recommendations make sense to you, but also consider whether the reader of your report will find that the recommendations make sense.

The final issue that I pay attention to is the question of bias. When I am asked to critique reports, it is common for the attorney who hires me, and that attorney's client, to believe that the evaluation is biased. As a result, I am often hired to provide my expert opinion about that question. I look for evidence of gender bias (e.g., I once read a report where the evaluator decided that the young child should be primarily with the mother because young children need their mother more than their father, in spite of the fact that the tender years doctrine disappeared from consideration in the early 1980s). I try to determine whether there was evidence of confirmatory bias, in which the evaluator seems to reach a conclusion early in the process and then looks primarily for data to support that conclusion. As described in Chapter 1, I strongly believe that evaluators must look for data that will disconfirm their early findings. In other words, did the evaluator keep an open mind until all data were collected? If interim recommendations were made and later findings were consistent with those interim recommendations, I will look for other evidence of confirmatory bias.

Other biases that I commonly see in evaluation reports are that there should not be overnight access with young children and the noncustodial parent, regardless of the data that might support such overnights; bias in favor of or against relocation, regardless of data that might support a position in the other direction; and bias in favor of keeping one parent as the primary parent in a relocation case, regardless of data that would suggest a change of custody is a legitimate consideration in that particular case. In each of those circumstances, I have seen numerous evaluations that showed evidence of such biases. Perhaps the most common is the evaluation report that identifies that a child should not move with

> The allegation of bias is common when a parent is unhappy with your conclusions. Pay attention to evidence of such bias in your evaluation process and report.

the parent who has a legitimate reason for relocation simply because the child needs to maintain a significant relationship with both parents. As described in Chapter 14, the only way to avoid such a bias is to focus on all the relevant factors before reaching a conclusion on the proposed relocation of the child.

# Boy Scout Oath

In concluding this chapter, I suggest that evaluators use the Boy Scout oath when critiquing their work as child custody evaluators. With thanks to the Boy Scouts, the adjectives emphasized in their oath are attributes that Boy Scouts are encouraged to achieve. After listing the item, I will suggest corresponding actions that can show that the evaluator has achieved that level of functioning:

- **Trustworthy:** Evaluators must be trustworthy, telling the truth, the whole truth, and nothing but the truth.
- **Loyal:** Evaluators must be loyal to the process and the needs of the court.
- **Helpful:** This can be a risk for evaluators, if being helpful leads to going beyond one's defined role.
- **Friendly/Courteous/Kind:** Evaluators need to be courteous, provide informed consent to parents, and discuss limits of confidentiality with parents, children, and collateral witnesses.
- **Obedient:** Evaluators need to be obedient to local or state court rules; psychologists to APA *Guidelines* and AFCC members to AFCC *Model Standards*.
- **Brave:** Evaluators need to bravely tell the truth, good or bad, about parents and their strengths and weaknesses as parents.
- **Clean:** Evaluators must be aware of biases and work to avoid interference from them, especially when they do not like a particular parent.
- **Reverent:** Evaluators must have respect for parents, attorneys, and the court system.
- **Be Prepared:** Evaluators must be prepared with the proper mind-set, which includes:

  o A healthy skepticism
  o A search for various truths within the family
  o Development of multiple hypotheses
  o Investigative attitude, seeking more details and leaving no stone unturned
  o An attitude of disconfirmation, rather than confirmation of what we are being led to believe
  o A recognition of factors that contribute to children's suggestibility
  o Willingness to be transparent and open

In addition to those traits, which evaluators should aspire to achieve, there are certain traits that I believe evaluators should aspire to avoid. These traits include:

- **Acceptance:** Evaluators should not blindly accept what parents, children, or attorneys tell them.
- **Overreliance:** Evaluators should not rely on nonvalid procedures or overly rely on psychological tests.
- **Impatience:** Evaluators must avoid the temptation to be impatient with parents who seem "scattered" or "overemotional."
- **Interpreting Children's Play:** Evaluators should avoid overinterpreting data, especially data from play, drawings, sand-tray play, and the like.
- **I'm in Charge/I Know Best:** Evaluators should avoid acting like a case manager instead of an evaluator.
- **I'll Do What I Want:** Evaluators need to be responsive to deadlines, requests from the court for information, requests from attorneys for information in file.

In conclusion, if evaluators strive to aspire to positive traits and avoid negative ones, then courts and attorneys, and parents as well, can have confidence that their evaluator has done a thorough, unbiased job; focused on all of the issues in the case; and truly reached conclusions that are in the best interests of the children involved.

# 17

# Conclusions

At the outset of this process, I planned to write one more chapter, focusing on issues that were important but were beyond the scope of this book. I have decided to address those issues here. All of these issues are important, yet they are either beyond my own expertise or there is not sufficient literature to guide readers to understanding those issues. I will focus on each of them in short detail.

## Special Needs Issues for Children

There is little in the custody evaluation literature focusing on this topic (Perryman, 2005; Saposnek, Perryman, Berkow, & Ellsworth, 2005). At the same time, with the apparent increase in children being diagnosed with various special needs, it is increasingly likely that evaluators will experience these special needs children in their evaluations. Between psychological and educational needs and medical needs, the range of issues can include:

- Children with ADD and ADHD
- Children who function somewhere along the autistic spectrum
- Children with significant psychiatric disorders (e.g., bipolar disorder)
- Children with medical needs, like cancer, diabetes, or other major illnesses
- Children with eating disorders
- Children with significant developmental delays, including those with serious learning disabilities

Each of these possible special needs requires the evaluator to have expertise. Few evaluators have expertise in all of these areas. In many communities, there may be no one who has expertise in both child custody evaluations and the particular special need of the child involved. If you do not have such expertise, it will be important for you to get consultation to help in understanding the child and her functioning. Good relationships with your local directors of special education, a trusted pediatrician, or others who work with these special needs children may be a tremendous help when conducting an evaluation where these issues are involved.

## Substance Abuse Issues

There are very few good articles on substance abuse issues in child custody work (McMahon & Giannini, 2003; Schleuderer & Campagna, 2004). I am not an expert in substance abuse, but I know who the substance abuse experts are in the communities where I do child custody work. When I am referred a case that involves allegations of substance abuse, I expect there to be some type of ongoing drug testing while I do the child custody evaluation. In addition to drug testing, if there are unusual allegations involved in the case, I would always have a more comprehensive substance abuse evaluation performed by a local expert. Situations where this might occur are when the child provides information about a parent falling asleep, passing out, or otherwise being unavailable to parent on a regular basis. In a recent case, there were allegations that a parent frequently urinated in wastebaskets after coming home after drinking. Such unusual allegations require more extensive understanding of the substance use or abuse. In those situations, I always try to differentiate between controlled use of alcohol or prescription medication versus abuse or dependency on alcohol or medications. With illegal drugs, it is always important to have a more comprehensive evaluation of abuse versus dependency on those drugs.

In my report, I integrate the data from the drug testing into my own findings and use all of that data to complete my evaluation. To the extent that I do not know something about the drug test results or need a more thorough substance abuse evaluation, I will consult with colleagues who know more than I do on that topic. After that consultation, I am likely to recommend a more thorough evaluation of the substance abuse issues or to explain to the court why there is no longer a need to be concerned about the drug test results.

## Sexual Abuse Allegations

Essentially, throughout my career, I have avoided child custody evaluations in which the major issue is the allegation of sexual abuse of one or more children. I have never felt competent to do evaluations where that is the central issue. I refer readers to the wonderful writing of Kathryn Kuehnle, PhD (Kuehnle, 1996; Kuehnle & Connell, 2009; Kuehnle & Kirkpatrick, 2005) for more on conducting those evaluations. I have always felt that Dr. Kuehnle's analysis of the multiple hypotheses one needs to keep while doing the sexual abuse evaluation is excellent and quite useful for all of the work that custody evaluators do, even in other types of cases. Because I do not do such evaluations, I will simply refer readers to those other resources for a better understanding of the necessary work to be done in these cases.

At the same time, I have occasionally done evaluations in which someone else did the evaluation of the sex abuse issues. Then, just as with substance abuse cases, I integrate the findings of the sexual abuse evaluator with the rest of my data to reach my ultimate conclusions in the case. I also have a group of colleagues in those communities where I do my custody evaluation work, whom I can consult to learn more about these cases when I am involved with them.

## Longitudinal Evaluations

In some families, either the chaos is so great or the issues so complex that it seems the best we can do at the end of the evaluation is to make short-term recommendations, with the recommendation that the family be reevaluated after a period of time, usually 9 months to a year, in order to see how the children are adjusting to those changes and how the parents are implementing the recommendations made at the end of the first evaluation. When that happens, it is critical that the evaluator be clear that *anyone* can do the updated evaluation. As noted in Chapter 16 on critiquing evaluations, I do not believe that an evaluator should recommend that she be the one to follow the family. This would be granting the evaluator too much power. At the end of the first evaluation, it is likely that one parent is not happy with the outcome, and with that in mind, that parent should have the right to request a new person to do the updated assessment of the issues. While this may cost more money or may lead to more time taken to do the update, it is critical that each parent be given a chance to consider a new evaluator. Along with that, if the original evaluator is asked to perform an update with the family, it is important to avoid confirmatory bias, such that the update is not overly influenced by the findings of the first evaluation. Each evaluation must be unique, and the findings of the first evaluation, while important, are important only for the snapshot of what occurred at that time. The update needs to look at what has changed since the original evaluation, focusing in particular on the qualities of each parent that either improved or did not improve, as well as the changes in the children that may have occurred.

## Conclusion

In 1994, at the end of my book *Conducting Child Custody Evaluations,* I wrote,

> I would like to close this chapter by stating that anyone who works in the field of custody needs on-going training in child development, family assessment, problems of divorce, the workings of the court, and the special ethical issues this work brings. We need to network with

one another to learn as much as we can about this burgeoning field. We need to develop our skills in interviewing, and we need better research on what makes a good-enough parent. We need to develop new instruments which help us understand the tasks of parenting and find ways to integrate them into our comprehensive evaluations.

It is our duty as professionals to learn the dynamics of divorcing families, maintain an understanding of the needs of children and the changing laws of the states in which we work, and maintain the highest of ethical, professional standards if we are going to work in this dynamic, highly conflicted, litigious, yet rewarding area of our fields. As mentioned at the beginning of the chapter, we need to be cognizant of the power that we have, and use it wisely. We need to respect parents and their children, respect the process of the courts, and continue to grow in our skills. We must always work for the betterment of our children, who remain the victims of divorce unless their parents can learn to free them from the battles of parental conflict.

If we meet these standards, maintain our professional integrity, hold to our ethical principals, and write reports which empower parents to strengthen their parenting skills, we will benefit from the rewards of helping families reduce the divorce conflict for their children. (pp. 153–154)

What I wrote then still stands true today. Over the past 15 years, I have observed a new generation of child custody evaluators at meetings of the Association of Family Conciliation Courts (AFCC). I have been involved in teaching thousands of new people at various workshops, either those sponsored by AFCC, those sponsored by other organizations in various states, those I have sponsored myself, or more recently online (e.g., www.sfrankelgroup.com). I still believe that regular attendance at continuing education programs and a focus on the ethical challenges in our work is critical. More than anything, I still believe that child custody evaluators should aspire to reach the pinnacle of success, working to improve conditions for families in courts across the country. In 2000, the American Bar Association (ABA) sponsored a program designed to better understand the needs of high-conflict families (ABA, 2001). Among their conclusions was that evaluators should work to improve continuing education, develop better standards, and support those standards in their local communities. I have always supported those efforts, wherever I have lived and worked. I urge all evaluators to do the same.

Over the same span of time, I have also seen many evaluators get burnt out by this work. We put our hearts into the work, while parents and attorneys are all too often upset by what we do. In many jurisdictions, evaluators are sued or have licensing complaints lodged against them. Sometimes I have seen professionals attack each other in very hostile ways. This is not healthy. It is incumbent on all professionals in the field to act like professionals, with the highest of ethical and moral behavior. Nevertheless, I do believe there is a place for the professional critique of a colleague's work product. This cannot be done in a hostile way, and it is important to avoid personal attacks on a colleague's work.

When stressed, we need to manage our stress. We can do this with a variety of behaviors, including but not limited to exercise, yoga, maintaining a good sense of humor, paying attention to our spiritual and social life, and remaining balanced in all aspects of our lives. For me, I do a variety of tasks in the field, including evaluating, consulting, serving as an expert witness, teaching, and writing to help me retain balance in my work, and I try and take both shorter and longer vacations while enjoying my nonwork life. Taking such actions has helped me to avoid burnout, and taking similar actions may help you do the same (P. Stahl, 2008a).

Finally, I continue to urge anyone working with high-conflict divorce to engage in both regular consultation with trusted colleagues in your local community and to join relevant associations in which you can feel supported, learn, and grow in your work. For me, that has translated to a lifetime commitment to AFCC. But even outside of AFCC, I have continued to grow and learn. I have worked to earn my Board Certification as a Forensic Psychologist through the American Board of Professional Psychology. To do that, I took many continuing education courses outside of AFCC, mostly through the education arm of the American Board of Forensic Psychology. I would not encourage anyone who has read just one book or taken only a few continuing education courses to consider him- or herself capable of working in this high-conflict field. Instead, I encourage all who read my books to continue to read books and articles by others, the multidisciplinary literature of AFCC's *Family Court Review,* and the child custody focused–literature of the *Journal of Child Custody.* Take local, national, and international continuing education. And most of all, enjoy doing what you do and do not let the high conflict of the families you are evaluating wear you down.

# Appendix A _____

*Sample Court Order Appointing*
*Mental Health Professional*

Parenting Consultation/Limited Family Assessment        FC635

Comprehensive Custody Evaluation                        Date 1/26/10

## Appointment of a
_____ **Behavioral Health Professional**

IT IS ORDERED appointing the following Behavioral Health Professional to conduct a (Parenting Consultation/Limited Family Assessment/Comprehensive Custody Evaluation) in this case:

&lt;name&gt;
&lt;address&gt;
&lt;phone&gt;

1. *Scope*

_____ PARENTING CONSULTATION _____

Parenting consultations typically involve 2–4 hours of professional services to identify areas of parenting agreement, and/or provide parenting education or, therapeutic dispute resolution. Parents and/or children are interviewed. Reports typically summarize parenting plan agreements and/or recommend additional services, but do not include recommendations for a parenting time schedule.

———————————— Options for Parenting Consultation ————————————

_____Educate parents re: parenting plan options

_____Identify parenting plan agreements

_____Identify issues for further evaluation

_____Assess need for Parenting Coordinator

_____Therapeutic dispute resolution

———————————— LIMITED FAMILY ASSESSMENT ————————————

Limited family assessments (LFAs) typically involve 6–12 hours of professional services. Fewer and more narrowly defined issues are investigated in LFAs. The evaluator limits the amount of time available to family members to present their concerns and what documents are accepted for review. Psychological tests are not typically administered. The number of collateral witnesses is restricted. The LFA report is issue specific. If appointed to conduct an LFA and the evaluator concludes the issues are beyond the scope of an LFA, the evaluator advises the Court and seeks clarification of the appointment.

———————————— Options for Limited Family Assessment ————————————

_____Child maltreatment allegations (e.g., inadvertent/isolated incidents of maltreatment)

_____Child interview (e.g., custodial preference and whether preference based on developmentally appropriate reasoning)

_____Domestic violence (e.g., occasional instances of push/shove/slap)

_____Educational needs of child

_____Grandparents' request for access time

_____Home study (e.g., safety concerns)

_____Mental health and parenting capacity evaluation of one parent (e.g., substance abuse, mood disorder, personality disorder, criminal history)

_____Legal custody recommendations (e.g., ability to co-parent)

_____Parenting time-share recommendations

_____Safe exchanges

_____Relationship of child with parents and/or significant others (e.g., siblings, stepparents, grandparents)

_____Other referral issues (e.g., stalking; need for parenting supervision; impact of relocation on child; sources of co-parenting conflict; safety concerns; exchange precautions; allegations of coaching)

_____Specific information re: above selected issues:

──────────── COMPREHENSIVE CUSTODY EVALUATION ────────────

Comprehensive custody evaluations (CCEs) typically involve 20+ hour of professional services. CCEs investigate long-standing and broadly based issues of family functioning and parenting capacity. Parents and children are interviewed more than once. Psychological testing is often administered. Parent/child relationships are examined in greater detail than in an LFA. Documents submitted by attorneys are accepted for review, usually without screening by the evaluator. More collateral witnesses are typically contacted than in an LFA and may be interviewed in the office. The report will likely be lengthier than in an LFA and provide a narrative of the family's historical context, parent–child dynamics, assessment of parenting capacity, assessment of the child's developmental needs, and a full range of recommendations addressing custody, a detailed parenting time schedule, and recommended therapeutic interventions, sometimes including treatment goals.

──────────── Options for Comprehensive Custody Evaluation ────────────

_____Child maltreatment allegations (e.g., molestation, abuse, neglect, abandonment)

_____Child rejecting a parent (e.g., alienation)

_____Coercive control/domestic violence

_____Fitness of both parents

_____Legal custody recommendations

_____Relocation request

_____Specific Information re: above selected issues or other issues:

_____

_____

2. *Timely Written Report.* The evaluator shall prepare a written report no later than 14 days prior to the next scheduled hearing. The report shall be delivered to the Court and counsel, or the parties, if self-represented, unless the evaluator asserts extraordinary circumstances, such as imminent life threat or the potential for serious harm to a person related to the case. In that event, the Court shall make a ruling regarding dissemination of the report. The acceptance of this appointment by the evaluator indicates a capability of completing a written report in a timely manner and the ability to appear and testify in court upon reasonable notice.

3. *Initial Contact.* Counsel for both parties, or the parties, if self-represented, shall make the initial contact with the evaluator through a joint conference or conference call within 10 days of receipt of this order. The initial conference with the evaluator shall be used to summarize the issues present in this

case, to arrange for the initial appointments of the persons the evaluator wishes to examine, and to allow the evaluator to request information he or she believes to be pertinent.

4. *Authority of Evaluator/Cooperation by Parties/Waiver of Confidentiality.* The evaluator shall have the following authority with regard to the minor child(ren) and family members:

  a.  The evaluator shall serve as an expert for the court in order to provide data and opinions relevant to the care of, custody of, and access to the minor child in this case pursuant to applicable Arizona statutes and case law.

  b.  The evaluator shall have reasonable access to the child(ren) and family members with reasonable notice; and shall have reasonable notice of any and all judicial proceedings including requests for any examination affecting the child(ren) and shall be provided copies of all minute entries, orders, and pleadings filed in this case.

  c.  The evaluator shall also have access to:
      i.   All therapists of the child(ren) and parties;
      ii.  All school and medical records of the child(ren) and parties;
      iii. Any and all psychological testing or evaluations performed on the child(ren) or the parties;
      iv.  Any and all teachers/child care providers for the child(ren).

  d.  At the request of the evaluator, each party shall execute any and all releases or consents necessary to authorize the evaluator's access to the information described herein. No new clinicians (i.e., therapists, psychologists, social workers, etc.) are to work on this case during the course of the evaluation without the consent or authorization of the evaluator, unless otherwise authorized by court order. The services of existing mental health providers may be suspended by the evaluator pending review by the Court.

  e.  The parties are informed that the Court is the identified client of the evaluator in this case. The evaluator serves the Court in this case; therefore, neither the parties nor their child(ren) are patients of the evaluator. There is no confidentiality relating to the parties' communications with or to the evaluator or concerning the evaluator's activities or recommendations. The evaluator may engage in written or verbal communication with any person he or she perceives capable of providing information relevant to the care and welfare of the child.

  f.  The evaluator may request that the parties and/or child(ren) participate in adjunct services, to be provided by third parties, including but not limited to physical or psychological examinations, assessment, psychotherapy, co-parenting work, or alcohol and drug monitoring/testing. The Court shall allocate between the parties the cost of any adjunct service.

g. The evaluator shall be promptly provided all records, reports, and documents requested and shall receive the cooperation of all parties and counsel involved to ensure that the report is submitted by the date requested. This Order shall act as a release by the parties of all information requested by the evaluator and shall further obligate the parties for any costs associated with the production of those records to the evaluator. Any such costs shall be paid promptly.

5. *No Ex Parte Contact.* Counsel shall not have substantive ex parte discussions with the evaluator, but shall conduct all communication through conference calls or conferences, unless agreed upon otherwise by all counsel. Copies of any documentation provided by counsel or the parties to the evaluator shall concurrently be sent by the providing person to the other side. Copies shall be sent to counsel if the other side is represented by counsel. The evaluator may have ex parte contact with the Court regarding scheduling matters. This does not prohibit the evaluator from having individual contact with each party in the performance of the evaluation.

6. *Fees.* The evaluator's fee and costs shall be paid _____% *by Father*, and _____% *by Mother* subject to other and further orders of the Court. Costs shall be paid as directed by evaluator and may be required to be paid prior to the first appointment. In the event any person (including a child) fails to appear at the time of an appointment, the person responsible for the missed appointment shall be obligated to pay any cost associated with the missed appointment.

7. *Evidence.* The written report of the evaluator may be received in evidence without the necessity of any foundation and without any objection to hearsay statements contained therein or any other objection.

8. *Testimony.* Each party shall have the right to call the evaluator as a witness. If only one party believes that the evaluator's live testimony is necessary in addition to the written report, that party shall initially be responsible for 100% of the costs incurred in connection with the evaluator testifying at the court hearing, subject to reallocation by the court if appropriate.

9. *Immunity.* The evaluator acts as a quasi-judicial officer in his or her capacity pursuant to this Order, and as such, the evaluator has limited immunity consistent with the Arizona case law applicable to quasi-judicial officers of the Court as to all actions undertaken pursuant to the Court

appointment and this Order. Any alleged impropriety or unethical conduct by the evaluator shall be brought to the attention of the Court in writing.

——————————————————— [Option] ———————————————————

IT IS FURTHER ORDERED signing this minute entry as a formal order of this Court pursuant to Rule 81, *Arizona Rules of Family Law Procedure.*

DONE IN OPEN COURT this date: _____

**Hon.** _____
          **Judge of the Superior Court**

*Source:* A.R.S. §§25-403, -405(B), -406, -408 & -409; Rule 76(A), Arizona Rules of Family Law Procedure.

# Appendix B

*Sample Custody Evaluation Informed Consent and Retainer Agreement*

(This form is e-mailed to parents and their attorneys before the evaluation begins, and the information in the form is discussed with parents at the start of the evaluation process.)

Dear Parents,

Thank you for contacting me regarding your child custody evaluation. This contract will explain my procedures for child custody evaluations referred by the court.

I believe that it is in a family's best interests to develop their own postdivorce parenting arrangements, whenever possible. I become part of the process when a family's own attempts to resolve these issues, via mediation or conferences with their attorneys, have reached an impasse. When that occurs, or when the judge orders a child custody evaluation, I am asked to assist the attorneys or the judge in determining the parenting plan that is in your child's best interests. It is my belief, and research shows, that it is best for children when parents can agree on parenting arrangements, and my evaluations are designed to promote resolution of conflicts in this area.

## Evaluation Procedures

In order to do a thorough evaluation, I will need to know information about each of you. I will be asking you to fill out a comprehensive form regarding yourself, your perceptions of the other parent, and your children. The evaluation includes appointments with both parents, your children, and perhaps other significant adults in your child's life. The interviews may be individual and/or in any combinations and as often as necessary for the purpose of the evaluation. I might do home visits in your evaluation. In general, I do them when one or more of your children are under the age of six or there are specific issues that can be answered only via the observations of a home visit. In addition to the time that I spend with all of you, I often administer psychological testing and parenting questionnaires as part of my evaluation. Pursuant to the court order appointing me as your evaluator, I will also ask you to sign a release of information form, which will provide me with access to medical, school, legal, and other professional information. These releases will give permission to others to provide necessary information to me. All of these steps are designed to give me a complete understanding of you and your family.

During the evaluation, it is common for parents to ask me advice or give interim recommendations. My purpose during the evaluation is to evaluate. Until I am done, I cannot give advice or provide interim recommendations because I don't have all of the data regarding your family. On rare occasions I might give a brief, limited, short-term recommendation and then evaluate your ability to follow through with the suggestion or its impact on the children.

I like to inform parents that you are unlikely to know what I am thinking during the course of the evaluation. I discourage parents from reading into my questions, because they are only designed to give me information and not to give parents a sense of what I am likely to recommend. While I generally give no clue what I am thinking during the evaluation, I try to be very clear on my recommendations, and I try to explain why I believe those recommendations are in your child's best interests when the evaluation is over. Please keep in mind that my role is not to support or substantiate either parent's position; conversely, it is not my role to disparage or denigrate either parent. Additionally, I will be asking many questions and you may feel that I am interrogating rather than interviewing you. In order to perform my court-ordered evaluation, I must be an examiner, not a therapist.

## Collateral Sources

Many parents ask about my policy regarding collateral contacts. I will generally phone those professionals with whom you have worked and who can give me necessary information about you or your children. Generally, these collateral sources might include teachers, childcare providers, law enforcement officers, pediatricians and other medical doctors, and therapists. I can also include others as well. If you have been ordered to participate in drug testing or anger management, I will likely be in contact with those sources. It is rare for me to interview all collateral parties that are suggested. I usually phone only those professional collateral sources I believe will add information to my evaluation. If you have one or two collateral sources that you believe are crucial to my evaluation, please let me know. Please note that I inform all collateral sources that the content of all interviews may be included in my written evaluation report, and I may be required to testify about these contacts in court.

It is rare for me to interview friends or relatives, each of whom is often partial to one of the parents. I encourage you to get letters from friends and/or relatives that you believe might have pertinent information. I reserve the right to contact any of those persons if I need clarification of any written information given to me, and your signature below authorizes me to contact any such relevant nonprofessional parties.

## Confidentiality

Many parents ask about confidentiality in a child custody evaluation. Quite simply, within the process, there is no confidentiality. I may share information that one parent tells me with the other parent or ask one of you questions about what I hear from a parent, child, or any collateral source. I may ask your children about things that I hear from either of you. I will inform your children that their statements may not be confidential, though I may inform you, your attorneys, and the court if I believe it is in your child's interest to protect that confidentiality. I will inform all collateral witnesses that there is no confidentiality in the process. This protects your due process rights and ensures that I can gather necessary information for my evaluation. It is understood that I will be providing the court, Family Court Services, and the attorney(s) with a written report of my child custody evaluation. In addition, after I have completed my evaluation report and sent it to the attorneys and the court, my entire file, including all notes, psychological test data, and anything else in my file, could be made available to the attorneys and the court upon a legitimate request by any of the parties.

Additionally, please note that California state law requires reporting to the appropriate agencies where there is reasonable suspicion of child abuse, elder abuse, stated intention to injure another person, and/or imminent danger of harming yourself or inability to care for yourself. Please keep in mind that I do not provide any psychological services other than this court-ordered evaluation, including emergency services, to individuals whom I am evaluating. If an emergency arises, assistance should be sought through the police, the nearest hospital, or your attorney.

Both attorneys and parents are invited to send me any written materials that they think will be useful. I accept documents only via fax or mail to the fax number or mailing address noted in my letterhead or at regularly scheduled appointments in my office. Please do not give me materials at home visits, and do not make any unscheduled visits to my office in order to deliver documents. Please do not give me originals, and please note that I do not make copies of this material for your attorney or the other side. I must retain any items that are presented to me for my consideration. Also please note that the court order appointing me as your evaluator requires that copies of any materials sent to me must also be provided to the other parent or his or her legal representative. With that in mind, I will not accept any documents without written assurance that documents submitted for my review have been provided to the other party.

## Fees

My fee for conducting this evaluation is $_____. This fee covers all interview time, home visits (if there are any), time spent phoning parents and collateral sources and/or reviewing written material, scoring psychological tests and parenting inventories, writing the evaluation report, and any other time spent in association with the evaluation. All fees are to be paid by the first session of the evaluation unless other arrangements have been made. The percentage of the fee paid by each parent is determined by your court order. Payment must be made by cash, check, or credit card. In the event that I have agreed to partial payment at the start of the evaluation, full payment must be made within 2 weeks. In the event that full payment is not received by that time, the evaluation process will be halted and will not continue until all fees are paid. In the rare event that I spend significantly more time than anticipated, I will inform you of any further charges. I understand that the fee for this evaluation is to pay for a legal and not a health-related procedure. No claims for health insurance reimbursement will be completed by this evaluator.

My fee does not include court appearances or depositions. If either party wishes me to testify, I require a subpoena for court testimony or deposition. If the testimony will be by phone, my fee for phone testimony is based on $_____ per hour and should be paid a week in advance. If I need to travel for testifying at court or for a deposition, I charge a minimum of $_____ per half day (or less) or $_____ per full day. I charge for travel time to/from the deposition or trial and time involved in preparation for the deposition or court appearance. I require payment for such appearances at least one week before the court date or deposition. All fees are the responsibility of the party issuing the subpoena. My standard evaluation fee *does* include being available on phone standby for the court at Recommendation Conferences, provided I can arrange to make the time available.

At least 24-hour notice is required to cancel or reschedule an appointment without being charged. Without 24-hour notice, the parent who misses the appointment may be billed an additional $_____ per appointment hour. If both parents miss a joint appointment, each will be billed for half of the scheduled time. Excessive missed appointments can result in termination of the evaluation with notification to the court of what portion of the evaluation has been completed.

## Recommendations

On my custody evaluation form, I will ask each of you how you would suggest settling your dispute with the other parent. It is possible that I might agree with you when I have completed my evaluation. It is also possible that I may disagree with you and recommend something closer to what the other parent wants. Please be aware that whatever I recommend, it will always be based on my analysis of all of the evaluation data and what I believe to be in your child(ren)'s best interests.

In move-away cases, it is important to note that I might not even make a specific recommendation, because relocation issues are driven by legal issues and factors. It is my job to evaluate the family and provide the evaluation data and my analysis of the data to the court. In move-away cases, there are many factors that converge before a decision can be made. I will certainly provide my analysis of the relevant factors that the California statutory and case law demand, as well as any other relevant psychological factors to be considered. However, it is the judge's job to give weighting to those factors and in a move-away case, it is often impossible for me to make as clear a recommendation as I might in other custody evaluations. It is not uncommon for me to describe my analysis of all relevant factors and then suggest a set of recommendations based on the potential weighting of the court. As such, if the court weighs certain factors as more relevant than certain other factors, I might recommend in one direction, but if the court weighs certain other factors as more relevant, I might recommend in the other direction. This ensures that I do my job (i.e., evaluate and analyze data and factors) while encouraging and supporting the judge to do his or her job (i.e., weigh those factors and reach a decision).

At the end of the evaluation process, I will send my written report to the court, to Family Court Services, and to the attorneys. If a parent is self-represented, I will send the report directly to that parent. Following the completion and submission of the report, I can no longer have contact with you. It is unethical of me to perform additional roles with your family after completing my evaluation. I am willing to confer with the attorneys if such a conference is desired by all involved and not objected to by the court. Be aware that the custodial dispute may not be resolved with the issuance of my report, as my report is advisory only and the court is not obligated to accept my recommendations.

If your case does not settle after completion of my report, please note that unless directed otherwise by the court, all items in my case file will be subject to examination by both parties, their attorneys, the attorney for the child(ren), and any expert(s) who may have been retained by counsel for either party. If there is a trial and if you request that I testify, it is important that you understand my obligations as an evaluator and as a testifying expert. I am obligated to maintain my impartiality and openness to new information throughout the course of the evaluation and during the trial. I am prohibited by state rules from having ex parte communications with one side, nor can I help in trial preparation with only one side. Though it is more likely than not that testimony offered by me will explain and be supportive of the contents of my report, no assurances can be made that this will be the case. Regardless of the questions asked, I will, of course, respond honestly. I will not be an advocate for the person who seeks my testimony. I will answer all questions regarding each parent's strengths and weaknesses. All fees for my testimony are directly related to my time in preparation, travel, and testifying, and not for any particular testimony.

## Settlement Prior to Conclusion or Early Termination of Evaluation

If at any time during the course of the evaluation parents settle their custody or visitation dispute on their own, or jointly agree, with the court's consent to the early termination of the evaluation, it will be discontinued, and the court will be so notified. If I have been paid a fee that exceeds the time I have spent (billed at $_____ per hour), I will refund any amount due at the end of the month following my receipt of a written statement that the evaluation has been halted. If at any point in the future either parent wishes to resume the evaluation process, a new evaluation will need to be ordered and new fees will need to be paid.

## Consent

By my signature below, I acknowledge that I have been encouraged to review this document with my attorney. I have read and I understand all of the terms within this contract and agree to abide it. I understand that Philip M. Stahl, PhD, is an independent practitioner and that this contract is only with him, not any other entity or individual. I authorize Dr. Stahl to complete the evaluation and provide recommendations to the court.

Signed: _____          Date: _____

Witness: _____          Date: _____

Please Make a Copy of This Contract for Your Own Records!

# Appendix C _____

## *SAMPLE CUSTODY*
## *EVALUATION FACE SHEET*

Name: _____ Birthdate: _____ D.L. # _____ S.S. # _____

Address: _____ City: _____ State: _____ Zip: _____

Home Phone: _____ Work Phone: _____

Employment: _____ Address: _____

Reason for Referral:   Custody: _____ Visitation: _____ Court Case #: _____

Referred by Whom: _____ Phone: _____

Other Parent's Name: _____ Birthdate: _____ Phone: _____ S.S. # _____

Address: _____ City: _____ State: _____ Zip: _____

| Children:<br>Name | Birthdate | School/<br>Grade | Current Living<br>Arrangement |
|---|---|---|---|
| 1) | | | |
| 2) | | | |
| 3) | | | |
| 4) | | | |
| 5) | | | |

| Others Living In Home | Age | Relationship/Status |
|---|---|---|
| 1) | | |
| 2) | | |
| 3) | | |
| 4) | | |

Date of Marriage: _____ Separation: _____ Date Divorce Filed: _____

Who Filed: _____ Date of Divorce (If Applicable): _____

Date of Remarriage (If Applicable) _____

## COURT ACTION: (USE BACK IF NECESSARY)

I. Date: _____ Initiated by? Father: _____ Mother: _____ Reason: _____

Result: _____

II. Date: _____ Initiated by? Father: _____ Mother: _____ Reason: _____

Result: _____

III. Date: _____ Initiated by? Father: _____ Mother: _____ Reason: _____

Result: _____

Father's Attorney: _____ Phone: _____ Fax: _____

Mother's Attorney: _____ Phone: _____ Fax: _____

Any prior arrests for anyone in the family? No _____ Yes _____ Describe
(include dates and jurisdiction):

_____

_____

_____

_____

List names, addresses, and phone numbers for current or former therapists
or substance abuse detection or treatment for you or anyone in your
family?

_____

_____

_____

_____

List professional references you would like contacted as part of this evaluation (in order of importance):

Name            Relationship (e.g., teacher/doctor)            Phone Number

_____

_____

_____

_____

_____

_____

_____

_____

## Number of Previous Marriages

Father: _____ Dates(s) of Marriage(s): _____ Divorce: _____ # Kids: _____

Mother: _____ Dates(s) of Marriage(s): _____ Divorce: _____ # Kids: _____

## Employment History: (List Most Recent First)

Father: _____

Father: _____

Mother: _____

Mother: _____

Previous Mediation/Evaluation?: Yes: ____ No: ____ Date(s) Seen: _____

Name of Mediator/Evaluator: _____ Phone: _____

Recommendations: _____

Who cares for your children when you aren't at home? _____ Phone: _____

_____

Concerns about domestic violence? No ____ Yes ____ Describe: _____

_____

_____

_____

_____

_____

_____

_____

Were these concerns ever reported? No ___ Yes ___ To Whom: _____

Concerns about neglect or sexual or physical abuse or the safety of your children? No _____ Yes _____

Describe: _____

_____

_____

_____

_____

_____

_____

Were these concerns ever reported?      No ___ Yes ___ To Whom: _____

Concerns about substance abuse or alcohol problems? No ____ Yes ____
Please describe: _____

_____

_____

_____

_____

_____

_____

Were these concerns ever reported?      No ___ Yes ___ To Whom: _____

Please describe your child(ren)—include information on special needs:

_____

_____

_____

_____

_____

_____

_____

_____

Please describe your relationship with your child(ren):

_____

_____

_____
_____
_____
_____
_____
_____

**Please describe the other parent's relationship with your child(ren):**

_____
_____
_____
_____
_____
_____
_____

**Please describe your style of parenting:**

_____
_____
_____
_____
_____
_____

**Please describe the other parent's style of parenting:**

_____
_____
_____
_____
_____
_____

**How do you discipline your child(ren)?**

_____

_____

_____

_____

_____

_____

_____

**How does the other parent discipline your child(ren)?**

_____

_____

_____

_____

_____

_____

_____

**Please describe your strengths as a parent:**

_____

_____

_____

_____

_____

_____

**Please describe your weaknesses as a parent:**

_____

_____

_____

_____

_____

_____

_____

_____

**Please describe the other parent's strengths as a parent:**

_____

_____

_____

_____

_____

_____

_____

**Please describe the other parent's weaknesses as a parent:**

_____

_____

_____

_____

_____

_____

_____

**What will the other parent say about you?**

_____

_____

_____

_____

_____

_____

_____

_____

**Please describe the communication between you and the other parent:**

_____

_____

_____

_____

_____

_____

_____

**Please describe your involvement in your child's activities, both past and present (include extracurricular activities, school events, medical and dental appointments, etc.):**

_____

_____

_____

_____

_____

_____

_____

**Who pays for these activities and do you have problems agreeing on them?**

_____

_____

_____

_____

_____

How do you and the other parent support your child's education?

_____

_____

_____

_____

_____

Please describe your current timeshare, including days and times of exchange, who provides transportation, and a details of the holiday and vacation schedule:

_____

_____

_____

_____

_____

_____

_____

_____

_____

Please describe your current work hours, when you would need daycare, and who would provide daycare under your proposed schedule:

_____

_____

_____

_____

_____

_____

Do you feel that the schedule needs to be different for different children (if applicable)? Please explain:

_____

_____

_____

_____

How would you recommend sharing the parenting with the other parent?

_____

_____

_____

_____

_____

_____

Any other comments/questions (use back of form, if necessary):

_____

_____

_____

_____

_____

_____

_____

_____

I have read and understand the attached informed consent form and authorize Dr. Stahl to evaluate me and my children and assist the court in determining the parenting plan which will be in the best interests of my children.

Signed: _____ Date: _____

# Appendix D _____

## *Sample List of Questions to Ask Children*

*Do you know my name? Why are you here? Do you know what I do (what psychologists do)? What did your mom (dad) tell you about me? How do you feel about being here?*

These are the first questions I ask children and they are used to break the ice, provide them with some information about me and what they are here for, and to begin to understand whether their parents have been open with them or given them propaganda about the evaluation. I am quite suspect when I hear in the first few moments statements about custody (e.g. "I want to live with my mom"), especially when asking these quite general questions.

*Where do you go to school? What grade are you in? How are your grades? What do you like (dislike) about school?*

Gets the focus off of the divorce, turning it onto the child's own life.

*Who is your best friend? Tell me something about your friends. What do you like to do with your friends?*

Same as above.

*What are some of your favorite activities? Do you play any sports (music)? What are some things that you love to do? What are some things that you sometimes have to do that you don't like doing? Do you have any favorite video games (TV shows, movies, etc.)?*

Same as above.

*Who gets you up in the morning? Who else is up then? How do you get breakfast? How do you get ready for school? How do you get to school?*

Basic questions about the morning routine.

*How do you get home from school? What do you usually do after school? When do you do your homework? Who helps you (or supervises) with your homework?*

Basic questions about the after-school routine.

*What time is dinner? Who fixes dinner? Where do you eat dinner and with whom?*

Basic questions about the evening routine.

*What time is bedtime? What do you do to get ready for bed? Does anyone read to you at bedtime?*

Basic questions about the bedtime routine.

*Do you know what divorce means? How do you feel about your parents' divorce?*

> Gives a clue about the child's understanding of divorce, how much parents or friends talk about divorce, and begins our understanding of the child's feelings about his or her parents' divorce

*Tell me something you like (don't like) about mom (dad).*

> Gives a clue to the child's ability to talk openly about feelings toward each of the parents; very important in our understanding of the nature of the child's splitting, if any.

*Who do you talk to when you get scared (worried, happy, etc.)?*

> Gives a clue to the emotional connectedness of the child with either parent, and/or other people in the child's life.

*How do you know when mom (dad) is mad/sad/worried/happy?*

> Gives a clue to how parents express their feelings.

*What does your mom (dad) do to help with homework?*

> Gives a clue to the parent–child relationships.

*What happens when you get mad at your mom (dad)?*

> Same as above.

*What does mom (dad) do when she gets mad at you?*

Same as above.

*What kinds of punishments does mom (dad) use?*

Same as above.

*How do you feel when mom says bad things about dad (& vice versa)?*

Gives a good clue about how the child handles angry parents and loyalty conflicts. My question assumes that this goes on. In those instances when it does not, the children are quick to tell me so.

*How do your parents treat/feel about each other?*

Similar to above; also gives a clue to how much the child sees of the parental stress or animosity.

*If there was one thing you could change about yourself, what would it be?*

Gives me an opportunity to assess self-esteem, fantasy life, and other inner feelings of the child.

*If you could have three wishes for anything in the world, what would you wish for?*

Same as above.

*If there was one thing you could change about mom (dad), what would it be? (After the answer—anything else you'd like to change?)*

Gives a further clue to the parent–child relationship (asked again when seen conjointly with mom (dad).

*How do you like to spend your time with mom (dad)?*

Same as above (asked again when seen conjointly with mom (dad).

*Do you and mom (dad) have any favorite things to do together?*

Same as above (asked again when seen conjointly with mom (dad).

*What ideas do you have about how to split your time with mom and dad?*

Gives a clue to the child's thoughts about this question, without asking who they want to live with. Especially useful for older latency, preadolescent, and adolescent children who have their own thoughts and ideas and may want the evaluator to hear them.

For young children, I tend to ask them fewer questions, and observe them more in their play. I use a dollhouse to set up various situations and encourage their interaction. By observing their affect and their play responses, I get a clue to parental availability and emotionality.

If there are siblings, I ask similar questions about sibling relationships and differences in their perceptions of how the parents treat each of them, and questions to understand how much support the siblings provide one another.

In addition to the questions that I ask children and parents when seen together, I often encourage them to engage in an activity together (such as play with Legos, draw a picture, play a board game, or some other task). This gives me a chance to directly see their one-on-one interaction and support of one another, as well as the parent's level of directiveness or freedom toward the child. Sometimes I see parents who claim to be active participants with their child who have little idea how to freely interact with their child in my office. While doing all of this, I look for clues to the affection between the parent and child, and how much their interaction resembles what both parents and child have been telling me.

# Appendix E_____

*Sample List of Questions
to Ask Parents*

**General Questions During the Evaluation:**

*"Why are we here?"* Used to generate discussion about all of the issues, especially the conflict between the parents. In almost all evaluations, it is the first question I ask parents in the initial individual interview. From that single question, I find myself asking other leading questions based on the information that I hear. Sometimes in the first interview, there is no other formal question asked, as I take the answers from the parent and go where they lead me.

*"What was your marriage like before the problems began?"* Gets the parents talking about their historical relationship with the ex-spouse. Gives an opportunity to find out if there were times of peace before the discord, and to find out when things started to go awry.

*"Tell me about your children."* Obviously, used to begin talking about the children. I often ask this question in the middle of complaining about the other parent—in this context, used to see if the parent can stop talking about flaws in the other parent. Look for changes in affect, for example, does the parent smile more and relax when talking about the children, or stay angry and demeaning?

*"What do you like about _____ (other parent)?"* Again, often used to see if the parent can focus on anything positive about the other parent.

*"How does your arguing with _____ (other parent) affect _____ (child)?"* Gives a clue to parent's ability to understand the effects of the couple's conflict on the children.

*"How do you suppose your feelings about _____ (other parent) affect your child?"* Provides sense of ability for insight into this issue.

*"Given what you say, I don't understand why you stayed married to _____ (other parent)."* Used to confront some of the issues being raised. See if the parent can accept any responsibility for problems between them.

*"What do you sometimes do to contribute to the problems between you and _____ (other parent)?"* Same as above.

## Questions Regarding Parent–Child Relationship and Parenting Strengths and Weaknesses

*"What does _____ (child) need?"* Gives overview of parent's ability to conceptualize and verbalize his or her child's many needs, including the need for a relationship with the other parent. I try to use the answer to that question to confront something that I have heard in other interviews, especially with parents who tend to idealize themselves or their children. Useful in determining which parents truly understand children and their needs as opposed to those parents who want to control, hurt, or punish the other parent by taking the child away from him or her. Pay special attention to parents who answer this question by staying focused on the negative qualities of the other parent rather than their own positive understanding of the children.

*"What gives you pleasure as a parent?"* Gives a clue about how parent benefits from relationship with children.

*"What were your mother's (father's) good qualities as a parent?"* Gives a clue to the feelings associated with the parenting that each parent received and some insight into the relationship between the parenting we received and the parenting that we give.

*"What were your mother's (father's) bad qualities as a parent?"* Same as above.

*"Tell me about (describe) your children."* As before, look for affective indicators of joy in the parent–child relationship.

*"Tell me about a typical day when the children are with you."* Helps me understand the structure a parent follows, if there are typical times for meals, bedtime, rules, and so forth.

*"What are some things you would like to change about _____ (child)?"* Helps find out about relationship with child, openness regarding problems, or idealization of the child, a sign of defensiveness.

*"What are some of your rules that _____ (child) doesn't like?"* Same as above.

*"How do you discipline _____ (child)?"* Same as above.

*"What can you do to make things better for _____ (child)?"* Same as above.

*"What would you like to change as a parent?"* Gives a clue to parents' willingness to look inward regarding their flaws.

*"What concerns, if any, do you have about the other parent's relationship with _____ (child)?"* Gives the parent an opportunity to express his or her concerns.

*"What can _____ (other parent) do to satisfy those concerns?"* Gives a clue to parent's ability to view the other parent as capable of growth and change.

*"What will _____ (child) need in five (ten) years?"* Gives a clue to parent's ability to look forward to the future developmental changes of his or her child.

*"How is _____ (child's) health?"* Obvious.

*"What are your child's favorite activities and interests?"* Gives a clue to parent's knowledge of child's activities and interests. Used to compare what parents say about the child with child's own description of favorite activities and interests.

*"What makes _____ (child) feel sad (happy, excited, scared, worried, etc.)?"* Gives a clue to parent's ability to understand child's feelings and respond on a feeling level with the child.

*"What are your child's favorite foods? What is the bath-time routine in your house? What is the bedtime routine in your house? Where does your child sleep? Tell me about your child's early development. Were there any problems with toilet training? Does your child have any speech problems or show other signs of regression or anxiety? Has your child started to play with friends?"* These are typical of the questions I ask parents of children of preschool age in order to understand their ability to deal with age-appropriate issues.

*"How does your child like school (his or her teachers)? How does your child get along with his (her) peers? How does your child express himself (herself) if he's (she's) angry? Is your child afraid to be alone for a short time? Does your child have nightmares or other signs of emotional distress? Has your child started to sleep over at friend's houses? How does your child follow rules (deal with authority)?"* These are typical of the questions I ask parents of school-age children in order to understand their ability to deal with age-appropriate issues.

*"How does your child deal with authority? Do you think your child is excited (afraid) to get more independent? Does your child push your rules and limits very much? Is your child open to talking with you about sex (drugs, peers, school, etc.)? Is your child responsible for her (his) age? Does your child have any ideas what she (he) will do when she (he) is finished with high school? Does your child have a job outside the home?"* These are typical of the questions I ask parents of adolescents in order to understand their ability to deal with age-appropriate issues.

## Questions About the Co-Parenting Relationship:

*"How do you and _____ (other parent) make decisions about school (doctors, vacations, religious training, etc.)?"* Explores the ability to make joint decisions, or not, between the parents on behalf of the children.

*"When you were married, how did you make decisions about school (doctors, vacations, religious training, etc.)?"* Explores any change in the co-parenting relationship from when they were married.

*"How are the rules in your household the same (or different) from the rules in _____ (other parent's) household?"* Gives clue to the way in which the parents are aware of the style of parenting in the other parent's household, and whether there are major differences that the child must encounter during transitions.

*"How do you communicate with _____ (other parent) / When you try and talk with _____ (other parent) about _____ (child), what happens?"* Gives a clue to the quality of the communication between parents.

*"If you have school or medical information for _____ (other parent) about _____ (child), how does it get to him (her)?"* Gives a clue to the style of sharing information (over the phone, in writing, through the child, or not at all).

*"How does _____ (child) treat you in front of _____ (other parent)–"* Gives a clue to quality of the child's loyalty conflicts when the parents are together.

*"Who attends _____ (child's) events, and how does _____ (child) deal with it when you and _____ (other parent) are at the same event?"* Same as above.

From material I have heard from the other parent or the children, I will always ask questions to confront things I have heard from each parent. This is critical in my understanding of "truth" for the family.

*"What can you do to help disengage from _____ (other parent) to help your children?"* A good clue for how each parent understands this necessary step for ending the conflict.

*"What can you do to share in the parenting with _____ (other parent) more cooperatively?"* A good clue for how each parent understands this next step in cooperative parenting.

Finally, at the end of my last interview, I always ask the following:

*"We've talked about a lot of things. Is there anything else you want me to know, or is there anything you would like to ask me?"* Gives parents a last opportunity to make sure I know everything that is important to them, and to ask me questions that are in their mind. For those parents who are extremely critical, it usually gives them one last time to criticize the other parent. For those who are child-focused, it gives them a last opportunity to express feelings and thoughts about their children and their needs.

# Appendix F

*Sample Alienation Analysis
and Recommendations*

## Special Issues for the Court

Domestic Violence

There are no allegations of domestic violence in this case.

Substance Abuse

There are no allegations of substance abuse in this case.

Mental Health Problems

As noted above, neither parent has significant mental health problems, yet each of their psychological functioning does contribute to the difficulties being experienced in this matter. These issues will be integrated into the discussion below.

Interference With Other Parent's Access

Dr. Smith believes that Ms. Jones interferes with and doesn't support his relationships with Katie and Julie. While he does not believe that she does so maliciously and overtly, he believes that Ms. Jones has significant emotional problems which interfere with her ability to actually support his relationships with the girls. This will be discussed in greater detail in the section below.

## Summary, Analysis, and Recommendations

The data gathered in this evaluation reveals certain consistent findings. Dr. Smith and Ms. Jones had a marriage that was both highly functional and moderately dysfunctional at the same time. It was functional in that both Dr. Smith and Ms. Jones had their respective roles and each of them performed those roles exceptionally well. From all appearances, Dr. Smith is a very good physician who works hard and has always supported the family financially. Ms. Jones is a very good mother who has done the tasks of parenting excellently. She even continues to work part-time in Dr. Smith's office, even after their separation, something that is rare in families going through moderate to high conflict. Within that functional family, the girls have succeeded, academically, socially, psychologically, and within their chosen extracurricular activities.

At the same time, there has been a dysfunctional component to the family, as well. Dr. Smith and Ms. Jones didn't communicate. Dr. Smith had little patience for Ms. Jones and the girls at times, and the girls and Ms. Jones were extremely close. At the same time, the girls and Dr. Smith grew increasingly distant in their relationships. Dr. Smith correctly recalls instances in which he was there for the girls and they did things together, but gradually he was growing more distant from everyone in the family. Dr. Smith grew increasingly depressed and isolated within the family. While he felt that this was due to a lack of communication with Ms. Jones, which was certainly true, it is also clear that he felt distant and isolated from the girls, as well. At the same time, there was little communication between anyone in this family about their feelings. According to Dr. Smith, no one knew that Julie didn't like competitive soccer until she finally gave it up. She thought her parents wanted her to play, and they thought Julie wanted to play. Lacking healthy communication, Julie played for several years without being happy about it. Similarly, there was little discussion or communication between Dr. Smith and Ms. Jones about feelings in their relationship. Ms. Jones, to this day, doesn't understand what Dr. Smith was feeling in the marriage, and this evaluator believes that she didn't really want to know what he felt. This is part of their dynamic, but it filters down to their daughters.

Within this backdrop, Dr. Smith went into therapy, hoping to work on the marital issues. However, Ms. Jones wasn't interested in participating, and Dr. Smith grew even more detached and lonely. He was torn about leaving Ms. Jones, worrying about the impact on the girls. Since he always perceived that Julie was a bit emotionally fragile, he waited until she left home after high school. He was pleased that she was doing well. He was less concerned about Katie, whom he correctly perceived as highly functioning. However, he wasn't aware of Katie's underlying negative feelings toward him, again because of the history of poor family communication. He decided that for his own well-being, he needed to leave Ms. Jones. He and Katie worked out an agreement in which he would continue to see her once a week in the evening where they could continue their consistent and positive routine. He fully expected that he and Katie would build their own, independent relationship after the separation.

Unfortunately, Katie had little patience for her father. He missed a couple of those Friday night visits and she became angry. Ms. Jones told Dr. Smith that Katie wasn't interested in seeing him, and for several months, there was little or no contact between Dr. Smith and Katie. Ms. Jones and Dr. Smith went to mediation and reached some limited agreement on what to do. Included in that agreement was some therapy for Katie and her father. Katie approached the therapy much the same as Ms. Jones did when Dr. Smith wanted Ms. Jones to work on the marital issues. In other words, she wasn't interested. Katie did talk with Dr. Smith about her frustrations and their origins, but by and large, was unable and unwilling to warm up to him. By the time they went back to mediation last December, Katie was saying she wanted to stop therapy and Dr. Smith was frustrated that their relationship had not progressed any further.

At that point, Dr. Smith couldn't accept that he and Katie would have limited time together. While expressing an understanding of her busy schedule, Dr. Smith wanted her to spend more time with him, and would really like to be a more actively involved father, the kind of father who would have Katie spend some time at his home. Katie has expressed no willingness to do any of that. This impasse led Dr. Smith to make a calculated decision. While being concerned that requesting the § 730 evaluation might make things worse, he decided to seek the evaluation to try and better understand what was occurring and try and get Ms. Jones to take some responsibility for her contribution to Katie's refusal to see him. However, this has backfired, as Katie blames him for the intrusions which this evaluation has caused and has been even less willing to see him than before.

With this backdrop, it's important to discuss the context in which this evaluator believes that these dynamics have occurred. Each participant has some contribution to Katie's refusal to see her father. In this evaluator's opinion, Dr. Smith's contribution lies largely in his rigidity, his tendency to reject Katie's feelings toward him, and his continued efforts to force a different solution. To his credit, he hasn't just walked away, largely because he loves Katie and wants a different kind of relationship with her. Additionally, even though he has trouble looking inward to see his own role in problems, he expresses a desire to understand his contribution to the problems with Katie and will work to try and redeem himself if he can.

Ms. Jones's contribution is her apparent lack of insight into emotions and her lack of ability to communicate with Dr. Smith over the years. She has always supported Katie, which is a positive in her role as Katie's mother, though it interferes in Dr. Smith's efforts to improve things with Katie because she doesn't take a stronger position with Katie [and Julie] in supporting their role with their father. To her credit, she does a wonderful job with Katie in all other aspects of Katie's life.

Finally, we need to understand Katie's role in the problems. Quite simply, she, like Ms. Jones, doesn't like to communicate or focus on her feelings. Like Dr. Smith, she tends to be stubborn and rigid. She is currently unforgiving, something that is not psychologically healthy for her. She is regressed defensively, in that she is currently splitting her parents into all good (her mother) and all bad (her father), regardless of the history which was not as negative as she currently states. Additionally, she is overly focused on anything she perceives as negative about her father, refusing to acknowledge or give him credit for his efforts at trying to have a relationship with and be a father to her. At the same time, she has a very busy life, with school and academically tough classes, competitive swimming, and a desire to spend time with friends. This doesn't leave much time for anything else in her life, including either of her parents.

Finding a solution to this situation will not be easy. The easiest solution is unlikely to occur, that is, for Katie to warm up to her father's efforts, recognize that he loves her and simply wants a relationship with her, and talk with each other and/or mediate how they can spend time together. As long as Katie remains rigidly unforgiving, this won't happen. A second solution would be for Dr. Smith to back away and allow Katie some space, with the hope that she, on her own volition, misses and wants to see her father. Given that Katie is 16 years old, is very busy in her life, and wants her father to only see her when she wants them to get together, such a plan could make sense. Unfortunately, that may spell the end of their relationship, as there is no evidence that Katie will willingly invite her father back into her life. A third possible solution, therapy for Katie and her dad, has already been tried and was unsuccessful. Given Katie's current level of animosity and unwillingness to budge, renewed efforts in therapy are likely going to fail. Fourth, family therapy, in which Ms. Jones, Dr. Smith, and Katie all attend therapy together, might be useful, but the most likely outcome of that is that Katie blames her father for being forced into it, Ms. Jones continues her detachment of emotions, and Dr. Smith becomes increasingly frustrated at the lack of progress.

There is a new effort being considered for families with such dynamics. A weeklong, therapeutic summer camp has been successful for many of the families who attend. This program, titled Overcoming Barriers, is relatively new, takes place in the northeastern United States, and seems promising. However, this would not be available for this family until next summer, and Katie has rejected consideration of this program when discussed in one of our interviews. Nonetheless, this program might help provide some improvement if things don't progress in a positive fashion over the next year.

A final option is for Dr. Smith to acknowledge to Katie that he accepts her negative feelings and begin to detach from his strong efforts to forge a relationship with her. Even if he does this, I'd recommend some level of contact between them, via phone and regular face-to-face meetings. Katie has followed court orders, albeit with some resistance, so continuing a court order that requires some time together is advisable. Within that context, they could get together on regular Friday nights and resume their routine together there. They could meet for occasional Saturday morning breakfasts (once or twice per month), Dr. Smith could come to Katie's swim activities, and Dr. Smith could invite her to basketball games or other such events that he likes to attend.

Ms. Jones should keep Dr. Smith informed about Katie's activities, swim schedule, and academics. Katie should know that Ms. Jones is informing Dr. Smith of these events in her life and that both of her parents are in agreement with this plan. To help facilitate this arrangement, Katie and Dr. Smith could go together to mediation on a monthly basis simply to talk about how they'll redefine their relationship and what activities they want to do together. In this evaluator's view, this option has the best chance of success since it keeps Dr. Smith connecting with Katie, yet gives Katie more power in their relationship. If things improve sufficiently over the next 6 months, I would recommend that this be all that happens, but if not, I would recommend consideration of the Overcoming Barriers camp program for a week next summer.

Given the above, I offer the following recommendations:

1. To clarify the recommendation noted above, I would urge the following take place:

   a. Dr. Smith and Katie to meet with a mediator, perhaps Dr. Thornton, once per month to discuss the parameters of their relationship. It would be best if Dr. Smith were to convey to Katie that he will accept less time and involvement than he wants, as long as they do *some* things together. He certainly needs to convey that he is giving up his hope that Katie will spend time with him at his residence, unless Katie decides she wants to spend time with him there, perhaps a minimum of one Friday overnight per month. It would be ideal if Katie would be forgiving of Dr. Smith.

   b. At a minimum, Dr. Smith and Katie should resume their Friday night routine at least twice per month. The particular Fridays could be agreed upon in the mediation between Katie and Dr. Smith. If they cannot agree, this should be rigidly kept as the 1st and 3rd Friday of each month.

   c. Also at a minimum, Dr. Smith and Katie should get together for breakfast for a minimum of 2 hours on Saturday mornings twice per month. Again, the particulars of this could hopefully be worked out during mediation. Again, if they can't agree, this should be rigidly kept as the 2nd and 4th Saturday of each month.

   d. Ideally, Dr. Smith and Katie can talk on the phone twice per week for at least 10 minutes per call. Again, they could discuss this during their mediation, but I would encourage the calls to occur the night before their time together, that is, every other Thursday before the Friday routine and every other Friday before the Saturday breakfast.

   e. If Dr. Smith and Katie can agree on any other events to do together, that would be ideal. As noted above, this could include Phoenix Suns games, a day trip for boating or some other such activity, or any other activity that Dr. Smith and Katie can agree upon.

   f. Dr. Smith needs to know about Katie's swim schedule and be given the opportunity to attend events and competitions.

2.  As noted above, Dr. Smith and Ms. Jones need to talk once per week about Katie and Julie and their functioning and activities. It would be ideal if they could do this in the office of a co-parent counselor who could encourage healthy and positive communication about Katie and Julie. Again, it would be ideal if Katie and Julie knew that their parents were talking with one another about them and their well-being.

3.  I would encourage Dr. Smith to continue his therapy to stay focused on improving his empathy for Katie and her experiences. I'd recommend that Ms. Jones be in therapy, except that she is not a very good candidate for therapy. Her attitudes are just as critical as Dr. Smith's and Katie's, so her participation in therapy is essential. She needs to learn what she can do to promote Katie's relationship improvements with Dr. Smith rather than leaving it totally up to Dr. Smith.

4.  I would recommend the appointment of a Parent Coordinator to coordinate the therapies and be sure that things are progressing along a positive path. If they falter, the PC could begin the process of coordinating referral to the Overcoming Barriers program next summer.

5.  If things are progressing reasonably well and Katie is treating Dr. Smith more positively, I would encourage that this simply continue with no changes, other than those that Dr. Smith and Katie agree to. However, if Katie remains resistant to even this limited time with Dr. Smith, and things don't improve within the family, I would recommend that the family attend the Overcoming Barriers program next summer.

Thank you for allowing me to be of assistance with this family.

# Appendix G_____

## Sample Relocation Analysis and Recommendations

### _____ Special Issues for the Court

Domestic Violence
  This is not an issue in this matter.

Substance Abuse
  There are no allegations of substance abuse in this case.

Mental Health Problems
  Neither parent appears to have any particular mental health problems.

Interference With Other Parent's Access
  This is not an issue in this matter.

Relocation
  Relocation issues will be discussed in the section below.

### _____ Summary, Analysis, and Recommendations

As noted above, the only reason this case has come for an evaluation is because of the relocation-related issues. For job reasons, Ms. Green and her husband have moved to Tennessee. They have a new baby, Ms. Green is pregnant, and they have a home. Ms. Green misses Sophia tremendously and wants her to be a larger part of her family. In contrast, Mr. Brown did not move and sees no reason why his relationship with Sophia should suffer simply because Ms. Green decided to move.

  As with many evaluations, there are a few things we do not know. Both parents claim that they were primary parents during the time when Ms. Green was sick. In some ways, it does not matter now, as that was many years ago and subsequent to that time, both shared custody of Sophia relatively equally for many years until Ms. Green moved. This evaluator did not talk with Sophia's teacher, who was unavailable, but no one suggested that Sophia had any particular problems in school. As noted above, Sophia is delightful, yet at her age, she does not voice a particular preference as to where to live, in spite of Ms. Green's belief that Sophia wants to live with her.

In considering the rest of the issues in this evaluation, I have listed many questions that are useful for consideration in move-away evaluations. Some of these answer relevant questions that must always be considered and others are relevant in the post-*LaMusga* era in California. These questions, and my responses to each, follow.

A move typically leads to greater instability and change. How can we expect Sophia to deal with these changes in her life?

As noted above, Ms. Green has already moved. Sophia misses her mother. It is expected that if Sophia were to move to be in the primary care of her mother, Sophia will then miss her father. Sophia appears to be fairly adaptable and will likely adapt to significant changes without problems.

Is the move representative of stability or a pattern of instability on the part of the moving parent?

There is no evidence that this is about instability on the part of Ms. Green.

Are there concerns about the mental health of the moving parent and whether or not Ms. Green will facilitate a positive relationship between Sophia and her father over time?

None.

Does Sophia have any special needs, siblings, activities, or friends that will be affected by the move?

The siblings are in Ms. Green's home, so moving will allow her greater opportunities to grow in those relationships.

What have been the actual custodial arrangements, how have they been working, and what are the problems?

Prior to Ms. Green and her husband's move, Mr. Brown and Ms. Green shared custody reasonably well and relatively equally. There were no significant problems, other than difficulty in the communication between them.

Are there concerns about restrictive gatekeeping?

Ms. Green and her husband tend to have relatively negative views of Mr. Brown and highlight their own positive attributes while highlighting his negative attributes. This is consistent with many custody litigants. If that translates into later restrictive gatekeeping, that could be an issue, but there is no clear evidence that this will be a problem in this matter. Similarly, there is no evidence that Mr. Brown is a restrictive gatekeeping parent.

Are there differences in social capital in either parent's location?

There is clearly more family in Tennessee than in California. In California, Sophia has her father, friends, and her father's current girlfriend and her son. There are no other relatives in California. In contrast, in Tennessee, there is Ms. Green and her husband, their daughter Amy, friends, and relatives of Ms. Green's nearby. Additionally, Ms. Green is pregnant again, so there will be another sibling along the way soon. This would suggest the probability of greater social capital in mother's location.

Among the post-*LaMusga* factors that the court would ordinarily consider when deciding whether to modify a custody order in light of the custodial parent's proposal to change the residence of the child are the following:

Is there some type of detriment to Sophia moving?

Sophia is in a bind regardless of where she lives. If she remains in California, she misses her mother, her stepfather, and her sister. If she moves to Tennessee, she will miss her father. Detriment will exist simply by virtue of the fact that Ms. Green has moved, regardless of how legitimate the move was.

Does Sophia have an interest in stability and continuity of the custodial arrangement?

There is some validity to continuing in California, as she will not have to make new friends or go to new schools. However, Mr. Brown may be leaving the military in several months and he may also need to move from the area, and if so, Sophia is going to leave her school and friends. The situation is unpredictable given Mr. Brown's desire to leave the military. Just a few years ago he wanted to move to Ohio to be close to his family. He may still want to do so after he leaves the military. Thus, independent of where Sophia lives during the school year, it is likely that Sophia will be making changes over the next year. In fact, the greatest stability could be making one move to her mother's house and then maintain stability and continuity there.

How does the distance of the move affect the recommendation?

This is a cross-country move so the flight is about 5–6 hours roundtrip in each direction. While Sophia could travel to the other parent's home for a long weekend, it would be best if it for were at least a week at a time.

How does the children's age affect the recommendation?

It is hypothesized that children of Sophia's age are able to make a move with the least problem. She is clearly able to hold on to the relationship with the distant parent via phone and Skype, she can travel easily, and she can even travel by herself if need be. At the same time, she is not yet entrenched in the community so if a move were to take place, this might be the ideal time.

Describe Sophia's relationship with both parents.

As noted above, Sophia appears to have a great relationship with each of her parents. She is well bonded to both, talks to both of her parents about her feelings, and enjoys her time with each of them. She feels similarly toward her stepfather. Along with this, both parents appear to be authoritative in their style, as they have a general routine and structure, with reasonable and predictable rules, and both of them are sensitive to Sophia and her emotions and developmental needs. This style of parenting is seen as the healthiest for children.

What is the relationship between the parents, including but not limited to their ability to communicate and cooperate effectively?

These parents do not communicate very well. They will need help in improving their communication for the benefit of Sophia.

How willing are they to put the children's interests above their individual interests?

While Mr. Brown does not believe that Ms. Green put Sophia's interests above her own when she moved to Tennessee, this move was for a good financial opportunity for her and her husband. There is no evidence available to this evaluator to suggest that either parent puts their own interests above Sophia's.

What are Sophia's wishes, and is she mature enough for such an inquiry to be appropriate?

At this age, Sophia's wishes about where to live are not as significant as other factors described. She is not mature enough for such an inquiry to be appropriate. At the same time, Sophia wishes to continue having a good relationship with both of her parents, something that is not easy to do at this distance.

What are the reasons for the proposed move?

As noted above, the reason for the move was due to Mr. Green's new job. In this evaluator's view, this was in good faith and there is no evidence that this move has any bad faith component to this good faith move.

To what extent are the parents currently sharing custody?

Prior to the move, they shared custody equally. It is expected that both parents will continue to share custody to the extent possible across distance and time.

# Analysis of Advantages and Disadvantages of Mother-Custody in Tennessee Versus Father-Custody in California

While children generally do best when both parents are actively involved in a wide range of their child's life experiences and activities, and if both parents can be nearer to one another in either California or in Tennessee, the potential risks associated with the possibility of a move would be moot. As noted above, a move, for all practical purposes, does create change in the parent–child relationship with the "left-behind" parent. Unless children can maintain frequent and continuing contact with that parent, there is some loss associated with the move and an automatic adjustment required by the move. In a perfect world, absent significant harm or abuse, children would never live very far from either of their parents so that they could benefit from frequent and continuing contact with both parents.

However, that is not the appropriate question in a move-away evaluation. The necessary analysis at this point is to focus on the potential risks and benefits of mother-custody in Tennessee or father-custody in California and relevant protective factors that might apply in both circumstances.

In looking at the benefits of mother-custody in Tennessee, the primary benefits are that Sophia will have a bigger family; she will be with her mother, stepfather, and sisters; and her mother will be home to take care of her after school, reducing or negating the need for before- and after-school day care. However, the primary risks of mother-custody in Tennessee lie in their negative attitudes toward Mr. Brown and the minimal risk that they might turn into restrictive gatekeeping parents if Sophia is in her mother's care. Of course, she will also have the risk of missing her father while in her mother's primary care.

In considering the benefits of father-custody in California, the primary benefit is that there will be no change in Sophia's major day-to-day life. She will continue in her school, maintain her present friends and the routines she is used to. However, the primary risk of father-custody in California is that she will continue to miss her mother, her stepfather, and Amy. The other primary disadvantages of being in California are that Sophia spends a significant portion of each day in daycare instead of in either parent's care and that no one knows what Mr. Brown will actually be doing after he leaves the military in a few months.

Ultimately, in this evaluator's opinion, the court needs to weigh the primary advantages of mother-custody in Tennessee against the primary advantages of father-custody in California. In this evaluator's view, the benefit to Sophia being with her sister may outweigh the benefit of ongoing stability in California. In addition, it is unclear whether that stability will be at risk when Mr. Brown leaves the military. However, the potential risks associated with Mr. and Ms. Green's negative views toward Mr. Brown make this a very close call.

Again, it will be best for Sophia if both parents could be nearer one another and resume relatively equally shared custody. This can be achieved only if, when Mr. Brown leaves the military, he gets employment in the Tennessee area whereby he will be much closer to Ms. Green and her husband. If that were to occur, I would recommend that they share custody more equally and based on the actual location of where Mr. Brown would be living. However, if Mr. Brown remains in California or gets a job elsewhere after he leaves the military, it would appear to this evaluator that, while a close call, it would be best for Sophia if she were to live in her mother's primary care in Tennessee, and spend considerable time with her father when not in school.

Given the above, this evaluator recommends the following:

1. Both Mr. Brown and Ms. Green to continue sharing joint legal custody of Sophia.

2. In the event that the parents can live near enough to one another, they should go back to sharing physical custody relatively equally.

3. If the parents do not live near one another and the court agrees with this evaluator's recommendation, Ms. Green to be the primary parent during the school year.

4. If the court does not agree and believes that the risks of moving to Tennessee outweigh the benefits, Mr. Brown to be the primary parent during the school year.

5. Regardless of that decision, the school parent to have primary physical custody of Sophia during the school year. That parent to also have primary custody of Sophia for half of the Christmas break (alternated annually between first half or second half of the break) and 2 weeks during the summer for a vacation. Sophia to remain with the primary parent for 5 days after school ends and be back with the primary parent 7 days before school begins.

6. Sophia to be in the physical custody of the non-school parent the rest of the time.

7. Regarding summer vacations, the primary school parent is to pick his or her vacation dates by April 1 of each calendar year. In the event that the parents cannot agree on those dates, father to have first choice of dates in even-numbered years and mother to have first choice of dates in odd-numbered years.

8. Mr. Brown and Ms. Green need to learn to communicate better with each other. I would recommend that they put aside their differences and start to communicate about Sophia and her day-to-day life. They can use the website www.ourfamilywizard.com to begin that communication. If that is not sufficient, they may benefit from periodic co-parent counseling. While such counseling might be difficult cross-country, it may be workable via phone, if needed.

9. Regardless of the outcome, if either parent believes that Sophia is having trouble adjusting to the custodial arrangement during the next year, or if Mr. Brown moves to a different location requiring a change in the parenting plan, this evaluator would recommend an updated brief evaluation to see what is in Sophia's best interests.

Thank you for allowing me to be of assistance with this family.

# Appendix H_____

## *Recommended Reading*

Ackerman, M. (2006). *Clinician's guide to child custody evaluations* (3rd ed.). Hoboken, NJ: John Wiley.

Amato, P., & Booth, A. (1997). *A generation at risk: Growing up in an era of family upheaval.* Cambridge, MA: Harvard University Press.

Arredondo, D., & Edwards, L. (2000). Attachment, bonding, and reciprocal connectedness: Limitations of attachment theory in the juvenile and family courts. *Journal of the Center for Families, Children, and the Courts, 2,* 109–127.

Austin, W. (2003). Relocation law and the threshold of harm: Integrating legal and behavioral perspectives. *Family Law Quarterly, 34,* 63–82.

Baker, A. (2010). Adult recall of parental alienation in a community sample: Prevalence and associations with psychological maltreatment. *Journal of Divorce and Remarriage, 51,* 16–35.

Clawar, S., & Rivlin, B. (1991). *Children held hostage.* Chicago: American Bar Association.

Gardner, R. (2001). Should courts order PAS children to visit/reside with the alienated parent? A follow-up study. *American Journal of Forensic Psychology, 19*(3), 61–106.

Garrity, C., & Baris, M. (1994). Caught in the middle: Protecting children of high-conflict divorce. New York: Lexington Books.

Gould, J., & Stahl, P. (2000). The art and science of child custody evaluations. *Family and Conciliation Courts Review, 38*(3), 392–414.

Jaffe, P. G., Crooks, C. V., & Wolfe, D. A. (2003). Legal and policy responses to children exposed to domestic violence: The need to evaluate intended and unintended consequences. *Clinical Child and Family Psychology Review, 6,* 205–213.

Johnston, J. R. (2005). Children of divorce who reject a parent and refuse visitation: Recent research and social policy implications for the alienated child. *Family Law Quarterly, 38,* 757–775.

Johnston, J. R., Walters, M. G., & Olesen, N. W. (2005). The psychological functioning of alienated children in custody disputing families: An exploratory study. *American Journal of Forensic Psychology, 23*(3), 39–64.

Markan, L. K., & Weinstock, D. K. (2005). Expanding forensically informed evalu-
    ations and therapeutic interventions in family court. *Family Court Review, 43,*
    466–480.

Martindale, D. (2006). Play therapy doesn't play in court. *Journal of Child Custody,*
    *3*(1), 77–86.

Poole, D., & Lindsay, D. (2001). Children's eyewitness reports after exposure to
    misinformation from parents. *Journal of Experimental Psychology: Applied, 7,*
    27–50.

Price, M. (2009). *The special needs child and divorce: A practical guide to evaluat-
    ing and handling cases.* Chicago: American Bar Association.

Tesler, P. (2001). *Collaborative law: Achieving effective resolution in divorce with-
    out litigation.* Chicago: American Bar Association.

Warshak, R. A. (2010). *Divorce poison: How to protect your family from bad-
    mouthing and brainwashing.* New York: Harper Paperbacks.

# References

Abidin, R. (1990). *Parenting Stress Index*. Charlottesville, VA: Pediatric Psychology Press.

Achenbach, T. M. (1991). *Child Behavior Checklist*. Burlington: University of Vermont, Department of Psychiatry.

Ackerman, M., & Ackerman, M. (1997). Custody evaluation practices: A survey of experienced professionals (revisited). *Professional Psychology: Research & Practice, 28*(2), 137–145.

AFCC Task Force on Parenting Coordination. (2005). *Guidelines for parenting coordination*. Madison, WI: American Association of Family and Conciliation Courts.

Ahrons, C. (2001). *Divorce and remarriage: The children speak out*. Research report submitted to the Judicial Council of California, Center for Families, Children and the Courts, San Francisco.

Ahrons, C. (2004). *We're still family: What grown children have to say about their parents' divorce*. New York: HarperCollins.

Allen, S., & Hawkins, A. (1999). Maternal gatekeeping: Mothers' beliefs and behaviors that inhibit greater father involvement in family work. *Journal of Marriage and the Family, 61*, 199–212.

Amato, P., & Hohmann-Marriott, B. (2007). A comparison of high- and low-distress marriages that end in divorce. *Journal of Marriage and Family, 69*(3), 621–638.

American Bar Association. (2001, Winter). High-conflict custody cases: Reforming the system for children. *Family Law Quarterly, 34*(4), 589.

American Law Institute. (2002). *Principles of the law of family dissolution: Analysis and recommendations*. Albany, NY: Matthew Bender.

American Psychiatric Association. (1994). *Diagnostic and statistical manual of mental disorders* (4th ed.). Washington, DC: Author.

American Psychiatric Association. (2010). *DSM-5 development: Conditions proposed by outside sources*. Retrieved February 15, 2010, from http://www.dsm5.org/ProposedRevisions/Pages/ConditionsProposedbyOutsideSources.aspx

American Psychological Association. (2002). *Ethical principles for psychologists*. Washington, DC: Author.

American Psychological Association. (2009). *Guidelines for child custody evaluations in family law proceedings*. Washington, DC: Author.

Arbuthnot, J., Kramer, K., & Gordon, D. (1997). Patterns of relitigation following divorce education. *Family and Conciliation Courts, 35*, 269–279.

Arizona. (2010). *Planning for parenting time: Arizona's guide for parents living apart.* Supreme Court of Arizona. Retrieved from http://www.supreme.state.az.us/nav2/ParentingPlansWorkgroup/Documents/PPWguidelines.pdf

Arizona Revised Statutes 25-403 and 25-408.

Association of Family and Conciliation Courts. (2006). *Model standards of practice for child custody evaluation.* Madison, WI: Author.

Attachment and child custody [Special issue]. (2009). *Journal of Child Custody, 6,* 1–2.

Austin, W. (2000). A forensic psychology model of risk assessment for child custody relocation law. *Family Court Review, 38*(2), 192–207.

Austin, W. (2002). Guidelines for utilizing collateral sources of information in child custody evaluations. *Family Court Review, 40*(2), 177–184.

Austin, W. (2008a). Relocation, research, and forensic evaluation, Part I: Effects of residential mobility on children of divorce. *Family Court Review, 46*(1), 137–150.

Austin, W. (2008b). Relocation, research, and forensic evaluation, Part II: Research in support of the relocation risk assessment model. *Family Court Review, 46*(2), 347–365.

Austin, W., & Gould, J. (2006). Exploring three functions in child custody evaluation for the relocation case: Prediction, investigation, and making recommendations for a long-distance parenting plan. *Journal of Child Custody, 3*(3–4), 63–108.

Austin, W., & Kirkpatrick, D. (2002, November). *Effective collateral sources of information.* Presentation at a workshop of the Association of Family and Conciliation Courts, Tucson, AZ.

Baker, A. (2005a). The long-term effects of parental alienation on adult children: A qualitative research study. *American Journal of Family Therapy, 33,* 289–302.

Baker, A. (2005b). Parent alienation strategies: A qualitative study of adults who experienced parental alienation as a child. *American Journal of Forensic Psychology, 23*(4), 41–64.

Baker, A. (2007a). *Adult children of parental alienation syndrome: Breaking the ties that bind.* New York: W. W. Norton.

Baker, A. (2007b). Knowledge and attitudes about the parental alienation syndrome: A survey of custody evaluators. *American Journal of Family Therapy, 35,* 1–19.

Bala, N., Hunt, S., & McCarney, C. (2010). Parental alienation: Canadian court cases 1989–2008. *Family Court Review, 48,* 164–179.

Bancroft, L., & Silverman, J. G. (2002). *The batterer as parent: Addressing the impact of domestic violence on family dynamics.* Thousand Oaks, CA: Sage.

Barsky, A. (2007). Mediative evaluations: The pros and perils of blending roles. *Family Court Review, 45*(4), 560–572.

Bathurst, K., Gottfried, A. W., & Gottfried, A. E. (1997). Normative data for the MMPI-2 in child custody litigation. *Psychological Assessment, 9*(3), 205–211.

Baumrind, D. (1996). The discipline controversy revisited. *Family Relations, 45*(4), 405–414.

Bauserman, R. (2002). Child adjustment in joint-custody versus sole-custody arrangements: A meta-analytic review. *Journal of Family Psychology, 16*(1), 91–102.

Berkow, J. (1996). "50 ways to leave your lover" or "Move-away" cases circa March 1996. *Contra Costa Lawyer, 9*(5), 18–19.

Bolen, R. (1993). Kid's turn: Helping kids cope with divorce. *Family and Conciliation Courts Review, 31*(2), 249–254.

Bornstein, R. F. (2006). The complex relationship between dependency and domestic violence: Converging psychological factors and social forces. *American Psychologist, 61*, 595–606.

Bourg, W., Broderick, R., Flagor, R., Kelly, D. M., Ervin, D. L., & Butler, J. (1999). *A child interviewer's guidebook.* Thousand Oaks, CA: Sage.

Boyan, S., & Termini, A. (2005). *The psychotherapist as parent coordinator in high-conflict divorce: Strategies and techniques.* Binghamton, NY: Haworth Clinical Practice Press.

Braver, S., Ellman, I., & Fabricius, B. (2003). Relocation of children after divorce and children's best interests: New evidence and legal considerations. *Journal of Family Psychology, 17*(2), 206–219.

Bray, J. (1991). Psychosocial factors affecting custodial and visitation arrangements. *Behavioral Sciences and the Law, 9*, 419–437.

Bricklin, B. (1995). *The custody evaluation handbook: Research-based solutions and applications.* New York: Brunner-Mazel.

Brodsky, S. (1991). *Testifying in court: Guidelines and maxims for the expert witness.* Washington, DC: American Psychological Association.

Brodsky, S. (1999). *The expert expert witness: More maxims and guidelines for testifying in court.* Washington, DC: American Psychological Association.

Brodsky, S. (2004). *Coping with cross-examination and other pathways to effective testimony.* Washington, DC: American Psychological Association.

Brodzinsky, D. (1993). On the use and misuse of psychological testing in child custody evaluations. *Professional Psychology: Research and Practice, 24*(2), 213–219.

Bruch, C. (2001). Parental alienation syndrome and parental alienation: Getting it wrong in child custody cases. *Family Law Quarterly, 35*(3), 527.

Bruniers, T. (2000). Luncheon speech to the Contra Costa Bar Association, Walnut Creek, CA, January, 2000.

California Family Codes, § 3111, § 3020, § 3040, § 3041, § 3042, § 3044, and § 7501.

*California rules of court.* (2009). Albany, NY: Matthew Bender.

California Rules of Court, Rule 5.220.

California Rules of Court, Rule 5.225.

California Rules of Court, Rule 5.230.

California Rules of Court, Rule 5.235.

Calloway, G. (2005). The Rorschach: Its use in child custody evaluations. *Journal of Child Custody, 2*(1–2), 143–157.

*Cassady v. Signorelli,* 49 Cal. App. 4th 55—state: court 1996.

Ceci, S., & Bruck, M. (1993). The suggestibility of the child witness: A historical review and synthesis. *Psychological Bulletin, 113*, 403–439.

Ceci, S., & Bruck, M. (1995). *Jeopardy in the courtroom: A scientific analysis of children's testimony.* Washington, DC: American Psychological Association.

Coates, C., Jones, W., Bushard, P., Deutsch, R., Hicks, B., Stahl, P., Sullivan, M., Sydlik, B., & Wistner, R. (2003). Parenting coordination: Implementation issues. *Family Court Review, 41*(4), 533–564.

Committee on Ethical Guidelines for Forensic Psychologists. (1991). Specialty guidelines for forensic psychologists. *Law and Human Behavior, 15*(6), 655–665.

Dalton, C., Drozd, L., & Wong, F. (2005). *Navigating custody and visitation evaluations in cases with domestic violence: A judge's guide.* Reno, NV: National Council of Juvenile and Family Court Judges.

Deutsch, R. (2008). Divorce in the 21st century: Multidisciplinary family interventions. *Journal of Psychiatry & Law, 36*(1), 41–66.

Drozd, L., & Olesen, N. (2004). Is it abuse, alienation, and/or estrangement? A decision tree. *Journal of Child Custody, 1*(3), 65–106.

Duggan, D. (2007). Rock-paper-scissors: Playing the odds with the law of child relocation. *Family Court Review, 45*(2), 193–213.

Dunford-Jackson, B., & Jordan, S. (2003, Winter). Context is everything: Domestic violence in the real world. *Newsletter of the National Council of Juvenile and Family Court Judges,* pp. 12–14.

Dunn, J., Davies, L., O'Connor, T., & Sturgess, W. (2001). Family lives and friendships: The perspectives of children in step-, single-parent, and nonstep families. *Journal of Family Psychology, 15*(2), 272–287.

Dyer, F. (1997). Application of the Millon inventories in forensic psychology. In T. Millon (Ed.), *The Millon inventories: Clinical and personality assessment* (pp. 124–139). New York: Guilford Press.

Edens, J. F., Cruise, K. R., & Buffington-Vollum, J. K. (2001). Forensic and correctional applications of the Personality Assessment Inventory. *Behavioral Sciences and the Law, 19,* 519–543.

Eisenberg, L. (1958). School phobia: A study in the communication of anxiety. *American Journal of Psychiatry, 114,* 712–718.

Elrod, L. (2006). A move in the right direction? Best interests of the child emerging as the standard for relocation cases. *Journal of Child Custody, 3*(3–4), 29–61.

Emery, R. (1999). *Marriage, divorce, and children's adjustment* (2nd ed.). Thousand Oaks, CA: Sage.

Emery, R., Otto, R., & O'Donohue, W. (2005). A critical assessment of child custody evaluations: Limited science and a flawed system. *Psychological Science in the Public Interest, 6*(1), 1–29.

Emery, R., Sbarra, D., & Grover, T. (2005). Divorce mediation: Research and reflections. *Family Court Review, 43*(1), 22–37.

Exner, J. E. (1995). *The Rorschach: A comprehensive system.* New York: John Wiley.

Fabricius, W., & Braver, S. (2006). Relocation, parent conflict, and domestic violence: Independent risk factors for children of divorce. *Journal of Child Custody, 3*(3–4), 7–24.

*Family Court Review.* (2010). [Special Issue on Alienated Children in Divorce and Separation: Emerging Approaches for Families and Courts], *48*(1).

Fidler, B. J., & Bala, N. (2010). Children resisting postseparation contact with a parent: Concepts, controversies, and conundrums. *Family Court Review, 48,* 10–47.

Fields, L., & Prinz, R. (1997). Coping and adjustment during childhood and adolescence. *Clinical Psychology Review, 17*(8), 937–976.

Flens, J. (2005). The responsible use of psychological testing in child custody evaluations: Selection of tests. *Journal of Child Custody, 2*(1–2), 3–29.

Florida Statutes 61.13.

Fox, R. (1994). *Parent Behavior Checklist.* Brandon, VT: Clinical Psychology Publishing.

Friedlander, S., & Walters, M. G. (2010). When a child rejects a parent: Tailoring the intervention to fit the problem. *Family Court Review, 48,* 97–110.

Garb, H., Wood, J., Lillenfeld, S., & Nezworski, M. (2002). Effective use of projective techniques in clinical practice: Let the data help with selection and interpretation. *Professional Psychology: Research and Practice, 33*(5), 454–463.

Garber, B. (2004). Parental alienation in light of attachment theory: Consideration of the broader implications for child development, clinical practice, and forensic process. *Journal of Child Custody, 1*(4), 49–76.

Gardner, R. (1987). *The parental alienation syndrome and the differentiation between fabricated and genuine child sex abuse.* Cresskill, NJ: Creative Therapeutics.

Gardner, R. (1995). *The parental alienation syndrome: A guide for mental health & legal professionals* (2nd ed.). Creskill, NJ: Creative Therapeutics.

Gerard, A. (1994). *Parent-Child Relationship Inventory.* Los Angeles: Western Psychological Services.

Glassman, J. (2007, December). Presentation at a workshop titled "Successful Joint Legal Custody, or, Is Joint Legal Custody Really Meant for Everyone?" Phoenix, Arizona.

Goldstein, J., Freud, A., & Solnit, A. (1984). *Beyond the best interests of the child.* New York: Free Press.

Gondolf, E. (2004). Evaluating batterer counseling programs: A difficult task showing some effects. *Aggression and Violent Behavior, 9*(6), 605–631.

Goodman, G. S., & Reed, R. (1986). Age differences in eyewitness testimony. *Law & Human Behavior, 10,* 317–332.

Gould, J. (1998). *Conducting scientifically crafted child custody evaluations.* Thousand Oaks, CA: Sage.

Gould, J. (1999). Conducting scientifically crafted child custody evaluations: Part two: A paradigm for the forensic evaluation of child custody determination. *Family and Conciliation Courts Review, 37*(2), 135–158.

Gould, J. (2006). *Conducting scientifically crafted child custody evaluations* (2nd ed.). Sarasota, FL: Professional Resource Press.

Gould, J., Kirkpatrick, H., Austin, W., & Martindale, D. (2004). Critiquing a colleague's forensic advisory report: A suggested protocol for application to child custody evaluations. *Journal of Child Custody, 1*(3), 37–64.

Gould, J., & Martindale, D. (2007). *The art and science of child custody evaluations.* New York: Guilford Press.

Gould, J., & Stahl, P. (2001). Never paint by the numbers: A response to Kelly and Lamb (2000), Solomon and Biringen (2001), and Lamb and Kelly (2001). *Family Court Review, 39*(4), 372–376.

Greenberg, L., Gould, J., Gould-Saltmann, D., & Stahl, P. (2003). Is the child's therapist part of the problem? What judges, attorneys, and mental health professionals need to know about court-related treatment for children. *Family Law Quarterly, 37*(2), 241–271.

Greenberg, L., Gould-Saltmann, D., & Schneider, R. (2006). The problem with presumptions—A review and commentary. *Journal of Child Custody, 3*(3–4), 139–172.

Greenberg, S., & Shuman, D. (1997). Irreconcilable conflict between therapeutic and forensic roles. *Professional Psychology: Research and Practice, 28*(1), 50–57.

Greenberg, S., Shuman, D., & Meyer, R. (2004). Unmasking forensic diagnosis. *International Journal of Law and Psychiatry, 27*(1), 1–15.

Grove, W. M., Barden, R. C., Garb, H. N., & Lillenfeld, S. O. (2002). Failure of Rorschach-Comprehensive-System-based testimony to be admissible under the Daubert-Joiner-Kumho standard. *Psychology, Public Policy and Law, 8*(2), 216–234.

Gutheil, T., & Simon, R. (2004). Avoiding bias in expert testimony. *Psychiatric Annals, 34*(4), 260–270.

*Hague Convention on the Civil Aspects of International Child Abduction.* (2010). Retrieved April 23, 2010, from http://en.wikipedia.org/wiki/Hague_Convention_on_the_Civil_Aspects_of_International_Child_Abduction

Halon, R. (2001). The Millon Clinical Multiaxial Inventory-III: The normal quartet in child custody cases. *American Journal of Forensic Psychology, 19*(1), 57–75.

Hanks, S. (1992). Translating theory into practice: A conceptual framework for clinical assessment, differential diagnosis and multi-modal treatment of maritally violent individuals, couples, and families. In E. Viano (Ed.), *Intimate violence: Interdisciplinary perspectives* (pp. 157–176). Washington, DC: Hemisphere Publications.

Hawes, S., & Boccaccini, M. (2009). Detection of overreporting of psychopathology on the Personality Assessment Inventory: A meta-analytic review. *Psychological Assessment, 21*(1), 112–124.

Hetherington, E., & Kelly, J. (2002). *For better or worse: Divorce reconsidered.* New York: W. W. Norton.

Hodges, W. (1986). *Interventions for children of divorce.* New York: John Wiley.

Holtzworth-Monroe, A., & Stuart, G. L. (1994). Typologies of male batterers: Three subtypes and the differences among them. *Psychological Bulletin, 116,* 476–497.

In re Marriage of Abargil, 131 Cal. Rptr. 2d 429—Cal: Court 2003.

In re Marriage of Burgess, 13 Cal. 4th 25—Cal: Supreme Court 1996.

In re Marriage of Campos, 108 Cal. App. 4th 839—Cal: Court date.

In re Marriage of Condon, 62 Cal. App. 4th 533—Cal: Court of Appeals, 2nd Dist., Div. 7 1998.

In re Marriage of Edlund v. Hales, 78 Cal. Rptr. 2d 671—Cal: Court of Appeals, 1st Dist., Div. 3 1998.

In re Marriage of LaMusga, 88 P. 3d 81—Cal: Supreme Court 2004.

In re Marriage of McGinnis, 7 Cal. App. 4th 473—Cal: Court of Appeals, 2nd Dist., Div. 6 1992.

In re Marriage of Seagondollar, Cal: Court of Appeal, 4th Dist., Div. 3 2006.

In re Marriage of Williams, 105 Cal. Rptr. 2d 923—Cal: Court of Appeal, 2nd Dist., Div. 6 2001.

Isman, D. (1996, Fall). Gardner's witch-hunt. *UC Davis Journal of Juvenile Law & Policy,* p. 12.

Jaffe, P. G., Johnston, J. R., Crooks, C. V., & Bala, N. (2008). Custody disputes involving allegations of domestic violence: The need for differentiated approaches to parenting plans. *Family Court Review, 46,* 500–522.

Johnston, J. (1994). High-conflict divorce. *Future of Children, 4*(1), 165–182.

Johnston, J. (1995). Children's adjustment in sole custody compared to joint custody families and principles for custody decision making. *Family & Conciliation Courts Review, 33*(4), 415–425.

Johnston, J., & Campbell, L. (1988). *Impasses of divorce: The dynamics and resolution of family conflict.* New York: Free Press.

Johnston, J., Kline, M., & Tschann, J. (1989). Ongoing postdivorce conflict in families contesting custody: Effects on children of join custody and frequent access. *American Journal of Orthopsychiatry, 59,* 576–592.

Johnston, J., & Roseby, V. (1997). *In the name of the child.* New York: Free Press.

Johnston, J., Roseby, V., & Kuehnle, K. (2009). *In the name of the child: A developmental approach to understanding and helping children of conflicted and violent divorce* (2nd ed.). New York: Springer.

Johnston, J., Walters, M., & Friedlander, S. (2001). Therapeutic work with alienated children and their families. *Family Court Review, 39,* 316–332.

Johnston, J., Walters, M. G., & Olesen, N. W. (2005). Is it alienating parenting, role reversal or child abuse? A study of children's rejection of a parent in child custody disputes. *Journal of Emotional Abuse, 5,* 191–218.

Kalter, N. (1990). *Growing up with divorce.* New York: Free Press.

Kelly, J. (1996). A decade of divorce mediation research: Some answers and questions. *Family and Conciliation Courts Review, 34,* 373–385.

Kelly, J. (2010). Commentary on "Family bridges: Using insights from social science to reconnect parents and alienated children" (Warshak, 2010). *Family Court Review, 48,* 81–90.

Kelly, J., & Emery, R. (2003). Children's adjustment following divorce: Risk and resilience perspectives. *Family Relations: Interdisciplinary Journal of Applied Family Studies, 52*(4), 352–362.

Kelly, J., & Johnson, M. P. (2008). Differentiation among types of intimate partner violence: Research update and implications for interventions. *Family Court Review, 46,* 476–499.

Kelly, J., & Johnston, J. R. (2001). The alienated child: A reformulation of parental alienation syndrome. *Family Court Review, 39,* 249–266.

Kelly, J., & Lamb, M. (2000). Using child development research to make appropriate custody and access decisions for young children. *Family Court Review, 38*(3), 297–311.

Kelly, J., & Lamb, M. (2003). Developmental issues in relocation cases involving young children: When, whether, and how? *Journal of Family Psychology, 17*(2), 193–205.

Kelly, R., & Ramsey, S. (2009). Child custody evaluations: The need for systems-level outcome assessments. *Family Court Review, 47*(2), 286–303.

Kirkland, K., McMillan, E., IV, & Kirkland, K. (2004). Use of collateral contacts in child custody evaluation. *Journal of Child Custody, 2*(4), 95–109.

Kirkpatrick, H. (2004). A floor, not a ceiling: Beyond guidelines—An argument for minimum standards of practice in conducting child custody and visitation evaluations. *Journal of Child Custody, 1*(1), 61–75.

Kline, M., Johnston, J., & Tschann, J. (1991). The long shadow of marital conflict. *Journal of Marriage & the Family, 53,* 297–309.

Kuehnle, K. (1996). *Assessing allegations of child sexual abuse.* Sarasota, FL: Professional Resource Press.

Kuehnle, K., & Connell, M. (Eds.). (2009). *The evaluation of child sexual abuse allegations: A comprehensive guide to assessment and testimony.* Hoboken, NJ: John Wiley.

Kuehnle, K., & Kirkpatrick, H. (2005). Evaluating allegations of child sexual abuse within complex child custody cases. *Journal of Child Custody, 2*(3), 3–39.

Lamb, M. E., Hershkowitz, I., Orbach, Y., & Esplin, P. (2008). *Tell me what happened: Structured investigative interviews of child victims and witnesses.* Hoboken, NJ: John Wiley.

Lamb, M. E., Orbach, Y., Hershkowitz, I., Esplin, P. W., & Horowitz, D. (2007). A structured forensic interview protocol improves the quality and informativeness of investigative interviews with children: A review of research using the NICHD Investigative Interview Protocol. *Child Abuse & Neglect, 31*(11–12), 1201–1231.

Lamb, M. E., Sternberg, K., & Thompson, R. (1997). The effects of divorce and custody arrangements on children's behavior, development, and adjustment. *Family & Conciliation Courts Review, 35*(4), 393–404.

Lampel, A. (1996). Child's alignment with parents in highly conflicted custody cases. *Family and Conciliation Courts Review, 34,* 232–235.

Lee, M. (1996, January). *The use of the Rorschach in child custody evaluations.* Paper presented at the 2nd Child Custody Symposium of the Association of Family & Conciliation Courts, Clearwater, FL.

Lee, M., & Olesen, N. (2001). Assessing for alienation in child custody and access evaluations. *Family Court Review, 39*(3), 282–298.

Lott, M. (2006). Relocation cases: Analyzing relevant evidence. *Journal of Child Custody, 3*(3–4), 125–137.

Ludolph, P. (2009). Answered and unanswered questions in attachment theory with implications for children of divorce. *Journal of Child Custody, 6*(1–2), 8–24.

Ludolph, P., & Viro, M. (1998, May). *Attachment theory and research: Implications for professionals assisting families of high conflict divorce.* Paper presented at the 35th Annual Conference of the Association of Family and Conciliation Courts, Washington, DC.

Lund, M. (1995). A therapist's view of parental alienation syndrome. *Family and Conciliation Courts Review, 33,* 308–316.

Lyon, T. D. (1999). The new wave of suggestibility research: A critique. *Cornell Law Review, 84,* 1004–1087.

Maccoby, E., & Mnookin, R. (1992). *Dividing the child: Social and legal dilemmas of custody.* Cambridge, MA: Harvard University Press.

Martindale, D. (2005). Confirmatory bias and confirmatory distortion. *Journal of Child Custody, 2*(1–2), 31–48.

Marvin, R., Cooper, G., Hoffman, K., & Powell, B. (2002). The Circle of Security Project: Attachment-based interventions with caregiver-pre-school child dyads. *Attachment and Human Development, 4,* 107–124.

Marvin, R., & Schutz, B. (2009). One component of an evidence-based approach to the use of attachment research in child custody evaluations. *Journal of Child Custody, 6*(1–2), 113–138.

McCann, J., Flens, J., Campagna, V., Collman, P., Lazzaro, T., & Connor, E. (2001). The MCMI-III in child custody evaluations: A normative study. *Journal of Forensic Psychology Practice, 1*(2), 27–44.

McIntosh, J. (2009, May). *Deconstructing shared parenting.* Presentation at the 46th annual conference of the Association of Family and Conciliation Courts, New Orleans, LA.

McIntosh, J., Wells, Y., Smyth, B., & Long, C. (2008). Child-focused and child-inclusive divorce mediation: Comparative outcomes from a prospective study of post-separation adjustment. *Family Court Review, 46*(1), 105–124.

McKinnon, R., & Wallerstein, J. (1987). Joint custody and the preschool child. *Conciliation Courts Review, 25*(2), 39–48.

McMahon, T. J., & Giannini, F. D. (2003). Substance-abusing fathers in family court. *Family Court Review, 41,* 337–353.

Medoff, D. (2003). The scientific basis of psychological testing: Considerations following Daubert, Kumho, and Joiner. *Family Court Review, 41*(2), 199–213.

Melton, G., Petrila, J., Poythress, N., & Slobogin, C. (2007). *Psychological evalua-tions for the courts: A handbook for mental health professionals and lawyers* (3rd ed.). New York: Guilford.

Miller, S. (1995). Whatever happened to the "best interest" analysis in New York relocation cases? *Pace Law Review, 15*(2), 339–389.

Millon, T. (1996). *Disorders of personality: DSM-IV and beyond.* New York: Wiley-Interscience.

Millon, T. (2006). *MCMI-III manual (Millon Clinical Multiaxial Inventory-III)* (3rd ed.). Eden Prairie, MN: NCS Pearson.

Montenegro v. Diaz, 27 P. 3d 289—Cal: Supreme Court 2001.

Morley, J. (2009, May). *International relocation.* Presentation at a program spon-sored by the New York State Chapter of the Association of Family and Conciliation Courts, Tarrytown, NY.

Murrie, D., Martindale, D. A., & Epstein, M. (2009). Unsupported assessment tech-niques in child sexual abuse evaluations. In K. Kuehnle & M. Connell (Eds.), *The evaluation of child sexual abuse allegations: A comprehensive guide to assessment and testimony.* (pp. 397–420). Hoboken, NJ: John Wiley.

Newmark, L., Harrell, A., & Salem, P. (1995). Domestic violence and empower-ment in custody and visitation cases. *Family and Conciliation Courts Review, 33,* 30–62.

O'Donohue, W., & Bradley, A. (1999). Conceptual and empirical issues in child cus-tody evaluations. *Clinical Psychology: Science and Practice, 6*(3), 310–322.

Ornstein, P., & Haden, C. (2001). Memory development or the development of memory? *Current Directions in Psychological Science, 10,* 202–205.

Otto, R. K., & Collins, R. (1995). Use of the MMPI-2/MMPI-A in child custody eval-uations. In Y. Ben-Porath, J. Graham, G. Hall, R. Hirschman, & M. Zaragoza (Eds.), *Forensic applications of the MMPI-2* (pp. 222–252). Thousand Oaks, CA: Sage.

Otto, R. K., Edens, J. F., & Barcus, E. (2000). The use of psychological testing in child custody evaluations. *Family and Conciliation Courts Review, 38,* 312–340.

Parental Kidnapping Prevention Act. (2008). Retrieved April 23, 2010, from http://en.wikipedia.org/wiki/Parental_Kidnapping_Prevention_Act

Perryman, H. (2005). Parental reaction to the disabled child: Implications for family courts. *Family Court Review, 43*(4), 596–606.

Poole, D., & Lamb, M. (1998). *Investigative interviews of children: A guide for help-ing professionals.* Washington, DC: American Psychological Association.

Pruett, M. K., Insabella, G., & Gustafson, K. (2005). The Collaborative Divorce Project: A court-based intervention for separating parents with young children. *Family Court Review, 43*(1), 38–51.

Pruett, M. K., Williams, T., Insabella, G., & Little, T. (2003). Family and legal indi-cators of child adjustment to divorce among families with young children. *Journal of Family Psychology, 17*(2), 169–180.

Rand, D. (1997a). The spectrum of parental alienation syndrome: Part I. *American Journal of Forensic Psychology, 15*(3), 23–52.

Rand, D. (1997b). The spectrum of parental alienation syndrome: Part II. *American Journal of Forensic Psychology, 15*(4), 39–92.

Ritzler, B., Erard, R., & Pettigrew, G. (2002). Protecting the integrity of Rorschach expert witnesses: A reply to Grove and Barden (1999) re: the admissibility of testimony under Daubert/Kumho analyses. *Psychology, Public Policy and Law,* *8*(2), 201–215.

Roseby, V. (1995). Uses of psychological testing in a child-focused approach to child custody evaluations. *Family Law Quarterly, 29,* 97–110.

*Ruisi v. Thieriot,* 53 Cal. App. 4th 1 197—Cal: Court 1997.

Salem, P., & Dunford-Jackson, B. (2008). Beyond politics and positions: A call for collaboration between family court and domestic violence professionals. *Family Court Review, 46*(3), 437–453.

Saposnek, D., Perryman, H., Berkow, J., & Ellsworth, S. (2005). Special needs children in family court cases. *Family Court Review, 43*(4), 566–581.

Saywitz, K. (1994). Questioning child witnesses. *Violence Update, 4*(7), 3–10.

Saywitz, K., & Lyon, T. (2002). Coming to grips with children's suggestibility. In M. L. Eisen, J. A. Quas, & G. S. Goodman (Eds.), *Memory and suggestibility in the forensic interview* (pp. 85–113). Mahwah, NJ: Lawrence Erlbaum.

Schleuderer, C., & Campagna, V. (2004). Assessing substance abuse questions in child custody evaluations. *Family Court Review, 42*(2), 375–383.

Shear, L. (1996). Life stories, doctrines, and decision making: Three high courts confront the move-away dilemma. *Family and Conciliation Courts Review, 34*(4), 439–458.

Shear, L. (2003). *Amicus brief submitted to the California Supreme Court in Re: Marriage of LaMusga.*

Shelton, K., & Harold, G. (2007). Marital conflict and children's adjustment: The mediating and moderating role of children's coping strategies. *Social Development, 16*(3), 497–512.

Solomon, J., & Biringen, Z. (2001). Another look at the developmental research: Commentary on Kelly and Lamb's "Using child development research to make appropriate custody and access decisions for young children." *Family Court Review, 39,* 355–364.

Solomon, J., & George, C. (1996). *The effect on attachment of overnight visitation in divorced and separating families.* Paper presented at the Biennial Meeting of the International Conference on Infant Studies, Providence, RI.

Stahl, P. (1994). *Conducting child custody evaluations: A comprehensive guide.* Thousand Oaks, CA: Sage.

Stahl, P. (1995). The use of special masters in high conflict divorce. *California Psychologist, 28*(3), 29.

Stahl, P. (1996). Second opinions: An ethical and professional process for reviewing child custody evaluations. *Family and Conciliation Courts Review, 34*(3), 386–339.

Stahl, P. (1999). *Complex issues in child custody evaluations.* Thousand Oaks, CA: Sage.

Stahl, P. (2004). Understanding and evaluating alienation in high-conflict custody cases. *Wisconsin Journal of Family Law, 24,* 1.

Stahl, P. (2005, April). The benefits and risks of child custody evaluators making recommendations to the court: A response to Tippins and Wittmann. *Family Court Review, 43*(2), 260–265.

Stahl, P. (2006). Avoiding bias in relocation evaluations. *Journal of Child Custody, 3*(3–4), 109–124.

Stahl, P. (2008a, Spring/Summer). Keeping the balance: Judicial stress and wellness. *Case in Point* [published by the National Judicial College], *7*(1), pp. 3–4.

Stahl, P. (2008b). *Parenting after divorce* (2nd ed.). Atascadero, CA: Impact Publishers.

Stahl, R. M. (2007). "Don't forget about me": Implementing Article 12 of the United Nations Convention on the Rights of the Child. *Arizona Journal of International and Comparative Law, 24,* 803–842.

Sternberg, K. J., Lamb, M. E., Esplin, P. W., Orbach, Y., & Hershkowitz, I. (2002). Using a structured interview protocol to improve the quality of investigative interviews. In M. Eisen, J. Quas, & G. Goodman (Eds.), *Memory and suggestibility in the forensic interview* (pp. 409–436). Mahwah, NJ: Lawrence Erlbaum.

Sullivan, M. (2004). Ethical, legal, and professional practice issues involved in acting as a psychologist parent coordinator in child custody cases. *Family Court Review, 42*(3), 576–582.

Sullivan, M., & Kelly, J. (2001). Legal and psychological management of cases with an alienated child. *Family Court Review, 39*(3), 299–315.

Sullivan, M., Ward, P. A., & Deutsch, R. M. (2010). Overcoming Barriers Family Camp: A program for high-conflict divorced families where a child is resisting contact with a parent. *Family Court Review, 48,* 115–134.

Talia, S. (1997, April). *To test or not to test: The use of psychological testing in child custody evaluations.* Paper presented at a meeting of the Contra Costa County (California) Bar Association meeting, San Ramon, CA.

Tesler, P. (2004). *Collaborative law FAQ's: What is collaborative law?* Retrieved January 24, 2010, from http://www.divorcenet.com/states/california/cafaq10

Tippins, T., & Wittman, J. (2005). Empirical and ethical problems with custody recommendations: A call for clinical humility and judicial vigilance. *Family Court Review, 43*(2), 193–222.

Troxel v. Granville—State: Court 2000, 530 U.S. 57, 137 Wash. 2d 1, 969 P.2d 21

Uniform Child Custody Jurisdiction and Enforcement Act. (2010). Retrieved April 23, 2010, from http://en.wikipedia.org/wiki/Uniform_Child_Custody_Jurisdiction_and_Enforcement_Act

United States, Uniform Child Custody Jurisdiction and Enforcement Act. (1997). Retrieved February 16, 2010, from http://en.wikipedia.org/wiki/Uniform_Child_Custody_Jurisdiction_and_Enforcement_Act

*UN Convention on the Rights of the Child.* (1989). Retrieved February 16, 2010, from http://en.wikipedia.org/wiki/Un_convention_on_the_rights_of_the_child

U.S. Department of State. (2009). *Reports on compliance with the Hague Abduction Convention.* Retrieved January 15, 2010, from http://travel.state.gov/family/abduction/resources/resources_4308.html

Ver Steegh, N. (2005). Differentiating types of domestic violence: Implications for child custody. *Louisiana Law Review, 65,* 1379–1431.

Ver Steegh, N., & Dalton, C. (2008). Report from the Wingspread Conference on Domestic Violence and Family Courts. *Family Court Review, 46,* 454–475.

Walker, A. G. (1999). *Handbook on questioning children.* Chicago: ABA Books.

Wallerstein, J. S. (2003). Amicus brief submitted to the California Supreme Court *in Re: Marriage of LaMusga.*

Wallerstein, J. S., & Kelly, J. (1980). *Surviving the breakup: How children and parents cope with divorce.* New York: Basic Books.

Wallerstein, J. S., Lewis, J. M., & Blakeslee, S. (2000). *The unexpected legacy of divorce: A 25-year landmark study.* New York: Hyperion.

Wallerstein, J. S., & Tanke, T. (1996). To move or not to move: Psychological and legal considerations in the relocation of children following divorce. *Family Law Quarterly, 30,* 305.

Warshak, R. A. (2000a). Blanket restrictions: Overnight contact between parents and young children. *Family and Conciliation Courts Review, 38,* 422–445.

Warshak, R. A. (2000b). Social science and children's best interest in relocation cases: Burgess revisited. *Family Law Quarterly, 34.*

Warshak, R. A. (2001). Current controversies regarding parental alienation syndrome. *American Journal of Forensic Psychology, 19*(3), 29–59.

Warshak, R. A. (2010). Family bridges: Using insights from social science to reconnect parents and alienated children. *Family Court Review, 48,* 48–80.

Whiteside, M. (1996). An integrative review of the literature pertinent to custody for children five years of age and younger. *AFCC California Newsletter, 7*(1), 24–25.

Wood, C. (1994, June). The parental alienation syndrome: A dangerous aura of reliability. *Loyola of Los Angeles Law Review,* pp. 1367–1415.

Zervopoulos, J. (2010). *Confronting mental health evidence.* Chicago: American Bar Association, Section of Family Law.

Zibbell, R. (2005). Common couple aggression: Frequency and implications for child custody and access evaluations. *Family Court Review, 43*(3), 454–465.

# Name Index

Abidin, R., 118
Achenbach, T. M., 120
Ackerman, M., xiii, 113, 117, 120, 122
AFCC Task Force on Parenting
    Coordination, 200
Ahrons, C., 37, 40, 46, 149, 150
Allen, S., 231
Amato, P., 44, 311
American Bar Association, 134, 191, 266
American Law Institute, 35
American Psychiatric Association, 115, 204
American Psychological Association,
    xiii, 8, 12, 13, 18, 20, 69, 94, 95, 111,
    112, 118, 256
Arbuthnot, J., 150, 199
Arizona, 26
Arizona Revised Statutes 25–403,
    xv, 212, 213, 274
Arizona Revised Statutes 25–408,
    xv, 212, 213
Association of Family and Conciliation Courts
    (AFCC), xiii, 7, 20, 46, 79, 159,
    166, 267
    critiquing evaluations and, 256, 258
Austin, W., 129, 213, 221, 235, 255
    gathering collateral data and, 130
    relocation evaluations and, 224
    relocation evaluations/literature and, 214,
    219, 220, 222

Baker, A., 188, 189, 191
Bala, N., 172, 204
Bancroft, L., 171
Barcus, E., 112
Barden, R. C., 114
Barsky, A., 30
Bathurst, K., 15, 91, 116, 257
Baumrind, D., 40, 46
Bauserman, R., 44

Berkow, J., 215, 216, 263
Biringen, Z., 56
Blakeslee, S., 44
Boccaccini, M., 216
Bolen, R., 180
Bornstein, R. F., 169
Bourg, W., 98
Boyan, S., 159
Bradley, A., 3
Braver, S., 17, 44, 220, 222
Bray, J., 55
Bricklin, B., 113, 118
Broderick, R., 98
Brodsky, S., 239
Brodzinsky, D., 112, 122
Bruch, C., 183
Bruck, M., 97, 98
Bruniers, T., 150
Buamrind, D., 39
Buffington-Vollum, J. K., 116
Bushard, P., 27

California Rule of Court 5.220, xiii, 8, 10,
    12, 29, 52, 53, 113, 141, 142, 256, 258
California Rule of Court 5.225, 8
California Rules of Court, 5.235, 9
California Supreme Court, 51, 54, 207,
    209, 210
Calloway, G., 114
Campagna, V., 94, 116, 264
Campbell, L., 149, 154, 190
*Cassady v. Signorelli*, 208
Ceci, S., 97, 98
Coates, C., 27
Collins, R., 113
Collman, P., 94, 116
Committee on Ethical Guidelines for Forensic
    Psychologists, 118
Connell, M., 264

Connor, E., 94, 116
Cooper, G., 57
Crooks, C. V., 172
Cruise, K. R., 116

Dalton, C., 166, 255, 256
Davies, L., 94
Deutsch, R. M., 22, 180, 203
Drozd, L., 186, 188, 255
Duggan, D., 224
Dunford-Jackson, B., 166, 167
Dunn, J., 94
Dyer, F., 114, 122

Edens, J. F., 112, 116
Eisenberg, L., 187
Ellman, I., 17, 220
Ellsworth, S., 263
Elrod, L., 212, 222
Emery, R., 3, 6, 16, 37, 43, 44, 45
Epstein, M., 106
Erard, R., 114
Esplin, P. W., 97, 98
Exner, J. E., 117

Fabricius, B., 17, 44, 220, 222
Fabricius, W., 17, 44, 220, 222
Family Court Review, xiii, 144, 166, 181,
        187, 204, 267
Fidler, B. J., 204
Fields, L., 155
Flens, J., 94, 112, 116
Florida Statutes, 35
Fox, R., 119
Freud, A., 14, 38, 55
Friedlander, S., 186, 189, 199, 204

Garb, H. N., 114
Garber, B., 199
Gardner, R., 183, 184, 186, 200, 201
George, C., 56
Gerard, A., 119
Giannini, F. D., 264
Glassman, J., 163
Goldstein, J., 14, 38, 55
Gondolf, E., 179
Goodman, G. S., 97
Gordon, D., 150, 199
Gottfried, A. E., 15, 91, 216, 257
Gottfried, A. W., 15, 91, 216, 257
Gould, J., xiii, 127, 191, 213, 255
    alienation and, 191
    bias and, 15

developmental needs and, 56
high-conflict families and, 154
overnights and, 59–61
preparing for testimonies and, 244
psychological testing and, 112
relocation evaluations/literature and,
        215, 222
therapists and, 21
Gould-Saltmann, D., 21, 154, 191, 222
Greenberg, L., 21, 154, 191, 222
Greenberg, S., 19, 204
Grove, W. M., 114
Grover, T., 6
Gustafson, K., 56
Gutheil, T., 13, 14

Haden, C., 97
Hague Convention on the Civil Aspects Of
        International Child Abduction, 14, 47
Halon, R., 116
Hanks, S., 165, 166, 173
Harold, G., 155
Harrell, A., 165
Hawes, S., 116
Hawkins, A., 231
Hershkowitz, I., 97, 98
Hetherington, E., 68, 218
Hicks, B., 27
Hodges, W., 55
Hoffman, K., 57
Hohmann-Marriott, B., 44
Holtzworth-Monroe, A., 169
Horowitz, D., 97, 98
Hunt, S., 204

In Montenegro v. Diaz, 51
In re Marriage of Abargil, 208
In re Marriage of Burgess, 53, 207–208, 209,
        209–210
In re Marriage of Campos, supra, 209
In re Marriage of Condon, 53, 208
In re Marriage of Edlund v. Hales,
        53, 208, 210
In re Marriage of LaMusga, xv, 4, 53, 143,
        209, 210–211, 236n 5, 325
In re Marriage of McGinnis, 207
In re Marriage of Williams, 71
In re Seagondolla, 51, 52
Insabella, G., 56, 231
Isman, D., 183

Jaffe, P. G., 172, 176, 178
Johnson, M. P., 168, 169, 170

Johnston, J., 56, 68, 69, 149, 154, 161, 165, 166, 186, 187, 189, 190, 199, 204
Johnston, J. R., 172, 183, 184, 185, 187, 189, 195, 200
Jones, W., 27
Jordan, S., 167

Kalter, N., 56
Kelly, J., 195
    alienation and, 183, 184, 185, 187, 189, 194, 199, 200, 203
    attachment and, 58
    best interests of the child and, 37
    children of divorce and, 44, 45
    children's reactions to parental conflict and, 68
    developmental needs and, 55, 56
    domestic violence and, 168, 169, 170
    family relationships and, 38
    harmfull evaluations and, 6
    Parent Coordinators and, 27
    relocation cases and, 16
    relocation evaluations and, 224
    relocation evaluations/literature and, 215, 217, 218, 220, 221
Kelly, R., 3
Kirkland, K., 125
Kirkpatrick, H., 7, 8, 255, 264
Kline, M., 68, 69
Kramer, K., 150, 199
Kuehnle, K., 56, 149, 187, 264

Lamb, M. E., 14
    attachment and, 58
    best interests of the child and, 37
    children of divorce and, 45
    developmental needs and, 56
    family relationships and, 38
    relocation evaluations and, 224
    relocation evaluations/literature and, 215, 218, 220, 221
    suggestibility and, 97, 98
Lampel, A., 183
Lazzaro, T., 94, 116
Lee, M., 114, 191
Lewis, J. M., 44
Lillenfeld, S. O., 114
Little, T., 231
Long, C., 43
Lott, M., 222
Ludolph, P., 38, 56, 58
Lund, M., 183
Lyon, T. D., 97

Maccoby, E., 46, 150
Martindale, D. A., xiii, 13, 106, 255
Marvin, R., 57
McCann, J., 94, 116
McCarney, C., 204
McIntosh, J., 43, 58
McKinnon, R., 56
McMahon, T. J., 264
McMillan, E., 125
Medoff, D., 114
Melton, G., 247
Meyer, R., 204
Miller, S., 214, 215
Millon, T., 151
Mnookin, R., 46, 150
Montenegro v. Diaz, 51
Morley, J., 233, 236n 6
Murrie, D., 106

Newmark, L., 165
Nezworski, M., 114

O'Connor, T., 94
O'Donohue, W., 3
Olesen, N., 186, 188, 191
Olesen, N. W., 186
Orbach, Y., 97, 98
Ornstein, P., 97
Otto, R., 3, 112, 113, 118, 122

Parental Kidnapping Prevention Act, 47, 48
Parent Awareness Skills Survey, 113
Perception of Relationship Test, 113
Perryman, H., 263
Petrila, J., 247
Pettigrew, G., 114
Poole, D., 97
Powell, B., 57
Poythress, N., 247
Prinz, R., 155
Pruett, M. K., 56, 231

Ramsey, S., 3
Rand, D., 183
Reed, R., 97
Ritzler, B., 114
Rorschach, Thematic Apperception Test (TAT), 114, 117, 118, 120–120, 121
Roseby, V., 56, 120, 121, 122, 149, 187, 189, 200
Ruisi v Theriot, 160

Salem, P., 165, 166
Saposnek, D., 263
Saywitz, K., 97
Sbarra, D., 6
Schleuderer, C., 264
Schneider, R., 222
Schutz, B., 57
Shear, L., 214, 221
Shelton, K., 155
Shuman, D., 19, 204
Silverman, J. G., 171
Simon, R., 13, 14
Slobogin, C., 247
Smyth, B., 43
Solnit, A., 14, 38, 55
Solomon, J., 56
Stahl, P., 31n 1, 125, 204n, 254n, 255, 267
    alienation and, 183, 187, 191
    bias and, 13, 15
    developmental needs and, 56
    domestic violence and, 165
    high-conflict families and, 154
    joint legal custody and, 163
    overnights and, 59–61
    parallel parenting and, 162
    Parent Coordinators and, 27, 159
    psychological testing and, 112
    recommendations and, 143–144
    relocation evaluations and, 224
    relocation evaluations/literature and,
        215, 220, 222
    therapists and, 21
Stahl, R. M., xvi
Sternberg, K. J., 14, 37, 45, 97, 98, 218
Stuart, G. L., 169
Sturgess, W., 94
Sullivan, M., 27, 159, 199, 200, 203
Sydlik, B., 27

Talia, S., 122
Tanke, T., 214, 216, 217, 218, 221
Termini, A., 159

Tesler, P., 22
Thompson, R., 14, 37, 45, 218
Tippins, T., 144
*Troxel v. Granville*, 48, 50
Tschann, J., 68, 69

*UN Convention on the Rights of the
    Child*, xvi
Uniform Child Custody Jurisdiction and
    Enforcement Act, 47
U.S. Department of State, 49, 232, 233

Ver Steegh, N., 166
Viro, M., 56

Walker, A. G., 99
Wallerstein, J. S., 183
    alienation and, 184
    children of divorce and, 44
    developmental needs and, 55, 56
    relocation evaluations and, 214, 227, 228
    relocation evaluations/literature and, 214,
        215, 216, 217, 218, 221
    research and, 44
Walters, M. G., 186, 189, 199, 204
Ward, P. A., 203
Warshak, R. A., 183, 203, 214, 236n 3
    attachment and, 57
    developmental needs and, 56
    relocation evaluations/literature and, 217,
        218, 219, 221
Wells, Y., 43
Whiteside, M., 56
Williams, T., 231
Wistner, R., 27
Wittman, J., 144
Wong, F., 255
Wood, C., 183
Wood, J., 114

Zervopoulos, J., 249, 250
Zibbell, R., 166

# Subject Index _____

Abductions:
    children/domestic violence and, 171, 176
    Hague Convention on, 14, 47
Abuse:
    alienation and, 188, 191, 196
    best interests of the child and, 37
    bias and, 18
    children/information gathering and, 100
    children/language and, 99
    confidentiality and, 277
    data and, 173–176, 248
    domestic violence and, 171. *See also*
        Domestic violence
    elder, 277
    emotional, 169, 173
    false allegations of, 231
    initial individual appointments and, 85
    insecure attachments and, 57
    parents and, 42
    reunification therapist and, 22
    spousal, 196
    suggestibility and, 98
    verbal, 100
    *See also* Child abuse; Sexual abuse;
        Substance abuse
Academic failure, 66
Academic needs, 74
Academic skills, 63
Access time, xvii
    developmental needs and, 55–56
    international relocations and, 233
    relocations and, 16, 206
    therapists and, 21
    *See also* Visitations
Achenbach Child Behavior Checklist
    (CBCL), 120
Ackerman Schoendorf Scales for Parent
    Evaluation of Custody (ASPECT),
    117–118

Adolescents, 65–68, 75
    alienation and, 200, 201
    assessing parent/child attachment and, 104
    best interests of the child and, 35–36
    children's needs and, 74
    confidentiality and, 69
    information gathering and, 101
    preferences of, 107, 108
    psychological evaluations and, 23
    reactions to parental conflict and, 69
    relocation evaluations and, 226
    relocation evaluations/literature and, 217
AFCC *Model Standards,* 7, 8, 9, 13, 18, 134
    collateral data and, 125–126
    collateral witnesses and, 129
    evaluation procedures and, 135
    evaluation reports and, 142, 143
    witnesses and, 131
    *See also* Association of Family Conciliation
        Courts (AFCC); Standards
Affection:
    best interests of the child and, 34
    preschoolers and, 61
Alcohol:
    abuse of, 264
    children/language and, 99
    psychological evaluations and, 23
    strengths/weaknesses of parents and, 39
    *See also* Drugs; Substance abuse
Alienation, 203–204
    analysis/recommendations and, 299–304
    bias and, 18
    children and, 184–185, 188–189, 195–197
    children/information gathering and, 100
    children's contributions to, 187
    children's reactions to parental conflict
        and, 69
    data and, 248
    education programs and, 199, 203

emotions and, 185, 188, 189–190
evaluation of, 191–197
evaluation reports and, 138, 142, 143
expert witness testimony and, 25
high-conflict families and, 150
parent's contributions to, 186–187
recommendations and, 198–201
rejected parents and, 194, 195, 199, 201,
    202, 203, 204
school-age children and, 63–64
severe, 200, 201
signs of, 192–193
American Bar Association, 134, 191
American Law Institute (ALI), 35
American Psychiatric Association, 115, 204
American Psychological Association (APA),
    7–8, 20, 118, 134
confidentiality and, 69
critiquing evaluations and, 256
dual relationships and, 12
guidelines and, 13
psychological testing and, 112
American Psychological Association
    Guidelines, 13, 18
See also Guidelines
Anger, 163
alienation and, 184, 186, 193
children/domestic violence and, 175
children/information gathering and, 100
domestic violence and, 168, 169,
    170, 172
domestic violence/data and, 173
evaluation reports and, 138, 142
high-conflict families and, 150
initial individual appointments and, 85
management programs for, 179
narcissistic parents and, 152
relocation evaluations and, 224
Anxiety:
adolescents and, 66
alienation and, 187, 189, 195, 198
children and, 93, 96, 97, 100, 102, 103,
    105, 106, 110
first conjoint appointments and, 82
home visits and, 106, 107
infants/toddlers and, 57
parents and, 81, 172
siblings and, 71
testifying in court and, 239
Approximation principle, 35
Arizona:
evaluation reports and, 143
relocation evaluations and, 212–213

Assault, 173, 174
Association of Family Conciliation Courts
    (AFCC), xiii, 7, 46, 79, 125, 200, 266
confidentiality and, 69
domestic violence and, 166
parent coordinators and, 26, 159
psychological testing and, 111, 112–113
relocation evaluations and, 206
therapists and, 20
See also AFCC Model Standards
Attachment:
assessing parent/child, 103–105
bias and, 18
children's needs and, 73–74
family relationships and, 38
infants/toddlers and, 56–58, 59, 75
preschoolers and, 61, 62
school-age children and, 65
Attorneys:
alienation and, 189, 191, 200
collaborative law and, 22–23
collateral information and, 90
collateral witnesses and, 128–129
communication and, 81
confidentiality and, 70
conflicts of interest and, 10–11
consultant to, 25
court orders and, 80
decision-making and, 158
domestic violence and, 166
evaluation procedures and, 136
evaluation reports and, 133, 141, 142, 146
ex parte communication and, 9, 18
gathering collateral data and, 126
high-conflict families and, 150, 154
hypothetical questions and, 250–251
initial contract and, 82
international relocations and, 232
interviews and, 110
parents and, 84
preparing for testimonies and, 243–244
psychological testing and, 122, 123
recommendations and, 143–144, 145
relocation evaluations and, 205
testifying in court and, 240–241, 242, 245
trick questions and, 251–252
Authoritative parenting:
children of divorce and, 39, 40, 46, 54
domestic violence and, 171
evaluation reports and, 138

Base Rate (BR), 115–116
Battering Partner Violence, 169

Behavioral issues:
    alienation and, 188–189. *See also*
        Alienation
    children/information gathering and, 101
    children of divorce and, 44
    children's reactions to parental conflict and,
        68, 69
    evaluation reports and, 138, 139
    psychological evaluations and, 23
    psychological testing and, 116
    school-age children and, 63
Best Interests Attorney, 70
Best interests of the child, 33–37
    abuse and, 37
    adolescents and, 35–36
    affection and, 34
    collateral witnesses and, 131
    court orders and, 80
    critiquing evaluations and, 259
    custody and, 33–37
    evaluation reports and, 133
    initial individual appointments and, 85
    international relocations and, 233
    relocation evaluations and, 234, 235
    testifying in court and, 246, 247, 254
    visitations and, 37
Bias, 13–18
    avoiding, 233–235
    confirmatory, 14–15
    critiquing evaluations and, 259
    cultural, 14
    evaluators and, 8, 10–11, 27
    first conjoint appointments and, 82
    gathering collateral data and, 130
    gender, 13–14
    initial contacts to parents and, 81
    primacy/recency, 14
    psychological testing and, 15, 111
    reducing risk of, 17–18
    relocation evaluations and, 207, 235, 236
    relocation evaluations/literature and, 222
    second interviews with parents and, 86
    testifying in court and, 246
Blame:
    alienation and, 193, 194, 195
    children/information gathering
        and, 102
    domestic violence and, 169
    domestic violence/data and, 174
    evaluation reports and, 137
    family law system and, 191
    high-conflict families and, 154
    initial individual appointments and, 85

    personality disorders and, 151, 152
    truth and, 88
Boy Scout Oath, 260–261
Bricklin Perceptual Scales (BPS), 113, 118

California:
    case law and, 51–54
    case law/relocation evaluations and, 207,
        208, 209
    confidentiality and, 277
    court orders and, 80
    family law and, 49–51
    mediators and, 24
    parent coordinators and, 26, 160
    psychological testing and, 113
    relocation evaluations and, 213, 230
    relocation evaluations/literature and, 214
    siblings and, 71
California Family Code, 37, 52, 207
California Rules of Court:
    bias and, 12
    collateral information and, 141
    confidentiality of communications
        and, 29
    critiquing evaluations and, 256, 259
    ethics and, 12, 13
    evaluation procedures and, 135
    evaluation reports and, 134, 142
    evaluators and, 8–9
    ex parte communication and, 9
    objectivity and, 10
    therapists and, 20
    *See also* Rules of Court
California Supreme Court, 210, 211, 212
    case law/relocation evaluations and,
        207, 209
    relocation evaluations/literature and, 214
    *In re Marriage of LaMusga and*, 4, 143,
        209, 236n 5
Case law:
    analysis sections and, 258
    international relocations and, 232
    relocation evaluations and, 205, 206–212,
        224, 235
    relocation evaluations/literature
        and, 219
    *See also* Legal issues
*Cassady v. Signorelli*, 208
Child abuse:
    alienation and, 185
    assessing parental, 118
    confidentiality and, 277
    *See also* Abuse

Child custody *See* Custody
Child Protective Services, 174
Children:
  age issues and, 55–59, 68, 72, 73
  alienation and, 183–184, 195–197. *See also*
    Alienation
  anxiety and, 93, 96, 97, 100, 102,
    103, 105, 106, 110
  assessing parent/child attachment and,
    103–105
  best interests of, 33–37. *See also* Best
    interests of the child
  case law/relocation evaluations and,
    207–208
  cautions in interviewing, 110
  collaborative law coaches and, 23
  confidentiality and, 29, 82, 95–96, 256
  co-parenting and, 40–41. *See also*
    Co-parenting
  courts and, xvi
  courts/punishment and, 201
  developmental needs and, 55. *See also*
    Developmental needs
  divorce and, 43, 54
  domestic violence and, 165, 166, 170,
    171, 175–176, 177–178, 179
  evaluation reports and, 136–137,
    139–141, 142
  evaluators and, 27–28
  first conjoint appointments and, 83
  gathering information about experiences of,
    100–103
  high-conflict families and, 150
  inconsistencies and, 98
  informed consent and, 9
  language skills and, 99–100
  listening to, 5
  living preferences and, 97
  needs of, 73–74. *See also* Child's needs
  observations and, 93–94
  overnights and, 59–61. *See also* Overnights
  parent coordinators and, 159
  play and, 103, 104, 105–106
  preferences of, 107–109
  preschoolers and, 61–63, 75
  privacy and, 69–71
  relocation evaluations and, 205, 206,
    223, 224, 226
  relocation evaluations/literature and, 219
  reunification therapist and, 22
  sample list of questions to ask, 291–294
  school-age, 63–65. *See also* School-age
    children

sexual abuse and, 264–265
siblings and, 71–73
special needs for, 226, 263–264
splitting, 72–73
suggestibility and, 97–98
tests for, 120–121. *See also* Testing
therapists and, 20
therapy and, 155
time-sharing and, 41–42
truth and, 94–96. *See also* Truth
understanding divorce and, 94
*See also* Family issues
Children's Apperception Test, 117, 120
Child's needs:
  academic issues and, 74
  domestic violence and, 172
  emotional issues and, 58
  evaluation reports and, 137, 138, 142
  medical issues and, 58
  special, 226, 263–264
  testing and, 121
  *See also* Developmental needs
Coaching:
  alienation and, 190
  collaborative law and, 23
  gathering collateral data and, 128, 129, 130
Coercive–Controlling Violence (CCV), 168,
    169–170, 171–172, 181
  domestic violence/data and, 174
  joint legal custody and, 163
  parenting plans and, 178–179
  patterns and, 176–177
  therapeutic recommendation and, 179
  therapy and, 180
Cognitive skills, 61, 63
Collaborative law, 22–23
Collateral data, 125–126
  benefits of using, 127–128
  concentric circle approach and, 129–131
  review of records and, 128
  *See also* Data
Collateral witnesses *See* Witnesses
Committee on Ethical Guidelines, 118
Common Couples Violence, 168
Communication:
  adolescents and, 67
  attorneys and, 81
  caregivers and, 58
  children of divorce and, 44, 45
  collaborative law coaches and, 23
  collateral witnesses and, 131
  confidentiality and, 29
  co-parenting and, 40–41

ex parte, 9
infants/toddlers and, 59
initial contacts to parents and, 79–82
overnights and, 60
parallel parenting and, 161, 162
parent coordinators and, 26, 27
parents/divorce and, 46
preschoolers and, 63
relocation evaluations and, 225
relocation evaluations/literature and, 221
school-age children and, 65
stress and, 75
testing for, 118
therapists and, 20, 21
Confidentiality, 277–278
children and, 69–71, 95–96, 139
collateral information and, 90
collateral witnesses and, 131, 141
conflicts of interest and, 11
court orders and, 80
critiquing evaluations and, 255–256
evaluation reports and, 135
evaluators and, 8–9, 18
gathering collateral data and, 126
initial contracts and, 82
mediators and, 24, 28–29
parents and, 129
roles of mental health experts and, 19, 31
siblings and, 105
therapists and, 20
See also Privacy issues
Conflict, 149
adolescents and, 66, 67, 68
background information and, 136
best interests of the child and, 37
bias and, 15–16
children of divorce and, 44, 45
children's needs and, 74
children's reactions to parental, 68–69
co-parenting and, 40–41
divorce and, 43, 54
first conjoint appointments and, 83
history of, 85
insecurity and, 57, 156
of interest, 10–11, 13
parents/divorce and, 46
preschoolers and, 61, 62, 63
recommendations and, 145, 146
resolution of, 23, 24
school-age children and, 63–64, 65
siblings and, 71
testifying in court and, 254
therapists and, 20

time-sharing and, 41
See also High-conflict families
Consent See Informed consent
Continuing education programs, 266
Control:
domestic violence and, 165–166, 167, 168, 169, 170
initial individual appointments and, 85
relocation evaluations and, 224
See also Power
Cooperative Colleagues, 150, 163
Co-parenting, 40–41
bias and, 17
evaluation reports and, 143
high-conflict families and, 161
parent coordinators and, 27
preschoolers and, 62
recommendations and, 145
relocation evaluations and, 225
school-age children and, 65
See also Parenting
Coping skills, 68, 160
Corporal punishment, 100
See also Discipline; Punishment
Costs:
evaluations and, 7, 9
initial contracts and, 82
parent coordinators and, 27
psychological testing and, 122
See also Fees
Counseling:
adolescents and, 67
co-parenting, 163
high-conflict families and, 155
marriage, 6–7
parents/divorce and, 46
recommendations and, 145
Court orders, 79–80
alienation and, 199
confidentiality/children and, 95
domestic violence and, 170, 181
evaluations and, xv, 5, 12, 18
evaluator's fees and, 7
first conjoint appointments and, 82
international relocations and, 232–233
joint legal custody and, 163
noncompliance of, 230
parent coordinators and, 27, 160
safe haven therapy and, 21, 28
sample of, 269–274
therapists and, 20

Court reporters, 240, 245
Courts:
    adolescents and, 66
    alienation and, 199, 201
    case law/relocation evaluations and, 208
    children and, xvi
    collaborative law coaches and, 23
    confidentiality and, 29, 70
    culture of, 8
    decision-making and, 158
    domestic violence and, 167
    evaluation reports and, 133
    evaluations and, 3, 4
    evaluators and, 7, 27–28
    high-conflict families and, 152–153
    initial contacts to parents and, 81
    listening to children and, 5
    parent coordinators and, 27
    parents/divorce and, 46
    psychological testing and, 123
    relocation evaluations and, 228, 234, 235, 236
    relocation evaluations/literature and, 220, 221
    reunification therapist and, 22
    rules/procedures and, 46–47, 241–243, 244
    stepparents and, 223
    testimony and, 25, 239. See also Testimony
    therapists and, 6–7, 21
Cross-sectional research, 43
Cultural issues:
    bias and, 14
    international relocations and, 233
Custody:
    best interests of the child and, 33–37
    California statutes and, 49–51
    change in, 200–201, 202
    confidentiality and, 70
    infants/toddlers and, 58
    international boundaries and, 48–49, 53
    language of, xvii
    mediators and, 24
    overnights and, 59–61
    psychological evaluations and, 24
    research and, 44
    reunification therapists and, 22
    school-age children and, 65
    sharing, 163
    visitation rights and, 48
Custody evaluations See Evaluations
Custody evaluators See Evaluators
Custody plan:
    first conjoint appointments and, 82–83
    therapists and, 20, 21
    See also Parenting plans

Data:
    analysis of, 134
    bias and, 14–15, 17–18
    children/domestic violence and, 176
    court orders and, 80
    critiquing evaluations and, 256, 257–258, 259
    domestic violence and, 167, 168–169, 170,
        173–176, 176–178
    evaluation reports and, 133, 134, 141,
        142, 143
    evaluations and, 4, 18
    evaluators and, 10, 55
    guidelines for, 13
    initial individual appointments and, 85
    interpreting, 123, 124
    multiple avenues of, 79
    preparing for testimonies and, 243
    psychological testing and, 90–91, 111,
        112, 116, 122, 123
    recommendations and, 144–145
    relocation evaluations and, 205, 214, 226,
        234, 235
    relocation evaluations/literature and, 217,
        220, 222
    standards for, 10
    testifying in court and, 239, 242, 245,
        247–249, 250, 252, 254
    See also Collateral data
Day-care:
    collateral information and, 90
    critiquing evaluations and, 256
    gathering collateral data and, 130
    infants/toddlers and, 58–59
    preschoolers and, 62
Decision-making:
    bias and, 17
    by children, 107–109
    domestic violence/parenting plans and,
        178–179
    high-conflict families and, 158–160, 164
    initial contacts to parents and, 81–82
    parallel parenting and, 161, 162
    parent coordinators and, 27
    parenting plan and, 35
    parents/divorce and, 46
    recommendations and, 144
    relocation evaluations/literature and, 219
    sole legal custody and, 162–164
Delinquency:
    adolescents and, 66
    children of divorce and, 44
    children's reactions to parental conflict
        and, 69

Depositions:
   fees for, 244
   objections and, 246
   testifying in court and, 240–241, 242
Depression:
   adolescents and, 66
   children of divorce and, 44
   domestic violence/data and, 173
   infants/toddlers and, 57
   personality disorders and, 152
   preschoolers and, 61
   school-age children and, 63
   testing for, 119, 120–121
Developmental issues:
   infants/toddlers and, 57
   overnights and, 60
   preferences of children and, 108
   preschoolers and, 61
   relocation evaluations and, 226
Developmental needs, 55, 73–74
   family relationships and, 38
   infants/toddlers and, 58, 59, 75
   parent coordinators and, 160
   relocation evaluations and, 225
   relocation evaluations/literature and, 221
   siblings and, 72
   *See also* Child's needs
Discipline:
   children/information gathering and,
      100, 101
   collateral witnesses and, 131
   preschoolers and, 62
   relocation evaluations/literature and, 218
   *See also* Punishment
Distress:
   alienation and, 195
   children/information gathering and,
      102, 110
   relocation evaluations and, 206
Divorce, xvi, xvii
   adolescents and, 66
   best interests of the child and, 37
   bias and, 18
   California statutes and, 49–51
   children and, 54
   children's understanding of, 94
   collaborative law coaches and, 23
   co-parenting and, 40–41
   family relationships and, 38
   harmful evaluations and, 6–7
   infants/toddlers and, 57
   mediators and, 24
   parent coordinators and, 27

   preschoolers and, 62
   research and, 43–44
   school-age children and, 63, 64
   therapists and, 20, 21
Domestic violence, 165–166
   alienation and, 185, 191
   background information and, 136
   best interests of the child and, 34, 37
   bias and, 18
   California statutes and, 50
   children and, 175–176
   critiquing evaluations and, 255, 256
   data and, 173–176, 248
   data/conclusions and, 176–178
   divorce and, 43
   evaluation reports and, 137, 138, 143
   evaluators and, 8
   expert witness testimony and, 25
   forms of, 166
   gathering collateral data and, 128
   harmful evaluations and, 6–7
   high-conflict families and, 150
   joint legal custody and, 163
   men and, 166, 168, 169, 170, 173
   parenting plans and, 178–179
   parenting problems and, 171–172, 177, 179
   parents/questions and, 174–175
   primary perpetrators and, 177
   relocation evaluations and, 236
   relocation evaluations/literature and, 222
   restraining orders and, 83
   testifying in court and, 254
   therapeutic/structural interventions and,
      179–181
   types of, 167, 168–170
   victims and, 172
   *See also* Violence
Drugs:
   children/language and, 99
   children's reactions to parental conflict and, 69
   parenting problems and, 172
   parents and, 42
   psychological evaluations and, 23
   strengths/weaknesses of parents and, 39
   *See also* Alcohol; Substance abuse
Drug testing:
   parent coordinators and, 27
   strengths/weaknesses of parents and, 39
   substance abuse and, 264

Economic issues:
   best interests of the child and, 34
   children of divorce and, 45

parent coordinators and, 27
relocation evaluations and, 223
*Edlund v. Hales,* 208, 210
Education:
    alienation and, 199, 203
    best interests of the child and, 34
    bias and, 18
    evaluators and, 8
    gathering collateral data and, 127
    parents and, 150, 199
    relocation evaluations/literature and,
        216, 218
Elder abuse, 277
E-mail:
    collateral witnesses and, 131
    initial contacts to parents and, 81
    parallel parenting and, 161, 162
    sample form informed consent and, 275
Emotional issues:
    adolescents and, 66, 67
    alienation and, 184, 185, 186, 187, 188,
        189–190, 194, 198, 203
    attachment and, 56
    best interests of the child and, 34, 37
    children/domestic violence and, 175
    children/information gathering and, 102
    children of divorce and, 45
    children's needs and, 73, 74
    children's reactions to parental conflict and,
        68, 69
    collaborative law coaches and, 23
    co-parenting and, 40–41
    developmental needs and, 55
    domestic violence and, 168, 169, 171
    emotional abuse and, 169, 173
    evaluation reports and, 137, 138
    gathering collateral data and, 129
    infants/toddlers and, 57, 58, 59
    initial individual appointments and, 85
    parent coordinators and, 27
    personality disorders and, 152
    preparing for testimonies and, 244
    psychological evaluations and, 23–24
    psychological testing and, 91
    relocation evaluations and, 206, 231
    school-age children and, 63, 64
    second interviews with parents and, 86
    strengths/weaknesses of parents and, 39, 40
    suggestibility/children and, 97–98
    truth and, 87–88
Empathy:
    alienation and, 194, 199
    assessing parent/child attachment and, 104

domestic violence and, 172, 180
domestic violence/data and, 174
domestic violence/parenting plans and, 179
high-conflict families and, 155
personality disorders and, 151
preschoolers and, 61
school-age children and, 64
Ethical Code, 95
Ethical issues:
    confidentiality and, 69
    custody evaluations and, 28
    evaluators and, 8
Evaluation procedures, 275–276
Evaluation reports, 6, 133–134, 146
    analysis/summary and, 141–143
    background information and, 136
    children and, 139–141
    collateral information and, 141
    parents and, 136–139
    procedures and, 135–136
    *See also* Reports
Evaluations:
    blending roles and, 30–31
    complaints about, 3
    concluding, 198–201
    developmental needs and, 55
    families and, 4–6
    longitudinal, 265
    prior relationships and, 28
    psychological, 23–24
    relocations and, 205–206. *See also*
        Relocation issues
Evaluators, 27–28
    adolescents and, 67
    alienation and, 189
    children's needs and, 74
    co-parenting and, 17
    court orders and, 79–80
    domestic violence and, 167
    ethical duty of, 7
    family relationships and, 38
    fees and, 7
    initial contract and, 82
    mediators and, 29–30
    parent coordinators and, 27
    parents and, 5, 6
    tasks of, 54
    training and, xvi
Ex parte communication, 9, 18

Family Apperception Tests, 117, 120
Family Code, 37, 52, 207
Family Court Advisors, 26

*Family Court Review,* xiii, 144, 166, 181, 187, 204, 267
Family Court Services, 277, 279
Family issues, xiii–xiv
  adolescents and, 65–66
  children/information gathering and, 100–101
  children's needs and, 73–74
  children's reactions to parental conflict and, 69
  collateral witnesses and, 128–129
  decision-making and, 158–160
  divorce and, 43
  domestic violence and, 165
  evaluation reports and, 133
  evaluations and, 3–4, 4–6
  low-conflict families and, 149, 205
  medium-conflict families and, 4–5, 150
  nonviolent high-conflict families and, 149–151
  psychological evaluations and, 24
  relationships and, 38
  school-age children and, 63
  siblings and, 71–73
  therapists and, 21
  *See also* Children; High-conflict families; Parents
Family law:
  alienation and, 191
  attorney/expert witness and, 25
  bias and, 13–14, 18
  California and, 49–51
  evaluators and, 8
  relocation evaluations and, 206–212
  *See also* Legal issues
Fathers:
  best interests of the child and, 36
  custody and, 35
  domestic violence and, 181
  evaluation reports and, 136–137, 138, 143
  family relationships and, 38
  gender bias and, 14
  infants/toddlers and, 56
  overnights and, 60
  relocation evaluations and, 223, 224
  relocation evaluations/literature and, 217, 218, 221
  reunification therapist and, 22
  truth and, 87–89
Father's-rights groups, 33
Federal Rules of Evidence, 249
Fees, 278
  court orders and, 80
  evaluations and, 7
  expert witnesses and, 244
  *See also* Costs
Fiery Foes, 150, 163
Florida, 35
Forensic evaluations, 111, 114, 116
*Forensic Practice Guidelines,* 118
Frequent fliers, 150, 152
Friendly parent provision, 34
Funding, 208
  *See also* Costs; Fees

Gangs, 69
Gatekeeping, 231–232, 236
Gender issues, xvii
  best interests of the child and, 33
  bias and, 13–14, 259
  identity and, 58
  relocation evaluations and, 226–227
Goodness of fit:
  alienation and, 197
  relocation evaluations and, 227
  testing and, 121
Grandparents:
  high-conflict families and, 155
  initial contacts to parents and, 81
  overnights and, 60
  visitation rights and, 48
Guardian Ad Litem (GAL), 70
Guidelines, 18, 20, 94
  collateral information and, 125
  evaluations and, 7–8, 13
  parent coordinators and, 159
  psychological testing and, 112, 113

Habitual residence, 48–49
Hague Convention, 49
  child abduction and, 14, 47
  international relocations and, 232–233
  relocation evaluations and, 214
Harm:
  alienation and, 188. *See also* Alienation
  confidentiality and, 277
  divorce and, 43
  domestic violence and, 181
  evaluations and, 6–7
  gatekeeping and, 231–232, 236
  relocation evaluations/literature and, 220
  relocations and, 17, 54, 207
  visitation rights and, 48
Health issues:
  best interests of the child and, 34, 37
  California statutes and, 49–50
  children and, 263

co-parenting and, 40–41
family relationships and, 38
parent coordinators and, 160
relocation evaluations and, 231
strengths/weaknesses of parents and, 39
Heterosexual relationships, xvii, 169
High-conflict families, 164
    adolescents and, 66, 67
    alienation and, 186, 191, 199
    background information and, 136
    children's reactions to parental conflict
        and, 68
    data and, 248
    evaluation reports and, 138, 143
    infants/toddlers and, 58
    nonviolent, 149–151
    parallel parenting and, 161–162
    parent coordinators and, 153, 157,
        158–160
    recommendations for, 155–162
    relocation evaluations/literature and, 221
    safe haven therapy and, 21, 28
    school-age children and, 63
    structured recommendations for, 156–158
    testing children and, 120–121
    See also Conflict; Family issues
Histrionic scale, 116
Home visits, 106–107
    critiquing evaluations and, 257
    evaluation reports and, 139
    evaluators and, 10
    preschoolers and, 61
Homicides, 165, 167, 169, 181

Identity:
    adolescents and, 65–66
    alienation and, 189
    gender issues and, 58
Independent Medical Examination
    (IME), 23
Individual Educational Plan (IEP), 23
Infants/toddlers, 55, 56–59, 75
Informed consent:
    collateral witnesses and, 128
    court orders and, 80
    critiquing evaluations and, 255
    evaluations and, 8–9, 18, 135
    guidelines for, 13
    initial contacts and, 81
    sample form for, 275–280
Ink-blot test, 15, 113, 117
In Montenegro v. Diaz, 51
In re Marriage of Abargil, 208

In re Marriage of Burgess, 53, 207–208,
    209–210, 211
    relocation evaluations and, 214
    relocation evaluations/literature and, 215,
        217, 221
In re Marriage of Campos, supra, 209
In re Marriage of Condon, 53, 208
In re Marriage of Edlund v. Hales, 53,
    208, 210
In re Marriage of LaMusga, xv, 4,
    53, 143, 209, 210–211, 212, 214, 221,
    236n 5, 325
In re Marriage of McGinnis, 207
In re Marriage of Williams, 71
In re Seagondollar, 51, 52
Instability See Stability/instability
Intelligence testing, 113
International relocations, 232–233
Internet, 3
    See also E-mail
Interpersonal scales, 116
Interventions:
    high-conflict families and, 153
    psychological evaluations and, 23–24
    therapeutic/structural, 179–181
Interviews:
    children and, 110. See also Children
    children/domestic violence and, 176
    collateral witnesses and, 131
    data and, 79
    evaluation reports and, 135, 138
    evaluators and, 10
    first, 82–84, 94
    parents and, 91
    psychological testing and, 112, 116
    relocation evaluations and, 205
    second, 86–87
    techniques for, 88–89
    truth and, 88–89
Intimate Partner Violence, 169
Isolation, 168

Joint custody, 163, 164, 200
Journals, 59, 63
Judges:
    alienation and, 189
    best-interests concept and, 163
    collaborative law coaches and, 23
    confidentiality and, 70
    co-parenting and, 17
    custody plan letter and, 21
    domestic violence and, 165, 166, 167, 181
    evaluation reports and, 133, 141, 142, 146

ex parte communication and, 18
high-conflict families and, 154
initial contracts and, 82
joint legal custody and, 163
medium-conflict families and, 150
parents and, 5
psychological testing and, 122
recommendations and, 91, 144–145
relocation evaluations and, 205, 206, 208
relocation evaluations/literature and, 222
testifying in court and, 242, 246
Judicial authority, 26, 144
Judicial Council, 113
Judicial orders, 150

Language skills:
children and, 93–94, 99–100
infants/toddlers and, 56, 57, 58
preschoolers and, 61
Lawyers See Attorneys
Legal issues:
best interests of the child and, 33–34
California and, 49–54
critiquing evaluations and, 259
divorce and, 46–47
domestic violence and, 165
lawsuits and, 80
relocation evaluations and, 205, 213
relocation evaluations/case law and,
206–212
relocation evaluations/literature
and, 222
relocation evaluations/statutory laws and,
212–214
state laws and, 222, 224
See also Case law; Family law; Statutory
laws
Licensing board, 11, 20
Likert-type scale, 119
Litigation:
alienation and, 191
high-conflict families and, 154
psychological testing and, 122
Longitudinal evaluations, 265
Longitudinal research, 44
Love/hate:
alienation and, 186, 202
best interests of the child and, 34
children/domestic violence
and, 175
high-conflict families and, 153
Low-conflict families, 149, 205
Loyalty issues, 102

Marital relationships, xvi–xvii
counseling and, 6–7
international relocations and, 233
therapists and, 21
Mediation, 30
families and, xiv
harmful evaluations and, 6
relocation evaluations/literature and, 221
research and, 43
Mediators, 24, 26
confidentiality and, 28–29. See also
Confidentiality
domestic violence and, 167
evaluators and, 29–30
medium-conflict families and, 150
relocation evaluations and, 205
Medical issues:
best interests of the child and, 34
domestic violence/data and, 173
infants/toddlers and, 58
preschoolers and, 62
See also Health issues
Medium-conflict families, 4–5, 150
Mental health:
best interests of the child and, 34
children of divorce and, 44
domestic violence and, 170
high-conflict families and, 5
relocation evaluations and, 231
Mental health professionals:
alienation and, 200
attorneys and, 25
best interests of the child and, 35
collaborative law and, 23
complaints against, 3
domestic violence and, 166
roles of, 19, 31
Mental illness:
children and, 263
children/language and, 99
psychological evaluations and, 23
Meta-analysis research, 44
Michigan, 34
Millon Clinical Multiaxial Inventory-III
(MCMI-III), 15, 113, 114, 115, 116,
117, 123
Minnesota Multiphasic Personality Inventory
(MMPI-2), 113, 114, 115, 116, 117,
118, 123
Model Standards of Practice for Child
Custody Evaluation, xiii, 8, 9, 10, 12
evaluation procedures and, 136
evaluation reports and, 134

relocation evaluations and, 206
therapists and, 20
*See also* Standards
*Montenegro v. Diaz*, 51
Mothers:
    evaluation reports and, 136–137,
        138, 143
    family relationships and, 38
    overnights and, 60
    relocation evaluations and, 223, 224
    relocation evaluations/literature and, 221
    truth and, 87–89
    *See also* Women
Mother's rights groups, 33
Moves/moving issues *See* Relocation issues
Murders, 165, 167, 169, 181

Narcissism, 117, 121, 152, 153
National Council of Juvenile and Family
    Court Judges (NCJFCJ), 165, 166,
    255, 256
National Conference of Commissioners of
    Uniform State Laws, 47
Needs *See* Child's needs; Developmental
    needs; Special needs issues
Neglect, 57, 87, 195, 271
New York, 214, 224
New York Court of Appeals, 215
Nonviolent high-conflict families, 149–151
Nurturance, 39

Observations, 91
    alienation and, 192, 197
    children and, 93–94, 110
    collateral witnesses and, 131
    critiquing evaluations and, 256–257
    data and, 79, 127, 248
    evaluation reports and, 138, 140
    evaluators and, 10
    parent/child attachment and, 103–105
    psychological testing and, 112, 116
    relocation evaluations and, 205
    siblings and, 105
Order to Show Cause (OSC), 51–52
Overnights, 59–61
    attachment and, 58
    critiquing evaluations and, 259
    developmental needs and, 56
    high-conflict families and, 156
    parent coordinators and, 160
    preschoolers and, 62
    siblings and, 71
    testifying in court and, 254

Parallel parenting:
    high-conflict families and, 161–162, 164
    parent coordinators and, 27
    recommendations and, 156
    school-age children and, 65
    *See also* Parenting
Parental Alienation Syndrome (PAS), 183
Parental Custody Index, 118
Parental Kidnapping Prevention Act (PKPA),
    47–48
Parent Awareness Skills Survey (PASS), 118
Parent Behavior Checklist (PBC), 119
Parent–Child Relationship Inventory (PCRI),
    119, 123
Parent Coordinator (PC), 26–27
    alienation and, 190, 200, 201, 204
    complaints against, 3
    high-conflict families and, 153, 157,
        158–160, 164
    infants/toddlers and, 59
    legal custody and, 163, 164
    parallel parenting and, 161
    parents/divorce and, 46
    therapists and, 21, 22
Parent groups, 3, 33
Parenting:
    authoritative style of, 39, 40, 46, 54,
        138, 171
    children of divorce and, 45
    domestic violence and, 171–172, 177
    evaluation reports and, 134, 137–138, 143
    gatekeeping and, 231–232, 236
    high-conflict families and, 159
    overnights and, 59–61
    psychological testing and, 111
    rights/responsibilities and, 35
    *See also* Co-parenting; Parallel parenting;
        Shared parenting
Parenting classes, 140, 180
Parenting instruments, 118–120
Parenting Pals, 149, 163
Parenting plans, 4–5
    adolescents and, 66, 67, 68
    best interests of the child and, 35, 37
    children/information gathering and, 103
    children's needs and, 74
    collaborative law coaches and, 23
    critiquing evaluations and, 255
    domestic violence and, 168, 177
    first conjoint appointments and, 83
    fundamental questions and, 33
    high-conflict families and, 150
    infants/toddlers and, 58–59

initial contacts to parents and, 81
initial individual appointments and, 86
mediators and, 24
parent coordinators and, 26, 159
preferences of children and, 108
preschoolers and, 62
recommendations and, 145–146
relocation evaluations and, 205, 236
school-age children and, 64
time-sharing and, 42
See also Custody plan
Parenting skills, 266
  alienation and, 186
  attachment and, 58
  family relationships and, 38
  relocation evaluations/literature and, 221
Parenting Stress Index (PSI), 118
Parenting styles, 57, 68
Parenting time, xvii
Parents, xv
  adolescents and, 68
  alienation and, 183–184, 186–187, 199.
      See also Alienation
  attachment and, 56–58, 103–105
  authorizations and, 129
  California case law and, 53
  California statutes and, 49–51
  case law/relocation evaluations and,
      207–208
  children/information gathering and,
      100–101
  children's needs and, 73–74
  confidentiality and, 69, 70, 71
  conflict and, 68–69
  conflicts of interest and, 10–11
  contacting, 79–82
  co-parenting and, 40–41. See also
      Co-parenting
  domestic violence/questions and, 174–175
  evaluation reports and, 136–139, 140, 142
  first interviews with, 82–84
  initial individual appointments and, 84–86
  interviews and, 91
  mediators and, 24
  medium-conflict, 4–5
  moral fitness of, 35
  participation of, 80–81
  recommendations and, 145
  rejected, 194, 195, 199, 201, 202, 203, 204
  relocation evaluations and, 205, 206, 235
  responsibility and, 178, 256
  rights of, 234
  sample list of questions to ask, 295–298

school-age children and, 63, 64
second interviews with, 86–87
siblings and, 72
strengths/weaknesses of, 39–40, 85, 91
substance abuse and, xiv, 264
therapists and, 20, 21
time-sharing and, 41–42
truth and, 87–89
See also Family issues
Pediatricians:
  critiquing evaluations and, 256
  gathering collateral data and, 130
  special needs children and, 263–264
Peer relationships, 68, 69, 74
Perceptions of Relationships
    Test (PORT), 118
Personality Assessment Inventory (PAI), 116,
    117, 123
Personality issues:
  alienation and, 186
  high-conflict families and, 149, 155
  personality disorders and, 39, 151–152, 169
  personality tests and, 112, 114, 117
  psychological testing and, 115, 116
  relocation evaluations and, 227
  strengths/weaknesses of parents and, 39
Play, 103, 104, 105–106
Police:
  domestic violence/data and, 173
  gathering collateral data and, 130
Posttraumatic Stress Disorder (PTSD):
  children/domestic violence and, 175
  domestic violence and, 170
  domestic violence/data and, 173
  parenting problems and, 172
Poverty:
  children of divorce and, 45
  insecure attachments and, 57
Power:
  domestic violence and, 165–166, 167, 168,
      169, 172
  initial individual appointments
      and, 85
  See also Control
Preschool children, 61–63, 75
Privacy issues:
  children and, 55, 69–71
  home visits and, 106
  preferences of children and, 108
  See also Confidentiality
Problem-solving skills, 154, 155
Promiscuity, 66, 69
Psychological Assessment Resources, 116

Psychological issues:
    children/domestic violence and, 175
    children's reactions to parental conflict
       and, 68
    high-conflict families and, 155
    psychological evaluations and, 23–24
    psychological growth/development and, 39
Psychological testing, 90–91, 111, 124
    bias and, 15
    collateral information and, 89
    critiquing evaluations and, 257
    data and, 79, 248
    domestic violence/data and, 173
    evaluation procedures and, 135
    evaluation reports and, 138
    evaluators and, 10
    first conjoint appointments and, 82, 83
    interpretation of, 113
    over reliance on, 123
    scales and, 121
    symbolic play and, 106
    traditional, 114–117
    *See also* Testing
Psychologists:
    children and, 35, 95
    evaluations and, 8
    testimony and, 25
Psychotherapy, 180, 273
Punishment:
    children/information gathering and, 100
    domestic violence and, 172
    *See also* Discipline

Quasi-judicial immunity, 7

Recommendations, xv–xvi, 278–279
    alienation and, 198–201
    background information and, 136
    California and, 10, 24
    children/divorce and, 54
    children's needs and, 74
    collaborative law coaches and, 23
    confidentiality and, 70
    critiquing evaluations and, 255, 258, 259
    custody evaluations and, 33
    data and, 248–249
    evaluation reports and, 133, 140, 142,
       143–146
    guidelines and, 13
    high-conflict families and, 156–158
    hypothetical questions and, 250–251
    initial individual appointments and, 85
    judges and, 91

longitudinal evaluations and, 265
mental health experts and, 25
parallel parenting and, 161
parents and, 3
preparing for testimonies and, 243
preschoolers and, 62
professionalism and, 251, 252
psychological testing and, 15
relocation evaluations and, 206, 230,
    234, 235
school-age children and, 64
sole legal custody and, 162–163
testifying in court and, 239, 240–241,
    242, 246
therapeutic, 179
time-sharing and, 41–42
Regression:
    alienation and, 187, 200
    children/domestic violence and, 175
    children's reactions to parental conflict and,
       68, 69
    infants/toddlers and, 57
    preschoolers and, 61, 62
    school-age children and, 63
Religious issues:
    best interests of the child and, 33–34
    co-parenting and, 40–41
Relocation issues, 205–206
    analysis/recommendations and, 305–310
    bias and, 16–17, 18, 233–235, 236
    case law and, 52, 53, 54, 206–212
    children/information gathering and, 102
    children's needs and, 74
    court orders and, 80
    critiquing evaluations and, 259–260
    data and, 248
    divorce and, 43
    evaluation reports and, 138, 143
    expert witness testimony and, 25
    gatekeeping and, 231–232, 236
    initial individual appointments and, 85
    international, 53, 232–233
    literature and, 206, 207, 214–222
    medium-conflict families and, 150
    opposing the move and, 229
    preferences of children and, 108–109
    preparing for testimonies and, 243
    recommendations and, 144
    research and, 44
    siblings and, 71
    societal issues and, 223–224
    statutory laws and, 212–214
    testifying in court and, 254

Reports:
  children and, 95
  data and, 249
  evaluators and, 8
  preparing for testimonies and, 243–244
  relocation evaluations and, 213
  time-sharing and, 41
Research, 43–44
  children of divorce and, 45
  overnights and, 60–61
  retrospective, 44
Restraining orders:
  domestic violence and, 83, 165, 181
  domestic violence/data and, 174
  high-conflict families and, 150
Retainer agreement, 81, 275–280
Rorschach, Thematic Apperception Test
      (TAT), 114, 117, 118, 120, 121,
      123, 257
Rorschach Inkblot Test, 15, 113, 117
*Ruisi v. Theriot,* 160
Rules of Court, 8, 9, 13, 18
  critiquing evaluations and, 256
  ethics and, 12
  evaluation reports and, 142
  *See also* California Rules of Court
Rural communities, 6

Safe-haven therapy, 21, 28
Safety issues:
  best interests of the child and, 37
  California statutes and, 49–50
  critiquing evaluations and, 255
  domestic violence and, 165, 167, 168, 181
School-age children, 63–65, 75
  alienation and, 200
  children's needs and, 74
  children's reactions to parental conflict
      and, 69
  relocation evaluations and, 225, 235
  siblings and, 72
School issues:
  adolescents and, 65–66, 67
  alienation and, 190
  children of divorce and, 44
  children's reactions to parental conflict
      and, 69
  collateral information and, 90
  co-parenting and, 40–41
  evaluation reports and, 140
  gathering collateral data and, 126
  parent coordinators and, 160
  preschoolers and, 62

relocation evaluations and, 235
relocation evaluations/literature and, 216
school-age children and, 64
siblings and, 72
Security/insecurity:
  caregivers and, 58
  children/domestic violence and, 176
  children/information gathering and,
      100–101, 102
  children's needs and, 74
  developmental needs and, 55
  family relationships and, 38
  infants/toddlers and, 56, 59
  relocation evaluations and, 231
Self-esteem:
  alienation and, 186, 190
  children of divorce and, 44
  children's needs and, 74
  children's reactions to parental conflict
      and, 68, 69
  domestic violence and, 172, 180
  narcissistic parents and, 152
  preschoolers and, 61
  school-age children and, 63
Separation:
  insecure attachments and, 57
  siblings and, 71
  splitting children and, 72–73
  *See also* Divorce
Separation Instigated Violence (SIV), 170,
      171, 176–177, 179
Sex role development, 58, 61
Sexual abuse:
  children and, 264–265
  children/language and, 99
  domestic violence and, 171
  suggestibility and, 98
  *See also* Abuse
Shared parenting, 6
  recommendations and, 145
  relocation evaluations and, 234
  school-age children and, 65
  *See also* Parenting
Siblings, 71–73, 105
  alienation and, 185
  children/domestic violence and, 175
  evaluation reports and, 139, 140
  relocation evaluations and, 226, 235
  relocation evaluations/literature and, 215
Situational Couples Violence (SCV),
      168–169, 171
  domestic violence/parenting plans and, 179
  patterns and, 176–177

therapeutic/structural interventions
   and, 179
therapy and, 180
Skills, 266
   overnights and, 60
   problem-solving, 154
   school-age children and, 65
   strengths/weaknesses of parents and, 39–40
   time-management, 160
   *See also* Language skills; Parenting skills
Social service workers, 130
Sole legal custody, 162–164
Spanking, 100
   *See also* Discipline; Punishment
Special Master, 26, 181
Special needs issues, 226, 263–264
Stability/instability:
   California statutes and, 50
   children of divorce and, 44, 45
   children's needs and, 74
   infants/toddlers and, 59
   overnights and, 60
   relocation evaluations and, 230, 231, 235
   strengths/weaknesses of parents and, 39
   time-sharing and, 41
Stalking, 168
Standards, 266
   child custody and, 47–48
   evaluations and, 8, 13, 79
   informed consent and, 9
   psychological testing and, 113, 124
   *See also* AFCC *Model Standards; Model*
      *Standards of Practice for Child*
      *Custody Evaluation*
State laws, 222, 224
Statutory laws:
   analysis sections and, 258
   relocation cases and, 16
   relocation evaluations and, 17, 207,
      212–214, 224, 235
   *See also* Legal issues
Stepparents:
   best interests of the child and, 36
   initial contacts to parents and, 81
   psychological testing and, 124
   relocation evaluations and, 223, 226
Stress, 267
   anger management programs and, 179
   assessing parental, 118–119
   children and, 110
   collaborative law coaches and, 23
   domestic violence and, 170
   family relationships and, 38

preschoolers and, 62
reduction of, 75
relocation evaluations, 230
school-age children and, 64, 65
Substance abuse, 138, 264
   adolescents and, 66, 67
   attachment and, 56
   domestic violence and, 170, 180
   high-conflict families and, 5, 150
   parents and, xiv
   testing and, 121
   *See also* Abuse; Alcohol; Drugs
Suicide:
   adolescents and, 66
   alienation and, 200
   children of divorce and, 44
   children's reactions to parental conflict
      and, 69
   domestic violence and, 165
Support:
   adolescents and, 67
   children/information gathering and, 102–103
   school-age children and, 65
   siblings and, 71
Symbolic play, 105–106

Teachers:
   children/domestic violence and, 176
   collateral information and, 90
   critiquing evaluations and, 256
   gathering collateral data and, 126, 129, 130
   relocation evaluations/literature and, 215
Tender years doctrine, 33
Testimony, 239, 254
   California statutes and, 51
   data and, 247–249
   depositions and, 240–241, 242
   evaluation reports and, 134
   evaluators and, 8
   gathering collateral data and, 130
   hypothetical questions and, 250–251
   preparing for, 243–244
   procedures for, 245–247
   trials and, 241–243
   trick questions and, 251–252
Testing:
   benefits of, 121
   bias and, 15
   children and, 120–121
   children's apperception and, 117
   computerized scoring and, 123
   critiquing evaluations and, 257
   custody evaluations and, 117–118

drug, 27, 39, 264
  evaluation reports and, 142
  family apperception and, 117, 120
  gathering collateral data and, 127
  initial contract and, 82
  ink-blot, 15, 113, 117
  intelligence, 113
  parent coordinators and, 27
  risks and, 122–123
  substance abuse and, 264
  *See also* Psychological testing
Thematic Apperception Test, 120
Therapists, 19–21
  collateral information and, 90
  confidentiality and, 69, 141
  conflicts of interest and, 11
  critiquing evaluations and, 256
  domestic violence/data and, 173
  gathering collateral data and, 126,
      127–128, 129, 130
  harmful evaluations and, 6–7
  high-conflict families and, 150, 154
  parent coordinators and, 26
  reunification, 22
Therapy:
  adolescents and, 67
  alienation and, 199, 200, 201, 204
  evaluation reports and, 140
  high-conflict families and, 154, 155–156
  initial contract and, 82
  parent coordinators and, 160
  recommendations and, 145
  safe haven, 21, 28
Time-management skills, 160
Time-sharing:
  adolescents and, 67
  plan for, 41–42
  school-age children and, 64, 65
Toddlers, 56–59
Training, 265
  critiquing evaluations and, 255
  evaluators and, xvi, 8
  parent coordinators and, 160
  testifying in court and, 239
Treatment:
  domestic violence and, 180
  plan for, 176
  psychological evaluations and, 23
  therapists and, 20
*Troxel v. Granville*, 48, 50
Trust:
  children and, 20, 96
  infants/toddlers and, 56

Truth:
  background information and, 136
  bias and, 15–16
  children and, 94–96
  domestic violence and, 173
  domestic violence/data and, 173
  evaluation reports and, 142
  joint legal custody and, 163
  parent coordinators and, 160
  parents and, 87–89
  psychological testing and, 90–91
  testifying in court and, 246, 251, 254
  testing and, 121
  therapists and, 20, 21
Tutoring:
  adolescents and, 67
  gathering collateral data and, 130

*UN Convention on the Rights of the Child*, xvi
Uniform Child Custody Jurisdiction and
      Enforcement Act (UCCJEA), 47
U.S. Department of State, 49, 232, 233
U.S. Supreme Court, 48

Verbal abuse, 100
Vertical parenting, 143
Violence:
  children's reactions to parental conflict and,
      68, 69
  emotional, 168
  families and, xiv, xv
  harmful evaluations and, 6–7
  high-conflict families and, 5
  initial individual appointments and, 85
  insecure attachments and, 57
  parents and, 42
  second interviews with parents and, 86
  testing and, 121
  *See also* Domestic violence
Visitations, xvii
  best interests of the child and, 37
  California statutes and, 49–50
  developmental needs and, 55–56
  grandparents and, 48
  recommendations and, 144
  *See also* Access time

Washington statute, 48
Wingspread Conference, 166, 167, 168, 181
Wise Person, 26
Withdrawal:
  children's reactions to parental conflict and, 69
  school-age children and, 63

Witnesses:
  children/domestic violence and, 175
  collateral, 128–129, 131
  conflicts of interest and, 11
  critiquing evaluations and, 256, 258
  evaluation reports and, 141
  fees for, 244
  gathering collateral data and, 130–131
  informed consent and, 9
  mediators and, 24
  parent coordinators and, 27
  psychological evaluations
      and, 24
  testimony and, 25, 241, 242–243
  therapists and, 21
Women:
  domestic violence and, 166, 168,
      169, 170, 173
  *See also* Mothers
Written reports *See* Reports

# About the Author_____

**Philip Stahl, PhD, ABPP (Forensic)**, is a psychologist in private practice who conducts child custody evaluations and provides expert witness testimony. He is a provider of continuing education for psychologists and other mental health providers, and for attorneys and Family Law Specialists in California. He has conducted trainings throughout the United States and internationally for child custody evaluators and others working with high-conflict families of divorce. He has presented workshops for judges throughout the country, is on the faculty of National Judicial College, and is a frequent presenter at programs of the National Council of Juvenile and Family Court Judges.

As a board member of the Association of Family and Conciliation Courts (AFCC), he was on the task force that drafted AFCC's *Model Standards of Practice for Child Custody Evaluation* (2006). He was a member of the American Bar Association Wingspread Task Force on High Conflict Families. Dr. Stahl is on the Editorial Review Board of AFCC's journal *Family Court Review* and the *Journal of Child Custody*. Along with his teaching, Dr. Stahl has written extensively on various issues in high-conflict divorce and custody evaluations. His previous books have been *Conducting Child Custody Evaluations: A Comprehensive Guide* (1994), *Complex Issues in Custody Evaluations* (1999), and *Parenting After Divorce* (2nd ed., 2008), and he is the coeditor of *Relocation Issues in Child Custody Cases* (2006). His child custody evaluation was cited by the California Supreme Court in its landmark decision modifying 8 years of relocation case law in 2004 (*In re Marriage of LaMusga* 32 Cal. 4th 1072, 12 Cal. Rptr. 3d 356, 88 P. 3d 81). Most recently, Dr. Stahl was on the workgroup appointed by the Arizona Supreme Court that rewrote Arizona's "Planning for Parenting Time" (Arizona, 2010).

When he has free time, Dr. Stahl enjoys traveling, playing golf, and relaxing with family and friends.

Dr. Stahl can be reached via e-mail at philipstahlphd@gmail.com.

# Supporting researchers for more than 40 years

**Research methods have always been at the core of SAGE's publishing program.** Founder Sara Miller McCune published SAGE's first methods book, *Public Policy Evaluation*, in 1970. Soon after, she launched the *Quantitative Applications in the Social Sciences* series—affectionately known as the "little green books."

Always at the forefront of developing and supporting new approaches in methods, SAGE published early groundbreaking texts and journals in the fields of qualitative methods and evaluation.

Today, more than 40 years and two million little green books later, SAGE continues to push the boundaries with a growing list of more than 1,200 research methods books, journals, and reference works across the social, behavioral, and health sciences. Its imprints—Pine Forge Press, home of innovative textbooks in sociology, and Corwin, publisher of PreK–12 resources for teachers and administrators—broaden SAGE's range of offerings in methods. SAGE further extended its impact in 2008 when it acquired CQ Press and its best-selling and highly respected political science research methods list.

From qualitative, quantitative, and mixed methods to evaluation, SAGE is the essential resource for academics and practitioners looking for the latest methods by leading scholars.

For more information, visit **www.sagepub.com**.